Popular 19th Century Painting

GERARD PORTIELJE. A good vintage. Signed, on panel. 15½ x 12½ins. (39.5 x 32cm). *Christie's.*

Popular
19th Century Painting

A Dictionary of European Genre Painters

Philip Hook and Mark Poltimore

Antique Collectors' Club

© 1986 Philip Hook and Mark Poltimore
First published 1986
World copyright reserved
ISBN 1 85149 011 6

British Library CIP Data
Hook, Philip
    Popular 19th century painting:
    a dictionary of European genre painters
    I. Painting, Modern — 19th century —
    Europe — Dictionaries
    I. Title   II. Poltimore, Mark
    III. Antique Collectors' Club
    759.94   ND457

Endpapers. ANDRÉ HENRI DARGELAS.
The school room. Signed, on panel.
15 x 18ins. (38 x 45.5cm). *Christie's.*

Designed by John and Griselda Lewis
Printed in England by the Antique Collectors' Club Ltd.
Church Street, Woodbridge, Suffolk

To Angelique and Sally

Acknowledgements

Our thanks are due to the museums and collectors who have provided us with photographs for reproduction in this book: to Alex Apsis and Elizabeth Peterkin of Sotheby's London; to Doreen Squilla of Sotheby's New York; to Birgid Seynsche-Vautz, Araminta Morris, Julia Korner, Caroline von Klitzing and Margie Christian of Christie's; to Elizabeth Miles and Sally Poltimore; and especially to Anne Crosse and Karen Cormack for all their help and patience.

Contents

Colour Plates

Introduction

The purpose of this book is an analysis of the subject matter of popular nineteenth century painting in Europe. The cardinals and cavaliers, serving wenches and Regency bucks, not to mention the cows and cats and dogs, which adorned the walls of drawing rooms from Stockholm to Madrid, from London to Vienna, have hitherto been dismissed without serious critical examination. There is a gap to be filled. More specifically, it is hoped that by dividing pictures into various categories of subject matter, and listing the artists who specialised in each category as extensively as possible, the information amassed here may have some practical value in the attribution of unidentified nineteenth century paintings.

With this in mind, the choice of categories has been a careful one. Sections have only been created if they constitute genuine areas of artists' specialisation. For instance, we have not included a category such as 'harvest scenes', for while there were undoubtedly memorable pictures painted of harvests during the nineteenth century, no artist can helpfully be described as primarily 'a painter of harvest scenes'. Such pictures and painters should be sought under the wider umbrella of 'Peasants and Country Life'. Similarly, while artists may well appear under more than one category, they are not included where they qualify only by virtue of odd pictures exceptional within their oeuvre. Thus Franz von Defregger, although he painted the occasional wildlife study, is only found in this book under 'Peasants' and 'Old Men'; Albert Anker is known to have produced one or two historical military subjects early in his career, but is only recorded here as a painter of 'Children' and 'Peasants'; and Eugène Verboeckhoven, although he once attempted a wholly uncharacteristic nude, is classified solely as a purveyor of animals.

Of course no book of this sort can aspire to be comprehensive. Indeed we have deliberately excluded certain branches of painting in order to make more manageable the volume of material presented in detail. We have concentrated on oil paintings depicting human figures or animals as their primary purpose which means that no landscapes, seascapes, still lifes or topographical views are to be found here. Portraits, too, are omitted, as are the more traditional religious subjects, and mythological and historical set pieces. The emphasis is on areas of subject matter which came specially to the fore in the nineteenth century, those which were in a sense creations of the popular imagination of the time. Even within the scope of the thirty-one categories remaining, the artists listed could still not represent more than a fraction of the total number engaged in a particular field across Europe. We hope, however, that the names mentioned and the illustrations chosen will indicate a wide cross-section of the artists involved and include all the more important ones. A select bibliography of major reference books is also offered for consultation if further information is required about any painter listed.

The precise definition of what constitutes a nineteenth century artist must remain elastic in terms of date — a few will be found here whose lives began in the eighteenth century, and rather more whose careers continued into the twentieth — but the unifying factor should become clearer from the following pages. A book such as this would not, in fact, have been worth attempting were it not for a remarkable uniformity of imagination amongst artists catering for popular taste across Europe in the nineteenth century, particularly in the second half of our period. It was a time of unprecedented international exchange of ideas and treatments, and a time when artists sucessfully built reputations as specialists in particular subjects and stuck with them so as not to confuse a conservative public. The reasons for this uniformity are examined in the introductory chapter on popular nineteenth century painting in general, while an attempt is made at the beginning of each category to explain why the area of subject matter emerged coherently as one of special significance. In this sense we hope that the book may also make a contribution to modern understanding of the popular imagination of a century of remarkable complexity and fascination.

Popular Nineteenth Century Painting

Many modern books devoted to the likes of Alma-Tadema, Meissonier and Gérôme rather than Renoir, Cézanne or van Gogh have tended to start with an aggressive apology. Perhaps this is no longer necessary: the conventional painters of the nineteenth century have received their fair measure of reappraisal, and that void in the history of European art between Neoclassicism and Impressionism is no longer seen as a black hole of bad taste, into which it did not do to look too closely for fear of finding something which exerted a guilty appeal. Critical opinion is now more indulgent; and while there has not been a wholesale return to the views of the 1870s and 1880s, which found Josef Israels more important than van Gogh, and Bouguereau, Gérôme and Bastien-Lepage surer of eternal greatness than 'eccentrics' like Manet, Monet or Degas, people's perspective has widened. The conventional mainstream of the nineteenth century, comprising those artists who courted and achieved great public acclaim in their own lifetime, is now recognised to be a worthwhile study not least because of the high regard in which it was held contemporarily. But such painting need not be approached too reverently: it is an alluring and frequently calculating mixture of technical brilliance, pretension, excess, sentimentality and comedy, both intentional and unwitting.

The character of European painting underwent a distinctive change in the nineteenth century. A new patronage emerged, demanding a new sort of picture, and creating an international popular market for works which catered for the new buyer. What appealed in Munich generally appealed in London, Paris, or in Rome: given minor regional differences, taste was remarkably uniform throughout all those European countries whose industrial revolutions and other upheavals had transformed the class of people who had money and the inclination to spend it on pictures. What was this new taste? Thackeray gave an accurate analysis of it in 1843:

> The heroic has been deposed; and our artists in place cultivate the pathetic and the familiar... The younger painters are content to exercise their art on subjects far less exalted; a gentle sentiment, an agreeable, quiet incident, a teatable tragedy, or a bread-and-butter idyll... Bread and butter can be digested by the very many,... unlike Prometheus on his rock, or Orestes in his strait-waistcoat, or Hector dragged behind Achilles' car, or Britannia, guarded by Religion and Neptune, welcoming General Tomkins in the temple of Glory.

In simplest terms, the phenomenon which popular nineteenth century painting represents is the triumph of genre, the depiction of everyday domestic scenes on as intimate — and often as trivial — a level as possible. Artists of the Academy still took off on the grand, ennobling flights of the imagination beloved of their forefathers, but the popular feeling was that they had had their day. Later many such painters reached some sort of *rapprochement* with popular taste by introducing a note of salacious realism or intimate eroticism to their academic nudes, but what the second half of the century saw most conspicuously was the proliferation of genre across Europe: from London to Moscow, from Madrid to Budapest to Stockholm, the official exhibitions were full of saccharine infants being dandled upon their mothers' knees, of rosy cheeked children engaged in more or less innocent pranks often involving animals whose heart rending expressiveness of feature bordered on the human, of old gentlemen exchanging dewy eyed reminiscences of younger days in the cosy interior of some establishment purveying alcoholic beverages. 'What is genre?' asked the French critic A. Barbier in 1836, and answered his own question neatly:

> It's the vaudeville of High Art, drawing room comedy as against grand drama, coquettish, witty, a little mannered, sometimes merry, sometimes sad, often true to life despite its comic-opera make-up, and always very popular.

In the pursuit of genre, artists found new areas in which to indulge their public's predilection for the 'pathetic and familiar'. The wide variety of these areas will become apparent from the categories into which this book in divided. In the process an additional and distinctively nineteenth century pleasure was discovered and exploited, a pleasure which one might describe as a pictorial delight in the invasion of privacy. What people were up to, particularly behind closed doors, became of consuming interest, and artists began to specialise in a keyhole vision of domestic incidents. Most important, the piquancy of such incidents was heightened by their placing in times or societies not immediately familiar to the contemporary spectator. The public took a constant delight in being reminded by artists that people's emotions and behaviour in the past were essentially no different from those of the present. Bulwer Lytton justified such painting when he spoke of 'the bond which unites (us to) the most distant eras — men, nations, customs perish: The Affections are immortal!' And the French art critic Grangedor echoed his words in 1868: 'Le fond des passions et des sentiments reste le même à travers les âges.' It is these pictures, containing that combination of the 'timeless' intimate element with a setting removed from most people's normal experience, which are essentially an invention of popular nineteenth century painting.

Thus genre entered history painting, for example: a typical scene is laid on a sun-drenched Aegean terrace, circa 400 BC, sumptuously bedecked in flowers and populated by languorous Grecian ladies in attitudes of ease, exchanging the latest scandalous speculations of smart Athenian society. In a second such picture, a splendidly arrayed cavalier, his sword and multi-plumed hat temporarily laid aside for the purpose, cradles to his breast yet one more of those timelessly sugary infants to the fatuous admiration of its onlooking mother. In yet another, a shimmeringly clad Regency lady, moons about the shadows of a luscious garden, torturing herself with recollections of a recent amour. All these scenes are historical in that they are drawn from the past, but they are a far cry from the grand, apocalyptic events traditionally felt to be the rightful subject matter of history painters. All are essentially personal, private revelations, calculated to maintain a popular link with the present by emphasising the timeless domestic or human element with which everyone could identify. This 'man-in-the-street' approach to the past is parallel by Taine's contemporary exhortation of modern historians to:

> give up the theory of constitutions and their mechanism, of religions and their system, and try to see men in their workshops, in their offices, in their fields, with their sky, their earth, their houses, their tillage, meals, as you

do when landing in England or Italy, you remark faces and gestures, roads and inns, a citizen taking his walk, a workman drinking.

It was not just the past which proved ripe for this brand of keyhole exploitation. Artists also turned for tempting subjects to areas removed from the contemporary spectator not so much by time as by geographical distance, custom, or elevation out of the normal. For instance, the large number of pictures of cardinals shown in intimate episodes in their palaces, or of monks at play in unguarded moments in the monastery, seem at first sight an iconographical curiosity hard to explain. In fact they are part of the same late nineteenth century urge to see behind closed doors, in this case of the Vatican or the cloister, to savour the intrusion on the privacy of others normally distant from the prying eye. The same voyeuristic vision, often mixed with an element of coy sentimentality, was turned on the Middle East, which throughout the century had exerted a strong attraction to European artists. Originally there had been a sense of genuine adventure about such painters' forays into the mystery and exoticism of the arab world, but the later orientalist school was more set on fanciful reconstructions of Islamic life, suggestively packaged for European consumption. If it was fun to penetrate the cardinal's palace or the kitchens of the friary, now much more fascinating to peer through into the innermost recesses of the sultan's harem.

The urge towards genre in the nineteenth century is inextricable from the urge towards sentimentality and trivialisation. We have seen how this affected classical and history painting; the tendency also influenced other branches of subject matter with an established tradition. Animal painting, for instance, was transformed from an objective record of the external appearances of beasts, sometimes in rural landscapes, into an anthropomorphic world of emotion and passion, and not infrequently of humour. Sheepdogs mourn the passing of their masters with tear jerking expressions of grief: adorable little kittens cavort with the same conscious mischief displayed by adorable little children; and even cows and sheep show distinct and disturbing evidence of the possession of souls. The peasantry, to previous generations mere adjuncts to country landscapes, coarse and garrulous types only a small step up from the animals they tended, were now sentimentalised into stereotypes such as smiling ploughmen or happy harvesters; old age is merry, disturbed by little more than an occasional broken milk jug or bottle of port which has passed its best. At its worst, a numbing blandness descends upon the popular pictorial imagination of the century.

There are many factors to explain the vogue for the domestic in marked contrast to the heroic in popular nineteenth century painting. A significant one, which accounts amongst other things for the hordes of children and pets as subjects, is the emergence of the cult of the home as an influential feature in middle class life and imagination. The Industrial Revolution altered the social balance: by the mid-century more and more households were moving into the strata that kept a numerous domestic staff because more and more industrialists and professional men were adding to their substance. Thus a wider public grew affluent enough to have the leisure that a large staff provided. The efficiency of the servant machine left the lady of the house with little to do to fill her day. No domestic work was demanded of her, and the chores of looking after the children were completely taken out of her hands. The ideal of the gentle wife in a tranquil drawing room surrounded by charming children and lovable pets was a nineteenth century creation, a delight to the paterfamilias. Children were charming, because there were enough domestic staff to remove them the moment they did anything to dent this image. The same applied to the lovable cats and dogs who increasingly found their way into the drawing room (and on to canvas). A disproportionate amount of time and attention was lavished on such animals by ladies with no better use for their waking hours. Pictures whose subject matter encompassed such things — impossibly attractive children, winningly sweet pets — were enormously popular because to most women they represented a large section of their normal experience, and to many men they reinforced the fond ideal of 'home' which they cherished.

Of course it would be inaccurate to suggest that the domestic held complete sway in nineteenth century painting. There is also a distinct tendency towards 'exotica' in the subject matter which appealed to popular taste, a delight in scenes of arab and cossack life, wild animals and distant history. Yet, in this paradoxical century, the exotic is often compromised by the domestic. This pleasure in the unfamiliar is counterbalanced by the pervasive urge to be reassured by the familiar and gently lapped by the sentimental. So the exotic is ensnared. Ancient Greeks play leapfrog; arabs play tic-tac; cavaliers moon about writing love poetry; and ferocious wild animals are shown not stalking their prey but cuddling their cubs.

There was money to be made in providing the vast new class of patrons with the sort of pictures they wanted. Artists grew rich, and commercial considerations became increasingly important. Barbier in Paris deplored this development as early as 1836:

> Here it is: art become bourgeois, and what is worse, commercial... it is no longer concerned with genius or glory; no, it has more profitable interests. It is a trader, a trafficker in the lower instincts, it caters for the small investor, if pressed it can provide you with works at a fixed price, in good, saleable quality, and I am amazed that its products have not yet been quoted on the commodity market along with sugar and coffee.

Barbier's fears about the commodity market were never quite realised, but the nineteenth century certainly proved fertile ground for the flowering of the dealer, a sweet scented middleman between artist and newly expanded clientele, the interpreter (accurate, but generally conservative in influence) between the two. Flaubert's roguish art dealer Arnoux in *A Sentimental Education* is an extreme case:

> With his passion for pandering to the public, he led able artists astray, corrupted the strong, exhausted the weak, and bestowed fame on the second rate.

Of course there were others less cynical than Arnoux, but as P.G. Hamerton wrote in 1867:

> Assuming the dealer wishes to sell, and recommends his goods in the manner which experience proves to be the most effective, we cannot be far wrong in concluding that a kind of art which, however degraded, is popular, will be encouraged by him, and rendered, if possible, more popular still.

Then there were the Art Unions: their creation and success in countries like Britain and Germany are part of the broadening of the base of patronage in the nineteenth century and a force for the yet greater popularisation of art. Even the humblest collector could join an Art Union by paying a small annual subscription. This entitled him to a certain number of engravings after well-known modern pictures each year, and on top of that gave him the chance to win oil paintings by famous contemporary artists in a periodic prize draw. Thus a huge new range of collectors had access to works of art; and conversely artists, conscious of their potential Art Union public, tended to select subjects which made as broad an appeal as possible. A modern equivalent is perhaps the author who chooses his theme with an eye to being able to sell it to the big American book clubs. In Munich, the change wrought by Art Unions was perceived early on by the animal painter Albrecht Adam. He had been instrumental in the setting up of an Art Union in his native city, but confessed:

> Often have I asked myself whether I have done good or not by this scheme, and to this hour I have not been able to make up my mind. The cultivation of art clearly received an entirely different bias from that which it had in earlier days. What was formerly done by artistic and judicious connoisseurs was now placed for the most part in the hands of the people.

Artists were typecast into specialists, and the public were taught to expect certain sorts of picture from them. Thus a cardinal from Brunery, a cow by Voltz, a Roman bath by Alma-Tadema were all pre-eminently desirable because they were typical. This was the dealer's influence at work. It is also what makes the format of this book feasible. The fact that the same specialist areas crossed national borders and occupied artists of many different countries is explained by the easy communication of pictorial ideas possible in the nineteenth century; imagination was remarkably uniform in the service of the popular market. At the highest level, the artistic communication of ideas took place in a series of international exhibitions in the second half of the century, in Paris, Berlin, Munich, and Vienna, for instance. Here artists and patrons could take note of the achievements of painters from other countries, and imitate and adapt what they saw. This was one way in which an international taste for certain subjects developed. Marginally lower down the scale, various 'multi-national' dealers emerged — Gambart, Gimpel, Sedelmeyer, Wimmer and Knoedler, for example, men who, having connections in different countries, were as likely to sell a Belgian picture to a German as a French one to an Englishman. And later on, of course, many of their most successful sales were made to the other side of the Atlantic. What they were marketing made its international appeal because it was neither too sophisticated nor too challenging. As Thackeray said, 'Bread and butter can be digested by very many.'

Art magazines also contributed to an awareness of what was going on in other countries. *The Art Journal* in London, *L'Art* in Paris, *Zeitschrift für bildende Kunst* in Germany, all frequently carried illustrations and appreciations of the work of foreign artists. Hand in hand with this went the wide distribution of prints after famous contemporary pictures: thus Meissonier reached London, Landseer penetrated to Berlin, and Ludwig Knaus decorated Parisian walls. On top of all this, artists themselves were travelling extensively, often as students and sometimes as exiles. There were numerous Scandinavians to be found in Düsseldorf, Munich, Paris and Rome; Spaniards came to Paris and Rome; many Eastern Europeans forsook the comparatively provincial academies of Warsaw, Prague, and Budapest to train in Vienna, Munich or Paris; even the insular English artist often felt that his education might be augmented by taking a studio in Paris, too. The compliment was repaid, more by accident than design, when many French painters took up residence in London in 1870-71 as refugees from the Franco-Prussian war and the Commune. Towards the end of the century, Germans, Scots and

Scandinavians were drawn to Holland. All these many contacts added up to a popular market for pictures which existed simultaneously on a national and international level. While an Englishman might turn instinctively for a scene of children to another Englishman, like Millais, he could also be pleasantly surprised to find that an Edouard Frère or a Meyer von Bremen presented just as satisfactory an image with precisely the same terms of reference.

Popular nineteenth century pictures can be sentimental, melodramatic, literary, and occasionally comic to the point of vulgarity. But to set them in perspective, it is only fair to investigate a little deeper the aesthetic theory behind such painting, the contemporary preconceptions which made it take the form it did. Why then was there such a strong tendency towards the sentimental? The popular imagination of the time as displayed in its pictures was heir to the romantic conviction that 'feeling is everything'. We have to look back to Greuze and the cult of 'sensibilité' for the immediate origins of this obsession; the result of it was a residual idea that the public was there first and foremost to have its heart-strings twanged. Laughter or tears should be provoked; it did not matter which, so long as the emotion was intense. Parallel to this French theory (which was of course exported to other countries, notably England) runs the German, characteristically Biedermeyer, feeling for 'gemütlichkeit'. Again, its roots are to be found at the end of the eighteenth century. 'Gemüt', says Goethe, is the essence, the nub of what is sympathetic to one. By extension, something is 'gemütlich' when it strikes a person's innermost chord, promoting a deep sense of well-being. The pursuit of this in art was a perilous one, leading painters on to an ever more sentimental view of life. Theirs was the sentimentality of cosiness, nostalgia for the good old days, and a good laugh together, the tipsy camaraderie that will soon become maudlin. Artists reared on these French or German theories, that pictures should either provoke emotion or render their audience 'cosy', began to cut corners with the inevitable consequence that passion becomes contrived and charm grows saccharine. And yet we should not overlook the fact that even contemporarily painters were castigated for sentimentality: it is a modern prejudice that such discrimination was beyond the range of nineteenth century art criticism.

There was a broad conventional consensus across Europe about the aims of painting. Judged by today's standards, these aims seem absurdly narrow, and indeed different in kind rather than degree from the priorities which govern modern art. Scarcely an artist considered in this book, for instance, would have admitted the possibility of expression in the form as opposed to the subject matter of a picture. If a thing was well painted, it was so because it was naturalistically painted: any deviation from this naturalistic norm in colouring or in drawing was looked at askance and with suspicion. The notion that such variation could be the vehicle of the content of a picture was an idea beyond comprehension, let alone the approval, of the average exhibitor at the Salon or the Royal Academy during our period. So the picture's meaning or significance lay almost entirely in its subject matter, and success or failure was judged by the expressiveness with which the characters were depicted, and the pithiness with which the action or point was communicated. Mere technical excellence was not enough: a work of art needed imagination, and imagination was to be displayed in the choice and presentation of the subject. The result was a very literary sort of painting, and art was never closer to literature than in the nineteenth century. Fromentin speaks disparagingly of:

the contemporary German school (and) English school, in which subject,

delicacy, purpose, are everything as in the drama, comedy, vaudeville —
in which painting is too much imbued with literature since it lives on
nothing else — and in the eyes of some people dies of it too.

Indeed, a nineteenth century novelist's view of his own craft would have struck
a chord in many painters of the time, English, German, and French. Robert
Louis Stephenson wrote:

This is the plastic part of literature, to embody character, thought or
emotion in some act or attitude that shall be remarkably striking to the
mind's eye. This is the highest and hardest thing to do in words.

The search for acts to depict which were 'remarkably striking to the eye' was
also carried on in paint. Finding subjects which forcefully embodied character,
thought or emotion would have been considered 'the highest and hardest thing'
for artists too. The supremacy of the subject is echoed in Alma-Tadema's
assertion that:

there are painters who represent a bit of nature and call it a picture, but
it is nothing of the kind. That is simply a study and nothing more. The
painter must first have a subject, all the rest must be subordinate.

Despite this affinity between art and literature, it is perhaps more helpful to
see the artist not so much as an author manqué, but rather as a play or film-
director before his time. It was the *mis en scène* which was crucial to these
painters: they manipulated the actors in their dramas, domestic and trivial
though they may have been, and in this manipulation lay their success or
failure to contemporary eyes. For the generation of the later nineteenth
century, pictures even began to fill the role now taken by television and the
cinema. A major new painting by one of the favoured painters of the day could
provoke a reaction similar to a major new film today. Crowds flocked to its
unveiling; it might go on tour to various parts of the country with admission
charged to see it; it would be widely discussed and written about. Dealers
would vie for the engraving rights in much the same way that film companies
bid for the distribution rights of a new production.

One further strand in the aesthetic theory behind popular painting in the
nineteenth century is indicated by Gautier's statement that 'the goal of art is
Beauty, or at least Character'. The pursuit of beauty was all very laudable, but
in certain contexts it just did not meet requirements. Allowing 'Character' as
a substitute ideal licensed more flexibility. Its pursuit legitimised humour, so
that the comic anecdote became a subject fit for the brush of even quite serious
artists: Gérôme, Millais, and Spitzweg, for instance, all painted pictures
calculated to rouse a chuckle of merriment. Popular nineteenth century
painting often aimed to amuse and divert rather than to improve or educate.
And if the aim was the amusement of the public, then why not go the whole
way and give them a good laugh? So we get endless pictures of cardinals
dropping priceless vases, soldiers playing tricks on overweight friars, girls
giggling at forbidden books, and bulls frightening maiden ladies. In many
ways the dichotomy between 'beauty' and 'character' as ends in art is a reflection
of the difference between traditional 'high art' and the new popular painting, or
even between 'highbrow' and 'middle or lowbrow', concepts which come into
being for the first time in the nineteenth century. For it was now that a popular
culture emerged, with different terms of reference from the old élitist art, meeting
the needs of a strong newly expanded middle class who were not ashamed of their
taste and preferences. The critic Spielman spoke for many in 1898:

'Middle class', some object; perhaps; but the nation as a whole is middle class, and from those ranks have sprung the greatest of her sons. So true is this that I believe not a single work of importance by Sir John Millais, not in a National or Municipal Gallery, is in the hands of other than 'middle class' people.

Meissonier, another artist whose appeal was particularly strong for the middle class, declared stoutly:

> Don't talk to me of works of art which are overlooked by the public and appeal solely to the academic taste of the initiated… it is a principle I have always controverted.

If there was one major challenge with which artists — including those geared to the popular market — had to come to terms as the century progressed, it was the question of Realism. One cannot properly understand the pictures dealt with in this book without bearing in mind the fact that every country in Europe either underwent or felt the effects of some sort of 'Realist' revolution during the nineteenth century, broadly a reaction in favour of 'truth to nature' against the stale artificiality of the Academy or the excesses of Romanticism. Ruskin, for instance, praised the Pre-Raphaelites for acting on the principle that:

> things should be painted as they probably did look and happen, and not as by rules of art as developed under Raphael, Correggio and Michelangelo they might be supposed gracefully, deliciously, or sublimely to have happened.

La Castagnary noted in 1857, in connection with Zola and the Barbizon school of painters, a praiseworthy tendency to realism:

> The excesses of romanticism, its debauches of colour, have precipitated this twin movement. It seems that, worn out with violent emotions, disgusted by its own corruption, society has made an immense return to the truth.

The Pre-Raphaelites in England and the Barbizon School in France are only two of the many different forms the realist revolution took. Others include anti-academic reactions typified by Courbet, or by Waldmüller in Austria; and the wave of 'pleinairism' which swept over Europe in the last quarter of the century, affecting painters as varied as Bastien-Lepage, the Newlyn School, Zorn the Swede, the Machaioli in Italy, Sorolla in Spain, and the Hague School in Holland. All had in common a desire to paint nature more directly, to present a more vivid and truthful rendering of the external world. Where they differed was in the degree of emotional objectivity aimed at. Some tried to eradicate all passion and look at the world with an innocent eye; other seized on realist techniques as an aid to more poignant treatments of emotional subjects. These were generally the painters whose attentions were fixed on the popular market.

The assimilation of realism by a fundamentally romantic imagination is one of the features of popular painting in the second half of the century. The result is often an uneasy compromise between two irreconcilables, both of which had their distinct attractions to the public. The 'romantic', manifesting itself in the manipulation of subject matter to elicit maximum emotional response, struck a residual chord in those whose artistic imagination tended towards the sentimental. The 'realist', in so far as it purported to recreate reality in all its wholeness, was found extremely exciting by an age already thrilled by technological advance and stimulated by materialism. The marriage of the two approaches, by artists keen to get the best of both worlds, produced for example that strange sort of 'historical genre' which we have already observed, in which immense antiquarian learning and genuine historical research, together with a new brilliance of realistic technique, were exerted on subjects which were essentially everyday, intimate, and trivial.

This was realism applied to the past, in itself a paradoxically romantic notion; but even when it was employed on contemporary life subjects, similar dangers lurked. The peasant, who started the century as an object of picturesque ornamentation to a landscape, was subjected to 'realistic' scrutiny; but artists still found it difficult to abandon their romantic prejudices, and so produced pictures apparently strikingly lifelike (because of technique) but falsified by a patronising sentimentality. Works presented as objectively true in this way were all the more misleading, bolstering the bourgeois middle class patron's cosy impression that the working class could not be so very badly off since here they were, realistically portrayed, grinning quite charmingly.

All this is a brief attempt to sketch in as background some of the priorities, prejudices and preconceptions which governed the approach of those artists in the nineteenth century who painted pictures which found a ready market with the public. If one salient feature of such pictures emerges, it is that they would have been nothing without a subject, and it follows that the obvious way to approach the popular painting of the time is by its subject matter. The pages which follow reveal something of the extraordinary variety of the imaginations at work, from those who sought to endow cows with souls or Romans with grocery lists, to those whose comedies were enacted in the Vatican and their tragedies at the teatable.

Arab Genre

The first painters who penetrated to the Middle East in the nineteenth century, the pioneer orientalists, opened up a rich seam of novel and colourful subject matter for their successors. Delacroix, Chasseriau, Decamps and others were drawn to the east as romantics in search of adventure and the exotic. The bravado which inspired such enterprise is expressed by the character in Flaubert who declares 'Exuberance is better than taste, the desert is better than a pavement, and a savage is better than a barber!' The first artist-travellers who arrived in North Africa found a civilisation relatively untouched by western culture; its rich colouring, extravagant costume and unfamiliar customs provided a wonderful new range of subject matter to brighten the austere walls of the Salon. The first generation of orientalists were observers and reporters, recording in fascination the extraordinary everyday scenes they saw before them; arab genre was different from more conventional genre at this early stage because its immediate appeal lay in its *un*familiarity rather than the reverse.

For the French, too, painting the genre of the arab world presented some sort of viable alternative to the twin evils of excessively arid classicism and the sort of realism which was depressingly lacking in nobility. There were aspects of the east which were noble and eternal; others were sensationally exotic and refreshingly new. Delacroix wrote home in wonder: 'Imagine, my friend, what it's like see Consuls, Catos, and Brutuses, who certainly don't lack that superior air you would expect from the lords of the earth, lying in the sun, walking through the streets, mending old shoes.' Flaubert was similarly entranced on his first visit in 1849, although struck by a different feature of arab life:

> There is one element which I hadn't expected to see and which is tremendous here, and that is the grotesque. All the old comic business of the cudgeled slave, of the coarse trafficker in women, of the thieving merchant — it's all very fresh here, very genuine and charming.... There are guttural intonations that sound like the cries of wild beasts, and laughter, and flowing white robes, and ivory teeth flashing between thick lips, and flat negro noses, and dusty feet, and necklaces, and bracelets!

The European eye of the writer was also caught by another strange and pervasive phenomenon: 'One of the finest things is the camel — I never tire of watching this strange beast that lurches like a turkey and sways its neck like a swan.'

The second half of the century saw artists from much further afield than France also converging on the arab world. Painters roamed through North Africa, Egypt, the Holy Land, Syria, Turkey, and, less frequently, Persia. There was a wide variety of Englishmen, from W.J. Muller and J.F. Lewis onwards; Spaniards, who were sometimes viewed as honorary arabs themselves because of their moorish connections; Dutchmen, Belgians and Scandinavians; and a surprising number of very accomplished Austrians,

OSMAN HAMDY BEY.
The gate of the Great
Mosque, Broussa. Signed
and dated 1881. 47 x 24ins.
(119 x 61cm). *Christie's*.

including Ludwig Deutsch, Rudolf Ernst, and Leopold Carl Müller. Munich-based painters included Gustav Bauernfeind and Ferencz Eisenhut; while the leading Italian contingent comprised artists like Alberto Pasini, Stefano Ussi, and Cesare Biseo. It is hard to think of a European country which could not boast some sort of school of orientalist painting. As Gautier observed, 'the journey to Algeria has become as indispensable to painters as the pilgrimage to Italy. There they will learn about the sun, study the light, find original characters, customs, and primitive, biblical attitudes.'

The second and third generations of orientalists were populous and prolific; the path from the Salon to the Sahara was already a well-worn one. As early as the middle of the century the popularity of the trip was beginning to create a loss of freshness and ultimately decadence. In 1854 Thomas Seddon wrote of Egypt: 'The country is a spectacle of a society falling into ruins, and the manners of the east are rapidly emerging into the encroaching sea of European civilisation.' As the arab world became more influenced by the west, it lost much of its mystery and elusiveness; and in turn the exoticism recreated by visiting painters grew more contrived. Artists began to produce images of the arab world which were increasingly Europeanised, that is to say packaged for easy consumption by the new bourgeois patron at home. Some even painted orientalist scenes without ever setting foot in an arab country. Why not? They had produced convincing renderings of classical Rome and seventeenth century Holland without ever having been there.

The ways in which later painters sugared the east for the consumption of their European clientele are similar to the ways in which painters of classical genre or historical genre handled their material, emphasising the intimate and domestic elements, sometimes to a point of sentimentality. Certain English painters, for instance, began to treat the genre of the east as little more than a cosy extension of the home life of the average Kensington resident. In W.C. Horsley's *Fighting His Battles O'er Again*, an ancient arab chieftain is shown brandishing a sword in misty-eyed recollection of the military triumphs of his youth. It seems something of a distortion to present a brutal pagan warrior in terms of a benign Chelsea pensioner, but no doubt the public found in such a picture grounds for reassurance about the humanity of the Arab. Karl Ooms in his *Un Soir au bord du Nil* of 1896 achieves a similar level of domestication. Here an Egyptian family is portrayed in much the same spirit as a Belgian one might be depicted contemporarily on the beach at Knokke-le-Zoute. Gone is the mystery of the East. In its place is a reassuringly human intimacy with mother and father showing the same sentimentalised delight in their young offspring which European patrons could readily identify with. There has been a fundamental change here; no longer is it the unfamiliarity of the eastern way of life which is emphasised for the spectator, but its alleged common ground with western bourgeois experience. The eastern traveller Robert Curzon wrote prophetically in 1865 of the adulteration of arab character by:

> the levelling intercourse with Europeans, which always, and in a very short time, exerts so strong an influence that picturesque dresses and romantic adventures disappear, while practical utility and a commonplace appearance are so generally disseminated, that in a few years more every country will be alike, and travellers will discover that there is nothing to be found in the way of manners and customs that they may not see with greater ease in their own houses in London.

Sure enough, by 1897 the Belgian painter Evenpoel was writing home in a letter from North Africa: 'Algiers is a city destroyed... everywhere minarets are being replaced by factory chimneys.'

The geological accident of vast oil deposits beneath the lands depicted in many nineteenth century pictures of arab genre has meant that the present-day descendants of the subjects portrayed have enormous wealth with which to acquire these desirable pictorial records of Islamic life a hundred years ago. They are eagerly pursued, with the result that the market for orientalist paintings is extremely strong. Ironically, the Goodalls and the Ernsts, the Gérômes and the Deutsches, the very pictures originally painted by Europeans to interpret the arab world for other Europeans, are now being sought out and borne home in triumph by arabs. Studied closely, they can tell their new owners almost as much about the nineteenth century European imagination.

Index of artists

CORMON, Fernand (French, 1845-1924)
CRAPELET, Louis Amable (French, 1822-1867)

DARJOU, Alfred Henri (French, 1832-1874)
DAUX, Charles Edmond (French, 1855-?)
* DECAMPS, Gabriel Alexandre (French, 1803-1860)
* DEHODENCQ, Edme Alexis Alfred (French, 1822-1882)
DELACROIX, Auguste (French, 1809-1868)
DELACROIX, Ferdinand Victor Eugène (French, 1798-1863)
* DEUTSCH, Ludwig (Austrian, 1855-?)
DIAZ DE LA PENA, Narcisse Virgile (French, 1808-1876)
* DILLON, Frank (British, 1823-1909)
* DINET, Alphonse Etienne (French, 1862-1909)
* DISCART, Jean B. (French, late 19th Century)
DOMINQUEZ BECQUER, Valeriano (Spanish, 1834-1870)
DUBOIS, Henri Pierre Hippolyte (French, 1837-1909)

EECKHOUT, Victor (Belgian, 1821-1879)
* EISENHUT, Ferencz (Austrian, 1857-1903)
ENDER, Edouard (Austrian, 1822-1883)
* ERNST, Rudolf (Austrian, 1854-1920)
* ESCAZENA Y DAZA, José (Spanish, 1800?-1858)
EVENPOEL, Henri Jacques Edward (Belgian, 1872-1899)

FABBI, Fabio (Italian, 1861-1946)
* FABRES Y COSTA, Antonio Maria (Spanish, 1854-?)
* FAED, John (British, 1820-1902)
FERRARI, Giuseppe (Italian, late 19th Century)
FERRARIS, Arthur von (Austrian, 1856-?)
FERRIER, Gabriel Joseph Marie (French, 1847-1914)
FINELLI, Edoardo (Italian, late 19th Century)
FISCHER, Ludwig Hans (Austrian, 1848-1915)
* FORCELLA, N. (Italian, late 19th Century)
FORTUNY Y CARBO, Mariano (Spanish, 1838-1874)
FRANCÉS, Juan (Spanish, late 19th Century)
FRANCES Y PASCUAL, Placido (Spanish, 1840?-1901?)
* FRANKE, Albert Joseph (German, 1860-1924)
* FRÈRE, Charles Théodore (French, 1814-1888)
* FROMENTIN, Eugène (French, 1820-1876)

* GABANI, Giuseppe (Italian, 1846-1899)
GALE, William (British, 1823-1909)
* GALLEGOS Y ARNOSA, José (Spanish, 1859-1917)
* GEDDES, Andrew (British, 1783-1844)
GENTZ, Karl Wilhelm (German, 1822-1890)
GERGELY, Imre (Austrian, 1868-?)
* GÉRÔME, Jean Léon (French, 1824-1904)
GINAIN, Louis Eugène (French, 1818-1886)
* GIRARDET, Eugène Alexis (French, 1853-1907)
GIRAUD, Pierre François Eugène (French, 1806-1881)
* GIRIGOTTI, P. (Italian, late 19th Century)
* GOLZ, Alexander Demetrius (Austrian, 1857-1944)
GOODALL, Edward Alfred (British, 1819-1908)
* GOODALL, Frederick (British, 1822-1904)
GRISON, François Adolphe (French, 1845-1914)
GUILLAUMET, Gustav Achille (French, 1840-1887)

HAAG, Carl (German, 1820-1915)
HAGEMANN, Godefroy de (French, ?-1877)
HAITÉ, George Charles (British, 1855-1924)
* HAMDY BEY, Osmân (Turkish, 1842-1910)
* HARDY, Dudley (British, 1867-1922)

HEDOUIN, Edmond Pierre Alexandre (French, 1820-1889)
HERBERT, John Rogers (British, 1810-1890)
HODGSON, John Evan (British, 1831-1895)
* HOPPE, Bruno (Swedish, 1859-1937)
* HORSLEY, Walter Charles (British, 1855-?)
HUGUET, Victor Pierre (French, 1835-1902)
HUNT, Edward Aubrey (British, 1855-1922)
HUYSMANS, Jan Baptiste (Belgian, 1826-?)

ISRAEL, Daniel (Austrian, 1859-1901)

JERICHAU, Holger Hvitfeldt (Danish, 1861-1900)
JERICHAU-BAUMANN, Elisabeth Maria Anna (Polish, 1819-1881)
JIMENEZ Y MARTIN, Juan (Spanish, 1858-?)
* JOANOVICH, Paul (Austrian, 1859-1913)

KALTENMOSER, Max (German, 1842-1887)
KERSTAN, Carl Ludwig Ferdinand (Austrian, 1857-?)
* KOSLER, Franz Xavier (Austrian, 1864-?)
KRÄMER, Johann Victor (Austrian, 1864-?)
KRETZSCHMER, Johann Hermann (German, 1811-1890)
KUHNERT, Wilhelm Friedrich Karl (German, 1865-1926)

LABBÉ, Charles Emile (French, 1810-1885)
* LALAISSE, François Hippolyte (French, 1812-1844)
* LAZERGES, Jean Raymond Hippolyte (French, 1827-1887)
LAZERGES, Paul Jean Baptiste (French, 1845-1902)
LECOMTE, Emile (Belgian, 1866-)
* LECOMTE DU NOUY, Jean Jules Antoine (French, 1842-1923)
LEFEBVRE, Jules Joseph (French, 1836-1912)
* LEIGHTON, Frederic, Lord (British, 1830-1896)
LEMATTE, Ferdinand Jacques François (French, 1850-?)
LEROUX, Louis Hector (French, 1829-1900)
LEWIS, John Frederick (British, 1805-1876)
* LOGSDAIL, William (British, 1859-1944)
LONG, Edwin (British, 1829-1891)
LOYE, Charles Auguste (called Montbard) (French, 1841-1905)
LUKER, William (British, fl. 1851-1889)
LYBAERT, Theophile Marie François (Belgian, 1848-?)
LYNKER, Anna (Austrian, 1834-?)

MAFFEI, David (Italian?, late 19th Century)
MAKART, Hans (Austrian, 1840-1884)
MANN, Joshua Hargrave Sams (British, fl. 1849-1884)
MARIANI, Pompeo (Italian, 1857-1927)
MARILHAT, Georges Antoine Prosper (French, 1811-1847)
* MIELICH, Alphons Leopold (Austrian, 1863-1929)
MONTI, Giuseppe de (Italian, 1871-?)
* MORAGAS Y TORRAS, Tomas (Spanish, 1837-1906)
MOUCHOT, Louis Claude (French, 1830-1891)
MOULIGNON, Leopold Henri Antoine de (French, 1821-1897)
MÜLLER, Charles Louis (French, 1815-1892)
* MÜLLER, Leopold Carl (German, 1834-1892)
* MÜLLER, William James (British, 1812-1845)
* MÜLLER-WEISBADEN, Rudolph Gustav (German, 1858-1888)

NATHAN, W.H. (British, late 19th Century)
NICOLET, Gabriel Emile Edouard (Swiss, 1856-1921)

ODELMARK, Franz Wilhelm (Swedish, 1849-1937)
* OOMS, Karel (Belgian, 1845-1900)
OTTENFELD, Rudolf Otto von (Italian, 1856-1913)
OUDERAA, Pierre Jean van der (Belgian, 1841-1915)
OUTIN, Pierre (French, 1839-1899)

* PARLADE Y HEREDIA, Andres (Spanish, 1859-?)
* PASINI, Alberto (Italian, 1826-1899)
* PAVY, Eugène (French, late 19th Century)
* PAVY, Philippe (French, late 19th Century)
* PELLEGRINI, Riccardo (Italian, 1866-1934)
PETZL, Joseph (German, 1803-1871)
* PHILIPPOTEAUX, Paul Dominique (French, late 19th
     Century)
PILNY, Otto (Swiss, 1866-?)
* PINEL de GRANDCHAMP, Louis Emile (French,
     1831-1894)
* POPELIN, Gustave Léon Antoine Marie (French, 1859-?)
PORTAELS, Jean François (Belgian, 1818-1895)
* PUJOL DE GUASTAVINO, Clément (French, late 19th
     Century)

RAFFAELLI, Jean François (French, 1850-1924)
* RALLI, Theodore Jacques (Greek, 1852-1909)
* ROBERTSON, Charles (British, 1844-1891)
RONOT, Charles (French, 1820-1895)
ROSATI, Giulio (Italian, 1853-1917)
ROUBTZOFF, Alexandre (French, 1884-1949)
* ROUSSEAU, Henri Emilien (French, 1875-1933)
RUBEN, Franz Leo (Austrian, 1842-1920)

* SANTORO, Rubens (Italian, 1859-1942)
SAUX, Sophie de (French, 1829-1901)
SCHEUERMANN, Ludwig Gustav Wilhelm (German,
     1859-1911)
SCHLIMARSKI, Heinrich Hans (Austrian, 1859-?)
* SCHORN, Theobald (German, 1865-?)
* SCHREYER, Adolf Christian (German, 1828-1899)
* SCOGNAMIGLIO, Cavaliero Antonio (Italian, late 19th
     Century)
SEEL, Adolf (German, 1829-1907)
* SEYMOUR, George L. (British, fl. 1876-1888)
SIEFFERT, Paul (French, 1874-?)
SIGNORINI, Giuseppe Joseph (Italian, 1857-1932)
* SIMONETTI, Amedeo Momo (Italian, 1874-1922)
SIMONETTI, Ettore (Italian, late 19th Century)

* SIMONI, Gustavo (Italian, 1846-?)
SIMONSEN, Niels (Danish, 1807-1885)
SOMMER, R. (Russian, late 19th Century)
* SPEYER, Christian Georg (German, 1855-1929)
* STAACKMANN, H.M. (Dutch, late 19th Century)
STARCK, Julius Josephus Gaspard (Belgian, 1814-1884)
STIEPEVICH, Vincent (Russian, late 19th Century)
STYKA, Jan (Polish, 1858-1925)
* SWOBODA, Rudolph (Austrian, 1859-1914)
SUYKENS, Henri (German, late 19th Century)

TARENGHI, Enrico (Italian, 1848-?)
* TESSON, Louis (French, late 19th Century)
TORNAI, Gyula (Austrian, 1861-1928)
* TROOD, William Henry Hamilton (British, 1848-1899)

* UHL, Emil (Austrian, 1864-?)
ULFSTEN, Nicolai Martin (Norwegian, 1854-1885)
* USSI, Stefano (Italian, 1822-1901)

* VALEROS, H. (French?, late 19th Century)
VARLEY (jun.), John (British, ?-1899)
VEILLON, Auguste Louis (Swiss, 1834-1890)
VENUTI, Filippo (Italian, late 19th Century)
VERBRUGGE, Emile (Belgian, 1856-1936)
* VERNET, Horace Emile Jean (French, 1789-1863)
VERNET-LECOMTE, Charles Emile Hippolyte (French,
     1821-1900)
VIBERT, Jehan Georges (French, 1840-1902)
VIDAL, Eugène Vincent (French, 1850-1908)
VILLEGAS Y CORDERO, Ricardo (Spanish, 1852-?)
VILLEMSENS, Jean Blaise (French, 1806-1859)

* WARREN, Knighton (British, late 19th Century)
* WASHINGTON, Georges (French, 1827-1910)
* WEBB, William J. (British, fl. 1853-1878)
* WEEKS, Edwin Lord (Anglo-American, 1849-1903)
* WEISSE, Rudolf (Austrian, 1869-?)
WERNER, Carl Friedrich Heinrich (German, 1808-1894)
* WILDA, Charles (Austrian, 1854-1907)
WILLAERT, Ferdinand (Belgian, 1861-1938)
* WURBEL, Franz Theodor (Austrian, 1858-?)
WUTTKE, Carl (German, 1849-1927)
WYBURD, Francis John (British, 1826-?)
* WYGRZYWALSKI, Feliks M. (Polish, 1875-1944)
WYLD, William (British, 1806-1889)

* ZAMAÇOIS Y ZABALA, Eduardo (Spanish, 1842-1871)

GIAN ALVAREZ. The gunsmith. Signed and inscribed
Roma. 20 x 14¼ins. (51 x 36cm). *Sotheby's.*

JEAN JULES BADIN. A young Arab boy. Signed and dated
1881. 28¾ x 20ins. (73 x 51cm). *Sotheby's.*

FILIPPO BARATTI. The prisoner. Signed and dated Paris 1883, and signed, inscribed and dated 1883 on the reverse. 41 x 31ins. (104 x 78.5cm). *Christie's.*

Opposite: GUSTAV BAUERNFEIND. A street in Jaffa. Signed and dated Munchen 1890, and inscribed Jaffa. 41 x 52¼ins. (104 x 133cm). *Christie's.*

DAVID BATES. Near the desert. Signed and dated 1893-1903 and signed, inscribed and dated 1893, retouched 1903 on the reverse. 24 x 39½ins. (61 x 100.5cm). *Christie's.*

LÉON ADOLPHE AUGUSTE BELLY. By the Nile. Signed and dated 1859. 26 x 39ins. (66 x 99cm). *Christie's.*

EDMUND BERNINGER. A coastal landscape with an Arab caravan on the move. Signed and inscribed Tunis. 37¼ x 64¼ins. (94.5 x 163cm). *Christie's.*

30

L. BERTON. Mounted Arab warriors by a pool. Signed. 22½ x 30¾ins. (57 x 78cm). *Christie's.*

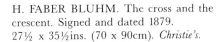

H. FABER BLUHM. The cross and the crescent. Signed and dated 1879. 27½ x 35½ins. (70 x 90cm). *Christie's.*

STANISLAUS VON CHLEBOWSKI. Arabs at prayer in a mosque in Brousse. Signed and dated 1880. 26¼ x 20¼ins. (67 x 51.5cm). *Christie's.*

GEORGES JULES VICTOR CLAIRIN. Allah! Allah! Signed. 45 x 65ins. (114 x 165cm). *Christie's.*

LUDWIG DEUTSCH. Two Arabs playing chess. Signed and dated Paris 1896. 20¾ x 16ins. (53 x 40.5cm). *Christie's.*

Top left: GABRIEL ALEXANDRE DECAMPS. An Arab fisherman on a river bank. Signed. 13½ x 9½ins. (34 x 24cm). *Christie's*

Left: EDME ALEXIS ALFRED DEHODENCQ. An Arab woman at a doorway. Signed. 24 x 17½ins. (61 x 44.5cm). *Christie's.*

Opposite: FERENCZ EISENHUT. An Arab slave market. Signed and dated München 1888. 53½ x 88ins. (136 x 224cm). *Christie's.*

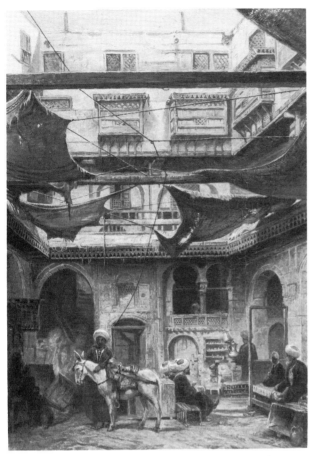

FRANK DILLON. An Arab courtyard. 16½ x 11½ins. (42 x 29.5cm). *Christie's.*

Top right: ALPHONSE ETIENNE DINET. Arab children playing. Signed and dated 1896, on board. 20 x 28¼ins. (51 x 71.5cm). *Christie's.*

JEAN B. DISCART. The toy seller. Signed and inscribed Tanger, on panel. 13 x 18ins. (33 x 45.5cm). *Christie's.*

RUDOLF ERNST. Two Arabs in an interior. Signed, on panel. 28½ x 36ins. (72.5 x 91.5cm). *Christie's.*

JOSÉ ESCAZENA Y DAZA. Arabs at a doorway. Signed and inscribed Gibraltar. 18¼ x 14ins. (46.5 x 35.5cm). *Sotheby's.*

ANTONIO MARIA FABRES Y COSTA. The prisoner. Signed and dated Tanger 1894. 35½ x 27¼ins. (90 x 69cm). *Christie's.*

JOHN FAED. The slave girl. On board. 17 x 24ins (43.5 x 61cm). *Christie's.*

GIUSEPPE FERRARI. The morning prayer.
Signed and dated 1881, watercolour. 52 x 55½ins.
(132 x 141cm). *Christie's.*

N. FORCELLA. The Hookah. Signed.
27¼ x 18ins. (69 x 46cm). *Christie's.*

ALBERT JOSEPH FRANKE. A conversation by the well. Signed and dated Muenchen '86, on panel. 13 x 9¾ins. (33 x 25cm). *Christie's.*

CHARLES THÉODORE. FRÈRE. Arabs by a gateway. Damascus. Signed and inscribed on the reverse. 25½ x 21¼ins. (65 x 54cm). *Christie's.*

EUGÈNE FROMENTIN. Thieves of the night. Signed and dated 1865. 51¾ x 80ins. (131.5 x 203.5cm). *Christie's.*

GIUSEPPE GABANI. A North African street scene. Signed and inscribed Roma, on board. 11 x 18ins. (28 x 46cm). *Christie's.*

JOSÉ GALLEGOS Y ARNOSA. An Arab street vendor. Signed and dated Tanger 1881, on panel. 15¾ x 8¼ins. (40 x 21cm). *Christie's.*

ANDREW GEDDES. Portrait of George Cumming in Turkish dress. Signed and dated 1847, on panel. 25 x 21ins. (63.5 x 53cm). *Christie's.*

EUGÈNE ALEXIS GIRARDET. An Arab caravan. Signed and dated 1875. 24½ x 35¾ins. (62 x 91cm). *Christie's.*

ALEXANDER DEMETRIUS GOLZ. Arab horseman outside a mosque. Signed and dated '88, on panel. 25 x 19½ins. (63.5 x 49.5cm). *Christie's.*

P. GIRIGOTTI. The story teller. Signed. 19 x 26ins. (48 x 66cm). *Christie's.*

FREDERICK GOODALL. Arabs crossing a flooded field by the Pyramids. Signed with monogram and dated 1895. 20 x 44ins. (51 x 111.5cm). *Christie's.*

JEAN LÉON GÉRÔME. Recrues Egyptiennes traversant le desert. Signed and dated 1857. 25¼ x 43¼ins. (64 x 110cm). *Christie's.*

RICHARD BEAVIS. Bedawin caravan descending the high ground at Wady Ghurundel en route to Mount Sinai. Signed and dated 1876, and signed and inscribed on an old label on the reverse. 65¼ x 122ins. (166 x 310cm). *Christie's.*

DUDLEY HARDY. The snake charmer.
Signed and dated 1896, on panel.
17½ x 13¼ins. (44.5 x 34cm). *Christie's.*

BRUNO HOPPE. A seated Arab smoking a pipe. Signed and
dated Paris '90, on panel. 18 x 14½ins. (46 x 36.5cm). *Sotheby's.*

40

WALTER CHARLES HORSLEY. Fighting his battles o'er
again. Signed and dated 1883. 48¾ x 38¼ins. (124 x 97cm).
Sotheby's.

FRANZ XAVIER KOSLER. The waterseller.
Signed and dated 1902. 25 x 17½ins.
(63.5 x 44.5cm). *Christie's.*

PAUL JOANOVICH. The music lesson. Signed and dated
Paris 1890. 38 x 58ins. (96.5 x 147.5cm). *Christie's.*

FRANÇOIS HIPPOLYTE LALAISSE. An Arab
with two horses. Signed. 25 x 31½ins. (63.5 x 80cm).
Christie's.

JEAN RAYMOND HIPPOLYTE LAZERGES. An Arab musician. Signed and dated 1876, on panel. 19½ x 12¾ins. (49.5 x 32.5cm). *Christie's.*

WILLIAM LOGSDAIL. The gates of the Khalif. Signed and dated '87. 43½ x 31½ins. (110.5 x 80cm). *Christie's.*

ALPHONS LEOPOLD MIELICH. An Arab tradesman. Signed, on panel. 3 x 4¼ins. (7.5 x 11cm). *Christie's.*

FREDERIC, LORD LEIGHTON. Old Damascus: Jew's quarter, or Gathering citrons. 51 x 41ins. (129.5 x 104cm). *Christie's.*

TOMAS MORAGAS Y TORRAS.
The trial of a murderer in the
square of an Arab town. Signed.
26¼ x 38ins. (67 x 96.5cm).
Christie's.

LEOPOLD CARL MÜLLER.
Food for the blind beggar. Signed
and dated 1879. 27 x 43ins.
(68.5 x 109cm). *Christie's.*

WILLIAM JAMES MÜLLER.
Interior of the Temple of Osiris at
Philae. 29 x 52ins. (73.5 x 132cm).
Christie's.

RUDOLF GUSTAV MÜLLER-WIESBADEN. An Arab street scene. Signed and inscribed München.
56¾ x 42½ins. (144 x 108cm). *Christie's.*

KAREL OOMS. Un soir au bord du Nil. Signed
and dated 1894. 63¼ x 101½ins. (161 x 258cm).
Koninklijk Museum Schone Kunsten, Antwerp.

ANDRES PARLADE Y HEREDIA. The barber.
Signed and dated Tanger 1888, on panel.
22 x 15¾ins. (56 x 40cm). *Sotheby's.*

ALBERTO PASINI. An Arab hawking party. Signed and dated 1866, on panel. 10 x 18ins. (25.5 x 46cm). *Christie's.*

EUGÈNE PAVY. The Moorish guard. Signed. 27¼ x 13ins. (69 x 33cm). *Christie's.*

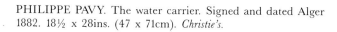

PHILIPPE PAVY. The water carrier. Signed and dated Alger 1882. 18½ x 28ins. (47 x 71cm). *Christie's.*

RICCARDO PELLEGRINI. The snake
charmer. Signed. 27½ x 19¼ins. (70 x 49cm).
Sotheby's.

PAUL DOMINIQUE PHILIPPOTEAUX.
The snake charmer. Signed and dated 1894.
23½ x 39¾ins. (60 x 101cm). *Christie's.*

LOUIS EMILE PINEL DE GRANDCHAMP An Arab boy with a donkcy. Signed, on board. 15 x 11¾ins. (38 x 30cm). *Christie's.*

GUSTAVE LEON ANTOINE MARIE POPELIN. An Arab guard. Signed and inscribed, à mon ami d'Argenie, and dated Juin 1878, on panel. 18 x 10ins. (45.5 x 25.5cm). *Christie's.*

CLÉMENT PUJOL DE GUSTAVINO. Regal gifts. Signed. 36¼ x 28ins. (92 x 71cm). *Sotheby's.*

THEODORE JACQUES RALLI. Lighting the Hookah. Signed and dated '79. 15½ x 12ins. (39.5 x 30.5cm). *Christie's.*

RUBENS SANTORO. Arabs by the riverside. Signed, on panel. 12½ x 9ins. (31.5 x 23cm). *Christie's.*

Top left: CHARLES ROBERTSON. Leaving the Mosque. Signed with monogram and dated 1881. 45 x 33ins. (114 x 84cm). *Christie's.*

HENRI EMILIEN ROUSSEAU. The return of the hawking party. Signed and dated '79. 21 x 17½ins. (53 x 44.5cm). *Christie's.*

THEOBALD SCHORN. An Arab encampment. Signed, on panel. 11½ x 18ins. (29 x 46cm). *Christie's.*

GEORGE L. SEYMOUR.
A consecration of arms.
On panel. 14 x 9ins. (35.5 x 23cm).
Christie's.

Above left: ADOLF CHRISTIAN
SCHREYER. Arab horseman in a
landscape. Signed. 23¼ x 32¼ins.
(59 x 82cm). *Christie's.*

CAVALIERO ANTONIO
SCOGNAMIGLIO. An Arab
encampment. Signed. 26 x 53ins.
(66 x 134.5cm). *Christie's.*

GUSTAVO SIMONI. Arabs in a
mosque. Signed and inscribed
Tlemcen. 28¾ x 41½ins.
(73.5 x 105.5cm). *Christie's.*

AMEDEO MOMO SIMONETTI.
The carpet market. Signed and inscribed
Roma. 23½ x 39¼ins. (60 x 99.5cm).
Christie's.

CHRISTIAN GEORG SPEYER.
A dismounted Arab horseman at camp.
Signed. 18 x 23ins. (45.5 x 58cm).
Christie's.

H.M. STAACKMANN. An Arab market
scene. Signed and dated 1885. On panel.
10¼ x 15¾ins. (26 x 40cm). *Christie's.*

LOUIS TESSON. An Arab market place. Signed. 25 x 30ins. (63.5 x 76cm). *Christie's.*

Left: RUDOLPH SWOBODA. The carpet dealer. Signed. 37 x 20¾ins. (94 x 53cm). *Christie's.*

WILLIAM HENRY HAMILTON TROOD. The Arab blacksmith. Signed and dated Morocco 1891. 12½ x 17¾ins. (31.5 x 45cm). *Christie's.*

EMIL UHL. In the sook. Signed, on panel. 18 x 14½ins.
(46 x 37cm). *Christie's.*

H. VALEROS. The water carriers. Signed. 26 x 21ins.
(66 x 53.5cm). *Christie's.*

STEFANO USSI. A girl at an oasis. Signed and dated
1872. 33 x 23ins. (84 x 58.5cm). *Christie's.*

HORACE EMILE JEAN VERNET. The lion hunter.
Signed and dated Roma 1833. 13¼ x 11ins. (34 x 28cm).
Christie's.

KNIGHTON WARREN. Guarding the harem.
Signed. 52 x 32ins. (132 x 81cm). *Christie's.*

WILLIAM J. WEBB. The Eastern sheep fold. Signed with
monogram and dated 1869. 41½ x 29½ins. (105.5 x 75cm).
Christie's.

GEORGES WASHINGTON. A mounted
Arab warrior in a landscape. Signed.
19¼ x 23½ins. (49 x 60cm). *Christie's.*

EDWIN LORD WEEKS. Leading the way. Signed and dated 1875. 35 x 45½ins. (89 x 115.5cm). *Christie's.*

RUDOLF WEISSE. A street scene in Cairo. Signed and inscribed Cairo, on panel. 20½ x 25ins. (52 x 63.5cm). *Christie's.*

CHARLES WILDA. The guard. Signed and dated Cairo 1888. 22 x 14½ins. (56 x 37cm). *Christie's.*

FRANZ THEODOR WURBEL. Arabs playing backgammon. Signed. 37¾ x 56ins. (96 x 142cm). *Christie's.*

FELIKS M. WYGRZYWALSKI. The carpet maker. Signed, on panel. 18¼ x 22ins. (46.5 x 56cm). *Sotheby's.*

EDUARDO ZAMACOIS Y ZABALA. Arabs outside a mosque. Signed and dated '69. 17 x 13ins. (43 x 33cm). *Christie's.*

JEAN JULES ANTOINE LECOMTE DE NOUY. The guard of the seraglio. Signed and dated 1876. 29 x 47ins.
(73.5 x 119.5cm). *Christie's.*

LUDWIG DEUTSCH.
Outside the palace.
Signed, on panel.
27½ x 38ins.
(70 x 96.5cm). *Christie's.*

Beauties

The sheer size of this section of subject matter bears witness to the fact that female beauty was much prized in the nineteenth century. For the first time, large numbers of pictures were painted whose sole raison d'être was the depiction of such beauty; not so much in the form of specific portraiture, but more as a homage to feminine beauty in its own right. Essentially, they were images created not to flatter the sitter but to please the eye of the beholder. Painters of beauties spread their net far and wide, to lay before an eager public examples from many different nationalities and social classes. There were idle rich beauties, whose surroundings were often as luxurious as their personal endowments; there were healthy outdoor beauties; there were cheeky servant beauties; and gypsy or peasant girls of 'unexpected' loveliness. These might be of a Latin race (to be exhibited at the Royal Academy as 'A Beauty from a Southern Clime'), French girls ('La Soubrette', 'La Coquette'), or English (the inevitable 'An English Rose').

Throughout the century ran a continuing fondness for the 'keepsake' tradition of the depiction of beauty, gentle, sweet and somewhat coy. But in the second half of the period a number of painters emerged in Paris who endowed the genre with considerably more sense of style. The culmination was reached in the Belle Epoque, when glittering stars like Boldini, de Nittis, Munkacsy, Flameng, Helleu and Stevens were all at work. Certainly these men were portraitists, but they were equally sought after as purveyors of nameless, ultra-fashionable female beauty. Beauty was heightened by dress, and haute couture played its part in such pictures. Painters found it necessary to become adept in the reproduction of dress materials as an aid to achieving the right blend of luxury and loveliness. Eugene Benson writes of Charles Baugniet in 1869:

> His pictures are remarkable for exquisite finish, purity of tone, and admirable rendering of the texture of silks and satins, of marble and gold.
> He enjoys painting these lovely women and girls in opulent nests.

A new sort of feminine beauty was perceived to have been invented by Parisian painters from about 1860 onwards. It was a treatment of beauty which concentrated heavily on externals, on surfaces, and on show. In the eyes of some critics, it contrasted unfavourably with the earlier approach which emphasised the more elevated, spiritual qualities of womankind. In former times, complained Castagnary in 1872,

> ladies had themselves painted for their husbands, for their children. Artists in painting them sought to express the sweetness of their souls, the elevation of their spirits, or the nobility of their feelings.

Now, Castagnary continued, a change had taken place (wrought in his opinion by Carolus-Duran, but others were not slow to follow his example):

> Whereas before a reserved and discreet demeanour was prized, now only the loudest colours are employed — never before has the human creature, its physiognomy and thought, been sacrificed so savagely to its garb. Heads are nothing — all space is taken up by material! The most showy

and sparkling satins! The painter doesn't just cover his models, he overwhelms them. The woman seems like a prize cow, to be dressed up and covered in ornaments. What vulgarity of taste, what fussiness of effect! Such a change was a reflection of the way the old order was giving way to the vulgar, plutocratic new; old virtues became submerged in the sea of satin. Spirituality was overwhelmed by materialism. That society was tending in this direction was observed by several critics, not just in Paris but also in London where Harry Quilter writing in the Spectator in 1879 spoke of 'the abominably articifial atmosphere of a certain style of society which might be called the Neo-French-English,' where 'the only things that are real are the dresses,' and 'the essential parts of which are to dress like a French actress.' To blame such developments entirely on the French, however, would not be totally fair. Berlin and Munich had artists — Lenbach, Kaulbach and other painters of the Grunderzeit, for instance — who popularised a style of female beauty which betrayed a similar degree of materialism.

If such images of female beauty were indeed products of an opulent materialism then it followed that these pictures would be appreciated as ideal adornments to the walls of rich interiors of the time, easily absorbed into the prevailing taste for full-blown luxury. As Edmond About wrote of a typical beauty by Charles Chaplin, an accomplished French specialist in such things:

> (He) has positively invented a genre of new, elegant, rich decoration, in harmony with the luxury and comfort of modern palaces. Princes have chosen him to brighten their apartments, and they have employed a happy hand. This fresh and laughing painting is truly a charm to the eyes.

Was it the painting which was a charm to the eyes, or was it the sitter? There can be no doubt that many of the pictures featured in this section were bought, rather like certain nudes, because they offered the opportunity to relish a beautiful girl under the cover of art appreciation. It was an easy and successful formula to paint a 'beautiful' picture by making it depict a beautiful human being. This confusion in patrons' minds had even been noted in the previous century by St. Julien when he remarked 'As long as pictures contain a few pretty women's faces, the public is happy.' It was this climate of receptivity which encouraged Greuze on his series of portraits of attractive girls in more or less thinly-veiled states of sexual arousal, the message of virginity breached often symbolised by eggs that have been broken or milk that has been spilt. Greuze is the precedent for Chaplin, Léon Herbo, and many others like them.

English painters were not so adept at rendering fashionable beauty as their French counterparts. Significantly, it was a refugee Frenchman, James Joseph Tissot, who conquered London in this respect during the 1870s. *The Times* described with awe his *Evening* of 1878:

> The crush of a West-end soiree, with a young lady in a daring 'arrangement'. . .a figure worthy of Worth. . .It is art brought to the doors and laid at the feet of the *monde*, if not sometimes of the *demi-monde*, with an almost cynical sincerity.

It is incontestable that the appeal of the more risquée Parisian beauties depicted in many French pictures lay in their citizenship of the demi-monde. In the 1860s and 1870s Zola's Nana might have figured as the model for any number of them. Indeed there was even a vogue for suggestions of more unconventional pleasures: Courbet's grappling nude ladies are an obvious example, but two beauties pictured together often carry subtler hints of forbidden passion. Tissot's Parisian *La Confidence* in which one lady melts dangerously into the bosom of another, is an example. So also is Jules Saintin's *In the Gloveshop*, where assistant and customer bend hotly together over the merchandise, earning the picture the unofficial later title 'The glove that dares not speak its name'.

In contrast to these metropolitan sophistications, at the opposite end of the scale from the Parisian boudoir, there was a vogue for loveliness which was 'simple and unvarnished', discernible amongst the country lasses of the peasantry. Minor English painters like Charles Sillem Lidderdale or William Oliver were clearly far more at home seeking out such rustic good-lookers than in smart drawing rooms. They presented a string of 'fair faggot-gatherers' for the public's delectation. Alluring shepherdesses and milkmaids were an international currency, being painted profitably in most countries of Europe. Italy was considered an especially fertile source for such beauties, and a variety of artists scoured the countryside for peasant models to pose for pictures with titles like *The Village Fornarina*, or *An Abruzzi Venus*.

A new element in the pictorial treatment of womanhood emerged as the century drew towards its close. Symbolism added this further dimension, emphasising the interior spiritual qualities of the female sex as well as — sometimes in contrast to — their decorative exterior. The tortured souls created by Rossetti and the Pre-Raphaelites were repeated and adapted across Europe by painters such as Levy-Dhurmer and Armand Point in France and Franz von Stuck in Germany. The vogue for titles like 'La Mysterieuse' or 'La Belle Dame sans Merci' presented women as intriguing creatures of mystery or cruelty, rather than mere beautiful objects. Even the least imaginative artists exploited this trend towards greater spirituality by rechristening their wares 'A pensive Beauty' or 'Far-away Thoughts'. The popularisation of symbolism gave a piquant new seasoning to the taste of the public at large for a pretty girl, the underlying appeal of all the pictures in this section.

Index of artists

BISSON, Edouard (French, 1856-?)
* BLAAS, Eugen de (Austrian, 1843-1931)
BLACKMAN, Walter (Anglo-American, fl.1878-1890)
BLANCHE, Jacques Emile (French, 1861-1942)
BLUME, Edmund (German, 1844-1911)
BOKS, Ernest Jan (Belgian, 1838-?)
* BOLDINI, Giovanni (Italian, 1842-1931)
BONAVIA, George (British, ?-1876)
* BOUGUEREAU, William Adolphe (French, 1825-1905)
BOUTIBONNE, Charles Edouard (Hungarian, 1816-1897)
* BOUVIER, Pietro (Italian, 1839-1927)
* BREAKSPEARE, William A. (British, 1855-1914)
BRESLAU, Marie Louise Catherine (Swiss, 1856-1928)
BRETT, Rosa (British, fl.1867-1881)
BROECK, Clémence van den (Belgian, 1843-1922)
BUCKNER, Richard (British, fl.1842-1877)
BULAND, Jean Eugène (French, 1852-1927)
BURGESS, John Bagnold (British, 1830-1897)

CAILLARD, Alfred Benoit (French, ?-1940)
* CALDERON, Philip Hermogenes (Anglo-Spanish, 1833-1898)
CAPRILE, Vincenzo (Italian, 1856-1937)
CAVE, Jules Cyrille (French, 1859-?)
* CAROLUS-DURAN, Charles Emile Auguste (French, 1838-1917)
CARRIERE-BELLEUSE, Pierre (French, 1851-1933)
CARROLL, William J. (British, late 19th Century)
CECCHI, Adriano (Italian, late 19th Century)
CHABAS, Paul (French, 1869-?)
* CHAPLIN, Charles (French, 1825-1891)
CHARTRAN, Théobald (French, 1849-1907)
* CHATEIGNON, Ernest (French, late 19th Century)
CHAVET, Victor Joseph (French, 1822-1906)
* CLAIRIN, Georges Jules Victor (French, 1843-1919)
* CLAUS, Emile (Belgian, 1849-1924)
COMERRE, Léon François (French, 1850-1916)
* CONTI, Tito (Italian, 1842-1924)
COPE, Charles West (British, 1811-1890)
* CORCOS, Vittorio Matteo (Italian, 1859-1933)
* COSTA, Giuseppe (Italian, 1852-1912)
COSTA, John da (British, 1867-1931)
COT, Pierre Auguste (French, 1837-1883)
COULON, Louis (French, 1820-1855)
CREMONA, Tranquillo (Italian, 1837-1878)
* CROEGAERT, Georges (French, 1848-?)
CZACHORSKI, Ladislas de (Polish, 1850-1911)

DANTIN, Paul (French, late 19th Century)
* DASTUGUE, Maxime (French, fl.1876-1908)
* DAVIES, Norman Prescott (British, fl.1890-1900)
DAVIS, Stuart G. (British, late 19th Century)
DEULLY, Eugène August François (French, 1860-?)
DIAQUE, Ricardo (Franco-Spanish, late 19th Century)
DICKSEE, Sir Frank (British, 1853-1928)
* DICKSEE, Thomas Francis (British, 1819-1895)
DOUCET, Henri Lucien (French, 1856-1895)
DOYEN, Gustave (French, 1837-?)
DUEZ, Ernest Ange (French, 1843-1896)
DVORAK, Franz (Austrian, 1862-1927)

EASTLAKE, Sir Charles Lock (British, 1793-1865)
* EGUSQUIZA, Rogelio de (Spanish, 1845-?)
* EICHSTAEDT, Rudolf (German, 1857-1924)

* ENJOLRAS, Delphin (French, 1857-?)
EPP, Rudolf (German, 1834-1910)
ERDFELT, Alois (German, 1851-1911)

FANFANI, Enrico (Italian, late 19th Century)
FELIX, Eugen (Austrian, 1837-1906)
FERRIES, Gabriel Joseph Marie (French, 1847-1914)
FEUERBACH, Anselm (German, 1829-1880)
* FILDES, Sir Samuel Luke (British, 1844-1927)
* FLAMENG, François (French, 1856-1923)
* FONTANA, Roberto (Italian, 1844-1907)

* GANDY, Herbert (British fl.1879-1920)
GARCIA Y MARTINEZ, Juan (Spanish, 1829-1890)
* GARRIDO, Eduardo Leon (Spanish, 1856-1906)
GARRIDO, Leandro Ramon (Spanish, 1868-1909)
* GERARD, Théodore (Belgian, 1829-1895)
GIESEL, Hermann (Austrian, 1847-1906)
GIOJA, Belisario (Italian, 1829-1906)
GIRARDET, Louis Auguste (French, 1858-1933)
GODWARD, John William (British, 1861-1922)
GOLA, Emilio (Italian, 1852-1923)
* GOLTZ, Alexander Demetrius Sandor (German, 1875-1944)
* GONZALES, Juan Antonio (Spanish, 1842-1914?)
GOODMAN, Maude (British, 1860-1938)
GOUPIL, Jules Adolphe (French, 1839-1883)
GRASSET, Auguste (French, 1829-?)
* GRENET, Edouard (French, 1857-?)
* GUGEL, Karl Adolf (German, 1820-1885)

HAANEN, Cecil van (Dutch, 1844-1914)
HAAXMAN, Pieter (Dutch, 1854-1937)
HALLE, Charles Edward (British, 1846-1914)
HALLE, Ludwig Samuel Baruch (German, 1824-1889)
* HARLAMOFF, Alexei Alexeievich (Russian, 1849-?)
HARRIS, Edwin (British, fl.1882-1904)
HEILBUTH, Ferdinand (German, 1826-1889)
HELLEU, Paul César (French, 1859-1927)
* HENNER, Jean Jacques (French, 1829-1905)
HENNESSEY, William John (British, 1839-1920?)
* HERBO, Léon (Belgian, 1850-1907)
* HERNANDEZ, Daniel (Peruvian-Italian, 1856-1932)
* HICKS, George Elgar (British, 1824-1914)
HILL, Arthur (British, fl.1858-1893)
* HILL, James John (British, 1811-1882)
* HODEBERT, Léon Auguste César (French, 1852-1914)
* HOFLINGER, Albert (German, 1855-?)
HOLWEG, Gustav (Austrian, 1855-1890)
HORRAK, Johann (Austrian, 1815-1870)
* HUISKEN, Herman (German, 1861-1899)
HURLSTONE, Frederick Yeates (British, 1801-1869)

INDONI, Filippo (Italian, late 19th Century)
* IRELAND, James (British, late 19th Century)

JACOBS, Emil (German, 1802-1866)
* JACQUET, Gustave Jean (French, 1846-1909)
* JENSEN, Theodore (British, mid 19th Century)
JONGHE, Gustave L. de (Belgian, 1829-1893)

* KAULBACH, Friedrich August von (German, 1850-1920)
* KEMM, Robert (British, fl.1874-1885)
* KENNINGTON, Thomas Benjamin (British, 1856-1916)

KERCKHOVE, Ernest van den (Belgian, 1840-1879)
KLEMPNER, Ernest (Austrian, 1867-?)
KNÖCHL, Hans (Austrian, 1850-?)
* KÖHLER, Carl (German, 1860-?)
KRØYER, Peter Severin (Danish, 1851-1909)

* LANCEROTTO, Egisto (Italian, 1847-1916)
LANDELLE, Charles Zacharie (French, 1821-1908)
* LAUNAY, Fernand de (French, ?-1904)
LEGA, Silvestro (Italian, 1826-1893)
* LEIGHTON, Frederic, Lord (British, 1830-1896)
LENBACH, Franz Seraph von (German, 1836-1904)
LENOIR, Charles Amable (French, 1861-?)
LEVORATI, Ernesto (Italian, fl.1880-1893)
LÉVY, Emile (French, 1826-1890)
* LIDDERDALE, Charles Sillem (British, 1831-1895)
LIST, Wilhelm (Austrian, 1864-1918)
LIVEMONT, Privat (Belgian, 1861-?)
LLANECES, José (Spanish, 1863-1919)
LONG, Edwin (British, 1829-1891)
LOUDAN, William Mouat (British, 1868-1925)
LOWCOCK, Charles Frederick (British, ?-1922)
* LUCAS, F. Hippolyte (French, fl.1841-1866)
LUNDGREN, Egron Sellif (Swedish, 1815-1875)
LYNCH, Albert (Franco-Peruvian, 1851-?)

MACHARD, Jules Louis (French, 1839-1900)
* MADRAZO Y GARRETA, Raimundo de (Spanish,
    1841-1920)
* MAKOVSKY, Constantin (Russian, 1839-1915)
* MALEMPRÉ, Leo (British, fl.1887-1901)
MANCINI, Antonio (Italian, 1852-1930)
MARCHETTI, Ludovico (Italian, 1853-1909)
* MARGETSON, William Henry (British, 1861-1940)
* MARSHALL, Thomas Falcon (British, 1818-1878)
MARTIN, Camille (French, 1861-1898)
MARTIN-KAVEL, François (French, late 19th Century)
* MENZLER, Wilhelm (German, 1846-?)
MERLE, Hugues (French, 1823-1881)
MILLAIS, Sir John Everett (British, 1829-1896)
MIRALLES, Francisco (Spanish, 1850-?)
MITCHELL, Charles William (British, fl.1876-1893)
* MODERAT D'OTÉMAR, Marie Adolphe Edouard
    (French, late 19th Century)
* MOLLICA, Achille (Italian, late 19th Century)
* MOLLICA, Emanuelle (Italian, late 19th Century)
MOORE, Albert Joseph (British, 1841-1893)
MUNKACSY, Michael von (Hungarian, 1844-1909)

NANI, Napoleone (Italian, 1841-1899)
NICZKY, Eduard (German, 1850-1919)
NITTIS, Giuseppe de (Italian, 1846-1884)
* NONNENBRUCH, Max (German, 1857-1922)

* OLIVER, William (British, fl.1867-1882)
OPIE, Edward (British, 1810-1894)
ORSELLI, Arturo (Italian, late 19th Century)
* OSSANI, Alessandro (Italian, fl.1860-1888)

PALLARES Y ALLUSTANTE, Joaquin (Spanish, late
    19th Century)
* PALMAROLI Y GONZALES, Vincente (Spanish,
    1834-1896)
PAPPERITZ, Georg Frederick (German, 1846-1918)
PASSINI, Ludwig Johann (Austrian, 1832-1903)

PAUSINGER, Clemens von (Austrian, 1855-1936)
* PELHAM, Thomas Kent (British, fl.1860-1891)
PEÑA Y MUÑOZ, Maximino (Spanish, 1863-?)
PENROSE, James Doyle (British, 1864-1932)
PERRAULT, Léon Bazile Jean (French, 1832-1908)
PERRET, Aimé (French, 1847-1927)
PERRY, William (British, fl. mid-19th Century)
* PERUGINI, Charles Edward (British, 1839-1918)
PIGLHEIN, Bruno Elimar Ulrich (German, 1848-1894)
PINCHART, Auguste Emile (French, 1842-?)
PIOT, Adolphe Etienne (French, 1850-1910)
POETZELBERGER, Robert (Austrian, 1856-1930)
POINT, Armand (French, 1861-1932)
POPE, Gustav (British, fl.1852-1895)
PORTAELS, Jean François (Belgian, 1818-1895)
PORTIELJE, Jan Frederik Pieter (Belgian, 1829-1908)
* POSTIGLIONE, Luca (Italian, 1876-1936)
PRINSEP, Valentine Cameron (British, 1836-1904)
PROBST, Karl (Austrian, 1854-1924)

QUIVIERES, Augustin Marcot de (French, 1854-1907)

RAUDNITZ, Albert (German, fl.1873-1892)
* RECK, Hermine von (German, 1833-1906)
REZNICEK, Ferdinand von (Austrian, 1868-1909)
* RHYS, Oliver (British, fl.1876-1893)
RIBERA, Pierre (French, 1867-?)
* RIBERA, Roman (Spanish, 1848-?)
* RICCI, Arturo (Italian, 1854-?)
RICHMOND, Sir William Blake (British, 1842-1921)
* ROBERTS, Edwin (British, fl.1862-1886)
ROMAKO, Anton (Austrian, 1832-1889)
* ROMANI, Juana (Italian, 1869-1924)
* RONDEL, Henri (French, 1857-1919)
* ROSSETTI, Dante Gabriel (British, 1828-1882)
* ROSSI, Lucius (French, 1846-1913)
* ROTA, Giuseppe (Italian, late 19th Century)
ROUGERON, Jules James (French, 1841-1880)
ROYER, Lionel (French, 1852-1926)
RUBEN, Franz Leo (Austrian, 1842-1920)
RUSS, Franz (Austrian, 1844-1906)
RUSSELL, Edwin Wensley (British, mid 19th Century)

SAENZ Y SAENZ, Pedro (Spanish, late 19th Century)
* SAIN, Edouard Alexandre (French, 1830-1910)
* SAINTIN, Jules Emile (French, 1829-1894)
SALMSON, Hugo Frederik (Swedish, 1843-1894)
SANDYS, Emma (British, 1834-1877)
* SANDYS, Frederick Anthony Augustus (British,
    1832-1904)
SAVAGE-COOPER, William (British, fl.1885-1903)
SCALBERT, Jules (French, 1851-?)
* SCHEURENBERG, Joseph (German, 1846-1914)
* SCHLESINGER, Henri Guillaume (French, 1814-1893)
SCHLIMARSKI, Heinrich Hans (Austrian, 1859-?)
SCHMALZ, Herbert Gustave (British, 1856-?)
SCHUSTER, Karl Maria (Austrian, 1871-1953)
SCHWARZENFELD, Adolf von (Austrian, 1854-?)
* SEIFERT, Alfred (German, 1850-1901)
* SEIGNAC, Guillaume (French, ?-1903)
* SEMENOWSKY, Emile Eisman (French, fl.1880-1900)
* SERRURE, Auguste (Belgian, 1825-1903)
SICHEL, Nathaniel (German, 1843-1907)
SIEFERT, Paul (French, 1874-?)
SIMONS, Frans Jan (Belgian, 1855-1919)

SKIPWORTH, Frank Markham (British, fl.1882-1916)
SOLOMON, Simeon (British, 1840-1905)
SOLOMON, Solomon Joseph (British, 1860-1927)
* SORBI, Raffaello (Italian, 1844-1931)
SOROLLA Y BASTIDA, Joaquin (Spanish, 1863-1923)
SPITZER, Emanuel (Austrian, 1844-1919)
STEINHARDT, Frederik Karl (German, 1844-?)
* STEVENS, Alfred (Belgian, 1823-1906)
STIFTER, Moritz (German, 1857-1905)
STONE, Marcus (British, 1840-1921)
STOREY, George Adolphus (British, 1834-1919)
STRYDONCK, Guillaume van (Belgian, 1861-1937)
* STYKA, Jan (Polish, 1858-1925)
SURAND, Gustave (French, 1860-?)

TANOUX, Adrien Henri (French, 1865-1923)
TANZI, Léon Louis Antoine (French, 1846-1913)
TAVERNIER, Andrea (Italian, 1858-1932)
TAYLOR, Ernest E. (British, 1863-1907)
TESCHENDORFF, Emile (German, 1833-1894)
* THADDEUS, Henry Jones (British, 1860-1929)
* TISSOT, James Joseph (French, 1836-1902)
* TOFANO, Eduardo (Italian, 1838-1920)
TORRES, Antonio (Spanish, 1851-?)
TOUDOUZE, Edouard (French, 1848-1907)
TOULMOUCHE, Auguste (French, 1829-1890)
* TOUSSAINT, Fernand (Belgian, 1873-1955)

TURINA Y AREAL, Joaquin (Spanish, 1847-1903)

UWINS, Thomas (British, 1782-1857)

VASARRI, Emilio (Italian, late 19th Century)
VERHAS, Frans (Belgian, 1827-1897)
* VERNON, Emile (French, fl.1890-1920)
VILLEGAS Y CORDERO, José (Spanish, 1848-1922)
VINEA, Francesco (Italian, 1845-1902)

* WAGEMANS, Maurice (Belgian, 1877-1927)
* WAGNER, Paul Hermann (German, 1852-?)
WAINWRIGHT, William John (British, 1855-1936)
WALLER, Mary Lemon (British, late 19th Century)
* WATERHOUSE, John William (British, 1849-1917)
WAUTERS, Emile Charles (Belgian, 1846-1933)
WEYDE, Julius (German, 1822-1960)
WICHERA VON BRENNERSTEIN, Raimund
   (Austrian, 1862-1925)
* WONTNER, William Clarke (British, fl.1879-1912)
WOOLMER, Alfred Joseph (British, 1805-1892)
* WYBURD, Francis John (British, 1826-?)

ZANDOMENEGHI, Federigo (Italian, 1841-1917)
ZULOAGA Y ZABELETA, Ignacio (Spanish, 1870-1945)

WILLIAM ALBERT ABLETT. On the terrace. Signed
and dated '05. 36¼ x 26ins. (92 x 66cm). *Christie's.*

EDMOND FRANÇOIS AMAN-JEAN. Le beau voyage.
Signed. 23 x 28¼ins. (58.5 x 71.5cm). *Christie's.*

FRIEDRICH VON AMERLING. The Oriental.
38¼ x 32ins. (97 x 81cm). *Christie's.*

SOPHIE ANDERSON. A spring beauty. Signed.
20½ x 16½ins. (52 x 42cm). *Christie's.*

FEDERIGO ANDREOTTI. A girl with a pigeon. Signed.
12¾ x 10ins. (32.5 x 25cm). *Christie's.*

CHARLES BAUGNIET. Reading the letter. Signed, on
panel. 26½ x 21ins. (67.3 x 53cm). *Christie's.*

CHARLES BAXTER. An elegant beauty. Signed and
dated 1855. 27½ x 23½ins. (70 x 60cm). *Christie's.*

EUGEN DE BLAAS. A summer beauty. Signed.
29¾ x 21½ins. (75.5 x 54.5cm). *Christie's.*

GIOVANNI BOLDINI. Portrait of Cecilia de Madrazo Fortuny, three-quarter length wearing a black dress. Signed. 45 x 27ins. (114.5 x 68.5cm). *Christie's.*

PIETRO BOUVIER. Off to the ball. Signed, inscribed di Milano and dated 1884, on panel. 10¼ x 7¾ins. (26 x 19.5cm). *Christie's.*

WILLIAM ADOLPHE BOUGUEREAU. The fair spinner. Signed and dated '73. 31¾ x 24ins. (80.5 x 61cm). *Christie's.*

WILLIAM A. BREAKSPEARE. The flower maiden. Signed. 30 x 19½ins. (76 x 49.5cm). *Christie's.*

PHILIP HERMOGENES CALDERON. Springtime 'For, lo, the winter is past, etc'. Signed and dated 1896. 60 x 41ins. (152 x 104.5cm). *Christie's.*

CHARLES EMILE AUGUSTE CAROLUS-DURAN.
Portrait of a girl, wearing a floral dress. Signed.
17½ x 14½ins. (44.5 x 37cm). *Christie's.*

CHARLES CHAPLIN. Lilac. Signed. 16¾ x 13¼ins.
(42.5 x 33.5cm.) *Christie's.*

ERNEST CHATEIGNON. A young lady in a park.
Signed. 39½ x 28¾ins. (100 x 73cm). *Christie's.*

GEORGES JULES VICTOR CLAIRIN. Autumn beauty.
Signed, on panel. 24¼ x 19¼ins. (61.5 x 49cm). *Christie's.*

TITO CONTI. An Italian beauty. Signed. 20 x 16ins.
(50.5 x 40.5cm). *Christie's.*

EMILE CLAUS. Arranging flowers. Signed, on panel. 7½ x 14ins. (19 x 35.5cm). *Christie's.*

VITTORIO MATTEO CORCOS.
Contemplation. Signed. 33 x 30ins.
(84 x 76.5cm). *Christie's.*

GIUSEPPE COSTA.
The miniature. Signed.
23 x 18ins.
(58.5 x 45.5cm). *Christie's.*

GEORGES CROEGAERT.
Portrait of a lady. Signed
and inscribed Paris.
12¾ x 9ins. (32.5 x 23cm).
Christie's.

MAXIME DASTUGUE. A rainy day.
Signed and dated '86. 24¼ x 20ins.
(61.5 x 51cm). *Christie's.*

NORMAN PRESCOTT
DAVIES. The maid of the
mill. Signed and dated
1891 and signed and
inscribed on an old label
on the reverse.
15¾ x 11¾ins.
(40 x 30cm). *Christie's.*

THOMAS FRANCIS
DICKSEE. Portrait of a
lady, half length, wearing
a white dress. Signed with
monogram and dated
1862. 15 x 12ins.
(38 x 30.5cm). *Christie's.*

RUDOLF EICHSTAEDT. A serving girl offering fruit. Signed. 37¼ x 25¾ins. (94.5 x 65.5cm). *Christie's.*

Right: DELPHIN ENJOLRAS. A lady at her dressing table. Signed. 21¾ x 15¼ins. (55.5 x 38.5cm). *Christie's.*

Bottom right: ROGELIO DE EGUSQUIZA. An elegant beauty. Signed. 18¼ x 22¼ins. (46.5 x 56.5cm). *Christie's.*

SIR SAMUEL LUKE FILDES. A girl, small bust length. Signed and dated '89, on panel. 14½ x 10½ins. (37 x 26.5cm). *Christie's.*

ROBERTO FONTANA. A peasant girl. Signed.
21¼ x 18ins. (54 x 46cm). *Christie's.*

Left: FRANÇOIS FLAMENG. A fashionable beauty. Signed.
65 x 33ins. (164 x 84cm). *Christie's.*

HERBERT GANDY. The love letter. Signed and dated '95.
25 x 45ins. (63.5 x 114.5cm). *Christie's.*

EDUARDO LEON GARRIDO. Deep thoughts. Signed, on panel. 15¾ x 11½ins. (40 x 29cm). *Christie's.*

THÉODORE GERARD. A Bavarian peasant girl. Signed and dated 1871, on panel. 15¼ x 10ins. (38.5 x 25.5cm). *Christie's.*

ALEXANDER DEMETRIUS SANDOR GOLTZ. A portrait of a young girl in a black hat. Signed and dated '96. 36½ x 32ins. (92.5 x 81cm). *Sotheby's.*

JUAN ANTONIO GONZALES. A lady with a fan. Signed and dated VI.75, on panel. 16 x 13ins. (40.5 x 33cm). *Christie's.*

74

EDOUARD GRENET. Contemplating her reflection.
Signed. 36 x 24ins. (91.5 x 61cm). *Christie's.*

KARL ADOLPH GUGEL. A girl with a basket of fruit.
Signed and inscribed München. 36 x 30ins. (91.5 x 76cm).
Christie's.

ALEXEI ALEXEIEVICH HARLAMOFF. Portrait of a
young girl, wearing a red dress holding a bunch of roses.
Signed and dated 1915. 28¼ x 23¼ins. (72 x 59cm).
Christie's.

JEAN JACQUES·HENNER. A young girl. Signed.
21¼ x 16¼ins. (54 x 41.5cm). *Christie's.*

JAMES JOSEPH TISSOT. Portrait of
Mrs. Kathleen Newton (Mavourneen).
Signed and dated 1877. 35½ x 20ins.
(90 x 51cm). *Christie's.*

LÉON HERBO. A daughter of the Lagoons. Signed. 29¼ x 40¼ins. (74 x 102cm). *Christie's.*

DANIEL HERNANDEZ. The billet doux.
Signed, on panel. 10 x 6¾ins. (25.5 x 17cm).
Christie's.

GEORGE ELGAR HICKS. A summer rose.
Signed and dated 1910. 24 x 20ins. (61 x 51cm).
Christie's.

JAMES JOHN HILL. The fortune teller. Signed and dated 1863, and signed on an old label on the reverse. 26¼ x 21¼ins. (66.5 x 54cm). *Christie's.*

LÉON AUGUSTE CÉSAR HODEBERT. A lady, head and shoulders, from the back. Signed and dated 1887. 26¼ x 21ins. (66.5 x 53cm). *Christie's.*

ALBERT HOFLINGER. Le loup. Signed. 19¾ x 12¾ins. (50.5 x 32.5cm). *Christie's.*

HERMAN HUISKEN. An Amsterdam beauty. Signed and dated '97 and signed, inscribed and dated 1897 on a label on the reverse. 32 x 25¼ins. (81 x 64cm). *Christie's.*

JAMES IRELAND. The questioning look. Signed and
dated 1887. 20¼ x 16¼ins. (51.5 x 41.5cm). *Christie's.*

GUSTAVE JEAN JACQUET. A young beauty.
Indistinctly signed. 11½ x 7½ins. (29 x 19cm). *Christie's.*

THEODORE JENSEN. The flower picker. Signed and
dated 1853, oval. 35 x 27ins. (89 x 68.5cm). *Christie's.*

FRIEDRICH AUGUST VON KAULBACH. An elegant
lady (portrait of the artist's wife). Signed and dated 1900.
51¼ x 38½ins. (130 x 97.7cm). *Munich, Neue Pinakothek.*

ROBERT KEMM. The fern gatherer. Signed and inscribed on the reverse 36 x 27½ins. (91.5 x 70cm). *Christie's.*

CARL KÖHLER. A lady seated on a sofa. Signed, canvas laid down on board. 30 x 25¼ins. (76 x 64cm). *Sotheby's.*

THOMAS BENJAMIN KENNINGTON. On the beach. Signed and dated 1887. 16 x 19½ins. (40.5 x 49.5cm). *Christie's.*

FERNAND DE LAUNAY. A lady with flowers in the Tuileries. Signed and dated Vente de Launay 1905. 23 x 28½ins. (58.5 x 72.5cm). *Christie's.*

EGISTO LANCEROTTO. Portrait of a young lady. Signed. 59 x 29¼ins. (150 x 74cm). *Christie's.*

FREDERIC, LORD LEIGHTON. The maid with the golden hair. 32¾ x 24¼ins. (83 x 61.5cm). *Christie's.*

CHARLES SILLEM LIDDERDALE. The country girl.
Signed with monogram and dated 1890. 26 x 17ins.
(66 x 43cm). *Christie's.*

F. HIPPOLYTE LUCAS. La Soubrette. Signed.
26½ x 16ins. (67 x 40.5cm). *Christie's.*

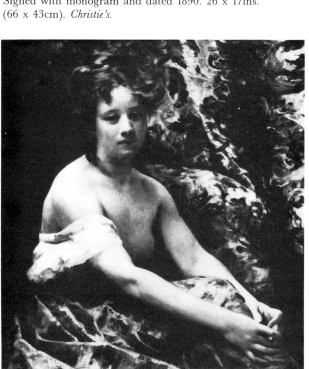

RAIMUNDO DE MADRAZO Y GARRETA. Portrait of
a model. Signed. 37½ x 31ins. (95 x 78.5cm). *Christie's.*

CONSTANTIN MAKOVSKY. A spring beauty. Signed,
on panel. 15 x 12½ins. (38 x 32cm). *Christie's.*

LEO MALEMPRÉ. A girl with flowers standing three-quarter length in a rose garden. Signed. 23¾ x 19¾ins. (60 x 50cm). *Sotheby's.*

THOMAS FALCON MARSHALL. A summer beauty. Signed and dated 1850, oval. 17 x 13ins. (43 x 33cm). *Christie's.*

WILLIAM HENRY MARGETSON. The murmur of the sea. Signed, and signed and inscribed on an old label on the reverse. 41¼ x 41¼ins. (104.5 x 104.5cm). *Christie's.*

MARIE ADOLPHE EDOUARD MODERAT
d'OTÉMAR. An elegant lady in the Place de la
Concorde, Paris. Signed, on panel. 16 x 9ins.
(40.5 x 23cm). *Christie's.*

Top left: WILHELM MENZLER. Idle thoughts.
Signed and inscribed München. 32¼ x 22¼ins.
(82 x 56.5cm). *Christie's.*

ACHILLE MOLLICA. An Italian beauty. Signed
and dated 1878. 26½ x 17½ins. (67 x 44.5cm).
Christie's.

EMANUELLE MOLLICA. A young peasant girl.
Signed and dated '78, on board. 6¾ x 4¼ins.
(17 x 10.5cm). *Christie's.*

MAX NONNENBRUCH. By the sea. Signed.
43 x 31½ins. (109 x 80cm). *Christie's.*

WILLIAM OLIVER. Contemplation. 22 x 16ins.
(56 x 40.5cm). *Christie's.*

ALESSANDRO OSSANI. The maid of Athens. Signed and dated 1880. 36½ x 29ins. (92.5 x 73.5cm). *Christie's.*

VINCENTE PALMAROLI Y GONZALEZ. Reading the future. Signed. 23 x 16¾ins. (58.5 x 42.5cm). *Christie's.*

THOMAS KENT PELHAM. Pride of the market. Signed and inscribed on the stretcher. 35 x 27½ins. (89 x 70cm). *Christie's.*

CHARLES EDWARD PERUGINI. A fair reflection. Signed with monogram. 32 x 24½ins. (81 x 62cm). *Christie's.*

LUCA POSTIGLIONE. The fair beauty. Signed.
20 x 15ins. (50.5 x 38cm). *Christie's.*

HERMINE VON RECK. Butterflies. Signed and dated
Carlsruhe 1874. 32½ x 24½ins. (82.5 x 62cm). *Christie's.*

OLIVER RHYS. The fruit seller. Signed and dated '95, on
board. 17 x 13ins. (43 x 33cm). *Christie's.*

ROMAN RIBERA. A pensive moment. Signed. 16 x 12ins.
(40.5 x 30.5cm). *Christie's.*

ARTURO RICCI. Good news. Signed. 23½ x 33ins. (59.5 x 84cm). *Christie's.*

EDWIN ROBERTS. Wild thyme. Signed. 23 x 19¾ins. (59.5 x 50cm). *Christie's.*

JUANA ROMANI. A dark haired beauty. Signed, on panel. 32 x 25¼ins. (81 x 64cm). *Sotheby's.*

DANTE GABRIEL ROSSETTI. Reverie. Signed with monogram and dated 1868. Coloured chalks. 33 x 28ins. (84 x 71cm). *Christie's.*

HENRI RONDEL. Portrait of a lady, bust length.
Signed. 21¼ x 18ins. (54 x 45.5cm). *Christie's.*

LUCIUS ROSSI. A young girl reclining on a sofa.
Signed and dated '86, on panel. 14 x 10½ins.
(35.5 x 26.5cm). *Sotheby's.*

GIUSEPPE ROTA. A young beauty. Signed, on panel.
15 x 12½ins. (38 x 31.5cm). *Christie's.*

EDOUARD ALEXANDRE SAIN. An elegant lady
strolling with her dog. Signed. 77 x 51¼ins.
(195.5 x 130cm). *Christie's.*

JULES EMILE SAINTIN. In the gloveshop. Signed.
36 x 25ins. (91 x 36cm). *Christie's.*

ANTHONY FREDERICK AUGUSTUS SANDYS. Love's
shadow; the artist's wife. On panel. 16 x 12¾ins.
(40.5 x 32.5cm). *Christie's.*

JOSEPH SCHEURENBERG. Sharing a book. Signed and
dated 1878. 16 x 12¼ins. (40.5 x 31cm). *Christie's.*

HENRI GUILLAUME SCHLESINGER. Reflections.
Signed and dated 1865, oval. 29 x 23ins. (73.5 x 58.5cm).
Christie's.

GUILLAUME SEIGNAC. A fair beauty. Signed.
17⅞ x 14¼ins. (45 x 36cm). *Christie's.*

EMILE EISMAN SEMENOWSKY. A Parisian
beauty. Signed and dated Paris 1889. 12¼ x 9¾ins.
(31 x 24.5cm) *Christie's.*

AUGUSTE SERRURE. A young girl in a ruined
garden. Signed and dated Paris 1853, on panel.
10 x 8¾ins. (25.5 x 22.5cm). *Sotheby's.*

ALFRED SEIFERT. A spring beauty. On panel.
19 x 15¼ins. (48 x 39cm). *Christie's.*

ALFRED STEVENS. La dame en jaune. Signed.
28¾ x 20½ins. (73 x 52cm). *Christie's.*

Top left: RAFFAELLO SORBI. Thoughts of the past. Signed
and dated 1873. 44½ x 30½ins. (113 x 77.5cm). *Christie's.*

JAN STYKA. A girl with a Japanese fan. Signed and dated
1889. (75 x 56.5cm).

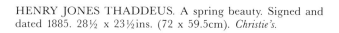
HENRY JONES THADDEUS. A spring beauty. Signed and dated 1885. 28½ x 23½ins. (72 x 59.5cm). *Christie's.*

EDUARDO TOFANO. A girl, head and shoulders. Signed. 17 x 12½ins. (43 x 31.5cm). *Christie's.*

FERNAND TOUSSAINT. A young lady reading. Signed 31¾ x 17⅞ins. (80.5 x 45cm). *Christie's.*

MAURICE WAGEMANS. La dame en noir. Signed and dated 1902. 87 x 43½ins. (221 x 110.5cm). *Christie's.*

Top left: EMILE VERNON. Spring. Signed and dated Paris 1913. 24¾ x 20¾ins. (63 x 52.5cm). *Christie's.*

JOHN WILLIAM WATERHOUSE. A study of a lady. 23¾ x 19½ins. (60 x 49.5cm). *Christie's.*

PAUL HERMANN
WAGNER. Gathering
water-lilies. Signed.
33 x 39ins. (84 x 100cm).
Christie's.

WILLIAM CLARKE WONTNER. The gypsy girl.
Signed and dated 1921. 24 x 20ins. (61 x 51cm).
Christie's.

FRANCIS JOSEPH WYBURD. A relaxing moment.
Signed with initials and dated 1870, framed as an oval.
18 x 15½ins. (45.5 x 39cm). *Christie's.*

96

Cardinals and Priests

The domestic antics of members of the higher echelons of the Roman Catholic Church exercised a powerful fascination for a number of popular painters and their patrons in the second half of the nineteenth century. These intimate scenes, set behind the closed doors of the private quarters of a cardinal's palace, constitute a clearly-defined genre of painting in their own right . Their popularity has remained remarkably constant, more so certainly than most other brands of nineteenth century painting over the years. In 1886 Collis Huntingdon paid the enormous sum of 25,000 dollars for Vibert's *The Missionary's Story*; equally extraordinary was the 1,400 guineas paid at auction in 1950 (a time at which it was difficult to attract any bid at all on a Meissonier, a Burne-Jones or an Alma-Tadema) for François Brunery's *The Toast of the Chef*.

The immediate reasons for the appeal of such pictures are not far to seek. Today's buyers are seduced by the high technique lavished upon them, and relish colour compositions which revel so unashamedly in large expanses of episcopal purple and crimson. On top of that the treatment is comic and full of character. But to understand the original motivation behind this choice of subject, one must not overlook the element, present in varying degrees in most such works, of anti-clericalism. There is no doubt that contemporary collectors and spectators took pleasure in the sight of noble figureheads of the church reduced to banal, even undignified proportions. The comedy was appealing, and the anti-clerical message suited the prevailing political mood of the buying public.

Initially artists turned to the Vatican for subject matter in a spirit of curiosity rather than anything more sinister. Merely to depict a cardinal in the privacy of his intimate surroundings was a recipe to delight the voyeuristic instincts of the nineteenth century clientele. There was an aura of intrigue, mystery and grandeur about the inner sancta of the Roman Catholic Church which could not fail to please when opened to keyhole scrutiny. Brunery's development is typical. After studying briefly under Gérôme in Paris, he followed a well-worn path to Rome where he painted classical and mythological scenes. This phase of his career was brought to a halt by marriage: his wife evinced a displeasure in the proximity to unclothed models necessitated by his line of work. He returned to Paris in 1877 in search of a new direction, and accepted a commission to paint a portrait of a cardinal. It seems that this initial contact with the Church in its temporal majesty provoked a curiosity about the more detailed trappings of its inner workings. There followed a highly successful series of ecclesiastical genre scenes, in which there grew out of the original curiosity in the mere externals a more insistent and beguiling element, that of comedy.

The approach of Brunery, and many painters like him, increasingly poked fun at the lords of the Church, and he delighted in portraying them in domestic dramas, which, while avoiding open scandal, nonetheless emphasised clerical susceptibility to the everyday trials and tribulations familiar to their humbler flock. A cardinal is seen accidentally sitting down on the palette of an embarrassed visiting portraitist, or leaping for the safety of a stool at the appearance of a mouse; Andrea Landini depicts a sumptuous dinner where fine wines and rich food are being dispatched with evident gusto to eminent bellies. Vibert presents a scene of meditation in which the cardinal concerned is not in his private chapel but at the end of a fishing rod. Unfortunately the tip of his rod has caught the bag holding his catch, and the fish are escaping back into the water.

The implications of such pictures are there to be drawn: if the Pope's right hand men are to be sent scampering for safety at the approach of one small mouse, what price the authority of the Church? If the princes of the Church live in styles reserved for kings and queens, what can they know of the reality of the working lives of their flock. And, the more extreme might argue, why should such wealth be available to a few irrelevant ecclesiastics simply for the purposes of enjoying themselves? If they are to play at royalty, they should mark the example of 1792. If they spend their days fishing, what time have they left to devote to their pastoral duties? And what is to be said for them at all if they cannot even fish properly?

It is no coincidence that the artists who painted this sort of comic ecclesiastical picture came almost exclusively from the predominantly Roman Catholic countries, France, Belgium, Italy, Spain and southern Germany. Anti-clericalism was a feature of the nineteenth century, generally the product of political conflict between liberal state and conservative church, exacerbated by a mounting jealousy of the wealth of certain religious orders. Pictorial anti-clericalism takes its extremest form in a work like Courbet's *Return from the Conference*, where drunken priests are seen rollicking home on a country road, gross rather than comic. A Brunery or a Vibert is underpinned less by hatred than by humour: it provoked a wry grin in the spectator, rather than sending him out to man the barricades.

Nonetheless, there was often a sting in the joke. Brunery shows a cardinal reading a newspaper distracted by a fly which settles on his nose. At first sight, this is merely comic. However, looking closer, one sees that the newspaper is *La Croix,* the reactionary catholic journal whose stance, for example, of anti-semitism in the Dreyfus affair won it few liberal friends; in this context the proximity of the fly to the cardinal's person can be read as an image of decay. In Vibert's *The Indulgence* a plutocratic cardinal happily examines a poster advertising indulgences; again, closer inspection reveals evidence of a different sort of indulgence on the part of the cardinal. He is smoking a cigarette; beyond is a table richly laden with food; there is no stinting in the supply of alcohol. In general the luxury of the surroundings, beautiful tapestries, fine furniture, superb wine, magnificent cuisine, is emphasised in these pictures. The painter's public, while enjoying fun being poked at cardinals, also derived pleasure from the sight of naked luxury; and at the same time the grandeur of the backdrop might more effectively show up the paltriness and triviality of the antics of the eminent actors.

The most successful cardinal painters were masters of innuendo rather than explicit slander. Courbet was felt to have gone too far when he showed inebriated curés carousing in the open countryside. On the other hand, cardinals might more acceptably be portrayed with the means for that inebriation close at hand, en route for the condition rather than displaying the more extreme characteristics of having arrived at it. Brunery's merry company of prelates at the dinner table is jolly rather than legless, funny rather than disgusting. There is also a more daring suggestiveness in the veiled implication of another Brunery, in which an eminent cleric dandles upon his knee, in somewhat awkward and embarrassed fashion, an infant of tender years while a pretty young nurse looks on. This is comic enough; but does the title of the picture, *The Cardinal's Nephew*, hint at the possibility that the relationship is even closer? Nothing is stated unequivocally, but the public would have enjoyed the artist's gentle nudge.

Spanish examples of ecclesiastical genre occur in the work of painters such as Gallegos and Salinas'. It is difficult to gauge precisely how far these men, through contact with Paris and Rome, were merely following a fashionable foreign trend. There is a tendency for such Spanish painting to be less outspoken in its criticism of the eminent actors, and rather to dwell ravishingly on the outward luxury of clerical trappings and furnishings. But Gallegos and Salinas certainly enjoy the close juxtaposition of priests and pretty young ladies, in a variety of scenarios. The confessional gave ample opportunity for a prurient delight (often manifested in exaggerated expressions of priestly horror) in the sins being admitted to by attractive females in shadowy churches. Salinas' cardinals attend tea parties given by rich and beautiful women, and grin lasciviously at their hostesses' opulent endowments.

There were also artists from Austria and the south of Germany who adorned rich bourgeois walls from Vienna to Munich with disporting cardinals and priests. The cardinals derive from Rome and Paris; but conflict between emerging state and conservative Catholic church is reflected in the distinctively Bavarian phenomenon of comic everyday scenes involving priests. If such pictures were the historian's sole source of information, he could be forgiven for concluding that the south German Catholic priest of the late nineteenth century did little else with his day but become involved in furious arguments in bars over political issues. On returning home he was invariably greeted by attractive peasant girls offering him succulent game on which to gorge himself.

Four painters emerge from the sea of crimson as the leading exponents of ecclesiastical genre: F. Brunery, Croegaert, Landini, and Vibert. As with other successful and popular branches of genre painting in the nineteenth century, there were many lesser followers differentiated from the better-known names by deficiencies in both technique and imagination. Marcel Brunery, the son of François, was no mean technician but largely repeated his father's tried and proven compositions. Painters such as Marais-Milton, Borione, and legions of minor Italians, sold pictures because they depicted cardinals doing nothing very much in vaguely grand settings. A splash of purple was enough.

Index of artists

AVITABILE, Gennaro (Italian, late 19th Century)

BAUMGARTNER, Pieter (German, 1834-1911)
* BENLLIURE Y GIL, José (Spanish, 1855-1914)
BENNETT, Frank Moss (British, 1874-1953)
* BORIONE, Bernard (French, late 19th Century)
* BRISPOT, Henri (French, 1846-1928)
* BRUNERY, François (Franco-Italian, fl.1870-1900)
* BRUNERY, Marcel (French, late 19th/early 20th Century)

* CACCIDRELLI, Victor (Italian, late 19th Century)
CASSELARI, Vincenzo (Italian, 1841-?)
CASTIGLIONE, Giuseppe (Italian, fl.1861-1900)
CEDERSTRÖM, Baron Ture Nikolaus de (Swedish, 1843-1924)
CHEVILLIARD, Vincent Jean Baptiste (French, 1841-1904)
COLEMAN, Francesco (Italian, 1851-?)
COURBET, Gustav (French, 1819-1877)
* CROEGAERT, Georges (French, 1848-?)

DAMIEN, François (Belgian, 1838-?)
DENEUX, Gabriel Charles (French, 1856-?)

* EICHINGER, Erwin (Austrian, late 19th Century)
EICHINGER, O. (Austrian, early 20th Century)

FALKENBERG, Georg Richard (German, 1850-?)
FRANKE, Albert Joseph (German, 1860-1924)
* FRAPPA, José (French, 1854-1904)
FRITSCH, Melchior (Austrian, 1826-1889)

* GALLEGOS Y ARNOSA, José (Spanish, 1859-1917)
GRÜTZNER, Eduard von (German, 1846-1878)
GUIDI, Guido (Italian, fl.1867-1911)
* GUZZONE, Sebastiano (Italian, 1856-1890)

* HEILBUTH, Ferdinand (French, 1828-1889)
* HERMANN, Leo (French, 1851-?)
* HOLMBERG, August Johann (German, 1851-1911)
* HOLWEG, Gustav (Austrian, 1855-1890)
HUMBORG, Adolf (Austrian, 1847-1913)

JIRASEK, Alfred (Austrian, 1863-?)
JORIS, Pio (Italian, 1843-1921)

* LAISSEMENT, Henri Adolphe (French, 1854-1921)
* LANDINI, Andrea (Italian, 1847-?)
LANZ, W. (Austrian, late 19th Century)
* LANZONI, P. (Italian, late 19th Century)
LAUPHEIMER, Anton (German, 1848-1927)
LESSI, Tito Giovanni (Italian, 1858-1917)
* LINDERUM, Richard (German, 1851-?)

LÖWITH, Wilhelm (German, 1861-1931)
LUZZI, C. (Italian, late 19th Century)

MANNUCCI, Cipriano (Italian, late 19th Century)
* MARAIS-MILTON, Victor (French, 1872-?)
MORETTI, R. (Italian, late 19th Century)
* MUNSCH, Josef (German, 1832-1896)

* ORFEI, Orfeo (Italian, fl.1862-1888)

PASTEGA, Luigi (Italian, 1858-1927)
* PENOT, Albert Joseph (French, fl.1896-1909)
PETTIE, John (British 1839-1893)
POSTIGLIONE, Salvatore (Italian, 1861-1906)
* PRIETO, Manuel Jiminez (Spanish, late 19th Century)

* REK, Christian (Belgian, late 19th Century)
* ROEGGE, Wilhelm Ernst Friedrich (German, 1829-1908)
ROYER, Charles (French, late 19th Century)

* SALINAS, Pablo (Spanish, 1871-1946)
SANCHEZ BARBUDO, Salvador (Spanish, 1857-1917)
SANCTIS, Giuseppe de (Italian, 1858-1924)
* SCALBERT, Jules (French, 1851-?)
* SCHAAN, Paul (French, late 19th Century)
* SCHILL, Adrien (German, late 19th Century)
* SCHOLZ, Max (German, 1855-1906)
* SCHREIBER, Charles Baptiste (French, ?-1903)
SCHROETTER, Alfred von (Austrian, 1856-1935)
SCHUSSER, Joseph (Austrian, 1864-1941)
* SERRA, Enrique (Spanish, 1859-1918)
SIGNORINI, Giuseppe (Italian, 1857-1932)
SINIBALDI, Jean Paul (French, 1857-1909)
SPRING, Alfons (German, 1843-1908)
* STEFANELLI, L. (Italian, late 19th Century)

* TAMBURINI, Arnaldo (Italian, 1843-?)

USSI, Stefano (Italian, 1822-1902)

VIANELLO, Cesare (Italian, late 19th Century)
* VIBERT, Jean Georges (French, 1840-1902)
* VINIEGRA Y LASSO, Salvador (Spanish, 1862-1915)

* WAGNER, Fritz (German, late 19th Century)
* WAGNER-HÖHENBERG, Josef (German, 1870-?)
WEBER, Alfred Charles (French, 1862-1922)
* WEISER, Joseph Emanuel (German, 1847-1911)
* WOLFLE, Franz Xavier (German, early 20th Century)

ZIMMERMAN, Reinhard Sebastian (German, 1815-1893)

JOSE BENLLIURE Y GIL. In the Cardinal's study. Signed, on panel. 14½ x 21ins. (37 x 53.5cm). *Christie's.*

BERNARD BORIONE. An eminent connoisseur. Signed and inscribed Paris. 21½ x 18½ins. (54.5 x 47cm). *Christie's.*

HENRI BRISPOT. Cardinals at table. Signed. 22¼ x 28¾ins. (57 x 73cm). *Christie's.*

FRANÇOIS BRUNERY. The unwanted intruder. Signed, on panel. 17 x 21ins. (43 x 53.5cm). *Christie's.*

FRANÇOIS BRUNERY. La mouche agacante. Signed, on panel. 23 x 20ins. (58.5 x 51cm). *Christie's.*

MARCEL BRUNERY. An eminent duet. Signed.
25½ x 31¾ins. (64.5 x 80.5cm). *Christie's.*

FRANÇOIS BRUNERY. A cardinal error. Signed.
35½ x 27ins. (90 x 68.5cm). *Christie's.*

VICTOR CACCIDRELLI. The Cardinal's first visit. Signed and inscribed Roma. 19¾ x 37¾ins. (50 x 96cm). *Christie's.*

GEORGES CROEGAERT. Pheasant for dinner. Signed and inscribed Paris, on panel. 19¼ x 23½ins. (49 x 59cm). *Christie's.*

ERWIN EICHINGER. In the library.
Signed and inscribed Wien, on panel. 14 x
22½ins. (35.5 x 57cm). *Christie's.*

SEBASTIANO GUZZONE. A Cardinal before
the High Altar. Signed, inscribed Roma and
dated '88, on board. 16¾ x 11ins.
(42.5 x 28cm). *Christie's.*

JOSÉ FRAPPA. A theological dispute. Signed.
21 x 25ins. (53.5 x 63.5cm). *Christie's.*

JOSÉ GALLEGOS Y ARNOSA.
The Cardinal's visit. Signed and dated 1897,
on panel. 15¼ x 24ins. (38.5 x 61cm). *Christie's.*

FERDINAND HEILBUTH. The Cardinal's farewell.
Signed, on board. 16½ x 20¼ins. (42 x 51.5cm). *Christie's.*

Right: LEO HERMANN. Feeding the swan. Signed.
13¼ x 9¾ins. (33.5 x 25cm). *Christie's.*

AUGUST JOHANN HOLMBERG. The music lesson.
Signed. 41½ x 30½ins. (105.6 x 77.5cm). *Christie's.*

GUSTAV HOLWEG. The letter. Signed and dated '80, on
panel. 10¼ x 6½ins. (26 x 16.5cm). *Sotheby's.*

ANDREA LANDINI. The stolen cap. Signed and inscribed Paris, on panel. 19 x 23½ins. (48.5 x 59.5cm). *Christie's.*

HENRI ADOLPHE LAISSEMENT. The letter. Signed, on panel. 17½ x 14½ins. (44.5 x 37cm). *Christie's.*

RICHARD LINDERUM. In the Cardinal's study. Signed, on panel. 19¾ x 26ins. (50 x 66cm). *Christie's.*

P. LANZONI. A portrait for posterity. Signed, on panel. 13 x 17ins. (33 x 43cm). *Christie's.*

VICTOR MARAIS-MILTON. La bonne histoire. Signed. 19 x 23½ins. (48.5 x 59.5cm). *Christie's.*

JOSEF MUNSCH. The Cardinal in consultation. Signed and dated München, 1891, on panel. 9½ x 11¾ins. (24 x 30cm). *Sotheby's.*

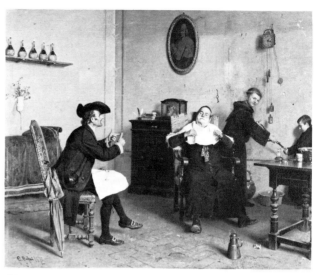

ORFEO ORFEI. The priest's shave. Signed and dated 1873. 20 x 25ins. (51 x 63.5cm).

ALBERT JOSEPH PENOT. A satisfying meal. Signed. 18 x 13ins. (46 x 33cm).

CHRISTIAN REK. A priest playing a cello. Signed, on panel. 7 x 5ins. (18 x 12.5cm). *Sotheby's.*

MANUEL JIMINEZ PRIETO.
Writing the dispatches. Signed and
dated Paris 1886, on panel.
17 x 25¼ins. (43 x 64cm). *Christie's.*

PABLO SALINAS. The audience. Signed and inscribed
Roma, on panel. 7½ x 11ins. (19 x 28cm). *Christie's.*

WILHELM ERNST FRIEDRICH ROEGGE. A game of
chess. Signed and dated 1869. 25 x 30¾ins. (63.5 x 78cm).
Christie's.

JULES SCALBERT. A good vintage. Signed, on panel.
18 x 21¾ins. (45.5 x 55cm). *Sotheby's.*

PAUL SCHAAN. A feathered friend. Signed and dated
1907, on panel. 18 x 14¾ins. (45.5 x 37.5cm). *Christie's.*

ADRIEN SCHILL. The Curé's visit. Signed, on
panel. 7¾ x 5¼ins. (20 x 13.5cm). *Christie's.*

MAX SCHOLZ. A game of
cards. Signed and inscribed
München. 22¼ x 24¼ins.
(56.5 x 61.5cm).

CHARLES BAPTISTE SCHREIBER. The new piece of music. Signed, on panel. 9 x 6¼ins. (23 x 16cm). *Christie's.*

ENRIQUE SERRA. The Cardinal's visit. Signed and dated 1892, on panel. 13 x 9¾ins. (33 x 24.5cm). *Christie's.*

L. STEFANELLI. Seeking knowledge. Signed and inscribed Roma. 14 x 20¾ins. (35.5 x 52.5cm). *Christie's.*

JEAN GEORGES VIBERT. The Cardinal's
favourite sport. Signed, on panel. 17⅞ x 21¾ins.
(45 x 55cm). *Sotheby's.*

Top left. ARNALDO TAMBURINI. A Cardinal at
his desk. Signed and inscribed Florence.
14 x 10¾ins. (35.5 x 27.5cm). *Christie's.*

SALVADOR VINIEGRA Y LASSO. A blessing
from his Eminence. Signed. 19 x 29½ins.
(48 x 75cm). *Christie's.*

FRITZ WAGNER. An interesting report.
Signed and inscribed Mch. 24¾ x 30½ins.
(63 x 77.5cm). *Christie's.*

JOSEF WAGNER-HÖHENBERG.
In the Cardinal's study. Signed.
21½ x 23½ins. (54.5 x 60cm).
Christie's.

JOSEPH EMANUEL WEISER. A reflective moment.
Signed, on panel. 9½ x 7ins. (24 x 18cm). *Christie's.*

FRANZ XAVIER WOLFLE. The connoisseur. Signed, on
board. 17 x 13¾ins. (43 x 35cm). *Christie's.*

WALTER HUNT. Good friends. Signed and dated 1903. 19½ x 29½ins. (49.5 x 75cm). *Christie's.*

Cats and Dogs

Before the nineteenth century, cats and dogs had certainly figured in pictures, but, with the exception of commissioned portraits of sporting dogs, their presence had been marginal to the main action. Cats impinge as details in larger compositions, sometimes vividly as in the snarling animal tempted by a caged bird in Hogarth's *The Graham Children,* sometimes prowling through seventeenth century Flemish still lifes of larders. Dogs sit at their masters' feet in grand portraits, or lurk disreputably in the corners of peasant scenes by Teniers and his followers. Nineteenth century patronage, however, created a demand for pictures in which cats and dogs occupied a more central area of the stage. The 'kittens' or 'small downy ducks' which George Eliot perceived to have such an infuriating beauty (see CHILDREN) became the raw material for artists intent on plucking at the sentimental heartstrings of a notoriously susceptible public.

The guiding light was without doubt Sir Edwin Landseer, not just in England (where Englishmen have traditionally found it easier to express emotion in relation to their dogs than their human dependents) but across the Continent. Baudelaire greeted Landseer as 'the painter of beasts "whose eyes are full of thought"'. Gautier observed in wonder: 'Landseer gives his beloved animals soul, thought, poetry, and passion. He endows them with an intellectual life almost like our own; he would if he dared take away their instinct and accord them free will.' This was Landseer's significant innovation: not only did he paint animals extremely well, but he also created in them an expressiveness bordering on the human. His work includes a string of famous pictures centred on canine character and emotion, from the tragic as in *The Old Shepherd's Chief Mourner* to the comic as in *Dignity and Impudence.*

Landseer's images are so familiar that it is easy to lose sight of their original novelty. He transformed animal painting in the nineteenth century from its traditional status as a record of beasts, sometimes in landscapes, to something approaching a mirror of human life. Human emotions are portrayed, but on the faces of animals which makes the mirror both comic and piquant. To say that Landseer had many followers would be an understatement, because most sentimental cat and dog pictures of the second half of the century would have been impossible without his example. Painters as diverse as Otto Eerleman in Holland, Carl Reichert in Vienna and Eugène Lambert in France all owe a clear debt to him. Certainly the original tradition of straight portraiture of sporting dogs, their features unsullied by human passion, persisted throughout the century, but painters of domestic pets found it increasingly difficult to avoid presenting their subjects in any other but a sentimental, anthropomorphic light. This was Landseer's legacy.

As the middle class expanded in the later nineteenth century, so did the number of cats and dogs kept as domestic pets. Since these animals reached an unprecedented level of domestication in the bosom of such human families, it is not surprising that the public, whose taste for the domestic in all types of painting is a feature of the century, should enjoy pictures which showed them in situations comic, sentimental and anthropomorphic. In 1857 Edmond About wrote of one such purveyor of domestic animal charm, Philippe Rousseau:

> Animals are wise little personages to Rousseau; each of his frames resembles an outlandish theatre in which the beasts play a comedy...I recognise with the public the originality and attraction of his works, but I am not able to approve of all the talent he expends in order to lower painting to the level of the vignette.

For such care and technical accomplishment to be expended on so trivial a subject as a domestic pet might well appear to the purist an abuse of talent. Nonetheless, Philippe Rousseau had many admirers; even more so Henriette Ronner, the queen of cat painters, who was acclaimed with wonder in her time. Spielmann, her biographer, declares that she was the first painter in the history of art to master the elusive cat in all its moods. The explanation for this is of course that no-one before had sought to attain mastery in such a field. An artist devoting his talents exclusively to cats would have been inconceivable in the eighteenth century. But this was the nineteenth century and bourgeois demand created the phenomenon of Henriette Ronner. She was the painter of pets par excellence, international in her appeal, and one of the most popular female artists of the century. Her cats and kittens disport in unmistakably bourgeois interiors, clambering over furniture and fashionable fittings which represent the latest in heavy middle-class luxury. Her clientele was no doubt delighted to find its taste so delightfully mirrored in this way. A list of the owners of her most important pictures in 1892 includes collectors in Rotterdam, Antwerp, New Orleans, Paris and Newcastle, all commercial centres where much new money had been made.

If Henriette Ronner was the queen of cat painters, she had many ladies-in-waiting across Europe. Cats as a subject were seen as eminently suitable for the female brush, and a greater congregation of women will be found in this section than in any other. Adrienne Lester, Hermine Biedermann-Arendts, Juliette Peyrol Bonheur, Augusta Talboys, Maud Earl and Blanche McArthur are but a few of those who strove to emulate Ronner's achievement, with varying degrees of success. Two men challenged female supremacy in cat painting. One was Eugène Lambert, who was highly regarded in Paris. The other was the Munich master Julius Adam. He was a younger generation of a famous family of Munich animal painters; his older relations such as Albrecht Adam had been successful horse painters along traditional lines, and it was perhaps a sign of the times that he should now forsake horseflesh for the domestic cat. Cat painting was the art of a new urban society, living a pampered life in rich apartments and town-houses; horse painting harked back to more rural days. At all events, Julius Adam clearly had a feeling for his subject; his self-portrait shows him manfully working on at his easel while a family of kittens climb over him.

The paradox of animals behaving like human beings, or at least showing evidence of recognisably human emotions, is inherent in many nineteenth century paintings of cats and dogs, and to some extent accounts for their appeal. It parallels other beguiling paradoxes in popular painting of the time: Greeks are shown behaving like Victorians, and Cavaliers like nineteenth century clubmen. English animal painters were fond of underlining the message with suitably comic explanatory titles. Briton Rivière calls his picture of a dog backing guiltily away from an upset vase 'Thus Conscience doth make Cowards of Us All'. The public, having learned from artists that the ancients were no different from them, that Cavaliers made dainty music and flirted in exactly the same way, were now enchanted to discover that dogs' consciences operated with the same terms of reference as their own. Alternatively, titles could enhance the comedy by sounding rather grand and high-flown. *Alexander and Diogenes* by Landseer shows merely a somewhat ill-tempered mongrel refusing to yield its place in a barrel to another canine claimant. *A Distinguished Member of the Humane Society* turns out to be a St. Bernard resting in stately fashion on a quay, the title an oblique reference to the breed's propensity for saving the lives of human beings in distress.

The roots of anthropomorphism in nineteenth century animal painting are to be found in fable: the cunning fox of Aesop is in some senses the ancestor of Landseer's scheming cur and even Henriette Ronner's romping kittens. Fable was the precedent for such pictures, in the same way that the historical novel opened the field for intimate historical painting. Thus animal painting was transformed by a sentimental vision directed on to the domestic pet, the furry charmer with a near-human expressiveness. Would Stubbs have recognised Maud Earl as his spiritual and artistic heir? Could Snyders have clasped hands across the centuries with Madame Ronner-Knip? Perhaps not; it is only by Landseer that we can see the chasm bridged between them.

Index of Artists

EARL, George (British, fl.1856-1883)
* EARL, Maud (British, fl.1884-1908)
EARL, Thomas (British, fl.1856-1883)
* EERELMAN, Otto, (Dutch, 1839-1926)
* EMMS, John (British, 1843-1912)
ENGELS, Robert (German, 1866-1926)
ESCUDIER, Charles Jean Auguste (French, 1848-?)
* EYCKEN, Charles van den (Belgian, 1859-1923)

FISHER, Percy Harland (British, 1867-?)
FULTON, Samuel (British, 1855-?)

GARLAND, Henry (British, fl.1854-1890)
GARLAND, Valentine Thomas (British, ?-1867)
GELIBERT, Paul Jean Pierre (French, 1802-1882)
* GIFFORD, John (British, late 19th Century)
GODDARD, Charles (British, mid-19th Century)
GODDARD, George Bouverie (British, 1832-1886)
GOOCH, R.A. (British, mid-19th Century)
GRASHEY, Otto (German, 1833-1912)

* HAMBURGER, Helen Augusta (British, 1836-1919)
* HAMBURGER, Julius (Austrian, 1830-?)
HARDEN, James (British, late 19th Century)
HARROWING, Walter (British, late 19th Century)
* HARTUNG, Johann (German, late 19th Century)
* HAYES, John (British)
HAZON, Jane d' (French, 1874-?)
HEAD, Edward Joseph (British, 1863-?)
HEPPLE, Wilson (British, 1854-1937)
* HERRING, Benjamin (British, 1830-1871)
* HERRING, Sen., John Frederick (1795-1865)
* HEYER, Arthur (German, 1872-1931)
HOLT, E.F. (British, mid-19th Century)
* HORLOR, George W. (British, fl.1849-1890)
* HUBER, Léon Charles (French, 1858-1928)
* HUGGINS, William (British, 1820-1884)
HUNT, Edgar (British, 1876-1953)
* HUNT, Walter (British, 1861-1941)

ISTVANFFY, Gabrielle Rainer (Austrian, 1877-?)

JADIN, Charles Emmanuel (French, 1855?-?)
JADIN, Louis Godefroy (French, 1865-1882)
JONES, Paul (British, 1860-?)

KEMP-WELCH, Lucy Elizabeth (British, 1869-1958)
* KOOL, B. (German, late 19th century)
KRUGER, Friedrich (German, 1797-1857)

LACHENWITZ, F. Sigmund (German, 1820-1868)
* LAMBERT, Eugène Louis (French, 1825-1900)
* LANDSEER, Sir Edwin Henry (British, 1802-1873)
* LAUR, Yvonne Marie Yo (French, 1879-?)
LAUX, Marie (German, 1852-?)
LEBLING, Max (German, 1851-?)
* LEROY, Jules (French, 1833-1865)
LESTER, Adrienne (British, late 19th Century)
LEWIS, John Frederick (British, 1805-1876)
* LOSSOW, Friedrich (German, 1837-1872)
* LUMINAIS, Evariste Vital (French, 1822-1896)
LUTYENS, Charles Auguste Henry (British, 1829-1915)

MACARTHUR, Blanche (British, lates 19th Century)
MATTEI, Guido von (German, 1838-?)

MERLIN, Daniel (French, 1861-1933)
MERY, Alfred Emile (French, 1824-1896)
* MEULEN, Edmond van der (Belgian, 1841-1905)
MONTEFIORE, E.B. Stanley (British, fl.1872-1890)
MOODY, Fanny (British, 1861-1896)
* MOORE, Ernest (British, 1865-?)
MORLEY, Robert (British, 1857-1941)
MORLEY-PARK, H. (British, mid-19th Century)
MORRIS, W. Walker (British, fl.1850-1867)
MUCHE, Karl Emile (German, 1847-1923)
MUTRIE, Annie Feray (British, 1826-1893)
MUZZOTTA, Federico (Italian, late 19th Century)

* NIGHTINGALE, Robert (British, 1815-1895)
* NOBLE, John Sargent (British, 1848-1896)

* OLARIA, Frederico (Spanish, 1849-1898)
OSWALD-BROWN, J.H. (British, late 19th Century)

PAICE, George (British, fl.1878-1900)
PARKER, Henry Perlee (British, 1795-1873)
* PASMORE, F.G. (British, fl.1875-1884)
PATON, Frank (British, 1856-1909)
PENNE, Oliver Charles de (French, 1831-1897)
PRATÈRE, Edmond Joseph de (Belgian, 1826-1888)
PRINGLE, Agnes (British, fl.1884-1893)

QUADRONE, Giovanni Battista (Italian, 1844-1898)

* RAAPHORST, Cornelis (Dutch, 1875-1854)
* REICHERT, Carl (Austrian, 1836-1918)
RIVIÈRE, Briton (British, 1840-1920)
* RONNER-KNIP, Henriette (Dutch, 1821-1909)
ROUSSEAU, Philippe (French, 1816-1887)
ROWLAND, G.D. (British, late 19th Century)

SCHMITZBERGER, Josef (German, 1851-?)
* SCHÜTZ, Heinrich (German, 1875-?)
SCHUSTER, Josef (Austrian, 1812-1890)
SCHWAR, Wilhelm F.J. (German, 1860-1898)
* SIMONSEN, Simon Ludovic Ditlev (Danish, 1841-1928)
SIMPSON, William (British, late 19th Century)
SPERLICH, Sophie (German, late 19th century)
* SPERLING, Heinrich (German, 1844-1924)
STEEL, John Sidney (British, 1863-1932)
* STEELL, David George (British, 1856-1930)
STEVENS, Joseph Edouard (Belgian, 1819-1892)
STOBBAERTS, Jan Baptiste (Belgian, 1838-1914)
STOCKS, Minna (German, 1846-1928)
STREBEL, Richard Hermann (German, 1861-?)
* STRETTON, Philip Eustace (British, fl.1884-1919)
* STRUTT, Alfred William (British, 1856-1924)

TALBOYS, Augusta W. (British, late 19th Century)
TANNER, C. (British, early 19th Century)
TASKER, William (British, 1808-1852)
* TAVERNIER, Paul (French, 1852-?)
TOOBY, Charles Richard (British, 1863-1918)
* TROOD, William Henry Hamilton (British, 1848-1899)

UCKERMANN, Karl (Norwegian, 1855-?)

VERLAT, Charles Michel Maria (Belgian, 1824-1890)
* VOS, Vincent de (Belgian, 1829-1875)

118

JULIUS ADAM. Kittens at play.
Signed and inscribed München.
14½ x 18ins. (37 x 46cm).
Christie's.

ROBERT L. ALEXANDER.
Studies of Collie pups. Signed
with monogram, canvas laid
down on board. 7 x 8¾ins.
(17.5 x 22cm). *Christie's.*

RICHARD ANSDELL RA. A mother and her puppies. Signed and dated 1840. 24½ x 29½ins. (62 x 75cm). *Christie's.*

GEORGE ARMFIELD. A hostile encounter. Signed and dated 1866(?). 29½ x 39½ins. (75 x 100.5cm). *Christie's.*

WRIGHT BARKER. Three yellow Russian Retrievers in a landscape. Signed and inscribed on an old label on the reverse. 52 x 69½ins. (132 x 176.5cm). *Christie's.*

120

MANUEL BARTHOLD. Le Pekinois. Signed.
24 x 19¾ins. (61 x 50cm). *Sotheby's.*

ROSA BONHEUR. A Toy dog on a sofa. Signed. 12¾ x 16ins.
(32.5 x 40.5cm). *Christie's.*

THOMAS BLINKS. A spaniel picking up.
Signed. 25 x 21ins. (63.5 x 53.5cm). *Christie's.*

HERMINE BIEDERMANN-ARENDTS. The catch. Signed and dated
München 1875. 23 x 28¾ins. (58.5 x 73cm). *Christie's.*

LUCIE BRIARD. Music hath charms. Signed. 12½ x 16¼ins. (31.5 x 41.5cm). *Christies.*

ABRAHAM BRUININGH VAN WORRELL. A spaniel with a dead
hare in a landscape. Signed, inscribed and dated 1836. On panel.
10½ x 12¾ins. (26.5 x 32.5cm). *Christie's.*

ALFRED ARTHUR BRUNEL
DE NEUVILLE. Kittens at play.
Signed. 28¼ x 15¼ins.
(72 x 38.5cm). *Christie's.*

122

HENRY CALVERT. Two greyhounds in a landscape.
Signed and dated 1850. 24½ x 29½ins. (62 x 75cm).
Christie's.

JOHN CHARLTON. A contrast. Signed, and signed
and inscribed on an old label on the reverse, on
board. 12 x 18¼ins. (30.5 x 46cm). *Christie's.*

ABRAHAM COOPER. Sancho, a greyhound in a
landscape on board. 8¾ x 12ins. (22 x 30.5cm).
Christie's.

HORATIO HENRY
COULDERY. Dog's Dinner.
Signed. 17¼ x 23¼ins.
(44 x 59cm). *Christie's.*

CONRADYN CUNAEUS.
Setters flushing a hare.
Signed, on panel.
10 x 15ins. (25.5 x 38cm).
Christie's.

DAVID DALBY OF YORK. An
Irish Wolfhound, a Toy Spaniel and
a Terrier in a park. Signed and
dated 1845. 17½ x 23½ins.
(44.5 x 59.5cm). *Christie's.*

FRANCISCO DOMINGO Y MARQUES. A kitten
watching a fly. Signed. 21½ x 18ins. (54.5 x 46cm).
Sotheby's.

A. DUKE. Full cry. Signed.
15¼ x 19¼ins. (38.5 x 49cm). *Christie's.*

Right: MAUD EARL. The lap of luxury. Signed.
21½ x 29½ins. (54.5 x 75cm). *Christie's.*

AGNES DUNDASE. A Dandie Dinmont Terrier.
Circular. 7¼ins. (18.5cm.) diameter. *Christie's.*

OTTO EERELMAN. Digesting the news. Signed.
34¾ x 51ins. (88 x 129.5cm). *Christie's.*

JOHN EMMS. Three spaniels after a days sport. Signed and dated 1903. 25 x 34½ins. (63.5 x 87.5cm). *Christie's.*

CHARLES VAN DEN EYCKEN. The spilt ink. Signed and dated 1892. 13 x 17½ins. (33 x 44.5cm). *Christie's.*

JOHN GIFFORD. Waiting for master. Signed 35½ x 27½ins. (90 x 70cm). *Christie's.*

HELEN AUGUSTA HAMBURGER. Feline Exploration. Signed and dated 1905. 16¼ x 23½ins. (41 x 60cm). *Sotheby's.*

JULIUS HAMBURGER. A King Charles Spaniel.
Signed. 13½ x 11ins. (34 x 28cm). *Christie's.*

JOHANN HARTUNG. The King of the castle.
Signed, on panel. 10 x 7½ins. (25.5 x 19cm).
Christie's.

JOHN HAYES. Winning fund raisers. Signed. 28 x 36ins. (71 x 91.5cm). *Christie's.*

BENJAMIN HERRING. Pointers and a sportsman in a landscape. Signed with monogram and dated '60. 7 x 10ins. (18 x 25.5cm). *Christie's.*

JOHN FREDERICK HERRING (SEN). A white Terrier with a hare in a landscape. Signed and dated 1852, on panel. 13 x 17ins. (33 x 43cm). *Christie's.*

ARTHUR HEYER. A curious cat. Signed.
38½ x 30¼ins. (97.5 x 77cm). *Christie's.*

GEORGE W. HORLOR. Retrievers in a landscape. Signed and dated 1866.
33 x 43ins. (84 x 109cm). *Christie's.*

WILLIAM HUGGINS. A cat. Signed and dated 1873.
On board, circular 8¼ins. (21cm.) diameter. *Christie's.*

LÉON CHARLES HUBER. Kittens in a basket. Signed.
18¼ x 15¼ins. (46.5 x 38.5cm). *Christie's.*

HENRIETTE RONNER-KNIP. Cats at play. Signed and dated 1897. 49¼ x 38½ins. (125 x 98cm). *Christie's.*

B. KOOL. A cat and three kittens in a stable. Signed and inscribed Mchn. 6¾ x 9ins. (17 x 23cm). *Sotheby's.*

EUGÈNE LOUIS LAMBERT. The intruders. Signed. 17½ x 22ins. (44.5 x 56cm). *Christie's.*

SIR EDWIN LANDSEER. Dignity and impudence. 35 x 27¼ins. (88.9 x 69.2cm). *Tate Gallery.*

YVONNE MARIE YO LAUR. Playful kittens. Signed.
19½ x 23¼ins. (49.5 x 59cm). *Christie's.*

JULES LEROY. Playful kittens. Signed. 34½ x 45¼ins.
(88 x 115cm). *Sotheby's.*

FRIEDRICH LOSSOW. Chasing the ducklings. Signed
and dated 1867. 35 x 31ins. (89 x 78.5cm). *Christie's.*

EVARISTE VITAL LUMINAIS. Feeding the dogs.
Signed and dated 1888. 25 x 31¼ins. (63.5 x 79.5cm).
Christie's.

ERNEST MOORE. Martyrs. Signed and dated 1890.
17½ x 25½ins. (44.5 x 65cm). *Christie's.*

EDMOND VAN DER MEULEN. Visitors to the
pantry. Signed. 80 x 59ins. (200 x 150cm). *Sotheby's.*

ROBERT NIGHTINGALE. The hound 'Guardian'.
39½ x 50ins. (100.5 x 127cm). *Christie's.*

JOHN SARGENT NOBLE. Otter hounds. Signed.
41 x 61¾ins. (104 x 157cm). *Christie's.*

FREDERICO OLARIA. A mother's pride. Signed.
45¾ x 31¼ins. (116 x 79.5cm). *Christie's.*

F.G. PASMORE. A Cocker Spaniel in a wooded landscape.
Signed. 13¼ x 17¼ins. (33.5 x 44cm). *Christie's.*

CORNELIS RAAPHORST. Playful Kittens. Signed. 24½ x 29½ins. (62 x 75cm). *Sotheby's.*

CARL REICHERT.
Duck shooting. Signed,
on panel. 8¼ x 12½ins.
(21 x 31.5cm). *Christie's.*

HEINRICH SCHÜTZ. Setters in a landscape. Signed. 31 x 22¾ins. (79 x 58cm). *Christie's.*

SIMON LUDOVIC DITLEV SIMONSEN. A portrait of Innocence. Signed and dated 1907. 13 x 9½ins. (33 x 24cm). *Christie's.*

HEINRICH SPERLING. A St. Bernard. Signed and dated 1886. 21½ x 25¾ins. (54.5 x 65.5cm). *Christie's.*

137

DAVID GEORGE STEELL. The Dumfriesshire Otter Hounds near Hoddon Castle. Signed and dated 1909. 62½ x 89ins. (159 x 226cm). *Christie's.*

PHILIP EUSTACE STRETTON. The best of friends. Signed and dated 1918. 29½ x 24½ins. (75 x 62.5cm). *Christie's.*

ALFRED WILLIAM STRUTT. The otter's holt. Signed. 22 x 30ins. (56 x 76cm). *Christie's.*

PAUL TAVERNIER. A group of hounds in a wooded landscape. Signed, on panel. 18 x 24ins. (46 x 61cm). *Sotheby's.*

WILLIAM HENRY HAMILTON TROOD. First steps.
Signed and dated 1880. 10 x 6ins. (25.5 x 15cm). *Christie's.*

VINCENT DE VOS. Dogs and a monkey in fancy dress. Signed and dated 1871, on panel. 22¾ x 29½ins. (58 x 75cm). *Christie's.*

LOUIS WILLIAM WAIN. Cats skating. Signed. 19¼ x 46¼ins. (49 x 117.5cm). *Christie's.*

ARTHUR WARDLE. The day's bag.
18 x 24½ins. (46 x 61.5cm). *Christie's.*

GEORGE WRIGHT. The Sinnington Hounds,
1902, in full cry. Signed and inscribed with date
and a key to the names on the reverse.
17½ x 35½ins. (44.5 x 90cm). *Christie's.*

JOSEPH ZÜRNICH. Two dogs by a kennel.
Signed and dated 1867. 31 x 41¼ins. (79 x 105cm).
Sotheby's.

Cavaliers

The past was of vivid fascination for the nineteenth century, and curiosity about it took a distinctive form: 'Gossip is charming', says Cecil Graham in *Lady Windermere's Fan,* 'History is merely gossip.' From the other side of the channel, Prosper Merimee echoes his words: 'In History, I love only anecdote.' Both men are displaying symptoms of a characteristic condition of their century, rampant Boswellism, that is to say obsession with the past on a human, intimate level, with history 'en deshabille'. It was after all a century which saw the development of the historical novel as a popular literary form; and in the same way that artists took pleasure in reducing heroic antiquity to the banal and the everyday, so also history was reinterpreted in terms of cavaliers playing with their children rather than fighting roundheads, of writing love letters rather than parliamentary edicts.

In France, the process of the trivialisation of history painting began early in the century: the school known as the Troubadours tended towards a romanticised, intimate view of the past; Ingres too was part of this movement, and a prime example is his picture of 1818, *Henry IV Surprised by the Spanish Ambassador while Playing with his Children*. There is of course a political motive here: the artist is concerned, as Roy Strong points out, to emphasise the human side of the earlier monarchy, and by analogy the gentle, paternalist qualities of the recently restored French monarchy. In the king who is shown scrabbling on the carpet with his energetic offspring, Ingres has also created the prototype of many later romping cavaliers, all too eager to sacrifice their dignity to the demands of domestic life. As the century progressed, these jolly successors adorned drawing room walls not just in France, but in Spain, Italy, Britain, Germany, Holland and Belgium.

The phenomenon of Sir Walter Scott and the subsequent vogue for historical romance also helped to open the market for the troops of cavaliers whose private moments are the subject matter of so many popular nineteenth century historical pictures. By their very nature historical novels dwelt more on the intimate, imaginary incident from history rather than the grand trend or event. And their attraction as an alternative to straight history, even as its supplanter, was recognised early on by Macaulay, writing in 1828:

> To make the past present, to bring the distant near... to call up our ancestors before us with all their peculiarities of language, manners and garb, to show us over their houses, to seat us at their tables, to rummage their old-fashioned wardrobes, to explain the uses of their ponderous furniture, these parts of the duty which properly belongs to the historian have been appropriated by the historical novelist.

The appeal of the glimpse into the intimate past, even the pleasure of prying into the houses and wardrobes of our ancestors, this fascination Macaulay has identified and understood. It was also a large part of the extraordinary appeal of Scott, which prompted Taine to describe him as:

> the favourite of his age, read over the whole of Europe, (who) was compared

and almost equalled to Shakespeare, had more popularity than Voltaire, made dressmakers and duchesses weep, and earned about £200,000.

British interest in cavaliers, as reflected in its popular nineteenth century painting, may, like the French, have had some political undertones. In the early part of the century, a combination of the example of the French Revolution, some weak and unpopular kings, and a degree of social upheaval undermined sympathy with the monarchy; this sympathy was only restored by a period of stability under Victoria. Gradually, monarchy and its past manifestations became popular again, and when subjects from the English civil war are treated they are often biased in favour of the romance of the Royalist cause as against the grim puritan. Thus we are given W.S. Burton's *The Wounded Cavalier*, Millais' *The Proscribed Royalist*, Frederick Goodall's *The Happier Days of Charles I*, and W.F. Yeames's famous *And When did you last See your Father?*, all concerned on an intimate level to curry sympathy for the cavalier. Nouveau riche Victorian taste was titillated by the domesticity of such reconstructions, but also pleased to espouse the Royalist cause as the upholder of traditional aristocratic values, those very values to which the new bourgeoisie ardently aspired.

In many of these pictures one has to admire the degree of historical accuracy attempted, the erudition displayed by artists in their quest for authenticity. This was as true of Roybet in France and Hendrik Leys in Belgium as it was of Seymour Lucas in England. Lucas indeed was the founder in 1880 of the Kernoozers Club, whose members were history painters with antiquarian ambitions. It was a group which met regularly of an evening, sustained by simple fare of beer and cheese, to study the details of historical costume and accoutrements: they were united by a love of arms and armour, examples of which were shown off and swapped as props for intimate pictorial recreations of the past.

Dumas had revealed to an appreciative public that cavaliers were debonair, flamboyant, and excellent visual material for artists in search of striking historical subject matter. Certainly some of the scenes chosen for illustration in the nineteenth century were swashbuckling and action packed; but as in so many other areas of the popular painting of the time, the spectator derived his keenest pleasure from spying on these illustrious figures from the past in trivial or sentimental private moments. It was as if their larger-than-life image had to be toned down to meet a more bourgeois Victorian sensibility. Could anything be more sublimely trivial than Paolo Bedini's scene of domestic bliss in which a cavalier and two ladies wind wool together, wrapped in expressions of joyous enthusiasm? The later nineteenth century was much given to romanticising contemporary affairs of the heart with historical associations: thus young ladies coyly refer to their admirers as variously 'swains' (Mediaeval), 'beaux' (Regency) and especially 'cavaliers'. Bedini seems to be pointing out here that cavaliers could equally well behave like soppy Victorian suitors. And what is to be made of G. Hildyard Swinstead's supremely unlikely recreation of cavaliers playing golf, dramatically entitled '*All Square and One to Play*'? It must have proved consoling to the late Victorian industrial magnate trudging back to the clubhouse after the eighteenth hole that he was following such exotic and romantic footsteps.

Perhaps it was the contemplation of pictures such as this which finally convinced G.A. Storey that his own attempts to make cavaliers live again, and indeed all the eager efforts at costume drama of his fellow artists across Europe, were doomed to failure:

> In the work of Velasquez I knew that not only were the costumes correct, but the actual men of the time were there before me, the period stamped, not only in the dress, but on every face, in the very attitudes even of the figures; the whole belonging so completely to its own day, even as the hand that wrought it, that I felt I had a true page of history before me, and not a theatrical make-up of a scene only dimly realised in the pages of a book written many years after the event.

Here was the moment of disillusion: if it was realism which such painters sought in their reconstructions of the seventeenth century, they were to be disappointed, because there were actual paintings of the time against which to judge. If, on the other hand, there were patrons to be satisfied with romanticised pastiches of a bygone era, an audience to be titillated with cosy suggestions of the jolly domesticity of cavaliers, there was no shortage of artists to meet these needs. Thus it is that the Cavalier, together with the Cardinal, the Monk, and the Regency Beau, takes his place as one of the archetypes of popular nineteenth century painting.

Index of Artists

HEGER, Heinrich Anton (German, 1832-1888)
* HERRING (Sen.), John Frederick (British, 1795-1865)
HESSE, Alexander (French, 1806-1879)
* HEYLIGERS, Gustav Anton François (Dutch, fl. 1860-1876)
HILLEMACHER, Ernest Eugène (French, 1818-1887)
* HILLINGFORD, Robert Alexander (British, 1828-1902)
HOFF, Conrad (German, 1816-1883)
HORSLEY, John Callcott (British, 1817-1903)

* INGRES, Jean Auguste Dominique (French, 1780-1867)
* ISABEY, Eugène Louis Gabriel (French, 1803-1866)

JAZET, Paul Léon (French, 1848-?)

KLIMSCH, Eugen Johann Georg (German 1839-1896)
KNOOP, Hermann August (German, 1856-1900)
KOERLE, Pancraz (German, 1823-1875)
KRONBERG, Julius Johan Ferdinand (Swedish, 1850-1921)

* LAGYE, Victor (Belgian, 1829-1896)
LAMI, Eugène Louis (French, 1800-1890)
LANGENMANTEL, Ludwig von (German, 1854-1922)
LANGEROCK, Henri (Belgian, ?-1885)
LANZONI, P. (Italian, late 19th Century)
LAVATI, Gusto (Italian, late 19th Century)
* LEIGH, Conrad (British, late 19th Century)
LELOIR, Alexandre Louis (French, 1843-1884)
* LEON Y ESCOSURA, Ignacio (Spanish, 1834-1901)
LESLIE, Charles Robert (British, 1794-1859)
* LESREL, Adolphe Alexandre (French, 1839-1890)
* LEWIN, Stephen (British,, fl. 1890-1910)
LEYENDECKER, Paul Joseph (French, 1842-?)
LITSCHAUER, Karl Joseph (Austrian, 1830-1871)
* LOMAX, John Arthur (British, 1857-1923)
LOUYOT, Edmund (German, 1861-1909)
* LUCAS, John Seymour (British, 1849-1923)

* McCORMICK, Arthur David (British, 1860-1943)
* MADOU, Jean Baptiste (Belgian, 1796-1877)
MANSFIELD, Heinrich August (Austrian, 1816-1901)
* MARCHETTI, Ludovico (Italian, 1853-1909)
* MARCH Y MARCO, Vincente (Spanish, 1859-?)
MAYER, Georges (French, fl. 1882-1912)
MEISSONIER, Jean Louis Ernest (French, 1815-1891)
MENOCAL, Armando (Spanish, late 19th Century)
MEYER, Claus (German, 1856-1919)
* MILLAIS, Sir John Everett (British, 1829-1896)
* MILLET, Francis David (Dutch-American, 1846-1912)
* MOORMANS, Frans (Dutch, 1831-1873)
* MOREAU, Adrien (French, 1843-1906)
MUNOZ Y CUESTA, Domingo (Spanish, 1850-1912)

NOBLE, James (British, 1797-1879)

* PARRIS, Edmund Thomas (British, 1793-1873)
PASMORE, Daniel (British, fl. 1829-1865)
PETTIE, John (British, 1839-1893)
POLIDORI, Gian Carlo (Italian, late 19th Century)
* PRAGA, Emilio (Italian, 1839-1875)

* QUADRONE, Giovanni Battista (Italian, 1844-1898)

* RAFFAELI, Jean François (French, 1850-1924)
RÄUBER, Wilhelm Carl (German, 1849-1926)
RENAZZI, Eugen von (Italian, 1863-?)

* REYNTJENS, Henricus Engelbertus (Dutch, 1817-1878)
* RICARDI, Attilio (Italian, late 19th Century)
* RICCI, Arturo (Italian, 1854-?)
RICCI, Pio (Italian, ?-1919)
RIVAS, Francisco Paolo (Italian, 1854-?)
RONGIER, Jeanne (French, fl. 1867-1900)
ROQUEPLAN, Camille Joseph Etienne (French, 1803-1855)
ROSENSTRAND, Vilhelm Jacob (Danish, 1838-1915)
ROSIER, Jean Guilaume (Dutch, 1858-1931)
* ROYBET, Ferdinand Victor Léon (French, 1840-1920)

SADLER, Walter Dendy (British, 1824-1923)
* SANI, Alessandro (Italian, late 19th Century)
SARTORIO, Giulio Aristide (Italian, 1860-1932)
* SCHAEFELS, Hendrik Frans (Belgian, 1827-1904)
SCHGOER, Julius (Austrian, 1847-1885)
* SCHIVERT, Viktor (Austrian, 1863-?)
* SCHROEDER, Albert Friedrich (German, 1854-?)
SCHROTTER, Alfred von (Austrian, 1856-1935)
SEGUI, José (Spanish 1821-?)
* SEILER, Carl Wilhelm Anton (German, 1846-1921)
SENEZCOURT, Jules de (French, 1818-1866)
SIMONE, Gustavo (Italian, 1846-?)
SOHN, Karl Wilhelm (German, 1853-1925)
SOULACROIX, Charles Joseph Frédéric (French, 1825-?)
STEPHANOFF, Francis Philip (Bavarian, 1790-1860)
* STEVER, Gustav Curt Friedrich (Russian, 1823-1877)
* STONE, Marcus (British, 1840-1921)
STOREY, George Adolphus Augustus (British, 1834-1919)
STROEBEL, Johann Anthonie Balthasar (Dutch, 1821-1905)
SWINSTEAD, George Hillyard (British, 1860-1926)
SYLVESTRE, Joseph Nöel (French, 1847-1926)

* TEN KATE, Herman Frederick Carel (Dutch, 1822-1891)
* TODT, Max (German, 1847-1890)
* TOMMASI, Publio de (Italian, 1849-?)

* VIBERT, Jean Georges (French, 1840-1902)
VILLEGAS Y CORDERO, José (Spanish, 1848-1922)
VINEA, Francesco (Italian, 1845-1902)
* VIOTTI, Giulio (Italian, 1845-1877)
VIRY, Paul Alphonse (French, fl.1861-1881)
VITA, Wilhelm (Austrian, 1846-1919)
* VOLKHART, Max (German, 1848-1924)

* WAGNER, Fritz (German, late 19th Century)
WARD, Edward Matthew (British, 1816-1879)
WATERLOW, Clifford (British, late 19th Century)
* WAUTERS, Emile Charles (Belgian, 1846-1933)
WEBB, Charles Meer (British, 1830-1895)
WEBER, Franz Xaver (Austrian, 1829-1887)
* WEBER, Heinrich (German, late 19th Century)
* WINGFIELD, James Digman (British, ?-1872)
WODZINSKI, Josef (Polish, 1859-?)

YEAMES, William Frederick (British, 1834-1919)

ZAMAÇOIS Y ZABALA, Eduardo (Spanish, 1842-1871)
ZIEBLAND, Hermann (German, 1853-1896)
ZIMMERMAN, Ernst Karl Georg (German, 1852-1901)

ALEX DE ANDRIES. A cavalier
smoking. Signed, on panel. 24 x 19¾ ins.
(61 x 50cm). *Christie's.*

Top left: FEDERICO ANDREOTTI. The
courtship. Signed, on panel.
16 x 12¼ ins. (40.5 x 31cm). *Christie's.*

HENRY ANDREWS. A hunting party
taking refreshment. Signed, shaped top.
33¼ x 32¼ ins. (84.5 x 82cm). *Christie's.*

FILIPPO BARATTI. The dance after supper: Cardinal Richelieu entertaining Louis XIII and the Musketeers at the Louvre. Signed and dated 1891 and inscribed on the reverse. 37½ x 52¾ins. (95.5 x 134cm). *Christie's.*

ANGELO ASTI. The toast. Signed. 17½ x 12ins. (44.5 x 30.5cm). *Sotheby's.*

PAOLO GIOVANNI BEDINI. Winding the skein. Signed, on panel. 13 x 9¾ins. (33 x 24.5cm). *Christie's.*

FRANK MOSS BENNETT. Cavaliers playing cards. Signed and inscribed 'sketch', and dated 1934, on board. 14¼ x 20¼ ins. (36 x 51.5cm). *Christie's.*

WILLIAM A. BREAKSPEARE. A toast. Signed, on board. 12½ x 18½ ins. (32 x 47cm). *Christie's.*

ADOLPHE ALEXANDRE LESREL. The connoisseurs. Signed and dated 1895, on panel. 23 x 19ins. (58.5 x 48cm). *Christie's.*

HEINRICH BRELING.
A woman offering drink to a
cavalier. Signed, on panel.
8 x 5ins. (20.5 x 12.5cm).
Christie's.

FRANÇOIS BRUNERY. Nouvelles Chansons. Signed. 30¾ x 41ins. (78 x 104cm). *Christie's.*

EDGAR BUNDY. The visitor. Signed and dated 1887. 29½ x 39ins. (75 x 99cm). *Christie's.*

MAXIMO CABALLERO. Off duty. Signed and inscribed Paris. 19¾ x 24½ ins. (50 x 61.5cm). *Christie's.*

ANTONIO CASANOVA Y ESTORACH. The gallant. Signed and dated Roma 1875, on panel. 12¾ x 7¾ ins. (32.5 x 19.5cm). *Christie's.*

THEODORE CERIEZ. A Pensive Cavalier. On panel, signed. 9 x 6¾ ins. (22.5 x 17cm). *Sotheby's.*

HERMAN FREDERICK CAREL TEN KATE. Soldiers plundering a mansion. Signed, on panel. 24¼ x 36¼ ins.
(61.5 x 92cm). *Christie's.*

FRANCESCO COLEMAN. The
elopement discovered. Signed and
inscribed Roma. 25 x 36¾ins.
(63.5 x 93.5cm). *Christie's.*

TITO CONTI. Two strings to her bow.
Signed. 31 x 41ins. (78.5 x 104cm).
Christie's.

ERNEST CROFTS. Before Naseby.
Signed and dated '78. 23 x 44ins.
(58.5 x 112cm). *Christie's.*

CESARE AUGUSTE DETTI. The favourite. Signed and dated Paris '83, on panel. 20 x 24ins. (50.5 x 61cm). *Christie's.*

FRANCISCO DOMINGO Y MARQUES. A halt at the inn. Signed and dated Paris 1898. 19½ x 23½ins. (49.5 x 60cm). *Christie's.*

HIPPOLYTE FRANÇOIS LÉON DULUARD. The farewell. Signed, on panel. 28½ x 22½ins. (72.5 x 57.5cm). *Christie's.*

ANTONIO MARIA FABRES Y COSTA. A cavalier drinking in a cellar. Signed. 37½ x 23½ins. (95.5 x 60cm). *Christie's.*

SAURO FOLCHI. Giving the toast. Signed and inscribed Roma. 19 x 22ins. (48 x 56cm). *Christie's.*

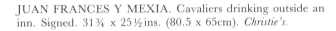

JUAN FRANCES Y MEXIA. Cavaliers drinking outside an inn. Signed. 31¾ x 25½ins. (80.5 x 65cm). *Christie's.*

ALFRED FRIEDLAENDER. A military encampment with soldiers. Signed, on panel. 8 x 12ins. (20 x 30.5cm). *Christie's.*

JAKOB EMMANUEL GAISSER. The card players. Signed and dated 1882, on panel. 15½ x 11½ins. (39.5 x 29cm). *Christie's.*

MAX GAISSER. The antiquarians.
Signed. 38½ x 45¼ ins.
(98 x 115cm). *Christie's.*

LOUIS-JOSEPH GRISÉE. The
Pipe smokers. Signed and dated
1845. 16 x 12¾ ins. (40.5 x 32.5cm).
Sotheby's.

JOHANN HAMZA. A cavalier
smoking a pipe in an interior.
Signed and dated Wien 1881, on
panel. 4¾ x 4ins. (12 x 10cm).
Christie's.

THOMAS FRANK
HEAPHY. Proscribed
Christmas. Signed
with monogram and
dated 1868.
47½ x 62¾ins.
(120.5 x 159.5cm).
Christie's.

JOHN FREDERICK
HERRING (SEN).
Cavaliers taking
refreshment outside an
inn. Signed and dated
1848. 40 x 50ins.
(101.5 x 127cm).
Christie's.

GUSTAV ANTON FRANÇOIS HEYLIGERS.
The Musicians. Signed and dated 1860, on panel.
11 x 13¼ ins. (28 x 34cm). *Christie's.*

JEAN AUGUSTE DOMINIC INGRES. Henry IV playing
with his children. 15½ x 19½ ins. (39 x 49cm). *Musée de Petit
Palais, Paris; Photo: Bulloz.*

ROBERT ALEXANDER HILLINGFORD.
The water party. Signed and dated 1864, on
panel. 18 x 13¼ ins. (45.5 x 33.5cm). *Christie's.*

EUGÈNE LOUIS GABRIEL ISABEY. Cavaliers
skirmishing. Signed and dated '67. 16½ x 25ins.
(42 x 63.5cm). *Christie's.*

Top right: VICTOR LAGYE. The standard bearer. Signed
and certified by the artist and stamped with the artist's seal
on the reverse, on panel. 21 x 15¼ ins. (53 x 39cm).
Christie's.

Centre right: CONRAD LEIGH. The cardinal's tale.
Signed. 17½ x 24ins. (44.5 x 61cm). *Christie's.*

ADOLPHE ALEXANDRE LESREL. A subtle move.
Signed and dated 1904, on panel. 20 x 25ins.
(51 x 63.5cm). *Christie's.*

Bottom right: IGNACIO LEON Y ESCOSURA.
Jovial Companions. Signed and dated 1883, on panel.
17 x 21½ ins. (43 x 54.5cm). *Christie's.*

STEPHEN LEWIN. The Guard. Signed and dated 1901. 12¾ x 10½ ins. (32.5 x 27cm). *Christie's.*

JOHN ARTHUR LOMAX. A question of Prudence. Signed, on panel. 11½ x 17ins. (29 x 43cm). *Christie's.*

JOHN SEYMOUR LUCAS. Charles I demands the surrender of Gloucester. Signed and dated 1881. 44½ x 72¼ ins. (113 x 183.5cm). *Christie's.*

ARTHUR DAVID
McCORMICK. Cavalier at an
inn. Signed. 15½ x 21½ins.
(39.5 x 54.5cm). *Christie's.*

Top left: JEAN BAPTISTE
MADOU. Quarrelling at
Cards. Signed and dated 1851,
and signed and authenticated
on an old label on the reverse,
on panel. 15½ x 19½ins.
(39.5 x 49.5cm). *Christie's.*

LUDOVICO MARCHETTI.
Elegant company by a lagoon.
Signed and dated 1882, on
panel. 13½ x 22½ins.
(34.5 x 57cm). *Christie's.*

VINCENTE MARCH Y
MARCO. The mountebank.
Signed and inscribed Roma.
12½ x 19ins. (31.5 x 48cm).
Christie's.

SIR JOHN EVERETT MILLAIS. The Proscribed Royalist, 1651. Signed and dated 1853. 40½ x 29ins. (103 x 73.5cm). *Christie's.*

FRANCIS DAVID MILLET. The piping times of peace. Signed and dated 1887. 28 x 38ins. (71 x 96.5cm). *Christie's.*

FRANS MOORMANS. A summer evening on the terrace. Signed and dated Paris, 1887, on panel. 5½ x 8ins. (14 x 20.5cm). *Christie's.*

EDMUND THOMAS PARRIS. The Duke and Duchess of St. Albans out falconing. Signed, inscribed and dated 1840, shaped. 84 x 62ins. (213 x 157.5cm). *Christie's.*

ADRIEN MOREAU. Les noces d'argent. Signed. 37 x 51ins. (94 x 129.5cm). *Christie's.*

GIOVANNI BATTISTA
QUADRONE. A cavalier. Signed
and dated '79, on panel.
8½ x 5¾ins. (21.5 x 14.5cm).
Christie's.

Top left: EMILIO PRAGA. The
fortune teller. Signed. 30¾ x 41¾ins.
(78 x 106cm). *Christie's.*

JEAN FRANÇOIS RAFFAELI.
Elegant figures in a garden. Signed.
12 x 15ins. (30.5 x 38cm). *Christie's.*

HENRICUS ENGELBERTUS
REYNTJENS. The card game.
Signed, on panel. 6¾ x 9ins.
(17 x 23cm). *Christie's.*

ATTILIO RICARDI. A family reunion. Signed. 18½ x 26¾ins. (47 x 68cm). *Christie's.*

ARTURO RICCI. A Cavalier. Signed. 12½ x 9ins. (32 x 23cm). *Christie's.*

FERDINAND VICTOR LÉON ROYBET. Divertissement Musicale. Signed and dated 1879. 58 x 47ins. (147 x 119cm). *Christie's.*

ALESSANDRO SANI. A musical interlude. Signed on panel.
19 x 23½ ins. (48 x 60cm). *Christie's.*

HENDRIK FRANS SCHAEFELS. A civic
company at ease outside a town house.
Signed and dated 1880, on panel.
8¾ x 7½ ins. (22 x 19cm). *Christie's.*

VIKTOR SCHIVERT. The conversation. Signed and
inscribed München. 25¼ x 20½ ins. (64 x 52cm). *Christie's.*

ALBERT FRIEDRICH SCHROEDER. A merry
company. Signed, on panel. 20½ x 16½ ins. (52 x 42cm).
Christie's.

CARL WILHELM ANTON SEILER. A game of chess. Signed and dated 1878, on panel. 10¾ x 15¾ ins. (27.5 x 40cm). *Christie's.*

GUSTAV CURT FRIEDRICH STEVER. Off to war. Signed, and signed and inscribed Dusseldorf on the reverse. 46 x 39ins. (117 x 99cm). *Christie's.*

MARCUS STONE. Bad News. Signed and dated 1882. 73 x 44¾ins. (184.5 x 113.5cm). *Christie's.*

HERMAN FREDERICK CAREL TEN KATE. Cavaliers in an interior. Signed and dated 1860, on panel. 11¾ x 16ins. (30 x 40.5cm). *Christie's.*

MAX TODT. The Messenger. Signed, on panel. 9¾ x 6¼ins. (25 x 16cm). *Christie's.*

PUBLIO DE TOMMASI. Cavaliers gambling. Signed. 26 x 18¾ins. (66 x 47.5cm). *Christie's.*

GIULIO VIOTTI. The flirtation. Signed, on panel. 19 x 13½ins. (48 x 34.5cm). *Christie's.*

JEAN GEORGES VIBERT. Les cadets de Gascogne. Signed, on panel. 27 x 37ins. (68.5 x 94cm). *Christie's.*

MAX VOLKHART. The eavesdropper. Signed and inscribed op.225. 34½ x 44¼ins. (87.5 x 112.5cm). *Christie's.*

FRITZ WAGNER. Sportsmen smoking in an interior. Signed. 26 x 31½ins. (66 x 80cm). *Christie's.*

HEINRICH WEBER. A musical gathering. Signed with initials, on panel. 16 x 9ins. (40.5 x 30cm). *Christie's.*

EMILE CHARLES WAUTERS. A Cavalier. Signed. 29 x 17½ins. (74 x 44.5cm). *Christie's.*

JAMES DIGMAN WINGFIELD. The Rehearsal; scene. The Garden, Elvaston, Derbyshire. Signed and dated 1857. 22¼ x 40ins. (56.5 x 101.5cm). *Christie's.*

170

Children

That the nineteenth century spectator could be reduced to a state of treacly ecstasy by the depiction of the antics of adorable little children was a weakness well understood and eagerly exploited by artists. A picture like James Hayllar's *I'm Mary Tween of Tots*, complete with childishly enunciated title, was enough to send Mrs New-Picture-Buyer swooning, her maternal feelings inflamed to the limit, while even her husband, the stern paterfamilias, might find it necessary to express his admiration of such a masterpiece in tones distinctly huskier than normal. Of course that archetype of a popular Victorian picture, Millais's *Bubbles*, exploits these very susceptibilities.

The English were not alone in their liking for such things. Every Continental country with a middle class voracious for domestic pictures had its painters particularly adept at heart-winning children. Some were artists of considerable merit. The Swiss Albert Anker, for instance, when he allowed straight observation to hold the balance in its fashionable combination with sentimentality, produced studies of children which can stand comparison with the highest achievements in the field. And Carl Larsson created a beguiling image of childhood whose influence was felt in nurseries of countries far beyond his native Sweden. Here were two artists of widely differing backgrounds, nationalities, and approaches equally transfixed by their subject. Anker, for instance, laid claim to being a serious student of child psychology, and contributed to a causerie on The Early Development of the Child conducted in La Suisse Liberale in 1898. Carl Larsson, on the other hand, was an advocate of the simple virtues of family, country life, and showed a missionary zeal in extolling them. Ultimately, however, both are acutely susceptible to children. Anker's contribution to the causerie rapidly dissolves from a high scientific tone into lyricism about 'the little ones playing their first games, laughing at their first jokes, upon their mother's lap.' Carl Larsson dilates ecstatically on the pleasures of recording 'how charmingly a little girl's braids snuggle against her little round neck, how the rays of sunlight fall on a little nose'.

For a more critical analysis of such juvenile charm, the tone of George Eliot writing forty years earlier is perhaps salutory:

> It is a beauty like that of kittens, or very small downy ducks making rippling noises with their soft bills, or babies just beginning to toddle and to engage in conscious mischief — a beauty with which you can never be angry, but that you feel ready to crush for inability to comprehend the state of mind into which it throws you.

This comparison of the human young with the young of animals is, pictorially, an apt one, because children are often shown with especially anthropomorphic domestic pets for maximum effect. Dogs and children were a particularly winning combination, and artists like Elsley and Charles Burton Barber in England, and Felix Schlesinger and Adolf Eberle in Munich, made a speciality of such scenes. The props may have been sheepdogs in one country and dachshunds in the other, but the essential message remains the same, speaking an international language.

The roots of this sort of sentimental painting of the child are to be found in the late eighteenth century. It was then, for instance, that the term 'espieglerie' was first coined in connection with those children's portraits by Greuze and Reynolds in which the sitters exhibit a self-consciously charming mischievousness. Sir Thomas Lawrence also found his patrons increasingly responsive to a treatment of children which rendered them just a bit too winning to be true, with curls that fell a little too entrancingly across the forehead, and pouts that played rather too simperingly upon the lips. Under the partial influence of Greuze, George Morland and the English early nineteenth century school of rustic genre created smiling peasant children who find numerous descendant cousins on the Continent in the works of painters like Lanfant de Metz in France, Jan Marie Ten Kate in Holland, and August Heyn in Munich. These are pretty, sanitised dolls, packaged for easy display in bourgeois drawing rooms, and bearing about as much relation to the reality of peasant life as Dumbo to an elephant of the African bush.

Whether Lawrence had any lasting influence on the approach of Viennese painters to children as a result of his stay there in 1815 is debatable. The spirit of Biedermeyer in Austria and Germany at this time was anyway extremely sympathetic to the domestic tenor of subjects encompassing the charming antics of little children. The ground was laid out of which flowered the proliferation of pretty children painted in the Munich school of popular genre of later in the century. Here again, the south German feeling for 'gemutlichkeit' was exercised to the full. But the Biedermeyer period did produce certain painters whose treatment of children had a less contrived charm and sensitivity, like the Austrian Peter Fendi. Later in the century came German painters such as Meyer von Bremen, who, starting from Biedermeyer innocence, developed a more explicitly sentimental formula which won him an enormous following, especially in the United States. He was nicknamed 'kinder-meyer' precisely because of his preference for children as subjects. These children are often well observed, but as he grew wiser in his public's preferences, Meyer von Bremen perfected certain tricks to elicit the maximum emotional response from his audience. One of these was a fondness for directing his prettiest subject's gaze straight at the spectator, drawing him irresistibly closer (resistance to such appeal being low at the best of times).

During the nineteenth century, popular attitudes to children crystallised into various stereotypes: innocence; the microcosm of adulthood; vulnerability; endearing naughtiness. It was also a time when the focus on childhood drew several older male writers dangerously close to the precipice in their adulation of the female young of the species. Ruskin, Lewis Carroll, and Kilvert, for instance, were victims of a condition which might charitably be described as galloping sentimentality in relation to little girls; a condition which was arguably prevalent in the nineteenth century partly because its popular imagery dwelt so rapturously on the adorable qualities of the child. Melbourne Art Gallery, to whom Ruskin acted as adviser for acquisitions during the 1880s, possesses as a result an inconveniently large holding of pictures of children by minor Victorian painters of little merit but a huge capacity for schmalz. Ruskin himself adopted a disproportionately laudatory tone to any painter who succeeded in indulging his weakness for childish beauty. Of the French artist Pierre Edouard Frère, the Parisian 'kinder-meyer' with a similar international popularity, Ruskin demanded ecstatically: 'Who would have believed it possible to unite the depth of Wordsworth, the grace of Reynolds, and the holiness of Angelico?'

Perhaps *Bubbles* is an appropriate epitaph to much nineteenth century painting of children: pretty, soapy, insubstantial, and excellent advertising material. An earlier Millais child portrait, *Cherry Ripe*, had been issued in colour reproduction with *The Graphic* in 1880, and 600,000 had been sold. Such exploitations of the public's susceptibility were intensely marketable. Millais, indeed, like a good advertising executive, was fully aware of his market, and knew what would and would not sell in the way of children even down to the question of nationality. 'What children do we care about?' he asked, in explaining why he could never paint a satisfactory realistic version of *Suffer Little Children to Come unto Me*. 'Why, our own fair English children of course; not the brown simious-looking children of Syria.'

A subsection of the genre of child-painting consisted of scenes enacted in schoolrooms or vestries. There was an international taste for such set-pieces, which offered scope for a multiplicity of anecdote, often featuring some endearing naughtiness on the part of the taught at the expense of the teacher; or, in the case of ecclesiastical settings, on the part of the choirboy at the expense of the choirmaster or even, on occasion, the priest. The vestry indeed in this context is the equivalent of the cardinal's palace in popular painting generally, offering a peep behind the scenes into a world reputedly serious and mysterious, but revealed as reassuringly full of practical jokes and appealing juvenile mischief. There is the same faint whiff of anti-clericalism. Certain artists, like the Italian Francesco Bergamini, the Frenchman Theophile Duverger, or the Englishman Thomas Webster, were specialists in school or vestry scenes. For others they were a useful standby when pictures were required which mixed humour, mischief, and sentimentality.

Index of artists

CALDECOTT, Randolph (British, 1846-1886)
CHEVILLIARD, Vincent Jean Baptiste (French, 1841-1904)
* CHIERICI, Gaetano (Italian, 1838-1920)
* CHOCARNE-MOREAU, Paul Charles (French, 1855-1931)
CLAUS, Emile (Belgian, 1849-1924)
COBBETT, Edward John (British, 1815-1899)
COLEMAN, William Stephen (British, 1829-1904)
* COLLINSON, James (British, 1825-1881)
* COMPTON, Charles (British, 1828-1884)
CONSTANTINI, Giuseppe (Italian, 1843-1893)
COPE, Charles West (British, 1811-1890)
CORNICELIUS, Georg (German, 1825-1898)
CURNOCK, James (British, 1812-1870)
CZECH, Emil (Austrian, 1862-1929)

DACRE, Susan Isabel (British, 1844-?)
DAFFINGER, Moritz Michael (Austria, 1790-1849)
DAMSCHROEDER, Jan Jacobus Matthijs (Dutch,
    1825-1905)
DANHAUSER, Joseph (Austrian, 1805-1845)
DANSAERT, Léon Marie Constant (Belgian, 1830-1909)
* DARGELAS, André Henri (French, 1828-1906)
DEGRAVE, Jules Alex Patrouillard (French, fl. 1875-1904)
DELACHAUX, Léon (French, 1850-1919)
DELAROCHE, Paul (French, 1797-1856)
* DELL, John H. (British, 1836-1888)
* DILLENS, Hendrick Joseph (Belgian, 1812-1872)
* DINET, Alphonse Etienne (French, 1861-1929)
DOBSON, William Charles Thomas (British, 1817-1898)
DODSON, Sarah Ball (British, late 19th Century)
DÜRCK, Friedrich (German, 1809-1884)
* DUVERGER, Théophile Emmanuel (French, 1821-?)
* DUWÉE, Henri Joseph (Belgian, late 19th Century)

ECHTLER, Adolf (German, 1843-1914)
* EDMONSTON, Samuel (British, 1825-?)
EDWARDS, Mia (British, fl. 1893-1900)
ELIAS, Emily (British, fl. 1882-1907)
* ELLIOTT, Robinson (British, 1814-1894)
ELSLEY, Arthur John (British, 1861-?)
ENGEL, John Frederick (German, 1844-1921)
ENTRAYGUES, Charles Bertrand d' (French, 1851-?)
EPP, Rudolf (German, 1834-1910)
ESCH, Mathilde (Austrian, 1820-?)

FARASYN, Edgard Pieter Joseph (Belgian, 1858-?)
FARRIER, Robert (British, 1796-1879)
FENDI, Peter (Austrian, 1796-1842)
FERON, William (Swedish, 1858-1894)
FIRLE, Walter von (German, 1859-1929)
FREDERIC, Léon Henri Marie (Belgian, 1856-1940)
* FRÈRE, Pierre Edouard (French, 1819-1886)
FRIEDLÄNDER VON MALHEIM, Hedwig (Austrian,
    1863-?)
FRÖSCHL, Carl (Austrian, 1848-1934)
* FULTON, David (British, 1848-1930)

* GABÉ, Edward Nicolas (French, 1814-1865)
GADSBY, William (British, fl. 1863-1893)
GARLAND, Henry (British, fl. 1854-1890)
GEERTZ, Julius (German, 1837-1902)
* GEOFFROY, Henry Jules Jean (French, 1853-1924)
* GESELSCHAP, Eduard (German, 1814-1878)
GILBERT JESPERSON, Anne Marie (Danish, late 19th
    Century)
* GLASGOW, Alexander (British, fl. 1859-1884)

174

GLÜCKLICH, Simon (German, 1863-?)
GOGIN, Charles (British, 1844-1931)
GORE, William Henry (British, fl. 1880-1920)
GOTCH, Thomas Cooper (British, 1854-1931)
GRAF, Paul Edmund (Swedish, 1866-1903)
GRANT, William James (British, 1829-1866)
* GREEN, Alfred H. (British, fl. 1844-1862)
GREENAWAY, Kate (British, 1846-1901)
GUZZONE, Sebastiano (Italian, 1856-1890)
GYSELINCKX, Jos (Belgian, late 19th Century)

* HAAG, Jean Paul (French, fl. 1870-1895)
* HALL, Thomas P. (British, fl. 1837-1867)
HARCOURT, George (British, 1869-1947)
HARDIE, Charles Martin (British, 1858-1916)
* HARDY, Frederick Daniel (British, 1826-1911)
HARDY, George (British, 1822-1909)
* HARDY, (Jun.) James (British, 1832-1889)
* HARLAMOFF, Alexei Alexeievich (Russian, 1849-?)
* HARPER, Edward S. (British, 1878-1951)
HAUSLEITHNER, Rudolf (Austrian, 1840-1918)
HAVENITH, Hugo (British, 1853-?)
* HAYLLAR, James (British, 1829-1920)
* HAYNES, John William (British, 1834-1908)
HEDLEY, Ralph (British, 1851-1913)
* HEMSLEY, William (British, 1819-1893)
HENSHALL, John Henry (British, 1856-?)
* HERDMAN, Robert (British, 1829-1888)
HEYERMANS, Jean Arnould (Belgian, 1837-1892)
* HEYN, August (German, 1837-?)
HIRT, Heinrich (German, late 19th Century)
* HOEGG, Joseph (German, 1826-?)
HOLMES, George Augustus (British, fl. 1859-1909)
HOOG, Bernard Johann de (Dutch, 1867-1943)
HOSEMANN, Theodor Friedrich Wilhelm (German,
    1807-1875)
* HUNT, Charles (British, 1803-1877)

IGLER, Gustav (Austrian, 1842-1908)

JASINSKI, Zdzislaw (Polish, late 19th Century)
* JEUNE, Henry le (British, 1820-1904)

KADEDER, Hans (German, 1852-1910)
KAULBACH, Hermann (German, 1846-1909)
KELS, Franz (German, 1828-1893)
KEYSER, Emil (Swiss, 1846-1923)
KINDT, Adéle (Belgian, 1804-1884)
* KISPERT, Gustav (German, 1856-1887)
KLIMT, Ernst (Austrian, 1864-1892)
KNAUS, Ludwig (German, 1829-1910)
KNIGHT, William Henry (British, 1823-1863)
KNÖCHL, Hans (Austrian, 1850-?)
KNOWLES, George Sheridan (British, 1863-1931)

LAMMENS, Jan Baptiste (Belgian, 1818-?)
* LANFANT DE METZ, François Louis (French,
    1814-1892)
LANGLOIS, Mark W. (British, fl. 1862-1873)
* LARSSON, Carl (Swedish, 1853-1919)
* LASSALLE, Louis (French, 1815-?)
* LEGA, Silvestro (Italian, 1826-1895)
LEJEUNE, Eugène Joseph (French, 1818-1894)
* LELEUX, Adolphe (French, 1812-1891)
LENBACH, Franz Seraph von (German, 1836-1904)
LESLIE, Charles Robert (British, 1794-1859)

* LÉVY, Emile (French, 1826-1890)
LEWIS, Charles James (British, 1830-1892)
* LINNIG, Willem (Belgian, 1819-1885)
* LOBRICHON, Timoleon Marie (French, 1831-1914)
* LOFFLER-RADYMNO, Leopold (Austrian, 1827-1898)
LORIMER, John Henry (British, 1857-1936)
LOUYOT, Edmond (German, 1861-1909)
LUDWIG, Auguste (German, 1834-?)

MACDUFF, William (British, fl. 1844-1876)
MACLEOD, Jessie (British, fl. 1845-1875)
* MCTAGGART, William (British, 1835-1910)
MAGNI, Giuseppe (Italian, 1869-?)
MALMSTRÖM, Johann August (Swedish, 1829-1901)
MANCINI, Antonio (Italian, 1852-1930)
* MARSHALL, Thomas Falcon (British, 1818-1878)
MERLE, Hugues (French, 1823-1881)
MEYERHEIM, Wilhelm Alexander (German, 1815-1882)
* MEYER VON BREMEN, Johann Georg (German, 1813-1886)
MICHETTI, Franscesco Paolo (Italian, 1851-1929)
* MILLAIS, Sir John Everett (British, 1829-1896)
* MOESELAGEN, Leon A. (German, late 19th Century)
MONIES, David (Danish, 1812-1894)
* MORGAN, Frederick (British, 1856-1927)
* MORGAN, John (British, 1823-1886)
* MORMILE, Gaetano (Italian, 1839-1890)
* MORO, Franz (Austrian, late 19th Century)
* MORRIS, Philip Richard (British, 1838-1902)
MUCKLEY, William Jabez (British, 1837-1905)
MÜLLER, August (German, late 19th Century)
* MULREADY, Augustus E. (British, ?-1886)
MUNIER, Emile (French, 1810-1895)

NEUSTATTER, Ludwig (German, 1829-1899)
* NIEDMANN, August Heinrich (German, 1826-1910)
NORDGREN, Anna (Swedish, 1847-1916)

OEHMICHEN, Hugo (German, 1843-1933)
* O'NEILL, George Bernard (British, 1828-1917)
OOMS, Karel (Belgian, 1845-1900)
ORFEI, Orfeo (Italian, late 19th Century)
OSTERLIND, Allan (Swedish, 1855-1938)

PACHER, Ferdinand (German, 1852-1913)
PAGET, Henry Marriott (British, 1856-1936)
* PAOLETTI, Antonio (Italian, 1834-1912)
PASSINI, Ludwig Johann (Austrian, 1832-1903)
* PATTEIN, César (French, late 19th Century)
PAUW, Robert de (Belgian, late 19th Century)
PEELE, John Thomas (British, 1822-1897)
PELEZ, Fernand Emmanuel (French, 1843-1913)
PERRAULT, Léon Jean Basile (French, 1832-1908)
PERRY, William J. (British, fl. 1870-1871)
PERSOGLIA, Franz von (Austrian, 1852-?)
* PERUGINI, Kate (British, 1839-1929)
PESKE, Géza (Austrian, 1859-1934)
* PETIT, Charles (French, late 19th Century)
* PIETERS, Evert (Dutch, 1856-1932)
PIGHLEIN, Bruno Elimar Ulrich (German, 1848-1894)
PILTZ, Otto (German, 1846-1910)
POOLE, Paul Falconer (British, 1807-1879)
PROVIS, Alfred (British, fl. 1843-1886)
PRZEPIORSKI, Lucien (Russian, 1830-1898)

RAUPP, Karl (German, 1837-1918)
* REINHOLD, Bernhard (German, 1824-1892)
REITER, Johann Baptiste (Austrian, 1813-1890)
RIBBING, Sofie Amalie (Swedish, 1835-1894)
* ROBERTS, Edwin (British, fl. 1840-1917)
ROBINSON, Matthias (British, fl. 1856-1884)
ROOSENBOON, Albert (Belgian, late 19th Century)
* ROSSI, Alexander M. (British, fl. 1870-1903)
* ROSSITER, Charles (British, 1827-?)
RUMPLER, Franz (Austrian, 1848-1922)

SALENTIN, Hubert (German, 1822-1910)
* SALMSON, Hugo Frederik (Swedish, 1843-1894)
* SANT, James (British, 1820-1916)
SAUVAGE, François Philippe (French, late 19th Century)
SAVILL, Gertrude May (British, fl. 1891-1893)
SCHICK, Karl Friedrich (German, 1826-1875)
* SCHLESINGER, Felix (German, 1833-1910)
* SCHLESINGER, Henri Guillaume (French 1814-1893)
SCHLOESSER, Carl Bernhard (German, 1832-1914)
* SCHUTZE, Wilhelm (German, 1840-1898)
* SEBEN, Henri van (Belgian, 1825-1913)
SEDILLOT, Anna (French, late 19th Century)
SEPHTON, George Harcourt (British, fl. 1885-1902)
SHIRLEY, Henry (British, fl. 1844-1859)
SIMM-MEYER, Marie (Austrian, 1851-1912)
SIMS, Charles (British, 1873-1928)
* SÖHN, Karl Rudolph (German, 1845-1908)
* SONDERMANN, Hermann (German, 1832-1901)
* SPENCELAYH, Charles (British, 1865-1958)
SPERL, Johann (German, 1840-1914)
STIFTER, Moritz (German, 1857-1905)
STIRNIMANN, Friedrich (Swiss, 1841-1901)
* SUTCLIFFE, Harriette (British, fl. 1881-1922).
SWINSTEAD, George Hillyard (British, 1860-1926)
SYMONDS, William Christian (British, 1845-1911)

TARRANT, Percy, (British, fl. 1879-1891)
* TEN KATE, Johan Marie Henri (Dutch, 1831-1910)
TILL, Johann (Austrian, 1827-1894)
* TORRE, Giulio del (Italian, 1856-1932)
TORRIGLIA, Giovanni Battista (Italian, 1858-?)
TROMP, Jan Zoetelief (Dutch, 1872-?)
TURLETTI, Celestin (Italian, 1845-1904)

VALOIS, Jean François (Dutch, 1778-1853)
VAUTIER, Marc Louis Benjamin (Swiss, 1829-1898)
VINEA, Francesco (Italian, 1845-1902)
VINTER, John Alfred (British, 1828-1905)
* VOLLMAR, Ludwig (German, 1842-1884)

WAGENER, Julius (German, mid-19th Century)
* WAGNER, Paul Hermann (German, 1852-?)
WAITE, James Clark (British, fl. 1863-1885)
* WALDMÜLLER, Ferdinand Georg (Austrian, 1793-1865)
WALKER, John Hanson (British, fl. 1869-1902)
* WALLER, Mary Lemon (British, fl. 1877-1916)
* WALRAVEN, Jan (Dutch, 1827-?)
WATSON, John Dawson (British, 1832-1892)
* WEBSTER, Thomas (British, 1800-1886)
WEEKES, Charlotte J. (British, fl. 1876-1890)
* WELLS, Mary Hayllar (British, fl. 1880-1885)
WENGLER, Johann Baptist (Austrian, 1815-1899)

175

WERGELAND, Oscar Arnold (Norwegian, 1844-1910)
WICKENBERG, Per (Swedish, 1812-1846)
WIESCHEBRINK, Franz (German, 1818-1884)
* WILHELMI, Heinrich (German, 1816?-1902)
* WRIGHT, Robert W. (British, fl. 1871-1906)
WUNSCH, Marie Mizi (Austrian, 1862-1898)
WYNVELD, Barend (Dutch, 1820-1902)

ZUBER-BUHLER, Fritz (Swiss, 1822-1896)

EDMUND ADLER. His first knitting lesson. Signed.
22 x 27¼ins. (56 x 69cm). *Christie's.*

ALBERT ANKER. Portrait of the artist's
son Ruedi, eating at table. 6¼ x 8¾ins.
(16 x 22cm). *Christie's.*

JAMES ARCHER. Summertime, Gloucestershire. 29 x 41ins. (74 x 104cm). *Christie's.*

JOSEPH ATHANASE AUFRAY. The young
wood gatherer. Signed, on panel. 10 x 8ins.
(25.5 x 20.3cm). *Christie's.*

EDWARD CHARLES BARNES. Building the snowman. Signed.
15¼ x 19¼ins. (38.5 x 49cm). *Christie's.*

KARL WILHELM FRIEDRICH BAUERLE. Sisterly love. Signed and dated 1881. 19¾ x 24¾ins. (50 x 63cm). *Christie's.*

WILLIAM BROMLEY. The present. Signed and dated 1864. 14 x 11½ins. (35.5 x 29cm). *Christie's.*

PIETER BAUMGARTNER. Boys playing with a goat.
Signed and dated München 1869. 34¼ x 28¾ ins.
(87 x 73cm). *Christie's.*

ARTHUR BECKER. Playing with kitten. Signed and dated
'68, on panel. 10 x 13¼ ins. (25.5 x 33.5cm). *Christie's.*

THEODOR VON DER BEEK. A
child eating an apple. Signed and
dated 77(?), on panel. 6¼ x 4½ ins.
(16 x 11.5cm). *Christie's.*

FRITZ BEINKE. The jubilee singers. Signed and inscribed
Düsseldorf, on panel. 9½ x 7¼ ins. (24 x 18.5cm). *Christie's.*

ERNEST BIELER. Little girls in an interior.
Signed and dated St. Barthélemy 1892.
59½ x 43¼ins. (151 x 110cm). *Christie's.*

FRANCESCO BERGAMINI. The arithmetic lesson. Signed and inscribed,
Rome. 10½ x 15½ins. (27 x 39.5cm). *Christie's.*

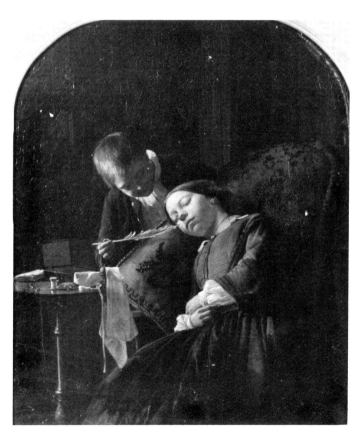

CARL HEINRICH BLOCH. Disturbed slumbers. Signed and
dated 1856, shaped top. 13 x 11ins. (33 x 28cm). *Christie's.*

NIKOLAI PETROVICH BOGDANOV-BJELSKY.
Children outside a barn. Signed and dated '84. 13 x
9¼ins. (33 x 23.5). *Christie's.*

KARL FRIEDRICH ADOLF BOSER. After church. Signed and dated 1861. 27½ x 22ins. (70 x 56cm). *Christie's.*

HARRY BROOKER. Busy hours. Signed and dated 1888. 26¾ x 35½ins. (70 x 90cm). *Christie's.*

WILLIAM BROMLEY. Feeding the bird. Signed. 14 x 12ins. (35.5 x 30.5cm). *Christie's.*

FRANÇOIS ANTOINE BRUYCKER. Two children playing with a boat. Signed, on panel. 17¼ x 21ins. (44 x 53cm). *Sotheby's.*

JOHANN GEORG BUCHNER. The bedtime story. Signed. 22½ x 23ins. (57 x 58.5cm). *Christie's.*

HENDRICUS JACOBUS BURGERS. Girls on a seashore. Signed and dated 1873, on panel. 15 x 8¼ins. (38 x 21cm). *Christie's.*

JOHN BURR. 'Wait till I get out'. Signed and inscribed on the reverse. 12¾ x 19ins. (32.5 x 48.5cm). *Christie's.*

GAETANO CHIERICI. The young smoker. Signed and dated 1887. 21½ x 16ins. (54.5 x 40.5cm). *Christie's.*

PAUL CHARLES CHOCARNE-MOREAU. In the studio. Signed and dated 1920. 31 x 39ins. (79 x 99cm). *Christie's.*

JAMES COLLINSON. A cat's cradle. Signed with monogram, on panel. 9¾ x 7¾ins. (24.5 x 19.5cm). *Christie's.*

CHARLES COMPTON. The young sculptor's first effort. Signed and dated Nov. 1850. 14 x 17⅞ins. (35.5 x 45cm). *Christie's.*

ANDRÉ HENRI DARGELAS. Laying the table. Signed, on panel. 18¼ x 14¾ins. (46.5 x 37.5cm). *Christie's.*

HENDRICK JOSEPH DILLENS. New tricks for an old dog. Signed and dated 1861. 37 x 29ins. (94 x 74cm). *Christie's.*

JOHN H. DELL. The young cartoonist. Signed, on panel. 10 x 15ins. (25.5 x 38cm). *Christie's.*

ALPHONSE ETIENNE DINET. The Sunday outing. Signed and dated 1882. 74 x 73ins. (188 x 185.4cm). *Christie's.*

HENRI JOSEPH DUWEE. The young tambourine player. Signed, oval. 35½ x 42¾ins. (90 x 108.5cm). *Christie's.*

Left: THÉOPHILE EMMANUEL DUVERGER. The young artist. Signed, on panel. 17½ x 14½ins. (44.5 x 37cm). *Christie's.*

SAMUEL EDMONSTON. Following the drum. Signed and dated 1860, on panel. 24½ x 30ins. (62 x 76cm). *Christie's.*

ROBINSON ELLIOTT. Strokes of genius. Signed and inscribed on the reverse, on panel. 10½ x 8½ins. (26.5 x 21.5cm). *Christie's.*

PIERRE EDOUARD FRÈRE. The girls' school. Signed and dated 1868, on panel. 36 x 27½ins. (91.5 x 70cm). *Christie's.*

DAVID FULTON. The poppy gatherer. Signed. 20½ x 13½ins. (52 x 34cm). *Christie's.*

EDWARD NICOLAS GABÉ. The little thieves. Signed with monogram and dated 1853. 26 x 36ins. (66 x 91.5cm). *Christie's.*

EDUARD GESELSCHAP.
Children looking at a
magic lantern. Signed and
dated 1856. 10 x 11¼ins.
(25.5 x 28.5cm). *Christie's.*

ALEXANDER GLASGOW.
Dressing the model. Signed
and dated (187(?) and
inscribed on a label on the
reverse. 27½ x 35½ins.
(70 x 90cm). *Christie's.*

ALFRED H. GREEN. The new doll. Signed with monogram, on panel. 9½ x 11¾ins. (24 x 30cm). *Christie's.*

JEAN PAUL HAAG. Young industry. Signed, on panel. 9½ x 7½ins. (24 x 19cm). *Christie's.*

THOMAS P. HALL. Please ring the bell, Sir! 23 x 18¼ins. (58.5 x 46.5cm). *Christie's.*

JAMES HARDY (JUN). Marching the recruits. On panel. 10 x 8ins. (25.5 x 20.5cm). *Christie's.*

FREDERICK DANIEL HARDY. The young photographers. Signed and dated 1862, on panel. 19 x 28ins. (48 x 71cm). *Christie's.*

EDWARD S. HARPER
The schoolboy. Signed.
35½ x 23¼ins. (90 x 59cm).
Christie's.

JAMES HAYLLAR. 'I'm Mary Tween of Tots''. Signed, and signed and inscribed on an old label on the stretcher. 33 x 21ins. (84 x 53cm). *Christie's.*

JOHN WILLIAM HAYNES. Military Preparation. Signed, and signed and inscribed on the reverse. 24 x 18¾ins. (61 x 47.5cm). *Christie's.*

WILLIAM HEMSLEY. The young artist. Signed, and signed on the reverse, on panel. 8 x 6½ins. (20.5 x 16.5cm). *Christie's.*

ROBERT HERDMAN. Portrait of a young girl, seated in a landscape. Signed with initials and dated 1857, on panel, oval. *Christie's.*

HEINRICH HIRT. One o'clock, two o'clock... Signed and dated '79. 17 x 11½ins. (43.5 x 29cm). *Christie's.*

AUGUST HEYN. The young cheat. Signed and inscribed München. 35½ x 30ins. (90 x 76). *Christie's.*

CHARLES HUNT. The rehearsal. Signed and dated 1861.
11 x 16ins. (28 x 40.5cm). *Christie's.*

JOSEPH HOEGG. The pet bird. Signed and inscribed
Dussldf. 16 x 13½ins. (40.5 x 34.5cm). *Christie's.*

GUSTAV KISPERT. Lesson time. Signed and
dated München, on panel. 11½ x 8¼ins.
(29 x 21cm). *Christie's.*

HENRY LE JEUNE. After drill. On panel.
15 x 20ins. (38 x 51cm). *Christie's.*

FRANÇOIS LOUIS LANFANT DE METZ. In the
nursery. Signed, on panel. 10½ x 7½ins. (26.5 x 19cm).
Christie's.

CARL LARSSON. Under Tisteln. Signed with initials
and dated Barbizon 77, on panel. 18 x 15ins.
(46 x 38cm). *Christie's.*

LOUIS LASSALLE. The young goatsherd. Signed.
8¾ x 6½ins. (22 x 16.5cm). *Christie's.*

SILVESTRO LEGA. The little barber. Signed.
18½ x 15ins. (47 x 38cm). *Christie's.*

ADOLPHE LELEUX. Making sand castles.
Signed and dated 1880. 30 x 42ins.
(76 x 106.5cm). *Christie's.*

EMILE LÉVY. The ivy chain. Signed and
dated 1876, on panel. 15¼ x 11½ins.
(38.5 x 29cm). *Christie's.*

WILLEM LINNIG. A watchful eye. Canvas laid down on board.
16½ x 14ins. (42 x 35.5cm). *Christie's.*

LEOPOLD LOFFLER-RADYMNO. The young truant.
Signed, on panel. 28 x 23ins. (71 x 58.5cm). *Christie's.*

TIMOLEON MARIE LOBRICHON.
Out to play. Signed. 44¼ x 26¾ins.
(112.5 x 68cm). *Christie's.*

WILLIAM MCTAGGART. The blackberry pickers. Signed. 27 x 39ins. (68.5 x 99cm). *Christie's.*

HENRY JULES JEAN GEOFFROY. Le retour de l'école. Signed and dated 1883. 37 x 15¾ins. (94 x 40cm).
Christie's.

ALEXEI ALEXEIEVICH HARLAMOFF. The young flower girls. Signed and dated 1885. 42¾ x 56¾ins.
(71 x 104cm). *Christie's.*

THOMAS FALCON MARSHALL. Children with May day garlands. Signed with initials and dated 1860, on board. 9¾ x 7¾ins. (24.5 x 19.5cm). *Christie's.*

LEON A. MOESELAGEN. The young artists. Signed and dated Ddf 62. 21½ x 17½ins. (54.5 x 44.5cm). *Christie's.*

FREDERICK MORGAN. Charity. Signed. 35 x 45ins. (89 x 114.5cm) *Christie's.*

196

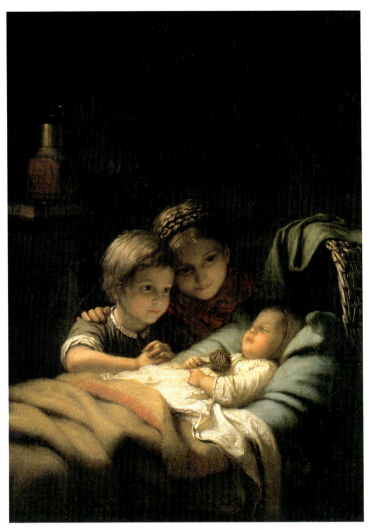

JOHANN GEORG MEYER VON BREMEN. The new baby.
Signed and dated 1855. 17 x 13½ins. (43 x 34.5cm). *Christie's.*

HARRIETTE SUTCLIFFE. Gathering plums. Signed.
37½ x 27½ins. (95 x 70cm). *Christie's.*

SIR JOHN EVERETT MILLAIS. Bubbles. Signed with monogram and dated 1886. *A. & F. Pears Ltd.*

JOHN MORGAN. Hide and Seek. Signed.
35½ x 23½ins. (90 x 59.5cm). *Christie's.*

GAETANO MORMILE. The young
musician. Signed and inscribed Napoli.
28 x 17¼ins. (71 x 44cm). *Christie's.*

PHILIP RICHARD MORRIS. A woodland babe. Signed.
36¼ x 28½ins. (92 x 72.5cm). *Christie's.*

AUGUSTUS E. MULREADY. When life is young.
Signed and dated 1881, and signed, inscribed and dated
on the reverse. 19½ x 14½ins. (49.5 x 37cm). *Christie's.*

GEORGE BERNARD O'NEILL.
First love. Signed with initials, on
panel. 15 x 11½ins. (38 x 29cm).
Christie's.

AUGUST HEINRICH NIEDMANN. An artist in his studio. Signed and indistinctly
dated. 36½ x 31¼ins. (92.5 x 79.5cm). *Christie's.*

ANTONIO PAOLETTI. The mishap. Signed and inscribed
Venezia, on panel. 12 x 18ins. (30.5 x 45.5cm). *Christie's.*

CÉSAR PATTEIN. The spoil sports. Signed and dated 1914.
34¼ x 50½ins. (87 x 128cm). *Christie's.*

KATE PERUGINI. A little woman. Signed and inscribed on an old label on the reverse. 23½ x 16¾ins. (59.5 x 42.5cm). *Christie's.*

Top right: CHARLES PETIT. Children playing round a chair. Signed and inscribed Bruxelles, and signed, authenticated and dated Bruxelles 1885 on the reverse. 44½ x 35¾ins. (113 x 91cm). *Christie's.*

EVERT PIETERS. Playing with dolls. Signed. 23 x 19½ins. (58.5 x 49.5cm). *Christie's.*

BERNHARD REINHOLD. Leaving school. Signed and dated 1869(?). 35½ x 43¼ins. (90 x 110cm). *Christie's.*

EDWIN ROBERTS. The duet. Signed, and signed and inscribed on the reverse. 16 x 12ins. (40.5 x 30.5cm). *Christie's.*

ALEXANDER M. ROSSI. The young anglers. Signed. 27½ x 35½ins. (70 x 90cm). *Christie's.*

CHARLES ROSSITER. The bird trap. Signed and dated 1857. 17½ x 13½ins. (44.5 x 34cm). *Christie's.*

HUGO FREDERIK SALMSON. In the meadow. Signed. 35½ x 45½ins. (90 x 115.5cm). *Christie's.*

JAMES SANT. Willie: The bedtime story. Signed with monogram and signed and dated 1861 on the reverse. 34½ x 24½ins. (87.5 x 62cm). *Christie's.*

FELIX SCHLESINGER. The pet bird. Signed, on panel. 10¾ x 8¼ins. (27.5 x 21cm). *Christie's.*

HENRI GUILLAUME SCHLESINGER. The
youthful proposal. Signed. 29 x 23½ins.
(73.5 x 59.5cm). *Christie's.*

WILHELM SCHUTZE. The little helpers. Signed. 19¾ x 23¾ins.
(50 x 60.5cm). *Christie's.*

HENRI VAN SEBEN. The kite flyers. Signed.
18 x 15ins. (46 x 38cm). *Christie's.*

KARL RUDOLPH SÖHN. A long wait.
Signed, on panel. 7½ x 4¾ins.
(19 x 12cm). *Christie's.*

CHARLES SPENCELAYH. Danger ahead. Signed and dated 1894 and inscribed on an old label on the reverse. 44 x 32¼ins. (112 x 82cm). *Christie's.*

HERMANN SONDERMANN. Feeding the goats. Signed and dated Dusseldorf '90, on panel. 12½ x 9¼ins. (32 x 23.5cm). *Christie's.*

JOHAN MARIE HENRI TEN KATE. The absence of the painter. Signed. 25½ x 37ins. (64.5 x 94cm). *Christie's.*

GIULIO DEL TORRE. Feeding the doll. Signed and dated 1894, on panel. 9¾ x 7½ins. (24.5 x 19cm). *Christie's.*

LUDWIG VOLLMAR. The lesson. Signed and inscribed München. 25 x 29ins. (63.5 x 74cm). *Christie's.*

PAUL HERMANN WAGNER. A moment of shyness. Signed and inscribed München Kochel. 24½ x 16½ins. (62 x 42cm). *Christie's.*

FERDINAND GEORG WALDMÜLLER. Baby worship. Signed and dated 1835, on panel. 23 x 20ins. (58.5 x 51cm). *Christie's.*

MARY LEMON WALLER. Gladys, daughter of Major Lutley Jordan. Signed and dated 1890. 35½ x 27¼ins. (90 x 69cm). *Christie's.*

JAN WALRAVEN. The sledge ride. Signed, on panel. 22 x 28¼ins. (56 x 71.5cm). *Christie's.*

THOMAS WEBSTER. The village school. Signed and
dated 1838, on panel. 17½ x 14½ins. (44.5 x 37cm).
Christie's.

MARY HAYLLAR WELLS. Little Flora's
wreath. Signed and dated 1884. 27 x 19ins.
(68.5 x 48.5cm). *Christie's.*

ROBERT W. WRIGHT. Blowing bubbles.
Signed and dated '94. 10 x 8ins.
(25.5 x 20.5cm). *Christie's.*

HEINRICH WILHELMI. Feeding the
fledglings. Signed and dated Df. 1877.
27½ x 22½ins. (70 x 57cm). *Christie's.*

Classical Genre

Each century, perhaps each generation, reinterprets antiquity according to its own lights; the nineteenth century found the classical world of special fascination, and its painters conjured a distinctive image of it. A continuing reverence for Greece and Rome as an ideal was one abiding strand in its attitude, certainly. The pictorial equivalent of this was High Art, a brand of rigorous academic painting whose arch English exponents were Leighton, Watts and Poynter, men whose classicism was at times so arid as to preclude animation. In France, too, Gleyre, Cabanel, Bouguereau and others produced a movement motivated by a like degree of high-mindedness, although it occasionally lapsed into a soapy lasciviousness found titillating at the Salon but less acceptable at the Royal Academy. But against this orthodox background, antiquity began to be interpreted in a new and increasingly popular way.

For the first time artists painted classical genre. An essentially popular vision of the ancient world emerged, one which was concerned with its everyday life rather than grand, apocalyptic events traditionally the subject matter of the classical painter. As Gibbon's *The Decline and Fall of the Roman Empire* is displaced by Lytton's *The Last Days of Pompeii,* so David yields to Alma-Tadema. Artists were at pains to create a more accessible antiquity, one in which the spectator might more readily indentify with the actors. The new patronage, for whom history painting had been rendered palatable by anecdote, now relished the same treatment of the ancient world. Artists found a happy aid in archaeology, a rapidly developing study which shed so much light on the ordinary as opposed to the epic. Pompeii, excavated progressively through the century, was a treasure trove and an inspiration.

It is possible to identify three main schools of 'antique genre', all flowering in the second half of the nineteenth century. In England Sir Lawrence Alma-Tadema dominated the field, right up till his death in 1913. He was unmatched in his ability to provide a vision of the prose of everyday life in antiquity, flavoured with a wonderfully English scent; he had many imitators and competitors, but all owed something to him. Any late Victorian attempting to visualise in his mind's eye the reality of life in Greece and Rome would have found it very hard to avoid doing so in terms dictated by Alma-Tadema: a tiger skin here, a flash of marble there, the pervasive perfume of the tepidarium. In Italy a group of painters emerged whose particular inspiration was Pompeii. Sorbi, Bazzani, Gianetti, Forti and others produced many pictures re-animating everyday life in its streets and flowershops, at its wells and fountains. Although their style is distinctive, their essential message, that the human side of Roman civilisation provides a titillating link with the present, remains the same. But perhaps the most influential contribution to the movement away from the heroic towards the intimate and trivial in classical painting came from Paris. It was here that Gérôme and the neo-grecs flourished, and it was here that painters of other nationalities — Belgian,

German and Eastern European — learned a derivative version of French intimate classicism which they took home with them.

The range of the painters of classical genre will be apparent from the subject matter of the illustrations which accompany this section. Some are seriously archaeological; others dwell sentimentally on saccharine-sweet children at play in togas, or lovers who languish on Aegean terraces; some draw parallels between the bourgeois life of ancient Rome and that of an upper middle class household in the nineteenth century Paris or London; others exploit the licence permitted by antiquity in revelations of the female form, a classical intimacy which was a proven receipe for success. All are concerned to recreate antiquity to a level of detail and naturalism, and often a depth of mundanity, not attempted in previous centuries.

Why were they doing it? Why was such painting so popular? Some of the answers can be found in the contemporary statements of the artists themselves, and the reactions of the more perceptive critics of the time. Gérôme himself gives an account of the laudable motives which prompted his early *The Cockfight*, a sensation of everyday classical naturalism at the Salon of 1849:

> At that time, generally, there was a complete lack of sincerity in art. ''Chic'' was highly regarded, when accompanied by slickness, which was no rare commodity, and my picture had the merit at least of being the work of a young fellow who, in his ignorance, had found no better scheme than to stick to nature and follow her step for step, without great power or grandeur, and timidly no doubt, but with a naïve sincerity.

A closer relationship with nature at the expense of the fashionable rhetoric of grander classical painting was no doubt refreshing, even (strange to say of the later arch-conservative Gérôme) avant-garde. Unfortunately the principle rapidly degenerated. An easy formula for success with the picture-buying public crystallised, one by which the question 'What was it really like to be there?' was answered not so much with naturalism as with an unhappy combination of sentimentality and archaeological pedantry. Ironically by 1875 Zola was finding fault with Gérôme and the neo-grecs for the lack of those very qualities which Gérôme was claiming for himself in 1849:

> ''Pseudo-antique'' pictures show Roman matrons at their toilet, Roman families eating dinner.... with pretensions to an absolute archaeological fidelity. All very well. I would even approve of the artists... if there was in their work the smallest particle of truth. But they only see in all this an inexhaustible source of sentimentality, of false grace, of gently ambiguous scenarios whose saleability is assured.

Even earlier, in 1859, Baudelaire criticised the degeneration of classical genre into a facile formula 'to disguise a lack of imagination', involving merely 'the transposition of the trivialities of life into antique circumstances'. Alma-Tadema or Gérôme would no doubt have maintained that they were in fact illustrating the timeless humanity of man, revealing the power of emotion to be the same whatever the period of history. In support, they could quote an influential and extremely popular historical novelist, Bulwer Lytton, whose *The Last Days of Pompeii* had first appeared in 1835. In those pages he declared unequivocally:

> We love to feel within us the bond which unites the most distant eras — men, nations, customs perish: the Affections are Immortal! — they are the sympathies which unite the ceaseless generations. The past lives again

when we look upon our emotions — it lives in our own!

This was a powerful attraction. Fans of Alma-Tadema, and there were many, applauded his avowed intention 'to express in my pictures that the Old Romans were flesh and blood like ourselves, moved by the same passions and emotions'. Here, before their very eyes, were classical men and women who lived and breathed, were subject to the same emotions of love and jealousy, prey to the same domestic and everyday problems as the nineteenth century, collectors of works of art like themselves, and by no means immune to the charms of the uncovered human form. To us today the figures in Alma-Tadema's pictures look comically like maidens from the St. John's Wood vicinity dressed up in sheets. The fallacy lies not in Bulwer Lytton's contention that the affections are immortal: human emotion may well remain constant through the ages, but these painters failed to grasp that the expression of it changes. No doubt the Romans fell in love — Catullus proves that — but it is doubtful that they expressed romantic attraction in quite the virginal Victorian manner which Alma-Tadema would have us believe.

Laborieu, writing about Gérôme in 1861, identifies one further element in the concoction of classical genre which contributed to its popularity: it flattered the spectator into an illusion of erudition:

> He interprets (classical) subjects with an exquisite taste and with a refined bourgeois delicacy, under a cloud of pedantry through which the public can see. The public is not averse to appearing erudite — and they can rely on M. Gérôme to give them a history lesson exactly tailored to their spirit and instincts.

Antiquity for the masses, certainly. But the fact that certain artists developed a slick formula to meet the popular hunger does not mean that it was merely the half-educated herd who felt curiosity about everyday antiquity. The eminent English scholar Porson had first given voice to this curiosity rather earlier, setting the tone for the coming nineteenth century, when he declared that he would gladly sacrifice all the commentaries on Aristophanes ever written for just one edition of an Athenian newspaper.

What English general of today would telegraph his conquest of Synd with the Latin pun 'peccavi' (I have sinned), as Lord Ellen did in 1857? On one level this illustrates the pervasiveness of the classics in the nineteenth century; but it also highlights a second contemporary obsession which may be relevant in this context, the pun itself. The humour of the time set great store by the pun: such wordplay was considered both clever and extremely funny, and the pages of *Punch* abound with puns, sometimes of an awful obviousness. Gérôme himself, when commissioned to design an optician's shop sign, came up with the — at first sight — incongruous motif of a little dog, subtitled in explanation O pti cien (O petit chien). There was something in the nature of the pun, the fact that the same (or same-sounding) word could have reference to two quite separate contexts simultaneously, which struck a pleasurable chord in the nineteenth century imagination. Alma-Tadema's pictures — indeed all pictures which showed the essential sameness of human nature in quite different times and places — had the appeal of a pun. Baudelaire was making the same point when he wrote in 1859:

> By their mania for dressing up trivial modern life in antique garments, the adherents of this school are forever perpetrating what I should be inclined to call 'counter-caricatures'.

Romantic rivalry, collecting works of art, enjoying a joke, all were activities widely familiar to the nineteenth century, and their transposition, almost intact, to an utterly different age and location fulfilled the prerequisites of a pun (or 'counter-caricature'), and created much the same frisson of delight.

Index of Artists

RICHMOND, Sir William Blake (British, 1842-1921)
ROBINSON, M. D. (British, fl.1885-1901)
ROCHEGROSSE, Georges Antoine (French, 1859-1938)
ROSELL, Alexander (British, late 19th Century)
RYLAND, Henry (British, 1856-1924)

SALINAS Y TERUEL, Augustin (Spanish, 1862-?)
* SARRI, Egisto (Italian, 1837-1901)
* SCHAFER, Henry Thomas (British, fl.1873-1915)
SCHMALZ, Herbert Gustave (British, 1856-?)
SCHNEIDER, Fritz (German, 1848-1885)
* SCIFONI, Anatolio (Italian, 1841-1884)
SCOTT, William Bell (British, 1811-1890)
SEIGNAC, Guillaume (French, late 19th Century)
SEMENOWSKY, Emile Eisman (French, fl.1880-1900)
* SIEMIRADZKI, Henryk (Polish, 1843-1902)
SKIPWORTH, Frank Markham (British, fl.1882-1916)
SNOWMAN, Isaac (British, 1874-?)

SOLOMON, Simeon (British, 1840-1905)
* SORBI, Raffaello (Italian, 1844-1931)
SPENCE, Thomas Ralph (British, 1855?-?)
STONE, Marcus (British, 1840-1921)
SULLIVAN, William Holmes (British, ?-1908)

UNGER, Eduard (German, 1853-1894)

* VASSARI, Emilio (Italian, late 19th Century)
* VINEA, Francesco (Italian, 1845-1902)

WATERHOUSE, John William (British, 1849-1917)
WEGUELIN, John Reinhard (British, 1849-1927)
* WERNER, Gotthard Gudfast Adolf (Swiss, 1837-1903)
WONNENBURG, M. (German, late 19th Century)
WONTNER, William Clarke (British, fl.1879-1912)

* ZOCCHI, Guglielmo (Italian, 1874-?)

SIR LAWRENCE ALMA-TADEMA. A
difference of opinion. Signed and inscribed
op CCCXXXIX on panel. 15 x 8¾ins.
(38 x 22cm). *Christie's.*

PIETRO ALDI. The cockfight.
Signed and dated Roma
MDCCCLXXXIII. 17¼ x 24¾ins.
(44 x 63cm). *Sotheby's.*

THOMAS ARMSTRONG. Three
female figures on a marble seat.
Signed with monogram and dated
1878. 34 x 62ins. (86.5 x 157.5cm).
Christie's.

ATTILIO BACCANI. Girls
playing jacks in a Mediterranean
landscape. Signed and dated 1874.
31¾ x 52½ins. (80.5 x 133.5cm).
Christie's.

STEPHAN BAKALOWICZ. The cloth merchant. On panel, signed and dated Rome MDCCCLXXXVII. 17½ x 12½ins. (44.5 x 32cm). *Sotheby's.*

FRIEDRICH BODENMÜLLER. At the fountain. Signed and dated Munchen 1883. 36¼ x 27ins. (92 x 68.5cm). *Christie's.*

ROBERTO BOMPIANI. Classical women arranging flowers. Signed and dated 1870, on panel. 13 x 9ins. (33 x 23cm). *Christie's.*

Left: LUIGI BAZZANI. A flower seller in Pompei. Signed and inscribed Roma, on panel. 22¾ x 15½ins. (58 x 39.5cm). *Christie's.*

RAFFAELLO SORBI. A marriage of convenience.
Signed and dated 1872. 35 x 46ins. (89 x 117cm).
Christie's.

PIERRE OLIVIER JOSEPH COOMANS.
A Pompeiian lady and her pet. Signed and dated 1868,
on panel. 18½ x 14½ins. (47 x 3)cm).
Christie's.

GUSTAVE CLARENCE RODOLPHE BOULANGER. Summer repast at the house of Lucullus at Tusculum. Signed and dated 1877. 39½ x 57½ins. (100.5 x 146cm). *Christie's.*

WILLIAM STEPHEN COLEMAN. A classical idyll. Signed and dated 1888. 25 x 16ins. (63.5 x 40.5cm). *Christie's.*

VINCENZO CAPOBIANCHI. A Pompeian antique dealer. Signed and dated Roma 1880, on panel. 19¼ x 25¼ ins. (49 x 64cm). *Christie's.*

AMOS CASSIOLI. A Roman family. Signed. 14 x 21ins. (35.5 x 53cm). *Sotheby's.*

EMANUELE COSTA. On the terrace. Signed.
28½ x 23¾ins. (72.5 x 60.5cm). *Christie's.*

COMTE ANGELO DE COURTEN.
The Sculptor's model. Signed.
46½ x 26½ins. (118 x 67.5cm).
Christie's.

NORMAN PRESCOTT DAVIES.
Classical figures on a terrace. Signed and
dated 1895. 11 x 8¾ins. (30 x 22cm).
Christie's.

CH. ETIENNE. A Grecian flower dance. Signed.
24 x 18ins. (61 x 45.5cm). *Christie's.*

JEAN LÉON GÉRÔME. The cockfight. Signed. 56¼ x 80ins. (143 x 204cm). *Louvre.*

RAFFAELE GIANETTI. Pompeii in all its glory. Signed and dated 1879, on panel. 20½ x 28ins. (52 x 71cm). *Christie's.*

SIMON GLÜKLICH. The poet's song. Signed and dated Wien '85. 52¾ x 66¼ins. (134 x 168cm). *Christie's.*

JOHN WILLIAM GODWARD. The favourite. Signed and dated 1901. 23 x 28ins. (58.5 x 71cm). *Christie's.*

M. GRIVA. The scent maker. Signed, canvas laid down on board. 31½ x 17¼ins. (80 x 44cm). *Christie's.*

EDWARD MATTHEW HALE. Musical repose. Signed and dated '83. 9¼ x 45¼ins. (23.5 x 115cm). *Christie's.*

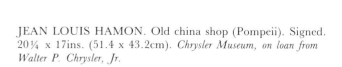

HENRI HOUBEN. A flower for cupid. Signed. 36½ x 48¾ins. (93 x 123cm). *Sotheby's.*

JEAN LOUIS HAMON. Old china shop (Pompeii). Signed. 20¼ x 17ins. (51.4 x 43.2cm). *Chrysler Museum, on loan from Walter P. Chrysler, Jr.*

LUDWIG VON LANGENMANTEL. The scent of roses.
Signed and dated 1901. 39½ x 31½ins. (100.5 x 80cm).
Christie's.

CONRAD KIESEL. The bath. Signed and dated 1888.
62½ x 42ins. (159 x 106.5cm). *Christie's.*

JULIUS JOHAN FERDINAND
KRONBERG. The young sentry.
Signed, inscribed and dated 1891.
9¼ x 14ins. (23.5 x 35.5cm).
Sotheby's.

FREDERIC, LORD LEIGHTON. Greek girl dancing.
35 x 46½ins. (89 x 118cm). *Christie's.*

HECTOR LOUIS LEROUX. The vestal virgins.
Signed and dated Rome 1864. 32½ x 55ins.
(82.5 x 139.5cm). *Christie's.*

ADOLPHE ALEXANDRE LESREL. Feeding the birds. Signed and dated 1873. 25 x 20¾ ins. (63.5 x 52.5cm). *Christie's.*

CHARLES FREDERICK LOWCOCK. In the temple. Signed and dated '81, and inscribed on the reverse, on panel. 18 x 8¼ ins. (45.5 x 21cm). *Christie's.*

ALBERT JOSEPH MOORE. Apples. Signed with a Greek anthemion and dated '75. 11¼ x 19¼ ins. (28.5 x 49cm). *Christie's.*

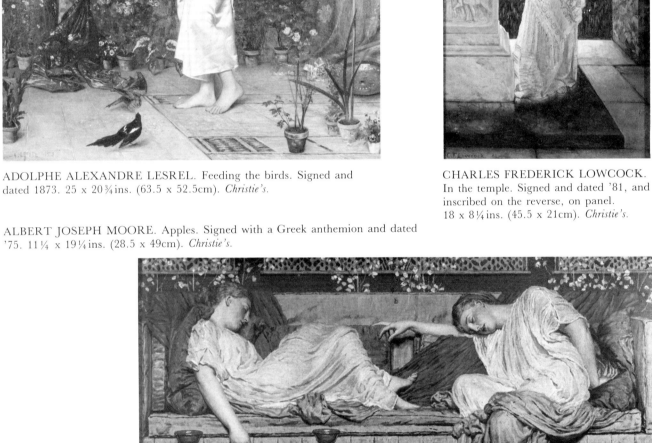

F. SYDNEY MUSCHAMP. A good game. Signed.
13¼ x 23½ ins. (33.5 x 59.5cm). *Christie's.*

EMANUEL OBERHAUSER. The pipes of love.
Signed. 26¼ x 40½ ins. (66.5 x 103cm). *Christie's.*

CHARLES EDWARD PERUGINI. The loom. 50 x 36ins.
(127 x 91.5cm). *Christie's.*

EMILE AUGUSTE PINCHART. The Armlet. Signed
and dated 1871. 21½ x 14¾ ins. (54.5 x 37.5cm).
Christie's.

SIR EDWARD JOHN POYNTER. A little mishap. Signed with monogram and dated 1912. 49½ x 39½ins. (125.5 x 100cm). *Christie's.*

AUGUSTE RAYNAUD. A cook from antiquity. Signed. 35¾ x 22ins. (90.5 x 56cm). *Christie's.*

THEODORE JACQUES RALLI. A classical beauty. Signed, on panel. 12¾ x 7¾ins. (32.5 x 19.5cm). *Christie's.*

EGISTO SARRI. Lovers in a Pompeian interior. 15¼ x 23¼ins. (39 x 59cm). *Christie's.*

HENRY THOMAS SCHAFER. The wreath. Signed
and dated 1877. 35 x 46ins. (89 x 117cm). *Christie's.*

ANATOLIO SCIFONI. The Artist's Studio. Signed and inscribed
Roma. 26¼ x 39½ins. (67 x 100cm). *Sotheby's.*

HENRYK SIEMIRADZKI. At the
well. Signed. 21 x 31ins. (53 x 79cm).
Christie's.

EMILIO VASSARI. Roman ladies
resting during a party. Signed.
15 x 21¾ins. (38 x 55cm). *Sotheby's.*

FRANCESCO VINEA. The Spinner.
Signed and dated Firenze 1898. Canvas
laid down on board. 17⅞ x 13¾ ins.
(45 x 35cm). *Christie's.*

GOTTHARD GUDFAST ADOLF WERNER. Roman dancing girls. Signed
and dated Capri 1875. 18½ x 26ins. (47 x 66cm). *Christie's.*

GUGLIELMO ZOCCHI. A warm greeting. Signed. 27½ x 39½ins. (70 x 100cm). *Sotheby's.*

Cossacks and Eastern European Exotica

This category can only brush the surface of the material available: in theory most of the artists active in Russia, Poland, Czechoslovakia, Hungary, Bulgaria and Rumania who painted contemporary genre during the nineteenth century qualify for inclusion. In practice, however, only those artists who emerged from behind an earlier version of the Iron Curtain to present to the 'sophisticates' of western Europe a specially packaged view of the life of the east are considered here.

As art centres Warsaw, Prague and Budapest were certainly active, but in the broad context provincial and cut off from the mainstream of popular nineteenth century painting. Many Polish, Czech, and Hungarian artists set off for Paris, Munich or Vienna in order to find this mainstream. Some became effectively French or German painters, but others found that it was not necessary to abandon their roots in order to succeed, treating subjects drawn from their native lands in a manner calculated to appeal to the fashionable western market. Thus Kowalski, the Pole, became hugely popular with his thrillingly realistic evocations of Cossacks galloping across the snowy steppes, while taking care always to inscribe them 'München', like some sort of guarantee stamp of quality and fashionability.

Russian Cossacks, Hungarian gypsies, Polish cavalry officers, all were picturesque, colourful and romantic figures. They had an exotic appeal to collectors not dissimilar to the attractions of arab subject matter, an appeal which was capitalised on by the artists who feature in this section.

Index of Artists

KARLOVSKY, Bertalan (Austrian, 1858-1938)
KASATKIN, Nikolai (Russian, 1859-1930)
KLECZYNSKI, Bohdah von (Polish, 1851-1916)
* KONARSKI, Janina (Polish?, late 19th Century)
KORIN, Alexei Michailovich (Russian, 1865-?)
KOROKNYAI, Otto (Austrian, 1856-1898)
KOSTANDI, Kiriak Constantinovich (Russian, 1853-?)
KOWALSKI, Leopold Franz (Polish, 1856-?)
KOZAKIEWICZ, Anton (Polish, 1841-?)

LASINSKY, Stanislaus Anthoni (Polish, 1867-1894)

MAKOVSKY, Vladimir (Russian, 1846-1920)
MARGITAY, Tihamer (Austrian, 1859-1922)
* MATHAUSER, J. (Czechoslovakian, late 19th Century)
MAXIMOV, Vassily (Russian, 1844-1911)
* MESZÖLY, Geza von (Austrian, 1844-1887)
MIACOIEDAFF, G.G. (Russian, 1835-?)
MICHALOWSKY, Piotr (Polish, 1801-1855)
MORAWOFF, Alexander Victorovich (Russian, 1879-?)

NESTEROV, Michail Vassilievich (Russian, 1862-1942)

PATAKY VON SOSPATAK, Lazlo (Austrian,
    1857-1912)
PIMONENKO, Nikolai Cornelievich (Russian,
    1862-1912)
PIOTROWSKI, Anthoni (Polish, 1853-1924)
PLATANOFF, Chariton Platonovich (Russian,
    1842-1907)
POLENOFF, Vassily Dimitrievich (Russian, 1844-1927)
PRIANICHNIKOFF, Illarion Michailovich (Russian,
    1840-1894)
* PRUCHA, Gustav (Austrian, 1875-?)

RAFFALT, Johann Gualbert (Austrian, 1836-1865)
RILSKY, A. (Polish?, late 19th Century)
* ROUBAUD, Franz (Russian, 1856-1928)
RUSKOVICS, Ignaz (Austrian, late 19th Century)
* RYBKOWSKI, Tadeusz (Polish, 1848-1926)
RYBKOWSKI, Jan (Polish, 1812-1850)
RZYSZCZEWSKI, Alexander (Polish, 1823-1891)

SAMOKICH, N. S. (Russian, 1860-?)
* SAWIN, Josef (Austrian, late 19th Century)
SAWITSKY, Konstantin Appollonovich (Russian, 1845-?)
* SCHREYER, Adolf Christian (German, 1850-1921)
SKUTECZKY, Dome (Austrian, 1850-1921)
* STOILOFF, Constantin (Russian, late 19th Century)
STOITZNER, Constantin (Austrian, 1863-1934)
STREITT, Franciszek (Polish, 1839-1890)
* SVERCHKOV, Nikolai Grigorevich (Russian,
    1817-1898)
SZERNER, Wladyslaw Karol (Polish, 1870-1936)
* SZIRMAI, Antal (Austrian, 1860-1927)
SZYKIER, Ksawery (Polish, 1860-1895)

* VAGO, Pal (Austrian, 1853-1928)
VENNE, Adolf von der (Austrian, 1828-1911)
* VENNE, Fritz van der (Austrian, late 19th Century)
* VESIN, Jaroslav Fr. Julius (Austrian, 1859-1915)
* VINOGRADOV, Sergei Arsenievich (Russian, 1869-?)
* VISKI, Janos (Austrian, late 19th Century)

* WIERUSZ-KOWALSKI, Alfred von (Polish, 1849-1915)
WITKIEWICZ, Stanislaus (Polish, 1851-1915)
WOLSKI, Stanislaus Pomian (Polish, 1859-1894)
WYCZOLKOWSKI, Leon (Polish, 1852-1936)
WYWIORSKI, Michael (Polish, 1861-1926)

JOSEF VON BRANDT. The huntsmen's return. Signed and inscribed. 13¾ x 25½ ins. (35 x 65cm). *Sotheby's.*

LUDWIG GEDLEK. Cossack troops. Signed and inscribed Wien. 14½ x 23ins. (37 x 58.5cm). *Sotheby's.*

BERTALAN KARLOVSKY. The herdsman. Signed, on panel. 8½ x 5¾ins. (21.5 x 14.5cm). *Christie's.*

JANINA KONARSKI. A winter landscape with horse-drawn sleighs. Signed. (9¾ x 13¼ins. (25 x 33.5cm). *Christie's.*

J. MATHAUSER. A horse and cart with peasants. Signed and dated Prag. 1895. 28¼ x 38¾ins. (71.5 x 98.5cm). *Christie's.*

GEZA VON MESZÖLY. Homewood bound. Signed and dated '872. 5¼ x 7½ ins. (12 x 19cm). *Christie's.*

GUSTAV PRUCHA. A cart ride. Signed. 24½ x 20ins. (62 x 51.5cm). *Sotheby's.*

FRANZ ROUBAUD. Cossacks charging into battle. Signed. 23 x 34¾ins. (58.5 x 88cm). *Christie's.*

TADEUSZ RYBKOWSKI. A market scene. Signed. 9¾ x 14¾ins. (25 x 37.5cm). *Christie's.*

JOSEF SAWIN. Cossacks on a horse-drawn sleigh. Signed.
7 x 11ins. (17.5 x 28cm). *Christie's.*

ADOLF CHRISTIAN SCHREYER. In der Wallachei.
Signed. 17 x 29ins. (43 x 73.5cm). *Christie's.*

CONSTANTIN STOILOFF. A winter landscape with a horse-drawn sleigh chased by a wolf. Signed. 19½ x 32ins.
(49.5 x 81cm). *Christie's.*

PAL BÖHM. A gypsy encampment. Signed and dated 1895. 39 x 51½ins. (99 x 131cm). *Christie's.*

NIKOLAI GRIGOREVICH SVERCHKOV. A Russian hunter with a dead wolf in a snowy landscape. Signed. 36¾ x 50½ins. (93 x 128cm). *Christie's.*

ANTAL SZIRMAI. Preparing the fish. Signed. 20⅞ x 22ins. (70.5 x 55.5cm). *Christie's.*

PAL VAGO. Breaking in a wild horse. Signed. 22½ x 31ins. (57 x 78.5cm). *Sotheby's.*

FRITZ VAN DER VENNE. A winter scene with wolves attacking a sleigh. Signed and inscribed München, on panel. 7 x 12¼ins. (17.5 x 31cm). *Christie's.*

JAROSLAV FR. JULIUS VESIN.
The Sleigh Ride. Signed and inscribed
Mnch. 21¼ x 36¾ins. (54cm x 93cm).
Sotheby's.

SERGEI ARSENIEVICH VINOGRADOV. Russian peasants on the bank of a
river. Signed and dated '92. 17½ x 33ins. (44.5 x 84cm). *Christie's.*

ALFRED VON WIERUSZ-
KOWALSKY. A Cossack on horseback.
Signed. 18½ x 8¼ins.(47 x 21cm).
Christie's.

JANOS VISKI. A horse round up.
Signed. 23 x 31ins. (58.5 x 78.5cm).
Christie's.

Cows, Sheep and Poultry

The depiction of farm animals had a long tradition, particularly in Dutch and Flemish painting, but it was in the nineteenth century that it achieved notably widespread popularity. Every country had its favoured specialist masters: the Palizzis in Italy, Voltz and Zügel in Munich, Brascassat and Bonheur in France, Thomas Sidney Cooper in England, and the incomparable Verboeckhoven in Belgium. All looked back in some degree to the seventeenth century example of Paulus Potter, an animal painter whom the nineteenth century held in the highest regard. Fromentin says (in 1876): 'With the *Anatomy Lesson* and the *Night Watch* (both by Rembrandt), the *Bull* of Paul Potter is the most celebrated picture in Holland.' It was the meticulousness of Potter which appealed most to the contemporary imagination. As Fromentin said, '[his] genius consists in taking measurements'. The sheer volume of nineteenth century painting of farm animals throughout Europe is extraordinary: the herds and flocks which found their way on to canvas hardly bear thinking about, still less counting.

Such pictures were, of course, part of the rural tradition, the difference being that now they were often bought by men who had made money in towns but yearned nostalgically for an image of the country. The prosaic nature of their subject matter was of little account: it was the material reality of the animals depicted, and the ease with which the new picture buyer could relate to them, which won such ready popularity. In his heart of hearts the new patron might baulk at a picture of Priam demanding Hector's body from Achilles, whereas sheep and cattle grazing was a concept reassuringly much more within his experience. For artists, too, the situation had its advantages: the docility of such beasts made them far easier models to cope with than, for instance, the kittens of Henriette Ronner.

Cows and sheep by Verboeckhoven almost became a currency in their own right, selling at easily quotable prices. A composition showing three sheep had a definite market value, significantly superior to one with only two. The artist himself was clearly a businessman, keen to encourage such a mercenary attitude to his pictures. An incident is recorded of a prospective buyer who visited him in his studio, and was offered a scene showing a mother ewe with two small lambs. The client was impressed and asked the price. 'A thousand francs for the ewe and two hundred per head of lamb', he was told, and his face fell because this was just above the limit of what he could afford. 'Never mind', said Verboeckhoven, seizing his brush, 'I'll make it two hundred francs cheaper', and promptly painted out one of the lambs.

For those who could not afford even the cheapest Verboeckhoven, there existed a band of followers in Belgium who could produce the goods at slightly lower rates: van Severdonck, Leemputten, Remy Maes, van Dieghem, and Verhoesen amongst others. For Verboeckhoven there was always the problem of faking, and on the reverse of many of his later works he affixed labels of authenticity; and even van Severdonck had to take similar measures, an indication of the hunger for such painting existing locally and internationally.

Verboeckhoven was a romantic in the sense in which the word tends to be used in Holland and Belgium to describe painters who viewed their subjects — particularly landscape and animals — through rose tinted spectacles. Foliage becomes a little too bosky, pasture a little too verdant, light a little too mellow, and cattle and sheep a fraction too serene. It is another aspect of the obsession with a rural golden age, one which was all the more attractive to the city dweller, who liked nature to be tidied up for him, shorn of its rough edges. As the century progressed, a reaction set in to the blandness of this vision. The somewhat more realistic mood which affected painting in most countries was felt even by painters of cows and sheep. The Hague School, for instance, produced a greyer and perhaps ultimately truer view of pastoral life in Holland, and Anton Mauve, Willem Maris, Westerbeek, van de Weele, and others began to paint cows and sheep with a closer relation to reality; not so much in anatomical detail, which was faultless with Verboeckhoven, but in the mood of presentation.

In France Constant Troyon and Charles Emile Jacque, with their Barbizon background, represented a similar movement away from traditional romanticism towards a greater degree of realist objectivity in the painting of livestock:

> Ah! Beautiful Realism! Pleasing and attractive Truth! How good is the countryside here, alive, animated, full of noise and movement, without losing its calmness, grandeur, and happiness!

This was R. de la Fizelière's somewhat ecstatic definition of Jacque's realism in 1864. A change was perceived to have taken place, although the critical response remains fulsomely romantic. The close observation of their subjects practised by painters like Jacque highlighted one further romantic preoccupation of the period, the burning question of whether animals had souls:

> Ah! Would that no-one would ever again declare that animals don't think. We would refer such prosaic objectors to the sheepfolds and farms of Charles Jacque, who saw nature as clearly as he knew how to observe her creations.

This was the opinion of one critic at the time of Jacque's death. Another artist who would surely have agreed with him was August Schenck, an animal painter who was a member of the artistic colony at Edouard Frère's farm at Ecouen. He was described by *Le Figaro* in 1878 as:

> One of our first animal painters. He is one of those originals, of a species not yet extinct, who prefers dogs to men, and finds more sweetness in sheep than in women.

Munich, that other great capital of cow painting, witnessed the same gentle progression from romanticism towards realism encountered elsewhere. The older tradition can be seen in the works of M.J. Wagenbauer and J.A. Klein; as the century progressed, the breeze of change blowing from France and Holland was felt in various quarters. Braith and Mali were certainly not unaware of the Barbizon school, and their own influence was widespread as together they ran what amounted to a school for aspirant cow and sheep painters. Others who achieved impressive reputations included Friedrich Voltz and Otto Gebler, as well as the Hungarian B. Pallik. It was Heinrich von Zügel who introduced the most 'advanced' approach; he rarely painted anything but cattle and sheep, but his awareness of the Barbizon and Hague schools prompted him to develop a direct impressionistic style which depended much more on sketches of his subjects on the spot, and less on reworkings in the studio. Even with Zügel, however, the ultimate verdict must be that he owed more to Paulus Potter than to Claude Monet.

Cow and sheep painting was essentially a conservative branch of artistic specialisation, and there were many painters operating late in the nineteenth and even into the twentieth century who remained innocent of any contamination with modern ideas of realism. Such men continued to turn out bland, pretty, edited versions of the farmyard or pastureland in which cows positively simper and sheep resemble large cuddly toys. Even poultry takes on a sentimental expressiveness of feature and gesture. Edgar Hunt and his brother Walter won great popularity with their cleaned-up, glossy farm scenes. What is missing from their pictures is any convincing sense of animality, any authentic whiff of manure. Perhaps such things were not for polite drawing rooms. The Hunts knew their market and were unlikely to produce anything to jeopardise it by offending the sensibilities of their patrons.

Thomas Sidney Cooper was another who knew his market and developed it with great success through a career which neatly spanned the century. He was the English Verboeckhoven, the acknowledged master in his field (or meadow). He, too, looked to the Netherlands for inspiration; not only did he consult seventeenth century originals, but he actually lived in Belgium for four years (1827-31), studying in Brussels with Verboeckhoven himself. It was only here that he discovered his true metier, animal painting, and although the academic hierarchy of values put animal painting at the lowest end of the scale as opposed to the high art of figure painting, this did not deter him, nor did it affect his earning power. At the height of his fame, in 1873, he sold *The Monarch of the Meadows* for the enormous sum of £2,500, and like other successful European cattle painters died a man of considerable wealth. Ultimately he perhaps had more in common with the prosperous farmers who were his neighbours in Kent than with his Olympian colleagues in the Royal Academy.

RICHARD ANSDELL. A Highland cattle fair, Isle of Skye. Signed and dated 1874. 54 x 92ins. (137 x 236cm). *Christie's.*

Index of Artists

ADAM, Benno (German, 1812-1892)
ADAM, Joseph Denovan (British, 1842-1896)
* ANSDELL, Richard (British, 1815-1885)
* ASKEVOLD, Anders Monsen (Swedish, 1834-1900)

* BAHIEU, Jules G. (Belgian, fl.1885-1895)
BAISCH, Hermann (German, 1846-1894)
BARKER, John Joseph (British, fl.1835-1866)
* BARKER, Wright (British, fl.1891-1941)
* BEAVIS, Richard (British, 1824-1896)
* BECKER, Albert (German, 1830-1896)
BERGH, Edward (Swedish, 1828-1880)
BERNIER, Geo (Belgian, 1862-1918)
* BEUL, Henri de (Dutch, 1845-1900)
BEUL, Laurent de (Dutch, 1821-1872)
BIANCHI, Mosé (Italian, 1840-1904)
BILDERS, Albert Gérard (Dutch, 1838-1865)
BOGH, Karl Hendrik (Danish, 1827-1893)
* BONHEUR, Auguste (French, 1824-1884)
BONHEUR, Rosa (French, 1822-1899)
BONNEFOY, Henri Arthur (French, 1839-1917)
* BONOMI, Giovanni (Italian, late 19th Century)
BRADLEY, Basil (British, 1842-1904)
* BRAITH, Anton (German, 1836-1905)
BRANDES, Hans Heinrich Jürgen (German, 1803-1868)
* BRASCASSAT, Jacques Raymond (French, 1804-1867)
* BRENDEL, Albert Heinrich (German, 1827-1895)
BRETLAND, Thomas W. (British, 1802-1874)
* BRISSOT DE WARVILLE, Félix Saturnin (French, 1818-1892)
BRUININGH VAN WORRELL, Abraham (Dutch, mid-19th Century)
* BRUZZI, Stefano (Italian, 1835-1911)
BÜHLMAYER, Conrad (Austrian, 1835-1883)
* BURGER, Anton (German, 1824-1905)
* BÜRKEL, Heinrich (German, 1802-1869)
* BURNIER, Richard (Dutch, 1826-1884)

CALIFANO, Giovanni (Italian, 1864-?)
* CAMPOTOSTO, Henry (Belgian,?-1910)
CARDON, Claude (British, fl.1892-1915)
CAULLET, Albert (Belgian, 1875-?)
CAVALLERI, Vittorio (Italian, 1860-1938)
* CERAMANO, Charles Ferdinand (French, 1829-1909)
* CHAIGNEAU, Jean Ferdinand (French, 1830-1906)
* CHAIGNEAU, Paul (French, late 19th Century)
CHARLEMONT, Hugo (Austrian, 1850-1939)
CHELIUS, Adolf (German, 1856-1923)
CHERUBINI, Andrea (Italian, late 19th Century)
* CHIALIVA, Luigi (Swiss, 1842-1914)
* CLAIR, Charles (French, 1860-?)
CLARK, James (British, 1858-1943)
COCK, Xavier de (Belgian, 1818-1896)
COIGNARD, Louis (French, 1810-1883)
* COLEMAN, Charles (British, ?-1874)
* COLLINS, Charles (British, 1851-1921)
* COOMANS, Auguste (Belgian, 1855-?)
* COOPER, Thomas Sidney (British, 1803-1902)
* COOPER, William Sidney (British, fl.1871-1908)
* CORTÉS, Andrés (Spanish, late 19th Century)

CORTÉS, Antonio (Spanish, fl.1887-1894)
COTTIN, F. Pierre (French, 1823-1886)
* COULAND, Martin (French, ?-1906)
COURTENS, Franz (Belgian, 1854-1943)
COUTURIER, Philibert Léon (French, 1823-1901)

DALLINGER VON DALLING, Johann Baptiste (Austrian, 1782-1868)
* DAMME-SYLVA, Emile van (Belgian, 1853-1935)
* DAVIS, Henry William Banks (British, 1833-1914)
DAVIS, W. H. (British, late 19th Century)
DELLEANI, Lorenzo (Italian, 1840-1908)
* DELVAUX, J. (French?, late 19th Century)
DESVIGNES, Herbert Clayton (British, fl.1833-1863)
DICKERT, Georg (German, 1855-1904)
* DIEGHEM, Jacob van (Belgian, late 19th Century)
* DIELMAN, Pierre Emmanuel (Belgian, 1800-1858)
* DIETERLE, Marie (van Marcke de Lummen) (French, 1856-1935)
DOBAN, Charles (British, mid-19th Century)
DOUBTING, James (British, 1841-1904)
DOUGLAS, Edwin (British, 1848-1914)
* DURST, Auguste (French, 1842-?)

EBEL, Fritz Carl Werner (German, 1835-1895)
EBERLE, Adolf (German, 1843-1914)
* EBERLE, Robert (German, 1815-1860)
* ENGEL, Frederik (Dutch, 1872-1958)
* ENGELEN, Piet van (Belgian, 1863-1924)
ENGELS, Robert (German, 1866-1926)
EXTER, Julius (German, 1863-1939)

FARQUHARSON, David (British, 1839-1907)
FARQUHARSON, Joseph (British, 1846-1935)
* FERNELEY (Sen.), John E. (British, 1781-1860)
* FRENZEL, Oskar (German, 1855-1915)

GARLAND, Henry (British, late 19th Century)
* GAUERMANN, Friedrich (Austrian, 1807-1862)
GAULD, David (British, 1866-1936)
* GEBLER, Friedrich Otto (German, 1838-1917)
* GILLARD, William (British, 1812-?)
* GRAHAM, Peter (British, 1836-1921)
GROBE, German (German, 1857-?)
GROENEWEGEN, Adrianus Johannes (Dutch, 1874-1963)
* GUILLEMINET, Claude (French, 1821-1860?)
* GUYOT, Louise (French, late 19th Century)
* GYSELMAN, Warner (Dutch, 1827-?)

HAAG, Hans Johann (Austrian, 1841-?)
* HAAS, Johannes Hubertus Leonardus de (Dutch, 1832-1908)
* HAENGER, Max (German, 1874-?)
HAGEMANS, Maurice (Belgian, 1852-1917)
HAMMAN, Edouard Michel Ferdinand (French, late 19th Century)
HARGITT, Edward (British, 1835-1895)
* HENRARD, Georges (Belgian, ?-1877)
HEYDEN, Hubert von (German, 1860-1911)

* HERRING (Sen.), John Frederick (British, 1795-1865)
* HERRING (Jun.), John Frederick (British, 1815-1907)
HOCHMAN, Franz Gustav (German, 1861-?)
* HOFNER, Johann Baptist (German, 1832-1913)
HOLDER, Edward Henry (British, fl.1864-1917)
HOLZ, Johann Daniel (German, 1867-1945)
* HORLOR, George W. (British, fl.1849-1891)
HORSLEY, Hopkins Horsley Hobday (British, 1807-1890)
HORSTIG, Eugen (German, 1843-1901)
* HUGGINS, William (British, 1820-1884)
HULK, William Frederick (Dutch, 1852-1882?)
HUMBERT, Jean Charles Ferdinand (Swiss, 1813-1881)
* HUNT, Edgar (British, 1876-1953)
* HUNT, Walter (British, 1861-1931)
* HURT, Louis Bosworth (British, 1856-1929)

INDONI, Filippo (Italian, late 19th Century)
INNOCENTI, Camillo (Italian, 1871-1961)

* JACOBS, Adolphe (Belgian, fl.1887-1910)
* JACQUE, Charles Emile (French, 1813-1894)
JANS, Edouard de (Belgian, 1855-1919)
JANSEN, Willem George Frederick (Dutch, 1871-1949)
* JONES, Charles (British, 1836-1892)
JUTZ, Carl (German, 1838-1916)

KAUFHOLD, August (German, late 19th Century)
KLEIN, Johann Adam (German, 1792-1875)
KOBELL, Jan III (Dutch, 1800-1838)
* KOBELL, Wilhelm Alexander Wolfgang von (German, 1766-1855)
KOCH, Joseph (German, 1819-1872)
KOLLER, Rudolph Johann (Swiss, 1828-1905)
KONINGH, Leendert de (Dutch, 1810-1887)
* KREGTEN, Johannes Aurelius Richard Fedor van (Dutch, 1871-1937)
KUNTZ, Carl (German, 1770-1830)

LANDSEER, Sir Edwin Henry (British, 1802-1873)
LAURENT-DESROUSSEAUX, Henri Alphonse Louis (French, 1862-1906)
LEBLING, Max Ludwig (German, 1851-?)
* LEEMPUTTEN, Cornelis van (Belgian, 1841-1902)
* LEEMPUTTEN, Jef Louis van (Belgian, late 19th Century)
LEMAIRE, C. (French, late 19th Century)
LOKHORST, Dirk van (Dutch, 1818-1893)
LOSSOW, Friedrich (German, 1837-1872)
LOTZE, Moritz Eduard (German, 1809-1890)
* LUKER, William (British, fl.1852-1889)
LUMINAIS-VITAL, Evariste (French, 1822-1896)

MADSEN, A. P. (Danish, 1822-1911)
* MAES, Eugène Remy (Belgian, 1849-1912)
* MAES, Philippe (Dutch, late 19th Century)
* MAHLKNECHT, Edmund (Austrian, 1820-1903)
* MALI, Christian Friedrich (German, 1832-1906)
* MARAIS, Adolphe Charles (French, 1856-?)
* MARCKE DE LUMMEN, Emile van (French, 1827-1890)
MARIS, Matthijs (Dutch, 1839-1917)
MARIS, Willem (Dutch, 1844-1910)
MARR, Joseph Heinrich Ludwig (German, 1807-1871)
* MAUVE, Anton (Dutch, 1838-1888)
MEISSNER, Ernst Adolph (German, 1837-1902)

MELCHIOR, Wilhelm Johann (German, 1817-1860)
* MEYER, Otto van (German, 1839-?)
MILONE, Antonio (Italian, late 19th Century)
MOODY, Fanny (British, 1861-1897)
* MORRIS, Alfred (British, fl.1853-1873)
MORRIS, J. C. (British, fl.1851-1863)

NEDER, Johann Michael (Austrian, 1807-1882)

* OBERMAN, Anthonijs (Dutch, 1781-1845)
OFFERMANS, Anthony Jacob (Dutch, 1796-1872)
OLARIA, Frederico (Spanish, 1849-1898)
* OMMERGANCK, Balthasar Paul (Belgian, 1755-1826)
OOSTERHOUDT, Daniel van (Dutch, 1786-1850)
OOSTERHOUDT, Dirk van (Dutch, 1756-1830)
OS, Pieter Frederick van(Dutch, 1808-1860)
OS, Pieter Gerardus van (Dutch, 1776-1839)

* PALIZZI, Filippo (Italian, 1818-1899)
PALIZZI, Francesco Paolo (Italian, 1825-1871)
PALIZZI, Giuseppe (Italian, 1813-1888)
* PALLIK, Béla (Austrian, 1845-1908)
PANERAI, Ruggero (Italian, 1862-1923)
PANHUYSEN, Ernest van den (Belgian, 1874-?)
PARK, Henry (British, 1816-1871)
PARMENTIER, Paul (Belgian, ?-1902)
PELLICCIOTTI, Tito (Italian, 1871-1950)
* PEZANT, Aymar Alexandre (French, 1846-?)
PHILIPSEN, Theodor (Danish, 1840-1920)
* PITTARA, Carlo (Italian, 1836-1890)
* PLAS, Johanna Diederica van der (Dutch, late 19th Century)
* PLUMOT, André (Belgian, 1829-1906)
* POINGDESTRE, Charles H. (British, ?-1905)
PRATERE, Edmond Joseph de (Belgian, 1826-1888)
PREHN, A. (French, late 19th Century)
PURTSCHER, Alfons (German, late 19th Century)

QUADRONE, Giovanni Battista (Italian, 1844-1898)

RANZONI, Gustav (Austrian, 1826-1900)
RAVENSWAAY, Jan van (Dutch, 1789-1869)
REGEMORTER, Ignatius Josef Pieter (Belgian, 1785-1873)
* REINHARDT, Ludwig (German, ?-1870)
* ROBBE, Louis Marie Dominique (Belgian, 1806-1887)
ROELOFS, Willem (Dutch, 1822-1897)
ROLL, Alfred Philippe (French, 1846-1919)
ROUSSEAU, Philippe (French, 1816-1887)
ROUX, Carl (German, 1826-1894)
ROY, Jean Baptiste de (Belgian, 1759-1839)
RYK, J. de (Dutch, early 19th Century)

* SANDE BAKHUYSEN, Hendrik van de (Dutch, 1795-1860)
* SAVRY, Hendrik (Dutch, 1823-1907)
* SCHENCK, August Friedrich Albrecht (German, 1828-1901)
SCHERREWITZ, Johan Frederik Cornelius (Dutch, 1868-1951)
* SCHEUERER, Julius (German, 1859-1913)
SCHEUERER, Otto (German, 1862-1934)
* SCHIEDGES, Petrus Paulus (Dutch, 1813-1876)
SCHLEISSNER, August (German, late 19th Century)
SCHMALZIGAUG, Ferdinand (German, 1846-1902)

SCHMIDTMANN, Hermann (German, late 19th Century)
SCHMITSON, Teutwart (German, 1830-1863)
SCHONIAN, Alfred (German, 1856-?)
SCHOUTEN, Henry (Anglo-Dutch, 1864-1927)
SCHRODL, Anton (Austrian, 1823-1906)
* SELLMAYR, Ludwig (German, 1834-1906)
SEVERDONCK, Frans van (Belgian, 1809-1899)
SEVERDONCK, Joseph van (Belgian, 1819-1905)
SHAYER, William (British, 1788-1879)
* SHAYER, William Joseph (British, 1811-1891)
SLUYS, Théo van (Dutch, late 19th Century)
* SMYTHE, Edward Robert (British, 1810-1899)
SOTTOCORNOLA, Giovanni (Italian, 1855-1917)
SPAENDONCK, Cornelis van (Dutch, 1756-1840)
* STEELINK, Willem (Dutch, 1856-1928)
STOBBAERTS, Jan Baptist (Belgian, 1838-1914)
STOCQUART, Ildephonse (Belgian, 1819-1889)
* STORTENBEKER, Pieter (Dutch, 1828-1898)
* STRÜTZEL, Leopold Otto (German, 1855-1930)

TENNANT, John Frederick (British, 1796-1872)
* TERMEULEN, Frans Pieter (Dutch, 1843-1927)
* THERKILDSEN, Michael Hans (Danish, 1850-1925)
* TOM, Jan Bedijs (Dutch, 1813-1894)
* TROYON, Constant (French, 1810-1865)
TSCHAGGENY, Charles Philogène (Belgian, 1815-1894)
TSCHAGGENY, Edmond Jean Baptiste (Belgian, 1818-1873)

UCKERMANN, Karl (Norwegian, 1855-?)

VALTER, Frederick E. (British, fl.1878-1900)
* VERBOECKHOVEN, Eugène Joseph (Belgian, 1799-1881)

VERBRUGGE, Jean Charles (Belgian, 1756-1831)
* VERHOESEN, Albertus (Dutch, 1806-1881)
VERLAT, Charles Michel Maria (Belgian, 1824-1890)
VERSCHUUR, Wouter (Dutch, 1812-1874)
VERVOORT, M. (Belgian, early 19th Century)
VERWEE, Alfred Jacques (Belgian, 1838-1895)
VERWEE, Louis Pierre (Belgian, 1807-1877)
* VOLTZ, Friedrich Johann (German, 1817-1886)
VOORDECKER, Henri (Belgian, 1779-1861)

* WAGENBAUER, Max Josef (German, 1774-1829)
WAGNER, Alexander von (Austrian, 1838-1919)
* WAINEWRIGHT, Thomas Francis (British, fl.1831-1883)
WASTROWSKI, Franciszek (Polish, 1843-1900)
* WATSON, Robert (British, late 19th Century)
* WATSON, William (British, ?-1921)
WEBBE, William J. (British, fl.1853-1887)
* WEBER, Otto (German, 1832-1888)
WEEKES, Henry (British, fl.1849-1888)
WEELE, Herman Johannes van de (Dutch, 1852-1930)
WEISHAUPT, Victor (German, 1848-1905)
* WEISSENBRUCH, Johannes Hendrick (Dutch, 1824-1903)
* WESTERBEEK, Cornelis (Dutch, 1844-1903)
* WILLIS, Henry Brittan (British, 1810-1884)
WOLF, Georg (German, late 19th Century)
WOLFRAM, Joseph (Austrian, fl.1860-1873)
WOODHOUSE, William (British, 1805-1878)
WOOLETT, Henry Charles (British, late 19th Century)
* WOUTERMAERTENS, Edouard (Belgian, 1819-1897)

ZIMMERMAN, Richard August (German, 1820-1875)
* ZÜGEL, Heinrich Johann von (German, 1850-1941)

ANDERS MONSEN ASKEVOLD. A peasant girl with cattle in a wooded landscape. Signed. 30 x 50ins (76 x 127cm). *Christie's.*

JULES G. BAHIEU. Poultry and sheep in a barn. Signed.
18½ x 24¾ins. (47 x 63cm). *Christie's.*

RICHARD BEAVIS. Milch goats, Granada. Signed and
inscribed Granada, and signed and inscribed on an old label
on the reverse. 14½ x 20½ins. (37 x 52cm). *Christie's.*

WRIGHT BARKER. Passing showers. Signed, and inscribed on an old label on the reverse. 51½ x 69ins. (131 x 175.5cm).
Christie's.

ALBERT BECKER. Poultry in a
landscape. Signed, on panel.
5½ x 9ins. (14 x 23cm). *Christie's.*

HENRI DE BEUL. Sheep in a
landscape. Signed and dated '71, on
panel. 6 x 8ins. (15 x 20cm). *Christie's.*

GIOVANNI BONOMI. A victorious fighting cock. Signed.
30 x 26ins. (76 x 66cm). *Christie's.*

AUGUSTE BONHEUR. A shepherd with his flock. Signed. 38 x 54½ins. (96.5 x 138.5cm). *Christie's.*

ANTON BRAITH. A girl at a gate with cattle. Signed. 20 x 38ins. (51 x 96.5cm). *Christie's.*

THOMAS SIDNEY COOPER. The midday rest. 40 x 64ins. (101.5 x 162.5cm). *Christie's.*

JACQUES RAYMOND BRASCASSAT. A Bull in an
extensive landscape. Signed and dated 1841. 51¼ x 63¾ ins.
(130 x 162cm). *Sotheby's.*

ALBERT HEINRICH BRENDEL. Sheep in a stable.
On board, signed and dated 1889.
10¾ x 15½ ins. (27.5 x 39.5cm). *Sotheby's.*

FÉLIX SATURNIN BRISSOT DE WARVILLE.
A shepherd and sheep on a path. Signed, on panel.
9 x 12ins. (23 x 30.5cm). *Christie's.*

ANTON BURGER. Sheep in a barn. Signed. 9¼ x 7½ ins.
(23.5 x 19cm). *Christie's.*

STEFANO BRUZZI. A shepherdess in the Campagna.
Signed and dated 1868. 21 x 27ins. (53.5 x 68.5cm). *Christie's.*

RICHARD BURNIER.
A meadow landscape with cattle and a milkmaid. Signed and dated '70. 15 x 22¾ins. (38 x 58cm). *Christie's.*

HEINRICH BÜRKEL. The return of the herd. Signed. 12½ x 15ins. (32 x 38cm). *Christie's.*

CHARLES FERDINAND CERAMANO. Sheep in a barn. Signed, on panel. 10¼ x 13¾ins. (26 x 35cm). *Christie's.*

HENRY CAMPOTOSTO. A rabbit and chickens by a hut. Signed. 13½ x 9½ins. (34 x 24cm). *Christie's.*

LUIGI CHIALIVA. A peasant family with sheep by a wooded pond. Signed, on panel. 18½ x 26¼ ins. (47 x 67cm). *Christie's.*

JEAN FERDINAND CHAIGNEAU. A wooded landscape with a shepherdess and sheep. Signed. 7¼ x 9¼ ins. (18.5 x 23.5cm). *Christie's.*

PAUL CHAIGNEAU. An extensive stormy landscape with a shepherd and his flock. Signed, on panel. 8¼ x 10¼ ins. (21 x 26cm). *Christie's.*

CHARLES CLAIR. 'Ma Bergerie des 4 Fenestres, 1906'. Signed and dated 1906, and inscribed and dated on the reverse, on panel. 9 x 12½ ins. (23 x 31.5cm). *Christie's.*

CHARLES COLEMAN. Oxen in an extensive landscape. Signed and dated Roma 1866. 21¼ x 41ins. (54.5 x 104cm). *Christie's.*

CHARLES COLLINS. The new calf. Signed and dated 1885. 13½ x 17½ins. (34 x 44.5cm). *Christie's*.

AUGUSTE COOMANS. Sheep and poultry in a landscape. Signed and dated 1881, on panel. 7 x 10¼ins. (18 x 26cm). *Christie's*.

THOMAS SIDNEY COOPER. Cattle and sheep grazing in a river landscape. Signed and dated 1870. 30¼ x 42ins. (77 x 107cm). *Christie's*.

WILLIAM SIDNEY COOPER. Cattle watering at a ford. Signed and dated 1894. 19¼ x 29½ins. (49 x 75cm). *Christie's*.

ANDRÉS CORTÉS. Cattle watering. Signed and dated 1888. 38 x 51½ins. (96.5 x 130.5cm). *Christie's.*

MARTIN COULAND. A shepherd and his flock in a landscape. Signed. 26 x 35½ins. (66 x 90cm). *Christie's.*

EMILE VAN DAMME-SYLVA. A herdsman and cattle on a path. Signed 18½ x 27⅞ins. (47 x 70.5cm). *Christie's.*

HENRY WILLIAM BANKS DAVIS. Rough Pasturage, Pas de Calais. Signed, and signed and inscribed on an old label on the stretcher. 23½ x 42ins. (59.5 x 106.5cm). *Christie's.*

J. DELVAUX. Cows watering. Signed. 19¾ x 33½ins. (50 x 85cm). *Christie's.*

JACOB VAN DIEGHEM. Sheep and poultry in a landscape. Signed, on panel. 6½ x 9¼ins. (16.5 x 23.5cm). *Christie's.*

PIERRE EMMANUEL DIELMAN. Sheep watering at a stream. Signed and dated 1851. 31 x 44¾ins. (79 x 113.5cm).
Christie's.

MARIE DIETERLE (VAN MARCKE DE LUMMEN).
Cattle watering in a wooded landscape. Signed.
16¼ x 23¼ins. (41 x 59cm). *Christie's.*

AUGUSTE DURST. Poultry in a farmyard. Signed.
19¼ x 28¾ins. (49 x 73cm). *Sotheby's.*

ROBERT EBERLE. A shepherd with his flock
in a landscape. Signed. 18 x 22ins.
(45.5 x 56cm). *Christie's.*

PIET VAN ENGELEN. Poultry by a hutch.
Signed, inscribed and dated Anvers '95.
42 x 58ins. (106.5 x 147cm). *Christie's.*

FREDERIK ENGEL. Cattle in a meadow.
Signed. 12 x 17½ins. (30.5 x 44.5cm). *Christie's.*

JOHN E. FERNELEY (SEN). Sir John Palmer's Prize Durham Shorthorn ox with the groom John Mentharn on his favourite grey horse. Signed and dated Melton Mowbray 1826. 33¾ x 42¾ins. (86 x 109cm). *Christie's.*

OSKAR FRENZEL. Cattle watering. Signed and inscribed Berlin. 27¼ x 39ins. (69 x 99cm). *Christie's.*

FRIEDRICH GAUERMANN. A horse and cattle fair. Signed and dated 1857. 41 x 54¼ins. (104 x 137.5cm). *Christie's.*

FRIEDRICH OTTO GEBLER. Sheep in a landscape. Signed, on panel. 6¼ x 9¼ ins. (16 x 23.5cm). *Christie's.*

WILLIAM GILLARD. Cattle, a goose and a child in a wheelbarrow by a shed. Signed. 22½ x 29½ ins. (57 x 75cm). *Christie's.*

CLAUDE GUILLEMINET. Poultry in a barn. Signed, on panel. 16 x 24½ ins. (41 x 62.5cm). *Christie's.*

PETER GRAHAM. A highland landscape with cattle. Signed and dated 1905. 40 x 53¼ ins. (101.5 x 135cm). *Christie's.*

LOUISE GUYOT. A wooded landscape with shepherds and sheep. Signed and inscribed Paris. 13¾ x 22ins. (35 x 56cm). *Christie's.*

WARNER GYSELMAN. A shepherd and sheep in a hilly landscape. Signed and dated '59. 9½ x 11½ins. (24 x 29cm). *Christie's.*

JOHANNES HUBERTUS LEONARDUS DE HAAS. Cattle and a milkmaid by a pond in a meadow. Signed. 19½ x 29½ins. (49.5 x 75cm). *Christie's.*

MAX HAENGER. Poultry by a pond. Signed, on panel. 7½ x 11ins. (19 x 28cm). *Christie's.*

GEORGES HENRARD. Sheep in a barn. Signed. 14 x 19¼ins. (35.5 x 49cm). Christie's.

JOHN FREDERICK HERRING (JUN). Sheep and sheepdog in a landscape. Signed, on board. 6 x 8ins. (15 x 20cm). *Christie's.*

JOHN FREDERICK HERRING (SEN). Cattle and goats by a pond in an extensive landscape. Signed and dated 1833(?), circular. 14¾ ins. (37.5cm) diameter. *Christie's.*

GEORGE W. HORLOR. Cattle and ducks in a mountain landscape. Signed and dated 1879. 24¼ x 40¼ ins. (61.5 x 102cm). *Christie's.*

JOHANN BAPTIST HOFNER. The shepherdess. Signed and dated 1866. 47½ x 35¾ ins. (120.5 x 91cm). *Christie's.*

WILLIAM HUGGINS. Ram and ewes. Signed on the reverse, on board. 17½ x 21½ins. (44.5 x 54.5cm). *Christie's.*

EDGAR HUNT. The unfamiliar visitor. Signed and dated 1936. 11 x 16ins. (28 x 40.5cm). *Christie's.*

WALTER HUNT. Calves and poultry outside a barn. Signed and dated 1913. 19½ x 29¾ins. (49.5 x 75.5cm). *Christie's.*

LOUIS BOSWORTH HURT. After the storm: Glen Dochart Perthshire. Signed and dated 1890, and signed and inscribed on the reverse. 39½ x 59½ins. (100.5 x 151cm). *Christie's.*

ADOLPHE JACOBS. Cattle grazing. 25½ x 38ins. (64.5 x 96.5cm). *Christie's.*

CHARLES JONES. Sheep in an extensive landscape. Signed with monogram and dated '89, and signed and dated 1889 on the reverse. 23¾ x 41½ins. (60 x 105.5cm). *Christie's.*

CHARLES EMILE JACQUE. A shepherdess with sheep on a rocky slope. Signed, on panel. 8¼ x 10½ins. (21 x 26.5cm). *Christie's.*

JOHANNES AURELIUS RICHARD FEDOR VAN KREGTEN. Cows in a landscape. Signed. 15 x 22ins. (38 x 56cm). *Christie's.*

WILHELM ALEXANDER WOLFGANG VON KOBELL. Isarlandschaft mit Schlösschen Harlacking. Signed with initials and dated 1819. 16 x 21ins. (40.3 x 53cm). *Munich, Neue Pinakothek.*

CORNELIS VAN LEEMPUTTEN. Poultry in a landscape. Signed and dated '63, on panel. 9½ x 13½ins. (24 x 34cm). *Christie's.*

JEF LOUIS VAN LEEMPUTTEN. Poultry by a haystack. Signed and dated 1865, on panel. 11¾ x 15¼ins. (30 x 38.5cm). *Christie's.*

WILLIAM LUKER. A highland landscape with a herdsman and cattle. Signed and dated 1882. 34½ x 55ins. (88 x 139.5cm). *Christie's.*

EUGÈNE REMY MAES. Poultry in a landscape. Signed, on panel. 9½ x 14ins. (24 x 35.5cm). *Christie's.*

PHILIPPE MAES. A goat, sheep and chickens in a barn. Signed, on panel. 7 x 9½ins. (17.5 x 24cm). *Christie's.*

EDMUND MAHLKNECHT. An alpine lake landscape with shepherdesses, cattle and goats by a house. Signed and dated '876. 27 x 37ins. (68.5 x 94cm). *Christie's.*

CHRISTIAN FRIEDRICH MALI. A river landscape with cattle watering near a town. Signed and inscribed München. 22 x 44½ins. (56 x 113cm). *Christie's.*

ADOLPHE CHARLES MARAIS. A cow in a landscape. Signed. 17¼ x 21¾ins. (44 x 55cm). *Christie's.*

OTTO VAN MEYER. In the Marshes. Signed. 37½ x 29½ins. (95.5 x 75cm). *Christie's.*

EMILE VAN MARCKE DE LUMMEN. Cattle in a stormy coastal landscape. Signed and dated '76. 45 x 61¼ins. (114 x 158cm). *Christie's.*

259

ANTON MAUVE. Cattle in a landscape. Signed. 25 x 39ins. (63.5 x 99cm). *Christie's.*

ALFRED MORRIS. Sheep in a landscape. Signed and dated 1878. 30 x 50ins. (76 x 127cm). *Christie's.*

ANTHONIJS OBERMAN. A wooded landscape with a herdsman and cattle. Signed and dated 1815, on panel. 15¼ x 13¼ins. (38.5 x 34cm). *Christie's.*

Centre left: BALTHASAR PAUL OMMEGANCK. An extensive wooded landscape with drovers, cattle and sheep. On panel. 19 x 26ins. (48 x 66cm). *Christie's.*

JOHANNA DIEDERICA VAN DER PLAS. A wooded landscape with cattle. Signed and dated 1871. 20½ x 33ins. (52 x 84cm). *Christie's.*

AYMAR ALEXANDRE PEZANT. Cattle in a meadow. Signed. 18 x 23½ins. (45.5 x 59.5cm). *Christie's.*

BÉLA PALLIK. The head of a ram. Signed and dated 1897. 31½ x 25½ins. (80 x 64.5cm). *Christie's.*

Centre right: CARLO PITTARA. Cattle in a hilly landscape. Signed. 19¼ x 28ins. (49 x 71cm). *Christie's.*

ANDRÉ PLUMOT. A mother and child with cattle and goats in a coastal landscape. Signed and dated 1877, on panel. 11¾ x 20ins. (30 x 51cm). *Christie's.*

CHARLES H. POINGDESTRE. Shooting near Rome unexpected game. Signed and dated 1878, and signed and inscribed on an old label on the reverse. 21¼ x 40¼ ins. (54 x 102cm). *Christie's.*

LUDWIG REINHARDT. A shepherd and sheep in a wooded landscape. Signed. 24½ x 28¾ ins. (62 x 73cm). *Christie's.*

LOUIS MARIE DOMINIQUE ROBBE. A cow and sheep in a barn. Signed, on panel. 8¼ x 10½ins. (21 x 26.5cm). *Christie's.*

Top right: HENDRIK VAN DE SANDE BAKHUYSEN. Cows and sheep watering in an extensive river landscape. Signed and dated 1846, on panel. 26¾ x 35ins. (68 x 89cm). *Christie's.*

HENDRIK SAVRY. Cattle in a meadow. Signed. 20 x 31¾ins. (50.5 x 80.5cm). *Christie's.*

AUGUST FRIEDRICH ALBRECHT SCHENCK. A shepherdess and sheep in a landscape. Signed. 13½ x 19¼ins. (34 x 49cm). *Christie's.*

JULIUS SCHEUERER. Ducks and poultry by a pond.
Signed, on panel. 7¼ x 9¾ins. (18.5 x 24.5cm).
Christie's.

PETRUS PAULUS SCHIEDGES. A wooded river landscape with
a shepherd and sheep. Signed. 10½ x 16ins. (27 x 40.5cm).
Christie's.

HERMANN
SCHMIDTMANN. In
the fields. Signed and
numbered 213 on the
reverse. 30 x 55½ins.
(76 x 141cm). *Christie's.*

LUDWIG SELLMAYR.
Cattle watering at a
lake. Signed and dated
München 1881.
23½ x 39½ins.
(60 x 100.5cm).
Christie's.

FILIPPO PALIZZI. Waiting. Signed and dated 1874. 18¾ x 28½ins. (48 x 72.5cm). *Christie's.*

EUGÈNE JOSEPH VERBOECKHOVEN. A shepherd, sheep and donkeys. Signed and dated 1878, on panel. 15 x 23ins. (38 x 58.5cm). *Christie's.*

WILLIAM JOSEPH SHAYER. A wooded river landscape with farmfolk and cattle, near Southampton. Signed and dated 1857. 23½ x 17½ins. (59.5 x 44.5cm). *Christie's*.

PIETER STORTENBEKER. A shepherd with sheep and cattle in an extensive landscape. Signed and dated 1854. 25 x 35¼ins. (63.5 x 89.5cm). *Christie's*.

LEOPOLD OTTO STRÜTZEL. A milkmaid and cows by a stream. Signed and dated 1913. 24½ x 39ins. (62 x 99cm). *Christie's*.

EDWARD ROBERT SMYTHE. Highland cattle in a rocky landscape. Signed. 15½ x 23½ins. (39.5 x 59.5cm). *Christie's*.

WILLEM STEELINK. A wooded landscape with a shepherd and sheep grazing. Signed. 12½ x 18½ins. (31.5 x 47cm). *Christie's*.

266

FRANS PIETER TERMEULEN. Sheep in a landscape. Signed. 25½ x 32ins. (64.5 x 81cm). *Christie's.*

JAN BEDIJS TOM. An extensive landscape with peasants loading hay on to an ox-driven cart. Signed and dated 1862. 33½ x 44¾ins. (85 x 113.6cm). *Christie's.*

CONSTANT TROYON. A cow in a wooded landscape. Signed with initials and with the atelier mark (L.2406) on panel. 12 x 15¼ins. (30.5 x 39cm). *Christie's.*

MICHAEL HANS THERKILDSEN. Cattle in a meadow. Signed with initials. 16½ x 24¾ins. (42 x 63cm). *Christie's.*

EUGÈNE JOSEPH VERBOECKHOVEN. Cattle, sheep, a goat and a donkey grazing by a stream. Signed and dated 1853, on panel. 10¾ x 14½ins. (27 x 37cm). *Christie's.*

ALBERTUS VERHOESEN. Poultry by a ruin. Signed and dated 1862. 13¾ x 18ins. (35 x 46cm). *Christie's.*

FRIEDRICH JOHANN VOLTZ. Cattle watering in a wooded landscape. Signed and dated 1875, on panel. 13½ x 34½ins. (34 x 87.5cm). *Christie's.*

HEINRICH JOHANN VON ZUGEL. Sheep watering in a wooded landscape. Signed and dated 88. 18¼ x 24¾ins. (46.5 x 63cm). *Christie's.*

MAX JOSEPH WAGENBAUER. A young steer in a
landscape. 57¼ x 68¾ins. (145.5 x 174.8cm). *Munich, Neue
Pinakothek.*

THOMAS FRANCIS WAINEWRIGHT. Sheep in an
extensive landscape. Signed and dated 1871, on panel.
8 x 12ins. (20 x 30.5cm). *Christie's.*

ROBERT WATSON. Highland cattle. Signed and dated
1904. 35½ x 27½ins. (90 x 70cm).

WILLIAM WATSON. Highland sheep, near Braemar. Signed and dated 1876. 20 x 30ins. (50.5 x 76cm). *Christie's.*

OTTO WEBER. Spring Time. Signed, and signed and inscribed on a label on the reverse. 39 x 64ins. (99 x 162.5cm). *Christie's.*

JOHANNES HENDRICK WEISSENBRUCH. Spring Time. Signed. 17⅞ x 23¾ins. (45 x 60.5cm). *Christie's.*

HENRY BRITTAN WILLIS. A wooded river landscape with cattle watering. 21¼ x 41¼ins. (54 x 105cm). *Christie's.*

CORNELIS WESTERBEEK. Cattle grazing by a river. Signed and dated '93. 9 x 15½ins. (23 x 39.5cm). *Christie's.*

EDOUARD WOUTERMAERTENS. A dog teasing two goats in a stable. Signed, on panel. 11 x 17⅞ins. (28 x 45cm). *Sotheby's.*

HEINRICH JOHANN VON ZÜGEL. Sheep in a pen. Signed and inscribed Munchen. 9¼ x 12¼ins. (23.5 x 31cm).

HEINRICH JOHANN VON ZÜGEL. Cattle watering with a cart beyond. Signed. 48¾ x 61ins. (124 x 155cm). *Christie's.*

Ducks

Even in a century of rigorous specialisation amongst artists, it is surprising to find painters whose reputations were largely founded on their adeptness in rendering the humble duck. Some of the names recorded in this section overlap with painters of poultry listed elsewhere in this book; but there was a definite demand for pictures specifically of ducks, and a number of painters across Europe strove to meet it. The best-known name in Munich was undoubtedly Alexander Koester, who was operating sufficiently late in the century to adopt an advanced impressionistic style on his somewhat repetitive subject matter. His equivalent in Holland was probably Constant Artz. The preferred milieu of both men was the riverbank, with ducks either swimming or disporting at the water's edge. A special note of pathos could be struck by the introduction of ducklings, soft, downy and adorable.

It is not difficult to mock artists bound by such limited horizons, but they were the products of the patronage of their time. People wanted uncomplicated pictures of things to which they could relate immediately and without troublesome intellectual effort. Their essentially materialist imagination required an easily recognisable, competently painted image of reality. If the subject chosen also incorporated an element of sweet sentimentality, then so much the better.

Index of Artists

ALEXANDER KOESTER. Ducks in a pond. Signed. 22¾ x 38ins. (58 x 96.5cm). *Christie's.*

CONSTANT ARTZ. Ducks in a meadow.
Signed, on panel. 9½ x 14¼ ins.
(24 x 36cm). *Christie's.*

ARTHUR VON BRANDES. Ducks.
Signed and inscribed. 25½ x 38¾ ins.
(64.5 x 98.5cm). *Christie's.*

FRANZ GRÄSSEL. Ducks by a river
bank. Signed, on panel. 6¼ x 8ins. (16 x
20cm). *Christie's.*

JOHN FREDERICK HERRING (SEN). Duck and ducklings by a pond. 20 x 27ins. (51 x 68.5cm). *Christie's.*

EDGAR HUNT. Ducks by a pond. Signed and dated 1922.
11½ x 15ins. (29 x 38cm). *Christie's.*

ALEXANDER KOESTER. Ducks on a river. Signed.
17⅞ x 29½ ins. (45 x 75cm). *Christie's.*

THÉOPHILE VICTOR EMILE
LEMMENS. Ducks in a river
landscape. Signed, on panel.
3¼ x 6ins. (8 x 15.5cm). *Christie's.*

BRUNO ANDREAS LILJEFORS.
Wild geese on the marshes. Signed
and dated 1921. 26 x 39½ins.
(66 x 100cm). *Christie's.*

GEORGE EDWARD LODGE.
Black necked Grebes on a pond.
Signed. 11½ x 17½ins.
(29 x 44.5cm). *Christie's.*

MAX RUDOLF SCHRAMM-
ZITTAU. Ducks on a sunlit pond.
Signed. 13¼ x 22¾ins.
(33.5 x 58cm). *Sotheby's.*

GUSTAV KONRAD SÜS.
Gaenseliesel. Signed and dated
'69. 24½ x 21ins. (62 x 53.5cm).
Christie's.

Dutch Historical Genre

Painters of 'Dutch Historical Genre' can be differentiated from painters of mere imaginary Cavaliers by their much closer dependence on original pictures from the Dutch and Flemish seventeenth century. Of course there were painters who strayed into either category, but certain popular nineteenth century pictures are so closely related to their seventeenth century forebears as to constitute a separate kind of historicism, combining elements of homage to, 'improvement' on, and even falsification of the originals concerned.

The parallels between Dutch seventeenth century society and the bourgeois societies which developed in most European countries in the nineteenth century do not need labouring. It is hardly a coincidence that a taste for Dutch seventeenth century pictures, with their strong domestic bias, emerged at the same time. Here was the prototype for intimate genre, and many nineteenth century painters turned directly to the original blueprint for inspiration. Some discretion was necessary: Teniers and Brouwer were perhaps a little too coarse for the drawing room, and were cleaned up, so that while artists like Braekeleer and Venneman in Belgium reproduced domestic genre set in the seventeenth century they excluded those indecorous figures relieving themsleves in public corners which so indelicately litter the compositions of the earlier masters. The merrymaking Cavaliers of Herman Ten Kate in Holland, and of his followers Reyntyens and Stroebel, clearly derive from interiors by painters like Palamedes and van der Laamen. Here and there the merrymaking is rendered more jolly, and therefore more anodyne, for the easier consumption of the contemporary public. Ferdinand Roybet, an artist of huge popularity, whom some of his patrons found difficult to separate from Rembrandt or Hals either in quality or in truthful representation of Dutch seventeenth century life, also took care to sugar the pill somewhat. Where a cavalier flirts with his lady, he does so with a saccharine primness which contrasts with the earthiness of earlier brothel interiors.

It was not only in Holland and Belgium that Dutch seventeenth century painting was consulted in this way. In Munich and Vienna there were more artists — Becker, Charlemont and Ramberg, for instance — who reproduced intimate Dutch life of the time by the same means. The originals to which they referred were easily found in the Alte Pinakothek or the Kunsthistorisches Museum. One more imaginary golden age, the Dutch seventeenth century of the peaceful interior and an elegant domesticity, had been created by popular nineteenth century painters and found international appreciation.

Baron Leys, at whose studio in Antwerp many painters studied in their formative years, turned out a string of artists who had learned to rehash Peter de Hooch and Terborch. Florent Willems was another who gained international popularity with realistic evocations of this golden age. But, in order to understand them, these pictures should be looked at more closely. At first sight, because of their technique and presentation, they appear seventeenth century, but this illusion is often destroyed because of the indelibly nineteenth century sentiment they betray. For this reason it is a mistake to see such painters as mere copyists of the old masters, copyists who were providing the customer with a pseudo-Dou to hang on his wall in lieu of the real thing which was beyond his means. Reference to contemporary art market prices belies this: often a work by a later 'imitator' like Willems was more sought after than a genuine Dou. Why did a large and influential section of the consumer market find Willems in some senses preferable to the original? One part of the answer is that in certain quarters Willems and his contemporaries were considered better painters than their predecessors. Consider the opinion expressed by L. Robinson writing in the *Art Journal* in 1887, an opinion which found wide acceptance at the time:

> Whilst in no degree underrating the services rendered to art by the (17th Century) Dutch school, one cannot but feel that its greatest masters were deficient in creative power, the true essence of genius.

Fromentin, too, remarked on the lack of subject in Dutch seventeenth century genre painting:

> We cannot see the least sign of anecdote. There is no well-determined subject, no action requiring thoughtful, expressive, or particularly significant composition... Drinking, smoking, dancing, kissing the maids can scarcely be called either rare or attractive incidents.

He contrasted this with the achievement of the contemporary French school in which 'the dramatic, pathetic, romantic, historical, or sentimental elements contribute to the success of its genre painting'. So it was that nineteenth century artists sought to remedy this deficiency, as they saw it, of 'creative power' in Dutch seventeenth century painting, by painting pictures set in that time and imitative of its techniques but adding the excitement of heightened incident or anecdote. Thus Charles van den Daele presents *The Suitor Surprised*, in which the ardent admirer of some blushing Netherlandish maiden has been forced to conceal himself under a table at the unexpected return of the girl's forbidding looking parents. It almost goes without saying that such comedy could equally well have been played out in the nineteenth century; but this 'time-punning', characteristic of classical genre and other intimate historical painting, was part of the attraction. Dou is reinterpreted as a drawing-room comedy.

Close study and imitation of the Dutch seventeenth century originals became a subtle aid to those painters, part of whose aim was to attain a vividness, an illusion of heightened reality, in their representations of what it was like to be an ordinary man in Holland two hundred years earlier. By reproducing the techniques and the mood of the old masters they achieved a spurious but superficially convincing feeling of period authenticity. In much the same way a film maker of today might set out to create an illusion of a hundred years ago by shooting a scene in sepia tints: such emphasis on the way we see a scene, on the spectacles through which we view it, in order to achieve an effect of authenticity, was a device — one might almost say a trick — developed by these nineteenth century painters.

Index of Artists

* ACCORD, Eugène (French, 1824-1888)
  ALMA-TADEMA, Sir Lawrence (Anglo-Dutch, 1836-1912)
* ANGUS, John (Belgian, 1821-?)
  ANGUS, William Louis (Belgian, 1823-?)

  BECKER, Carl Ludwig Friedrich (German, 1820-1900)
  BOON, Constant (Belgian, mid-19th Century)
  BOSBOOM, Johannes (Dutch, 1817-1891)
* BRAEKELEER, Adrien Ferdinand de (Belgian, 1818-1904)
  BRAEKELEER, Ferdinand de (Belgian, 1792-1883)
* BRAEKELEER (the younger), Ferdinand de (Belgian, 1828-1857)
* BRAEKELEER, Henri de (Belgian, 1840-1888)
  BREE, Jos. van (Belgian, early 19th Century)
  BREE, Philippe Jacques van (Belgian, 1786-1871)
  BRELING, Heinrich (German, 1849-1872)
  BRIAS, Charles (Belgian, 1798-1884)
  BUCHBINDER, Simon (Polish, 1853-?)

  CANON, Hans von (Austrian, 1829-1885)
* CANTA, Johannes Antonius (Dutch, 1816-1888)
  CHARLEMONT, Eduard (Austrian, 1848-1906)
  CLEYNHENS, Théodore Joseph (Belgian, 1841-1916)
* CORNET, Jacobus Ludovicus (Dutch, 1815-1882)
  CRAEYVANGER, Reinier (Dutch, 1812-1880)
  CROSIO, Luigi (Italian, 1835-1915)

* DAELE, Charles van den (Belgian, fl.1852-1873)
* DUBOIS, Henri (French, 1837-1909)
  DYCKMANS, Josephus Laurentius (Belgian, 1811-1888)

* ELMORE, Alfred W. (British, 1815-1881)

  FRIEDLÄNDER, Alfred Ritter von Malheim (Austrian, 1860-?)

  GEIRNAERT, Josef (Belgian, 1790-1859)
  GIRL, Helisena (German, 1831-1916)
  GRIPS, Charles Joseph (Belgian, 1825-1920)

  HAAXMAN, Pieter Alardus (Dutch, 1814-1887)
  HAMME, Alexis van (Belgian, 1818-1875)
* HEGER, Heinrich Anton (German, 1832-1888)
* HEIJLIGERS, Gustav Antoon François (Dutch, 1828-1897)
* HOESE, Jean de la (Belgian, 1846-1917)
* HOHENBERG, Rosa (German, 1852-?)
* HOLMBERG, August Johann (German, 1851-1911)
  HOVE, Hubertus van (Dutch, 1814-1865)

  JOLLY, Henri Jean Baptiste (Belgian, 1814-1853)

  KIRBERG, Otto Karl (German, 1850-1926)
* KNARREN, Petrus Renier Hubertus (Dutch, 1826-1896)
* KREMER, Petrus (Belgian, 1801-1888)

  LAAR, Jan Hendrik van de (Dutch, 1807-1884)

  LAGYE, Victor (Belgian, 1829-1896)
  LEBRUN, Louis (Belgian, 1844-1900)
* LEYS, Baron Hendrik (Belgian, 1815-1869)
  LIES, Josef Hendrik Hubert (Belgian, 1821-1865)
  LINGERMAN, Lambertus (Dutch, 1829-1894)
* LINNIG, Willem (Belgian, 1819-1885)
  LOOSE, Basile de (Belgian, 1809-1885)

  MARKELBACH, Alexandre (Belgian, 1824-1906)
  MADIOL, Adrien Jean (Dutch, 1845-1892)
  MADOU, Jean Baptiste (Belgian, 1796-1877)
  MEER, Ch. van (Belgian, late 19th Century)
* MERTZ, Johannes Cornelius (Dutch, 1819-1891)
* MEYER, Claus (German, 1856-1919)
* MOORMANS, Frans (Dutch, 1831-1873)

  NEUHUYS, Albert Johann (Dutch, 1844-1914)
  NOTER, David Emile Joseph de (Belgian, 1825-1875)

* PLAATZER, Hubert Willem van der (Dutch, 1810-1862)
  PLATTEEL, Jean (Belgian, 1839-1867)
* PLUMOT, André (Belgian, 1829-1906)
  PUTTEANI, Friederich von (Austrian, 1849-1917)

* RAMBERG, Arthur Georg von (Austrian, 1819-1875)
* RATINCKX. Jos. (Belgian, mid-19th Century)
  REYNTYENS, Henricus Engelbertus (Dutch, 1817-1878)
  ROYBET, Ferdinand Victor Léon (French, 1840-1920)

  SCHEERES, Hendricus Johannes (Dutch, 1829-1864)
  SCHMIDT, Willem Hendrik (Dutch, 1809-1849)
* SCHOLTEN, Hendrik Jacobus (Dutch, 1824-1907)
* SCHRÖTTER, Alfred von (Austrian, 1856-1935)
* SEGHERS, Corneille (Belgian, 1814-1869)
* SÖHN, Carl (German, 1853-1923)
  STACEY MARKS, Henry (British, 1829-1898)
  STROEBEL, Johannes Antonie Balthasar (Dutch, 1821-1905)

  TEN KATE, Herman Frederik Carel (Dutch, 1822-1891)
* TIELEMANS, Louis (Belgian, 1826-1856)
* TURKEN, Henricus (Dutch, 1791-1856)

  VAARBERG, Johannes Christoffel (Dutch, 1825-1871)
* VENNEMAN, Karel Ferdinand Charles (Belgian, 1802-1875)
* VERHOEVEN-BALL, Adrien Joseph (Belgian, 1824-1882)
  VERHULST, Charles Pierre Karel (Belgian, 1774-1820)
  VIGNE, Felix de (Belgian, 1806-1862)
* VINCK, Frans Kaspar Huibrecht (Belgian, 1827-1903)
* VOLKHART, Max (German, 1848-1935)
  VRIENDT, Albrecht Frans Lieven de (Belgian, 1843-1900)

* WAGNER, Ferdinand (German, 1819-1881)
* WAGNER, Fritz (Swiss, 1872-?)
* WILLEMS, Florent (Belgian, 1823-1905)
* WOLFE, Frans Xavier (German, late 19th Century)

EUGÈNE ACCORD. The farewell. Signed and dated 1861, on panel. 18 x 14ins. (45.5 x 35.5cm). *Christie's*.

JOHN ANGUS. A Dutch family at table. Signed, on panel. 8¼ x 7ins. (21 x 18cm). *Christie's*.

FERDINAND DE BRAEKELEER (THE YOUNGER).
A kitchen interior. Signed, on panel. 17½ x 21ins.
(44.5 x 53.5cm). *Christie's.*

ADRIEN FERDINAND DE BRAEKELEER. Figures
playing Tric-Trac outside a tavern. Signed and dated 1847,
on panel. 23 x 18ins. (58.5 x 45.5cm). *Christie's.*

Opposite left: JACOBUS LUDOVICUS CORNET. A secret
kept forever. Signed and dated 1848, on panel.
36½ x 12½ins. (93 x 32cm). *Christie's.*

Opposite right: CHARLES VAN DEN DAELE. The suitor
surprised. Signed, on panel. 27⅞ x 36¼ins. (70.5 x 92cm).
Christie's.

HENRI DE BRAEKELEER. A welcome message. Signed,
on panel. 20 x 18ins. (50.5 x 47cm).

JOHANNES ANTONIUS CANTA. The wedding party. Signed and dated 1843, on panel. 30¾ x 40ins. (78 x 101.5cm). *Sotheby's.*

FERDINAND WAGNER. The vegetable market. Signed.
61½ x 95½ins. (156 x 242.5cm). *Christie's.*

HUBERTUS VAN HOVE. A Dutch interior. Signed and
dated 1842, on panel. 26½ x 21¼ins. (67.5 x 54cm).
Christie's.

HENRI DUBOIS. The evening meal. On panel, signed and
dated 1861. 23½ x 18ins. (60 x 45.5cm). *Sotheby's.*

ALFRED W. ELMORE. An interesting story. Signed with
monogram, on panel. 17¼ x 20½ins. (44 x 52cm). *Christie's.*

HEINRICH ANTON HEGER. The connoisseur. Signed,
on panel. 17⅞ x 24ins. (45 x 61cm). *Christie's.*

GUSTAV ANTOON FRANÇOIS HEIJLIGERS. An
elegant lady standing at the foot of a staircase. Signed and
dated Brussels 1873, on panel. 18½ x 14¼ins. (47 x 36cm).
Christie's.

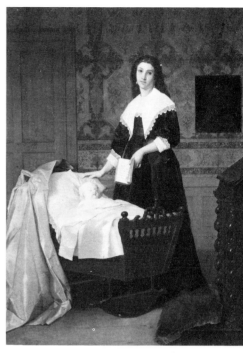

JEAN DE LA HOESE. Feeding the parrot. Signed and dated 73, on panel. 26¾ x 17½ins. (68 x 44.5cm). *Christie's.*

ROSA HOHENBERG. Bedtime. Signed and inscribed München, on panel. 25½ x 16¼ins. (65 x 41cm). *Christie's.*

PETRUS RENIER HUBERTUS KNARREN. The first born. Signed, on panel. 31 x 25ins. (78.5 x 63.5cm).

PETRUS KREMER. Rachel Ruysch in her studio. Signed and dated 1857, on panel. 35½ x 28ins. (90 x 71cm). *Christie's.*

AUGUST JOHANN HOLMBERG. Reciting the catechism. Signed. 29¾ x 34¾ins. (75.5 x 88cm). *Christie's.*

BARON HENDRIK LEYS. A Dutch interior with an old woman, a maid and child. Signed, on panel. 33½ x 29½ ins. (85 x 75cm). *Christie's.*

WILLEM LINNIG. A woman in an interior. On panel. 19¾ x 15ins. (50 x 38cm). *Christie's.*

JOHANNES CORNELIUS MERTZ. Two elegant ladies at table. Signed and dated 1858, and signed and authenticated and dated Bruges aôut 1858 on a label on the reverse. 20 x 16½ins. (51 x 42cm). *Sotheby's.*

CLAUS MEYER. The smoker. Signed, on panel. 13½ x 10½ins. (34 x 26.5cm). *Christie's.*

FRANS MOORMANS. An interesting story. Signed, indistictly inscribed and dated 1856(?) on panel. 27⅞ x 35½ins. (70.5 x 90.5cm). *Christie's.*

ANDRÉ PLUMOT. An elegant family in an interior. Signed and dated 1864. 22¼ x 31¾ ins. (56.5 x 80.5cm). *Christie's.*

HUBERT WILLEM VAN DER PLAATZER. Lovers in an interior. Signed and dated 1836. 15¼ x 12¼ ins. (38.5 x 31cm). *Sotheby's.*

JOS RATINCKX. The alchemist. Signed, on panel. 14 x 10½ ins. (35.6 x 26.5cm). *Christie's.*

ARTHUR GEORG VON RAMBERG. Nach Tisch. Signed, on panel. 31¼ x 40¼ ins. (79.7 x 102.3cm). *Munich, Neue Pinakothek.*

HENDRIK JACOBUS SCHOLTEN. At the inn. Signed, on panel.
16 x 21¼ins. (41 x 54cm). *Sotheby's.*

ALFRED VON SCHRÖTTER. At the notary. Signed and
dated Mch. '85, on panel. 15 x 18½ins. (38 x 47cm).
Sotheby's.

CORNEILLE SEGHERS. The music lesson. Signed, on
panel. 17½ x 14½ins. (44.5 x 37cm). *Sotheby's.*

CARL SÖHN. Dessert. Signed and
dated D'dorf 81. 25¾ x 32¾ ins.
(65.5 x 83cm). *Christie's.*

LOUIS TIELEMANS. The garden
party. Signed and dated 1853.
22 x 27¼ ins. (56 x 69cm). *Christie's.*

KAREL FERDINAND CHARLES VENNEMAN. Peasants drinking in an interior. Signed, on panel. 10¼ x 8¼ ins. (26 x 21cm). *Christie's.*

Bottom left: ADRIEN JOSEPH VERHOEVEN-BALL. Rubens at work in his studio. Signed and dated 1852. 39½ x 49¼ ins. (100 x 125cm). *Christie's.*

HENRICUS TURKEN. An elegant family in an interior. Signed, on panel. 31¼ x 26¼ ins. (79.5 x 66.5cm). *Christie's.*

FRANS KASPAR HUIBRECHT VINCK. An elegant Dutch couple seated near a canal. Signed with monogram, on panel. 14¼ x 11ins. (36 x 28cm). *Sotheby's.*

MAX VOLKHART. His mistress's voice.
Signed. 17 x 10¾ins. (43 x 27cm). *Christie's.*

FRITZ WAGNER. The lute player. Signed and inscribed
Mchn. 24 x 20ins. (61 x 51cm). *Christie's.*

FLORENT WILLEMS. Baby brother. Signed and dated
1864, on panel. 23½ x 19¾ins. (60 x 50cm). *Christie's.*

FRANZ XAVIER WOLFE. A musical interlude. Signed and
stamped with the artist's seal on the reverse, on panel.
23 x 19½ins. (58.5 x 49.5cm). *Christie's.*

Eighteenth Century Genre

Eighteenth century genre comes in many shapes and forms; interminable scenes from *The Vicar of Wakefield*; elegant beaux mooning about in agonies of unrequited love; dashing gentlemen of the Directoire enjoying a practical joke. There can be no doubt that the later nineteenth century looked back a hundred years with enthralment, and artists catered for this fascination with pictures set in the later eighteenth century which emphasied, on as intimate and trivial level as possible, those aspects of the time which particularly captured the imagination. Of course, the obsession with the century that had gone before was part of the wider reinterpretation of history painting which saw cavaliers, Greeks and Romans all reduced to banal levels for the edification of the bourgeoisie. But contemporarily this process was welcomed and justified (by Richard Muther, for instance) as 'the victory over pseudo-idealism'. It was claimed that artists like Meissonier in France and Menzel in Germany attained a realism which emancipated history painting from empty academic histrionics.

It is easy to see how such a claim could have been made at the time. Menzel's series of scenes from the life of Frederick the Great, which recreated many of the monarch's private moments as opposed to his heroic ones, must have come as singularly refreshing to a public worn out with 'grand' history painting of indifferent quality. As for Meissonier, his contemporary popularity, both in France and internationally, was extraordinary. He combined brilliant technique with painstaking research to produce pictures of eighteenth century readers, philosophers and cardplayers, generally on a minute scale, which had connoisseurs reaching for their magnifying glasses in much the same way that art lovers were wont to observe the minute touch of Terborch. The very Meissonier that they were studying in such detail might very well itself show a scene of bewigged and powdered connoisseurs closely examining a picture (a Terborch or van Mieris?); thus the Meissonier collector felt himself agreeably part of an honourable aesthetic tradition, saw himself indeed reflected in his own picture, a recipe for commercial success on Meissonier's part that it would have been hard to better.

Today, it would be impossible to mistake a Meissonier for a Chardin, but contemporary admirers were under a familiar illusion of authenticity about his recreations of the eighteenth century:

> It is not a man of today that he clothes with the vestments of another time; there is a perfect accord between the physiognomy, the carriage, the costume of him as represented, and the accessories with which he enriches his picture.

This was Rene Menard's confident opinion. With the aid of a new erudition and antiquarian scholarship, painters like Meissonier felt prepared to give renderings of the domestic side of history which would in their expectation stand up to the scrutiny of the future. He was to be disappointed. In fact his legacy to his followers (of whom there were many of little talent) was to set a precedent for trivial costume drama. As one French commentator at the end of the century rather bitterly put it:

> He is directly responsible for the distortion of models into men of muscular calves and noses like trumpets, for the maids who dust the fake Meissen, the Marquises dreaming over yesterday's stew, and the soldiers less inclined to fight than to have one too many to drink.

The trouble was that Meissonier was infinitely imitable: in London, Munich, Rome and Vienna painters recreated the eighteenth century on a scale of intimacy which would have been beyond them had it not been for the example of the master. Indeed, national stylistic characteristics were submerged in this striving to emulate, and it is hard to tell apart on this basis works by Johan Hamza (Austrian), Carl Seiler (German), the Belgian Madou, Cesare August Detti (Italian) and Meissonier himself. In their eagerness to attain the much-vaunted Meissonier 'serenity' (considered a particularly authentic characteristic of the eighteenth century), his followers often captured no more than a sense of futile inactivity. Costume was everything: as Alfred Stevens remarked, 'the public are attracted to costume subjects in the same way that they fall in love with the fancy-dress of a masked ball.'

English painters frequently favoured anecdotalism in their treatments of eighteenth century subjects, perhaps as a result of their initial reliance on literary sources for subject matter. C.R. Leslie, for instance, drew on Pope, Addison, Swift, Fielding, Sterne, Smollett and Goldsmith for incidents to illustrate. From the representation of eighteenth century domestic scenes with a literary pretext to entirely imaginary reconstructions was a small jump, and it was soon taken. The way was open for Marcus Stone: no Royal Academy show of the 1880s or 1890s was complete without an offering from him set in Regency England or Directoire France, generally centered upon some affair of the heart. The idea of that time being one of full-blooded romance and passionate intrigue is doubtless legitimate, but what Stone gives us is not Byron but Barbara Cartland. A typical title would be 'Il y en a toujours un autre'. A link is forged with the spectator by that 'toujours'. Times may change, Stone is saying, but certain abiding human truths remain, and being in love is the same in 1790, 1890, or any other date.

The eighteenth century assumed an almost mythic significance for bourgeois Europe of a hundred years later. The Goncourts rediscovered it and elevated it into an Arcadia on a par with antiquity. And indeed its attractions were manifold. It was the age of elegance, a commodity which a surprising number of people felt to be sorely lacking contemporarily. The artist G.A. Storey claimed

> There can be no doubt that want of taste in dress and other surroundings often obliges the artist to present his fancies in the costumes of periods when articles of clothing were in themselves works of art, instead of in the shifting fashions of the day that in a year or two not only look out of date, but stand forth in all their native ugliness and vulgarity.

He was echoing a favourite contention of Meissonier himself:

> In former times men respected their own persons. The graceful gesture, the harmonious attitude... was not a mere pose. Men in those days were careful about their bearing.

Nor was it surprising that the new rich should look back with admiration and even nostalgia to a society in which the aristocrat held sway. Emulation of aristocratic taste, and acquisition of social respectability was surely at the root of the vogue for English eighteenth century portraiture at the end of the nineteenth century. Bourgeois patrons were also entranced by an image of the sheer luxury of the previous century. On the Continent there developed a genre of picture set in that time in which the importance of the human action diminished. Such scenes might have titles like *A Whispered Confidence* or *The Billet Doux*, none of them themes arresting in their novelty, but existing more as a pretext for showing extremely elegant people in utterly luxurious surroundings. Reggianini, Ricci, Soulacroix and others dwelt lovingly on the richness of texture in the ladies' dresses and in the upholstery and draperies. Magnificent furniture was rendered in all its pristine glory. A materialistic society was paying its respects of another society of wealth in which money had not created more and more factories and coal-mines but more and more muslin and brocade, not railways but sedan chairs, not grossness but refinement.

Taste, elegance, and luxury, then, were keynotes in the pictorial reinterpretation of the age which artists undertook a hundred years later. Another was a rather prissy joie-de-vivre which was felt to be a characteristic of life in, for instance, the Directoire. F.H. Kaemmerer was a Paris-based Dutchman who claimed to chronicle its 'highways and byways'. He was particularly praised contemporarily for his 'little ladies' of that period, beings who 'do not stand or walk or sit, they trip and dance and jaunt'. This image of the Directoire seems hard to reconcile with what we know of it from David's portraiture, for example. Madame Recamier does not seem likely to 'trip and dance and jaunt', but no matter. Artists like Kaemmerer are a curious phenomenon. They were interpreting an earlier age for a later one, in terms in which the later one thought the former should have seen itself.

There was one further element which conditioned attitudes to the later eighteenth century. This was a wistful sense of 'so near and yet so far'. On the one hand Ward and Roberts wrote in 1904 of

> that society of the eighteenth century which had realised such a perfect art
> of living and with which we can clasp hands across the gulf as we cannot
> with the men and women of Charles II's time or even of Queen Anne's.

And on the other hand there was a widespread realisation that the industrial revolution had changed life, and perhaps the quality of life, irrevocably. The golden age of simple cosiness, rural prosperity, and picturesque innocence was gone forever, and therefore the more tantalisingly attractive. But artists strove to recapture it in genre scenes set in the period which attempted to highlight these qualities. The Biedermeyer period in Germany and Austria did actually produce some pictures which are genuine elegies to a rural golden age; later artists, however, were separated by too great an abyss — the chasm of the industrial revolution — to recreate anything more than mawkish costume pieces with titles like *The World went very well then*.

'I have always been struck by the aphorism that elegance and absurdity are divided from each other by a hair's breadth. Nothing could be truer,' wrote Meissonier, a remark which is singularly apt in relation to painters of eighteenth century genre. On which side of this narrow division Meissonier himself and his many followers are to be found may now be judged more clearly from the illustrations on the following pages.

Index of artists

AERNI, Franz Theodor (German, 1853-1918)
ALONZO-PEREZ, Mariano (Spanish, late 19th Century)
ALVAREZ, Luis (Spanish, 1836-1901)
AMBERG, Wilhelm (German, 1822-1899)
ANDREOTTI, Federico (Italian, 1847-1930)
ANDREWS, Henry (British, fl.1830-1860)
ANTONIO, Cristobal de (Spanish, late 19th Century)
APPERT, Pauline (French, 1810-?)
AYLWARD, James D. (British, late 19th Century)

BAKALOWICZ, Ladislaus (Polish, 1833-?)
BARBAGLIA, Giuseppe (Italian, 1841-1910)
BARNES, Edward Charles (British, ?-1882)
BARRAUD, Francis (British, ?-1924)
BAYARD, Emile Antoine (French, 1837-1891)
BAYES, Alfred Walter (British, 1832-1909)
BEDA, Francesco (Italian, 1840-1900)
BEDINI, Paolo Giovanni (Italian, 1844-1924)
BENNETT, Frank Moss (British, 1874-1953)
BESSON, Faustin (French, 1821-1882)
BEUCHOT, Jean Baptiste (French, 1821-?)
BLES, David Joseph (Dutch, 1821-1899)
BLUM, Maurice (French, 1832-?)
BOLDINI, Giovanni (Italian, 1842-1931)
BORNTRÄGER, Ludwig (German, ?-1852)
BOUCHERVILLE, Adrien de (French, ?-1912)
BOUGHTON, George Henry (British, 1833-1905)
BOUVIER, Pietro (Italian, 1839-1927)
BRACK, Emil (German, 1860-1905)
BREAKSPEARE, William A. (British, 1855-1914)
BRUGO, Giuseppe (Italian, late 19th Century)
BUCHNER, Hans (German, 1856-1941)
BULLOUIN, L. G. (French, late 19th Century)
BURMEISTER, Paul (German, 1847-?)

CACCIDRELLI, Victor (Italian, late 19th Century)
CALOSCI, Arturo (Italian, 1855-1926)
CANELLA, A. (Italian, late 19th Century)
CARAUD, Joseph (French, 1821-1905)
CAROLUS, Jean (Belgian, late 19th Century)
CASANOVA Y ESTORACH, Antonio (Spanish, 1847-1896)
CECCHI, Adriano (Italian, late 19th Century)
CECCONI, Lorenzo (Italian, 1867-?)
CEDERSTRÖM, Baron Ture Nikolaus (Swedish, 1843-1924)
CERIEZ, Théodore (Belgian, 1832-1904)
CERVI, G. (Italian, late 19th Century)
CHANET, Gustave (French, late 19th Century)
CHAVET, Victor Joseph (French, 1822-1906)
CHAVEZ Y ARTIZ, José de (Spanish, late 19th Century)
CIARDI, Emma (Italian, 1879-1933)
CIPOLLA, Fabio (Italian, 1854-?)
CODINA Y LANGLIN, Victoriano (Spanish, 1844-1911)
COESSIN DE LA FOSSE, Charles Alexandre (French, 1829-?)

COL, Jean David (Belgian, 1822-1900)
CONTI, Tito (Italian, 1842-1924)
COOKESLEY, Margaret Murray (British, ?-1927)
CORTAZZI, Oreste (Italian, 1836-?)
COSTA, Oreste (Italian, 1851-?)
CROEGAERT, Georges (French, 1848-?)

DALLA NOCE (Italian, late 19th Century)
DALSGAARD, Christen (Danish, 1824-1907)
DANSAERT, Léon Marie Constant (Belgian, 1830-1909)
DAVIDSON, Thomas (British, fl.1863-1893)
DELFOSSE, Eugène (Belgian, 1825-1865)
DETTI, Cesare Auguste (Italian, 1847-1914)
DEULLY, Eugène Auguste François (French, 1860-?)
DIDIONI, Francesco (Italian, 1859-1895)
DIVINI, Augusta (Italian, late 19th Century)
DOLLMAN, Herbert P. (British, 1856-?)
DOVASTON, Marie (British, late 19th and early 20th Century)
DOWNING, Delapoer (British, fl.1885-1902)
DRIENDL, Thomas (German, 1807-1853)
DULUARD, Hippolyte François Léon (French, 1871-?)
DYCK, Hermann (German, 1812-1874)

EERELMAN, Otto (Dutch, 1839-1926)
ENDE, Felix von (German, 1856-?)
ERDMANN, Otto (German, 1834-1905)

FAUVELET, Jean Baptiste (French, 1819-1883)
FAVRETTO, Giacomo (Italian, 1849-1887)
FERRAGUTI, Arnaldo (Italian, 1862-1925)
FICHEL, Benjamin Eugène (French, 1826-1895)
FLAMENG, François (French, 1856-1923)
FORNARI, E. (Italian, late 19th Century)
FORTUNY Y CARBO, Mariano (Spanish, 1838-1874)
FOX, George (British, fl.1873-1889)
FRANGIAMORE, Salvatore (Italian, 1853-1915)
FRANKE, Albert Joseph (German, 1860-1924)
FRITH, William Powell (British, 1819-1909)

GABRINI, Pietro (Italian, 1856-1926)
GAISSER, Jakob Emanuel (German, 1825-1899)
GAISSER, Max (German, 1857-1922)
GARLAND, Charles Trevor (British, ?-1901)
GARRIDO, Eduardo Leon (Spanish, 1856-1906)
GATTI, Annibale (Italian, 1828-1909)
GAUGENGIGL, Ignaz Marcel (German, 1855-1932)
GAUPP, Gustav Adolf (German, 1844-1918)
GIACHI, E. (Italian, late 19th Century)
GIERYMSKI, Alexander (Polish, 1849-1901)
GILARDI, Pier Celestino (Italian, 1837-1905)
GIMENO, Andrés (Spanish, 1879-?)
GISBERT, Antonio (Spanish, 1835-1870)
GIULIANO, Bartolomeo (Italian, 1825-1909)
GLIBERT, Albert (Belgian, 1832-1917)
GLINDONI, Henry Gillard (British, 1852-1913)
GONZALES, Juan Antonio (Spanish, 1842-?)

GORDON, Robert James (British, fl.1871-1893)
GRISON, François Adolphe (French, 1845-1914)
GRÖNVOLD, Marcus Fredrik Steen (Norwegian, 1845-1929)
* GUARDEBASSI, Guerrino (Italian, 1841-?)
* GUILLEMIN, Alexandre Marie (French, 1817-1880)

HAINES, William Henry (British, 1812-1884)
* HAMZA, Johann (Austrian, 1850-1927)
HAUG, Robert von (German, 1857-1922)
HEILBUTH, Ferdinand (German, 1826-1889)
* HENNINGS, Johann Friedrich (German, 1838-1899)
* HERNANDEZ, Daniel (Peruvian-Italian, 1856-1932)
* HERPFER, Carl (German, 1836-1897)
HERRISON, Louis François (French, 1811-1859)
HILLINGFORD, Robert Alexander (British, 1828-1902)
HOFFMAN, Anton (German, 1863-1938)
* HOLYOAKE, Rowland (British, 1834-1894)
HORSLEY, John Calcott (British, 1817-1903)
HUGHES, Arthur (British, 1832-1915)
* HUGHES, Edwin (British, fl.1861-1892)
HUGHES, Talbot (British, 1869-1942)

* INDUNO, Gerolamo (Italian, 1827-1890)
* INNOCENTI, Guglielmo (Italian, late 19th Century)
* ISABEY, Eugène Louis Gabriel (French, 1803-1886)

* JIMINEZ Y ARANDA, José (Spanish, 1837-1903)
JIMINEZ Y ARANDA, Luis (Spanish, 1845-1928)

* KAEMMERER, Frederik Hendrik (Dutch, 1839-1902)
* KEMENDY, Jeno Eugen (Austrian, 1860-1925)
KENNEDY, Edward Sherard (British, fl.1863-1890)
KERCKHOVE, Ernest van der (Belgian, 1840-1879)
* KILBURNE, George Goodwin (British, 1839-1924)
KLEINMICHEL, Ferdinand Theodor (German, 1846-1892)
KLIMT, Ernst (Austrian, 1864-1892)
KLIMT, Gustav (Austrian, 1862-1918)
KNOOP, Hermann, August (German, 1856-1900)
KNOWLES, George Sheridan (British, 1863-1931)
* KOCH, Hermann (German, 1856-?)
* KRATKÉ, Charles Louis (French, 1848-1921)
KRONBERG, Julius Johan Ferdinand (Swedish, 1850-1921)
KUEHL, Gotthardt Johann (German, 1850-1915)

LANCEROTTO, Egisto (Italian, 1847-1916)
* LANDINI, Andrea (Italian, 1847-?)
LARCHER, Emile (French, mid-19th Century)
* LEIGHTON, Edmund Blair (British, 1853-1922)
LELOIR, Maurice (French, 1853-1940)
LEON Y ESCOSURA, Ignacio (Spanish, 1834-1901)
* LEPAGE, J. (French, late 19th Century)
LESLIE, Charles Robert (British, 1794-1859)
LESREL, Adolphe Alexandre (French, 1839-1890)
* LESUR, Victor Henri (French, 1863-1900?)
LEVIS, Max (German, 1863-?)
LEWIN, Stephen (British, late 19th and early 20th Century)
LEYENDECKER, Paul Joseph (French, 1842-?)
LINDER, Lambert (German, 1841-1889)
* LOGSDAIL, William (British, 1859-1944)
* LOMAX, John Arthur (British, 1857-1923)
* LOSSOW, Heinrich (German, 1843-1897)
* LOWCOCK, Charles Frederick (British, ?-1922)

* LÖWITH, Wilhelm (German, 1861-1931)
LUCAS, John Seymour (British, 1849-1923)
LUZZI, Cleto (Italian, late 19th Century)

MACLISE, Daniel (British, 1860-1943)
* McCORMICK, Arthur David (British, 1860-1943)
* MADOU, Jean Baptiste (Belgian, 1796-1877)
MAGGIORANI, Luigi (Italian, late 19th Century)
* MAILLOT, Théodore Pierre Nicolas (French, 1826-1888)
MANTEGAZZA, Giacomo (Italian, 1853-1920)
MARCHETTI, Ludovico (Italian, 1853-1909)
MARKELBACH, Alexandre Pierre Jacques (Belgian, 1824-1906)
MARSTRAND, Wilhelm Nicolai (Danish, 1810-1873)
MARTENS, Willem Johann (Dutch, 1838-1895)
* MARTINETTI, Angelo (Italian, late 19th Century)
MASSANI, Pompeo (Italian, 1850-1920)
* MATANIA, Fortunino (British, late 19th and early 20th Century)
MEISEL, Ernst (German, 1838-1895)
MEISSONIER, Jean Charles (French, 1848-1917)
* MEISSONIER, Jean Louis Ernest (French, 1815-1891)
* MELZMACHER, E. (German, late 19th Century)
* MENZEL, Adolph Friedrich Erdmann von (German, 1815-1905)
MENZLER, Wilhelm (German, 1846-?)
MEYER, Beatrice (French, late 19th Century)
* MOCHI, Giovanni (Italian, 1829-1892)
MONFALLET, Adolphe François (French, 1816-1900)
MOREAU, Adrien (French, 1843-1906)
MORO, Ferrucio (Italian, 1859-?)
* MORRIS, Philip Richard (British, 1836-1902)
* MULREADY, Augustus E. (British, fl.1863-1905)
* MUNSCH, Joseph (German, 1832-1896)

NAVONE, Edoardo (Italian, fl.1873-1887)
* NUNES-VAIS, Italo (Italian, 1860-?)

OLIVER, William (British, fl.1867-1882)
* ORCHARDSON, Sir William Quiller (British, 1832-1910)
* ORSELLI, Arturo (Italian, late 19th Century)
* OUTIN, Pierre (French, 1839-1899)

PALMAROLI Y GONZALES, Vincente (Spanish, 1834-1896)
PANERAI, Ruggero (Italian, 1862-1923)
* PARADES, Vicenta de (Spanish, ?1850-?)
PASCUTTI, Antonio (Austrian, late 19th Century)
PASSINI, Ludwig Johann (Austrian, 1832-1903)
PAYTON, Joseph (British, fl.1861-1870)
* PECRUS, Charles François (French, 1826-1907)
PELLEGRIN, Louis Antonin Victor (French, 1836-1884)
PELUSO, Francesco (Italian, 1836-?)
PIPPICH, Carl (Austrian, 1862-1932)
PLASSAN, Antoine Emile (French, 1817-1903)
* POMPEUS, Carlo (Italian, late 19th Century)
* PONCELET, Maurice Georges (French, late 19th Century)
* PONTES, André de (Spanish, late 19th Century)
POTT, Laslett John (British, 1837-1898)
PRIECHENFRIED, Alois Heinrich (Austrian, 1867-1953)
PRIETO, Mario Jiminez (Spanish, late 19th Century)

RANDADINI, Carlo (Italian, ?-1884)
RASCH, Heinrich (German, 1840-1913)
RAUDNITZ, Albert (German, fl.1873-1892)
* REGGIANINI, Vittorio (Italian, 1858-?)
* REID, George Ogilvy (British, 1851-1928)
* REISZ, Hermann (Austrian, 1865-?)
REYNTJENS, Henricus Engelbertus (Dutch, 1817-1878)
* RICCI, Arturo (Italian, late 19th Century)
* ROEHN, Jean Adolphe Alphonse (French, 1799-1864)
ROSATI, Giulio (Italian, late 19th Century)
ROSIER, Jean Guillaume (Dutch, 1858-1931)
* ROSSI, Lucius (French, 1846-1913)
* RUBEN, Franz Leo (Austrian, 1842-1920)

* SADLER, Walter Dendy (British, 1854-1923)
SALA, Emilio (Spanish, 1850-1910)
SANCHEZ BARBUDO, Salvador (Spanish, 1857-1913)
* SANDERSON-WELLS, John (British, 1872-1955)
SANTA CRUZ Y BUSTAMENTE, Ramiro de (Spanish,
    late 19th Century)
SCHEURENBERG, Josef (German, 1846-1914)
SCHIVERT, Victor (Austrian, 1863-?)
* SCHRAMM, Alois Hans (Austrian, 1864-1919)
SCHURIG, Felix (German, 1852-1907)
* SCHWENINGER, Carl (Austrian, 1818-1887)
SEEBACH, Lothar Hans Emmanuel von (German,
    1853-1930)
SEILER, Carl Wilhelm Anton (German, 1846-1921)
* SERRA Y PORSON, José (Spanish, 1824-1910)
SERRURE, Auguste (Belgian, 1825-1903)
* SHADE, William Auguste (German-American,
    1848-1890)
SIMM, Franz Xaver (Austrian, 1853-1918)
SIMMONS, Paul Henri (French, 1865-1932)
SLOCOMBE, Frederick Albert (British, 1847-?)
SOLDENHOFF, Alexander Jules Jakob (Polish,
    1849-1902)
SORBI, Raffaello (Italian, 1844-1931)
* SOULACROIX, Charles Joseph Frederic (French,
    1825-?)

* SPIRIDON, Ignace (Italian, late 19th Century)
STELTZNER, Heinrich (German, 1833-1910)
* STIEPEVICH, Vincent (Russian, late 19th Century)
* STOLTENBERG-LERCHE, Vincent (Danish,
    1837-1892)
* STONE, Marcus (British, 1840-1921)
STOREY, George Adolphus (British, 1834-1919)

TARENGHI, Enrico (Italian, 1848-?)
* TEN KATE, Herman Frederik Carel (Dutch, 1822-1891)
TENRÉ, Charles Henry (French, 1864-1926)
TICHY, Hans (Austrian, 1861-1925)
* TISSOT, James Joseph (French, 1836-1902)
TORDI, Sinibaldo (Italian, 1876-1955)
* TORRINI, Pietro (Italian, 1852-?)
TOUDOUZE, Edouard (French, 1848-1907)

* VERNON, Arthur Langley (British, fl.1871-1922)
* VILLEGAS Y CORDERO, José (Spanish, 1848-1922)
VINIEGRA Y LASSO, Salvador (Spanish, 1862-1915)
VIRY, Paul Alphonse (French, late 19th Century)
VOLKHART, Max (German, 1848-1935)

* WALLER, Samuel Edmund (British, 1850-1903)
WATTIER, Charles Émile (French, 1800-1868)
* WEISS, Emile Georges (French, 1861-?)
* WEISZ, Adolphe (Austrian, 1838-?)
WERNER, Alexander Friedrich (German, 1827-1908)
* WILLIS, Charles (British, late 19th Century)
* WOLF, Franz Xavier (Austrian, late 19th Century)
* WOOD, Charles Haigh (British, 1856-1927)
* WRIGHT, Gilbert Scott (British, late 19th Century)
* WYNGAERDT, Petrus Theodorus (Dutch, 1816-1893)

* YEAMES, William Frederick (British, 1835-1918)

ZEWY, Karl (Austrian, 1855-1929)
* ZOPPI, Antonio (Italian, 1860-1926)

FRANZ THEODOR AERNI. Elegant figures on a terrace on the Palatine Hill, Rome. Signed and dated 'Rom 95'.
19 x 37½ins. (48 x 95cm). *Christie's.*

MARIANO ALONZO-PEREZ. Spring Love. Signed.
28¼ x 22½ins. (71.5 x 57cm). *Christie's.*

LUIS ALVAREZ. The dancing lesson. Signed and inscribed
Roma, on panel. 18½ x 14ins. (47 x 35.5cm). *Christie's.*

FRANZ LEO RUBEN. An elegant boating party. Signed. 25 x 40ins. (63.5 x 101.5cm). *Christie's.*

FEDERICO ANDREOTTI.
The suitor. Signed. 40 x 30ins.
(101.5 x76cm). *Christie's.*

HENRY ANDREWS. A fête champêtre with numerous figures playing cards and drinki
in a park. Signed. 42 x 66½ins. (106.5 x 169cm). *Christie's.*

CRISTOBAL DE ANTONIO.
The dandy and the flower girl.
Signed, on panel. 15¼ x 12¼ins.
(38.5 x 31cm). *Christie's.*

PAULINE APPERT. The flowerstall. Signed. 17½ x 23½ins. (44.5 x 59.5cm).
Sotheby's.

FRANCESCO BEDA. Elegant figures in a drawing room. Signed, and inscribed on the reverse. 39 x 59½ins. (99 x 151cm). *Christie's.*

PAOLO GIOVANNI BEDINI.
An attractive suggestion. Signed, on board.
10 x 6¼ins. (25.5 x 16cm). *Christie's.*

FRANK MOSS BENNETT. The hunt breakfast. Signed and dated 1949.
23½ x 29½ins. (59.5 x 75cm). *Christie's.*

FAUSTIN BESSON. The cherry pickers. Signed and dated 1858. 42¾ x 32ins. (108.5 x 81cm). *Christie's.*

JEAN BAPTISTE BEUCHOT. The new maid. Signed. 21½ x 19½ins. (54.5 x 49.5cm). *Sotheby's.*

MAURICE BLUM. The letter. Signed and dated '73, on panel. 17½ x 12¾ins. (44.5 x 32.5cm). *Christie's.*

LUDWIG BORNTRÄGER. Taking coffee with friends. Signed and dated Anvers 1858. 15¼ x 12½ins. (38.5 x 32cm). *Sotheby's.*

EMIL BRACK. The gift. Signed. 32 x 27¼ins.
(81 x 69.5cm). *Sotheby's.*

WILLIAM A. BREAKSPEARE. The tiff.
Signed. 27¼ x 20¼ins. (69 x 51.5cm). *Christie's.*

GIUSEPPE BRUGO. The eavesdropper. Signed and dated 1894.
27 x 16½ins. (68.5 x 42cm). *Christie's.*

HANS BUCHNER. The suitor. Signed and inscribed München.
22 x 26½ins. (56 x 67cm). *Christie's.*

A. CANELLA. An elegant sitter. Signed.
24 x 32ins. (61 x 81.5cm). *Christie's.*

JEAN CAROLUS. The dressmaker's visit.
Signed and dated Bruxelles 1866. 34 x 48¼ins.
(86.5 x 122.5cm). *Christie's.*

ADRIANO CECCHI. An appreciative audience.
Signed and inscribed Florence. 16¾ x 22¼ins.
(42.5 x 56.5cm). *Christie's.*

LORENZO CECCONI. A conversation in a classical garden. Signed and inscribed Roma. 20 x 36½ins. (51 x 93cm). *Christie's.*

EMMA CIARDI. Primavera. Signed
and dated Venezia 1923, and inscribed
on the reverse. 29 x 26½ins.
(73.5 x 67cm). *Christie's.*

VICTORIANO CODINA Y LANGLIN. News from a friend. Signed, on panel. 17⅞ x 14½ins. (45 x 37cm). *Christie's.*

TITO CONTI. The secret admirer. Signed and dated 1871, on panel. 13¼ x 9¾ins. (34 x 24.5cm). *Christie's.*

ORESTE CORTAZZI. Playing the lute. Signed. 16 x 13ins. (40.5 x 33cm). *Christie's.*

ORESTE COSTA. A musical party. Signed and inscribed Firenze and again on the reverse. 25¼ x 41¾ins. (64 x 106cm). *Christie's.*

GEORGES CROEGAERT. The letter. Signed and inscribed Paris, on panel. 13¼ x 9½ins. (34 x 24cm). *Christie's.*

DALLA NOCE. An amusing correspondence. Signed. 18 x 14ins. (46 x 35.5cm). *Christie's.*

EUGÈNE DELFOSSE. The laughing stock. Signed and dated 1859. 28¼ x 22¾ins. (71.5 x 58cm). *Christie's.*

CHRISTEN DALSGAARD. The suitor's arrival.
Signed and dated Søro 1880, and inscribed on a
label on the reverse. 36 x 28½ins. (91.5 x 72.5cm).
Sotheby's.

Top right: CESARE AUGUSTE DETTI. Flowers
for her ladyship. Signed and dated Roma '75.
12 x 16ins. (30.5 x 40.5cm). *Christie's.*

EUGÈNE AUGUSTE FRANÇOIS DEULLY.
The fortune teller. Signed. 18 x 23½ins.
(45.5 x 60cm). *Christie's.*

FRANCESCO DIDIONI. Raisons d'Etat.
Signed, signed with monogram and dated
Milano 1877 on the reverse. 27½ x 59ins.
(70 x 150cm). *Sotheby's.*

FELIX VON ENDE. The suitor. Signed and inscribed München.
26 x 39ins. (66 x 99cm). *Christie's.*

THOMAS DRIENDL. The letter. Signed and
dated München 1878, on panel. 19¼ x 12½ins.
(49 x 31.5cm). *Sotheby's.*

OTTO ERDMANN. Reading the will. Signed and dated DF 86. 38½ x 49½ins.
(97.5 x 125.5cm). *Christie's.*

JEAN BAPTISTE FAUVELET.
The connoisseur. Signed, on panel.
9½ x 7¼ins. (24 x 18.5cm).

BENJAMIN EUGÈNE FICHEL.
The conjuror. Signed and dated
1882. 14½ x 21ins. (37 x 53.5cm).
Christie's.

FRANÇOIS FLAMENG. The reception for Napoleon I, Isola Bella, in the fifth year of his reign. Signed, on panel.
41¼ x 55½ins. (105 x 141cm). *Christie's.*

E. FORNARI. Elegant figures seated by a fountain. Signed and inscribed Roma, on panel. 17⅞ x 30ins. (45 x 76.5cm). *Christie's*.

GEORGE FOX. A legal wrangle. Signed, and signed on the reverse, on board. 9¾ x 13¾ins. (24.5 x 35cm). *Christie's*.

SALVATORE FRANGIAMORE. The unwelcome suitor. Signed and inscribed Roma. 23½ x 19¼ins. (59.5 x 49cm). *Christie's*.

ALBERT JOSEPH FRANKE. The connoisseurs. Signed, on panel. 11¼ x 9¼ins. (28.5 x 23.5cm). *Christie's*.

EDUARDO LEON GARRIDO. The ball. Signed.
31 x 38½ins. (78.5 x 98cm). *Christie's.*

Left: PIETRO GABRINI. In the gondola. Signed.
18¾ x 13¾ins. (47.5 x 35cm). *Christie's.*

E. GIACHI. The flirtation. Signed. 38½ x 28ins.
(98 x 71cm). *Christie's.*

PIER CELESTINO GILARDI. The gem of the portfolio.
Signed and dated 1881, on panel. 9 x 8ins. (23 x 20.5cm).
Sotheby's.

BARTOLOMEO GIULIANO. The embarkation. Signed and dated 1899. 16¼ x 21½ins. (41 x 54.5cm). *Christie's*.

Right: GUERRINO GUARDEBASSI. Fishing in the lily pond. Signed and dated 1875, and signed, inscribed Roma and dated 1875 on the reverse. 16¾ x 11¼ins. (42.5 x 28.5cm). *Christie's*.

ALEXANDRE MARIE GUILLEMIN. The finishing touch. Signed and dated '49, on panel. 12½ x 9¼ins. (32 x 23.5cm). *Christie's*.

JOHANN HAMZA. The connoisseur. Signed and inscribed Wien, on panel. 10¼ x 8ins. (26 x 20cm). *Christie's*.

JOHANN FRIEDRICH HENNINGS. After church. Signed and inscribed München. 33¾ x 44¼ins. (85.5 x 112.5cm). *Christie's.*

DANIEL HERNANDEZ. Flirtation. Signed and inscribed Roma, on panel. 10½ x 7ins. (26.5 x 18cm). *Christie's.*

CARL HERPFER. The wedding party. Signed and inscribed Munchen. 62 x 44ins. (157 x 111.5cm). *Christie's.*

ROWLAND HOLYOAKE. The arrival. Signed.
16 x 11¾ins. (40.5 x 31cm). *Christie's.*

EDWIN HUGHES. No fool like the old fool. Signed and dated
1889, and signed and inscribed on a label on the reverse.
24½ x 23¼ins. (62 x 59cm). *Christie's.*

GEROLAMO INDUNO. The private recital. Signed and dated
1872. 21¼ x 29ins. (54 x 73.5cm). *Christie's.*

GUGLIELMO INNOCENTI. The puppet. Signed and
dated Roma 1872, on panel. 17¼ x 21¼ins. (44 x 54cm).
Christie's.

EUGÈNE LOUIS GABRIEL ISABEY. Madame est servie.
Signed with initials and dated '53. 14 x 10¼ins. (35.5 x 26cm).
Sotheby's.

JOSÉ JIMINEZ Y ARANDA. The news. Signed and dated
Paris 1884, on panel. 21 x 27¼ins. (53 x 69cm). *Christie's.*

JENO EUGEN KEMÉNDY. Bibliophiles. Signed and dated
München 1888. 8 x 10ins. (20.5 x 25.5cm).

FREDERIK HENDRIK KAEMMERER. The wedding,
church of Saint Roch, Paris. Signed. 39½ x 32ins.
(100.5 x 81.5cm). *Christie's.*

ARTURO RICCI. The reception. Signed. 26 x 36ins. (66 x 91.5cm). *Christie's.*

MARCUS STONE. Love at first sight. Signed. 12 x 20ins. (30.5 x 51cm). *Christie's.*

GEORGE GOODWIN KILBURNE.
Hearts are trumps. Signed. 40¼ x 30¼ins.
(102 x 77cm). *Christie's.*

HERMANN KOCH. The young lovers. Signed and inscribed München.
36¼ x 63ins. (92 x 160cm). *Christie's.*

CHARLES LOUIS KRATKÉ. An attentive audience. Signed and dated 1875. 35¼ x 45¾ins. (89.5 x 116cm).
Christie's.

ANDREA LANDINI. Patience. Signed. 17⅞ x 14¾ins. (45 x 37.5cm). *Christie's.*

Right: EDMUND BLAIR LEIGHTON. My next-door neighbour. Signed and dated 1894. 32 x 19½ins. (81 x 49.5cm). *Christie's.*

J. LEPAGE. The connoisseurs. Signed. 13½ x 10ins. (34 x 25.5cm). *Christie's.*

VICTOR HENRI LESUR. Rendez-vous in the Tuileries, Paris. Signed, on panel. 17 x 23½ins. (43 x 59.5cm). *Christie's.*

WILLIAM LOGSDAIL. In the Piazzetta; eighteenth century. Signed. 64 x 47½ins. (160.5 x 120.5cm). *Christie's.*

JOHN ARTHUR LOMAX. The art critic. Signed, on panel. 11½ x 15¼ins. (29 x 39cm). *Christie's.*

HEINRICH LOSSOW. The Sphinx. Signed and dated 1868. 45½ x 34ins. (115.5 x 86.5cm). *Christie's.*

CHARLES FREDERICK LOWCOCK. The duet. Signed and dated '83. 17½ x 13ins. (44.5 x 33cm). *Christie's.*

WILHELM LÖWITH. The artist's studio. Signed, on panel. 11½ x 9½ins. (29 x 24cm). *Christie's.*

ARTHUR DAVID McCORMICK. The promenade. Signed. 39¼ x 49¼ins. (99.5 x 125cm). *Christie's.*

JEAN BAPTISTE MADOU. La cruche casée. Signed and dated 1866, on panel. 22½ x 32½ins. (57 x 82.5cm). *Christie's.*

THÉODORE PIERRE NICOLAS MAILLOT. Chez le perruquier. Signed and dated 1861, on panel. 20½ x 25ins. (52 x 63.5cm). *Christie's.*

ANGELO MARTINETTI. A tantalising present. Signed.
25 x 18½ins. (63.5 x 47cm). *Christie's.*

FORTUNINO MATANIA. A fine performance. Signed.
21¾ x 30ins. (55 x 76.5cm). *Christie's.*

JEAN LOUIS ERNEST MEISSONIER. An artist showing
his work. Signed with monogram. 14½ x 11¼ins. (37 x 29cm).
*Reproduced by permission of the Trustees, The Wallace Collection,
London.*

ADOLPH FRIEDRICH ERDMANN VON MENZEL. The flute concert. 56½ x 81ins. (142 x 205cm). *National Gallery, Staatliche Museen Preussischer Kulturbesitz, West Berlin. Photo: Jörg P. Anders.*

E. MELZMACHER. An ardent suitor.
Signed and dated 1873, on panel.
20 x 14½ins. (51 x 36.5cm). *Christie's.*

GIOVANNI MOCHI. A walk in the garden.
Signed and dated 1874, on panel. 16¼ x 12¼ins.
(41 x 31cm). *Sotheby's.*

327

PHILIP RICHARD MORRIS. Waiting for the ferry. Signed. 14¾ x 23½ins. (37.5 x 60cm). *Christie's.*

AUGUSTUS E. MULREADY. The connoisseur. Signed and signed with initials, and signed and inscribed on an old label on the reverse, on panel. 10 x 12ins. (25.5 x 30.5cm). *Christie's.*

JOSEPH MUNSCH. The distraction. Signed, on panel. 11¾ x 15½ins. (30 x 39.5cm). *Christie's.*

ITALO NUNES-VAIS. The string of pearls. Signed. 26½ x 19½ins. (67 x 49.5cm). *Christie's.*

SIR WILLIAM QUILLER ORCHARDSON. The bill of sale. Signed and dated '76. 21½ x 32½ins. (54.5 x 82.5cm). *Christie's.*

ARTURO ORSELLI. Elegant figures picnicking. Signed. 30 x 40ins. (76 x 101.5cm). *Christie's.*

PIERRE OUTIN. Outside the inn. Signed. 34 x 26½ins. (86.5 x 67cm). *Christie's.*

VICENTA DE PARADES. The minuet. Signed. 15 x 21ins.
(38 x 53.5cm). *Christie's.*

MAURICE GEORGES PONCELET. The duet. Signed,
paper laid down on panel. 19½ x 14¼ins. (49.5 x 36cm).
Christie's.

CHARLES FRANÇOIS PECRUS. A sympathetic audience.
Signed and dated 58, on panel. 7½ x 5¾ins. (19 x 14.5cm).
Christie's.

ANDRÉ DE PONTES. Waiting on the ladies.
Signed, on panel. 19¾ x 15¾ins. (50 x 40cm).
Christie's.

Top right: CARLO POMPEUS. In the studio.
Signed. 20 x 31½ins. (50.5 x 80cm). *Christie's.*

Centre right: VITTORIO REGGIANINI. An
intimate conversation. Signed. 26¼ x 38ins.
(66.5 x 96.5cm). *Christie's.*

HERMANN REISZ. Entertaining the suitors.
Signed and dated '94 on panel. 12¼ x 10¼ins.
(31 x 26cm). *Sotheby's.*

GEORGE OGILVY REID. A quiet word. Signed. 11½ x 16¼ins.
(29 x 41cm). *Christie's.*

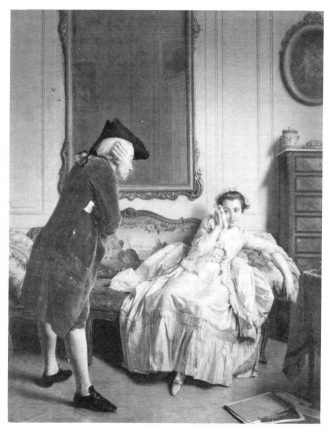

JEAN ADOLPHE ALPHONSE ROEHN. The scolding. Signed, on panel. 18 x 15ins. (46 x 38cm). *Sotheby's.*

LUCIUS ROSSI. A musical evening. Signed, on panel. 15¾ x 12½ins. (40 x 31.5cm). *Christie's.*

WALTER DENDY SADLER. Old and crusted. Signed and dated '88. 47½ x 33½ins. (120.5 x 85cm). *Christie's.*

JOHN SANDERSON-WELLS. The new tune. Signed, on panel. 9¾ x 13½ins. (24.5 x 34cm). *Christie's.*

ALOIS HANS SCHRAMM. Elegant girls on a terrace. Signed and dated 1897. 38 x 55ins. (96.5 x 140cm). *Sotheby's.*

CARL SCHWENINGER. The duet. Signed and inscribed Wien. 27 x 21¾ins. (68.5 x 55cm). *Christie's.*

JOSÉ SERRA Y PORSON. Admiring the Boucher. Signed and dated 1877, on panel. 9½ x 6ins. (24 x 15cm). *Christie's.*

CHARLES JOSEPH FREDÉRIC SOULACROIX. The lovers' tryst. Signed. 25½ x 32¾ins. (65 x 83cm). *Christie's.*

WILLIAM AUGUSTE SHADE. He loves me, he loves me not. Signed and dated 1877. 31 x 23½ins. (78.5 x 59.5cm). *Christie's.*

IGNACE SPIRIDON. The convalescence. Signed, on panel. 15¾ x 12½ins. (40 x 31.5cm). *Christie's.*

VINCENT STIEPERICH. Grandfather's joy. Signed and inscribed. Venice. 18 x 24¼ins. (46 x 61.5cm). *Sotheby's.*

HERMAN FREDERIK CAREL TEN KATE. The connoisseurs. Signed and dated 1859, on panel. 9¼ x 13ins. (23.5 x 33cm). *Christie's.*

VINCENT STOLTENBERG-LERCHE. The connoisseurs. Signed and dated '83. 24½ x 20¼ins. (62 x 51.5cm). *Christie's.*

JAMES JOSEPH TISSOT. Unaccepted. Signed and dated 1869. 15¾ x 12½ins. (40 x 32cm). *Christie's.*

PIETRO TORRINI. The tea party. Signed. 29½ x 24ins. (75 x 61cm). *Christie's.*

ARTHUR LANGLEY VERNON. The ferry. Signed. 11¾ x 18¼ins. (30 x 46.5cm). *Christie's.*

JOSÉ VILLEGAS Y CORDERO. Admiring the rapier. Signed and dated Sevilla 1876. 32½ x 24¾ins. (82.5 x 63cm). *Christie's.*

SAMUEL EDMUND WALLER. The empty saddle. Signed and dated 1879. 61 x 45½ins. (155 x 115.5cm). *Christie's.*

ADOLPHE WEISZ. The music lesson. Signed, on panel. 18 x 15ins. (45.5 x 38cm). *Christie's*.

EMILE GEORGES WEISS. Filling the pitchers. Signed and dated 89. 18 x 15ins. (46 x 38cm). *Christie's*.

CHARLES WILLIS. Rare prints. Signed and inscribed on the reverse. 20 x 26½ins. (51 x 67.5cm). *Christie's*.

PETRUS THEODORUS WYNGAERDT.
The recital. Signed 1866, on panel. 9¼ x 7½ins.
(23.5 x 19cm). *Christie's.*

Top left: FRANZ XAVIER WOLF. The concert.
Signed and inscribed on an old label on the
reverse, on panel. 19¼ x 21½ins. (50 x 54.5cm).
Christie's.

CHARLES HAIGH WOOD. In time of roses.
Signed. 37 x 48¾ins. (94 x 123cm). *Christie's.*

GILBERT SCOTT WRIGHT. The elopement.
Signed. 19¼ x 35¼ins. (49 x 89.5cm). *Christie's.*

WILLIAM FREDERICK YEAMES. The finishing touch. 49¾ x 79ins. (126.5 x 200.5cm). *Christie's.*

ANTONIO ZOPPI. A bouquet for the master. Signed and inscribed Firenze. 27¼ x 35¼ins. (69 x 89.5cm). *Christie's.*

Fairies and Fairy Tales

Fairies enjoyed a considerable vogue in the nineteenth century, and England especially nurtured painters whose speciality was scenes in which fairies disported. A century whose general characteristic is widely held to have been its materialism nonetheless took pleasure in such curious manifestations of the fantastic, both as an escape from modern life and in satisfaction of that demand for the exotic which is a constant if not always evident feature of the period.

The immediate roots of the phenomenon can be found in the rise of romanticism at the turn of the eighteenth to nineteenth century. 'The sleep of reason' encouraged many painters towards fantasy in their subject matter, and this taste is perhaps paralleled in literature by the feeling for the weird and supernatural in the gothic novels of Horace Walpole and William Beckford. Once again Shakespeare was mined for themes by painters, who now came up with the fairy scenes from *A Midsummer Night's Dream* and *The Tempest*. A literal minded critic who took Shakespeare to task for introducing fairies into the time of Theseus was himself set straight by the poet Thomas Campbell:

> If there were fairies in modern Europe, which no rational believer in fairy-tales will deny, why should these fine creatures not have existed previously in Greece, although the poor blind heathen Greeks, on whom the gospel of Gothic mythology had not yet dawned, had no conception of them?

Those whose taste inclined towards the Gothic rather than the classical were pleased to seize on fairies as 'the Gothic Mythology', an alternative to the mythology of the gods of Olympus. Thus Oberon and Titania superseded Apollo and Venus as the divinities of their imagination.

The English pictorial trait of devotion to detail, which reached its apotheosis in the Pre-Raphaelites, is well suited to fairy paintings. It is a technique which works well with pictures whose action is set in minutely observed foliage, where sparrows are giants and blades of grass are trees. The master of such things was surely Richard Dadd, whose intense labour on pictures like *The Fairy-Feller's Master Stroke* or *Titania and Oberon* betrays the single-mindedness of insanity.

The nineteenth century also saw a tremendous impetus given to the fairy tale, whose popularity spread across Europe. A large collection of traditional French stories was published in 41 volumes under the title *Cabinet des Fés* in 1785-89. In 1823-26 the Brothers Grimm first published their *Household Tales*, whose appeal and success were immediate and international, and later in the century Hans Christian Andersen delighted the world with his stories which were a mixture of traditional themes and works of his own imagination, flavoured with both satire and sentiment.

The written word stimulated artists across Europe to illustrate what they read. Comparison of their work suggests that certain national characteristics can be broadly attributed to the fairy painters of different countries. The German influence, for instance, as manifested in the Brothers Grimm, tended to emphasise hobgoblins, pixies and hags at the expense of the fairy ladies of the romances. Thus a painting such as Heinrich Schlitt's *The gnome artist* is

RICHARD DADD. Titania sleeping. 25½ x 30½ins. (65 x 77.5cm). *Christie's.*

typical: it shows a gnome at his easel in the shadow of a toadstool with a frog as his sitter. The gnarled, bearded and bespectacled little painter is very much in the Munich school tradition of 'gemütlich' old men, and might indeed have wandered out of a scene by Carl Spitzweg. The French on the other hand were more sophisticated, and enjoyed pictures of fairy ladies whose fleshly charms are more conspicuous than those of the ethereal wraiths who flit through the works of English painters like Huskisson and Noel Paton. Thus the fairies of Mazerolle and Seignac are disturbingly akin to girls from Montmartre with paper wings rather arbitrarily attached to their backs.

The degeneration of fairy painting towards pantomime and vaudeville can be dated from the 1870s. However, the best fairy paintings from the earlier golden age transcend the nagging doubts about paper wings and chorus girls, creating a powerful and convincing world of their own.

Index of Artists

DAVID BATES. A fairy grotto. Signed and dated 1862, shaped top. 4¾ x 7ins. (12 x 18cm). *Christie's.*

ARTHUR JOHN BLACK. Fairies' whirl. Signed and dated 93, and signed and inscribed on the reverse. 23½ x 29¾ins. (59.5 x 75.5cm). *Christie's*

JOSEPH BOUVIER. Fairies by moonlight. Signed, on oval panel. 8¼ x 6ins. (21 x 15.5cm). *Christie's.*

RICHARD EISERMANN. Sleeping Beauty. Signed and dated München 1881. 35½ x 50½ins. (90 x 128cm). *Christie's.*

GABRIEL JOSEPH MARIE
FERRIER. The water sprite. Signed.
40 x 25ins. (101.5 x 63.5cm). *Sotheby's.*

JOHN ANSTER FITZGERALD. Who killed Cock Robin? Signed,
oval. 12 x 15ins. (30.5 x 38cm). *Christie's.*

JOHN ATKINSON GRIMSHAW. Endymion on Mount Latmus. Signed and dated 1879, and signed, inscribed and dated
1879-1880 on the reverse. 32 x 47½ins. (81 x 120.5cm). *Christie's.*

ROBERT HUSKISSON. Come unto these yellow sands. On panel. 13½ x 17½ins. (34 x 44.5cm).
Christie's.

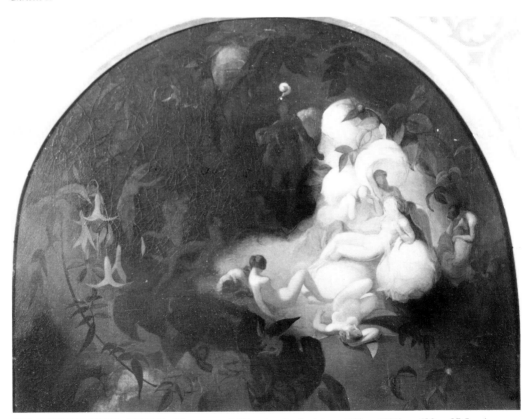

SIR JOSEPH NOEL PATON. Oberon and Titania. Arched top. 11¾ x 14¾ins. (30 x 37.5cm).
Christie's.

HEINRICH SCHLITT. The gnome artist. Signed and inscribed München, on panel. 21¼ x 15¾ins. (54 x 40cm).
Wiesbaden Museum.

ROLAND RISSE. Snow White. Signed. 19 x 15ins. (48 x 38cm). *Christie's.*

GUILLAUME SEIGNAC. Titania. Signed. 25½ x 21ins. (64.5 x 53cm). *Christie's.*

JOHN SCOTT. The reverie. Signed. 16¼ x 29¾ins. (41 x 75.5cm). *Christie's.*

Fish

Painters of fish who were in any sense specialists existed only in very small numbers, but those who can be included in this category divide into two groups. One group, almost entirely British, painted fish as sporting trophies, often on the riverbank with titles like *The Day's Catch*. These angling artists are led by Henry Leonidas Rolfe and Roland-Knight. The second group is larger and less easily definable in that it includes a certain proportion of still life painters. These were often men with realist tendencies, like Antoine Vollon, who saw fish as suitably humble and unpretentious subjects as against the affected elegance of flowers and expensive knick-knacks. In this they were echoing — once again — the Dutch seventeenth century and painters such as Abraham van Beyeren.

Index of Artists

JOHN FERNELEY (JUN). A salmon on a river bank. Signed and inscribed York.
25 x 49½ins. (63.5 x 125cm). *Christie's.*

WILLIAM GEDDES. A still life of fish
on a boat. Signed, canvas laid down on
board. 19 x 36ins. (48 x 91.5cm).
Christie's.

A. ROLAND-KNIGHT. Four to one on
Jack. Signed and inscribed on the reverse.
20 x 30ins. (51 x 76cm). *Christie's.*

FREDERICK RICHARD LEE. Pike
and perch on a bank with fishing tackle.
Signed and dated 1858, on panel.
21½ x 29¼ins. (54.5 x 74cm). *Christie's.*

HENRY LEONIDAS ROLFE. Perch feeding: the dinner hour. Signed twice and dated 1872. 24 x 35¾ins. (61 x 91cm). *Christie's.*

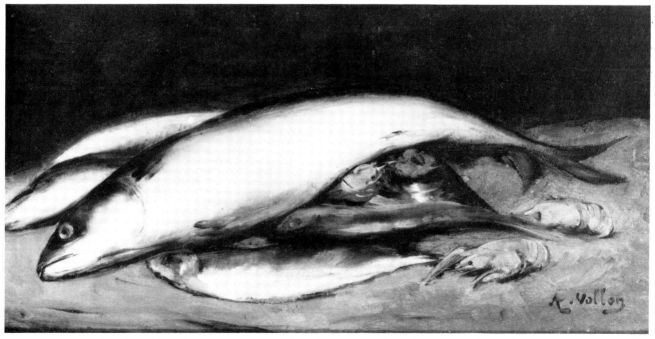

ANTOINE VOLLON. A still life of fish. Signed, canvas laid down on panel. 10½ x 20¾ins. (27 x 53cm). *Sotheby's.*

Harems

From the stately odalisques of Ingres through to the sensationalist pin-ups of Ernst and Rosati, the aspect of the Middle East which especially fascinated artists was the Harem, and its concomitants the Slave Market and the Baths. When Maxime du Camp wrote of the Cairo slave markets 'people go there to purchase a slave as they go here to the market to buy a turbot', the average European might outwardly gasp with horror, but then again he might speculate rather wistfully to himself the next time he passed the fishmarket. Harems, after all, answered 'civilised' western man's most enduring private fantasy, the idea of a variety of utterly captive women existing solely for their master's pleasure. Officially, the fact that these ladies of the seraglio frequently disported themselves naked was certainly regrettable, but nonetheless such scenes were permissible subjects for the artist's brush because (a) the participants in these scenes of the heathen Orient knew no better and (b) they were far distant from the experience of the European spectator. And of course pictures set in harems met *par excellence* the craving common to much popular nineteenth century painting, to pry behind closed doors and peer through keyholes.

Artists, particularly in France, were not slow to appreciate such pictorial dynamite. The result was an abundance of scenes set in harems, slave markets, or the public baths. The last were reserved for women in the afternoons, and were visited by members of harems who brought their own personal slaves to rub them down. Such scenes of massage were popular in the Salon: often the slave would be black and the concubine white, this contrast in naked female flesh being an especial source of delight. Most harem pictures are unashamedly erotic, shielded from anything too damaging in the way of normal censure by the fact that they are also exotic, and distanced. But the naturalism of the depiction of the girls, their physical reality, was not thereby compromised. Indeed one factor which conveniently heightened the realism for the European audience was that Muslim women were forbidden to sit for artists. Thus most of the ladies portrayed are European models, suitably disguised with eastern accessories.

Earlier in the century a few intrepid spirits attempted a greater degree of authenticity by sketching on the spot in the slave market. W.J. Müller, at work in this way, was assumed to be writing out bids for the merchandise and was repeatedly approached by prospective sellers. He later recorded his shock at the proceedings:

> When anyone desires to purchase, I not infrequently saw the master remove the entire covering of the female — a thick woollen cloth — and expose her to the gaze of the by-stander. Many of these girls are exceedingly beautiful — small features, well formed, with an eye that bespeaks the warmth of passion they possess.

Such flagrant exhibitionism was riveting to the European imagination. In their efforts to exploit it, many later artists were less scrupulous than travellers like Müller and Delacroix, painting harems and slave markets without actually leaving their Parisian studios. Indeed the line of division between the Parisian boudoir and the eastern harem becomes increasingly blurred as the century

JOHN FREDERICK LEWIS. An intercepted correspondence, Cairo. Signed and dated 1869, on panel. 30 x 35ins. (76 x 89cm). *Christie's.*

wears on. The inhabitants of the seraglio, with their cigarettes and languid poses, grow to resemble the ladies of easy virtue available in the French capital: only their setting is a little more exotic. And if the west was invading the east, then the east was also exerting its influence on the life style of the *demi-monde* of Europe. Flaubert describes a Parisian courtesan lighting a hookah:

> She suddenly grew languid and lay motionless on the divan, with a cushion under her armpit, her body slightly twisted, one knee bent, and the other outstretched. The long snake of red morocco formed loops on the floor and coiled round her arm. She pressed the amber mouthpiece to her lips and gazed at Frederic with half-closed eyes, through the spirals of smoke which enveloped her.

He could be looking at any number of Orientalist pictures of the latter part of the century allegedly set in harems.

There were other artists — English and Belgian, for instance — who treated harems with more circumspection. In Franz Charlet's *Favourites of the Harem*, an atmosphere of such gentility has been imposed upon proceedings that the favourites in question turn out to be particularly fluffy and simpering kittens, with which the ladies of the seraglio are playing as demurely as if in a Brussels drawing room. The same coyness pervades Frederick Goodall's *A New Light in the Harem*: a happy event for one of the Sultan's favourites (in this case human not feline) is treated with all the sentimentality normally applied to childbirth in an orthodox Victorian genre painting, where legally joined father and mother coo over the cradle of their offspring. According to eye-witness accounts, harem life could certainly be surprisingly domestic in its idle hours, when the occupants might while away the time in games of cards or chess, or embroidery or weaving. It was this intimate note which some nineteenth century painters sought to sound, almost as a reassurance to their public that all was not necessarily licence and immorality.

Even John Frederick Lewis, in many ways the greatest English Orientalist painter and a man whose personal experience of the east was much more extensive than most (he actually lived in Egypt for ten years from 1842-1851), painted harem scenes later in his career which are specially packaged for the English market, that is to say given that whiff of domesticity guaranteed to whet the appetites of the patrons of the Royal Academy. *An Intercepted Correspondence*, for instance, by its very title indicates the intimate drama that is unfolding. One of the Pasha's beautiful young ladies has been conducting a clandestine and forbidden romance; billets doux have been exchanged and fallen into the wrong hands; the incriminating evidence has been presented to the Pasha; and now the unfortunate and somewhat petulant looking culprit is being brought in to stand judgement before him. Just so might a Victorian head of the household reprimand a kitchen maid who has formed an unsuitable alliance on her afternoon off.

The pictorial image of the harem created by the nineteenth century painters had a rich and varied progeny in popular culture. Without their example, it is doubtful that there would have been the vogue for the romantic novels of Elinor Glyn involving passionate eastern princes and innocent European maidens; neither would we have had the archetypal cinematic sheikh of Rudolf Valentino; musicals like *The Desert Song*; even advertisements for popular brands of Turkish Delight might have taken a different form. All can trace their roots to the later nineteenth century urge to popularise and sensationalise the exotic arab world.

Index of Artists

AMADO Y BERNADET, Ramon (Spanish, 1844-1888)
ARNOUX, Charles Albert (French, 1820-1863)
AURELI, Giuseppe (Italian, 1858-1929)

BALLESIO, F. (Italian, late 19th Century)
* BARATTI, Filippo (Italian, late 19th Century)
* BAUGNIÈS, Eugène (French, 1842-1891)
BEAUMONT, Charles Edouard de (French, 1812-1888)
BELLY, Léon Adolphe Auguste (French, 1827-1877)
BOMPARD, Maurice (French, 1857-1936)
BOSCHI, Achille (Italian, 1852-1930)
BOUCHARD, Prudent Léon (French, 1817-?)
* BREDT, Ferdinand Max (German, 1860-1921)
BRIDGMAN, Frederick Arthur (Anglo-American, 1847-1928)
BRUNET, Jean Jacques Baptiste (French, 1850-1920)

CALA Y MOYA, José de (Spanish, 1850-?)
* CARLINI, Giulio (Italian, 1830-1887)
CHARLET, Franz (Belgian, 1862-1928)
* CLAIRIN, Georges Jules Victor (French, 1843-1919)
* COLLINA, Alberto (Italian, late 19th Century)
* COMERRE, Léon François (French, 1850-1916)
* COMERRE-PATON, Jacqueline (French, 1859-?)
* CONSTANT, Jean Joseph Benjamin (French, 1845-1902)
CORMON, Fernand (French, 1845-1924)
COULON, John (British, late 19th Century)
CUVILLON, Louis Robert de (French, 1848-?)

DARRICAU, Henry Léonce (French, 1870-?)
DEBAT-PONSON, Edouard Bernard (French, 1847-1913)
DELACROIX, Ferdinand Victor Eugène (French, 1798-1863)
DELAYE, Alice (French, late 19th Century)
DELOBBE, François Alfred (French, 1835-1920)
* DICKSEE, John Robert (British, 1817-1905)
DIRANIAN, Serkis (Turkish, late 19th Century)
DUFAU, Clémentine Hélène (French, 1869-1937)

ENDER, Eduard (Austrian, 1822-1883)
ERNST, Rudolf (Austrian, 1854-1920)

* FABBI, Fabio (Italian, 1861-1946)
* FONT, Constantin (French, late 19th Century)

GELLI, Eduardo (Italian, 1852-1933)
GENTZ, Karl Wilhelm (German, 1822-1890)
* GÉRÔME, Jean Léon (French, 1824-1904)
* GIMENEZ Y MARTIN, Juan (Spanish, 1858-?)
* GIRAUD, Sebastien Charles (French, 1819-1892)
GOODALL, Frederick (British, 1822-1904)

HABERT, Eugène (French, ?-1916)
HAYEZ, Francesco (Italian, 1791-1882)
HUYSMANS, Jan Baptist (Belgian, 1826-?)

INDONI, Filippo (Italian, late 19th Century)
* INGRES, Jean Auguste Dominique (French, 1780-1867)

* JERICHAU-BAUMANN, Anna Maria Elisabeth (Danish, 1819-1881)

* KLINCKENBERG, Eugen (German, 1858-?)

LANDELLE, Charles Zacharie (French, 1821-1908)
* LECOMTE-VERNET, Charles Emile Hippolyte (French, 1821-1900)
* LEFEBVRE, Jules Joseph (French, 1836-1912)
* LEROY, Paul Alexandre Alfred (French, 1860-1942)
* LEWIS, John Frederick (British, 1805-1876)
LEYDET, Victor (French, 1861-1904)
* LORIA, Vincenzo (Italian, 1849-?)

* MANCINELLI, Gustavo (Italian, late 19th Century)
MANTEGAZZA, Giacomo (Italian, 1853-1920)
MARCHETTI, Ludovico (Italian, 1853-1909)
MARSHALL, Charles Edward (British, 1872-1922)
MARTIN, Pierre (French, late 19th Century)
* MASRIERA Y MANOVENS, Francisco (Spanish, 1842-1902)
MEYS, Marcel Paul (French, late 19th Century)
MÜLLER, William James (British, 1812-1845)
* MUNOZ OTERO, Manuel (Spanish, 1850-?)
MUNOZ Y CUESTA, Domingo (Spanish, 1850-1912)
MURRAY-COOKSLEY, Margaret (British, ?-1927)

NONNENBRUCH, Max (German, 1857-1922)

* OLIVA Y RODRIGO, Eugenio (Spanish, 1854-1925)

* PARROT, Philippe (French, late 19th Century)
PERALTA DEL CAMPO, Francisco (Spanish, ?-1897)
PERCHI, Achille (French, late 19th Century)
* PILNY, Otto (Swiss, 1866-?)

* RAFFAELLI, Jean François (French, 1850-1924)
* RALLI, Theodore Jacques (Greek, 1852-1909)
RICHTER, Edouard Frederick Wilhelm (German, 1844-1913)
* ROQUEPLAN, Camille Joseph Etienne (French, 1803-1855)
* ROSATI, Giulio (Italian, 1853-1917)

SAINTPIERRE, Gaston Casimir (French, 1833-1916)
* SCHLIMARSKI, Heinrich Hans (Austrian, 1859-?)
SCHOPIN, Henri Frédéric (German, 1804-1880)
* SIMONETTI, Attilio (Italian, 1843-1925)
SIMONETTI, Ettore (Italian, late 19th Century)
* SIMONI, Gustavo (Italian, 1846-?)
SNOWMAN, Isaac (British, 1874-?)
STEVENS, Agapit (Belgian, late 19th Century)
* STIEPEVITCH, Vincent (Russian, late 19th Century)

FILIPPO BARATTI. La sultane.
Signed and dated 1901, and signed
and inscribed on the reverse.
46½ x 35¼ins. (118 x 89.5cm).
Christie's.

EUGÈNE BAUGNIÈS. The concubine and her servant. Signed. 21½ x 27½ ins. (54.5 x 70cm). *Sotheby's*.

FERDINAND MAX BREDT. The queen of the harem. Signed. 31½ x 20ins. (80 x 51cm). *Christie's*.

GIULIO CARLINI. The sultan's favourite. Signed and dated Venice 1861. 37¼ x 30½ ins.(94.5 x 77.5cm). *Christie's*.

GEORGES JULES VICTOR CLAIRIN. The harem. Signed. 29¼ x 37ins. (74 x 94cm). *Christie's.*

ALBERTO COLLINA. In the harem. Signed. 19 x 24¾ins. (48 x 63cm). *Christie's.*

LÉON FRANÇOIS COMERRE. The favourite of the harem. Signed. 49 x 31ins. (124.5 x 79cm). *Christie's.*

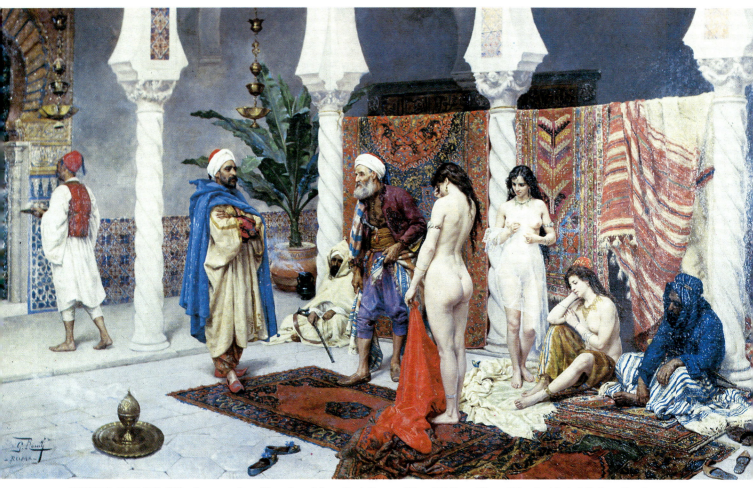

GIULIO ROSATI. The slave market. Signed and inscribed Roma. 24 x 39½ins. (61 x 100cm). *Mathaf Gallery, London.*

JEAN JOSEPH BENJAMIN CONSTANT.
An odalisque in a harem. Signed. 20 x 38ins.
(51 x 96.5cm). *Christie's.*

JOHN ROBERT DICKSEE. The harem
favourite. Signed with monogram. 32 x 40ins.
(81.5 x 101.5cm). *Sotheby's.*

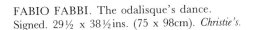

JACQUELINE COMMERRE-PATON. The
Moroccan girl. Signed. 21¾ x 55¼ins.
(55 x 140cm). *Sotheby's.*

FABIO FABBI. The odalisque's dance.
Signed. 29½ x 38½ins. (75 x 98cm). *Christie's.*

CONSTANTIN FONT. An odalisque. Signed. 57 x 112ins. (145 x 284.5cm). *Christie's.*

JUAN GIMENEZ Y MARTIN. The harem. Signed and inscribed Roma, on panel. 11½ x 17ins. (29 x 43cm). *Christie's.*

JEAN LÉON GÉRÔME. An odalisque. Signed. 19¾ x 15½ins. (50.5 x 39.5cm). *Christie's.*

SEBASTIEN CHARLES GIRAUD. Lighting the hookah. Signed, on panel. 20½ x 15ins. (52 x 38cm). *Christie's.*

JEAN AUGUSTE DOMINIQUE INGRES. An odalisque with a slave. Signed and dated 1842. 30 x 41¼ ins.(76 x 105cm).
Walters Art Gallery, Baltimore.

ANNA MARIA ELISABETH
JERICHAU-BAUMANN. The
odalisque. Signed. 39 x 29¼ ins.
(99 x 74cm). *Christie's.*

EUGEN KLINCKENBERG. Dolce far niente. Signed and dated München 1886.
17 x 27¼ ins. (43.5 x 69.5cm). *Sotheby's.*

JULES JOSEPH LEFEBVRE. A Turkish beauty.
Signed and dated 1880. 56¾ x 32½ ins. (144 x 82.5cm).
Christie's.

Top left: CHARLES EMILE HIPPOLYTE
LECOMTE-VERNET. A Moroccan beauty. Signed
and dated 1873. 16¾ x 11¼ ins. (42.5 x 28.5cm).
Christie's.

PAUL ALEXANDRE ALFRED LEROY. A conversation
in the seraglio. Signed and dated 1901. 25¼ x 25¼ ins.
(64 x 64cm). *Christie's.*

363

VINCENZO LORIA. A harem scene. Signed, canvas laid down on board. 23¼ x 39½ins. (60.5 x 100cm). *Christie's.*

GUSTAVO MANCINELLI. In the harem. Signed and dated 1875. 36 x 25¼ins. (91.5 x 64cm). *Christie's.*

FRANCISCO MASRIERA Y MANOVENS. The favourites of the harem. Signed and dated 1881. 74½ x 70ins. (189 x 178cm). *Christie's.*

EUGENIO OLIVA Y RODRIGO. The favourite. Signed, on panel. 17⅞ x 11½ins. (45 x 29cm). *Sotheby's.*

MANUEL MUNOZ OTERO. Harem musicians. Signed and dated Roma 1885. 28¼ x 73¾ins. (71.5 x 187.5cm). *Christie's.*

PHILIPPE PARROT. Moorish women. Signed, on panel. 22 x 12ins. (56 x 30.5cm). *Christie's.*

OTTO PILNY. The belly dancer. Signed. 43 x 63ins. (109.5 x 160cm). *Christie's.*

JEAN FRANÇOIS RAFFAELLI. An Eastern
odalisque. Signed and dated '76, on panel.
19¼ x 10¼ins. (49 x 26cm). *Christie's.*

THEODORE JACQUES RALLI. Repos au
bain. Signed and dated '88, and signed and
inscribed on an old label on the reverse.
18 x 15ins. (45.5. x 38cm). *Christie's.*

CAMILLE JOSEPH ETIENNE
ROQUEPLAN. An odalisque. Signed,
stamped with the 'cachet de vente' on the
stretcher, oval. 20¾ x 17ins. (52.5 x 43cm).
Sotheby's.

HEINRICH HANS
SCHLIMARSKI.
An Eastern dancer.
Signed, canvas laid
down on panel.
58½ x 32¾ins.
(148.5 x 83cm).
Christie's.

GUSTAVO SIMONI. The interior of a
harem. Signed, inscribed and dated 1881,
watercolour. 26 x 17½ ins. (66 x 44.5cm).
Christie's.

Top right: ATTILIO SIMONETTI. In the
seraglio. Signed and inscribed Roma, on
panel. 10¼ x 14¼ ins. (26 x 36cm).
Sotheby's.

MORITZ STIFTER. In the harem.
Signed and dated 1890, on panel.
12¾ x 19¾ ins. (32.5 x 50cm). *Christie's.*

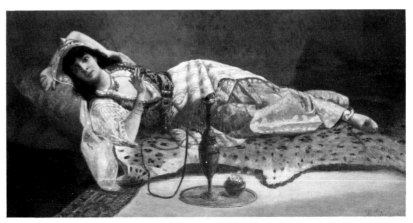

VINCENT STIEPEVITCH.
The favourite. Signed, inscribed and dated
on the reverse. 10 x 20ins. (25.5 x 51cm).
Christie's.

CHARLES STOECKLIN. A reclining odalisque. Signed. 30¾ x 42¾ ins. (78 x 108.5cm). *Sotheby's.*

VIRGILIO TOJETTI. The favourite. Signed and dated '86. 60¼ x 37ins. (153 x 94cm). *Christie's.*

FRANCIS JOHN WYBURD. Xarifa: the Zegri lady rose not, etc. Oval. 25 x 30ins. (63.5 x 76cm). *Christie's.*

ADRIEN HENRI TANOUX. A bejewelled eastern beauty. Signed. 21¼ x 14½ins. (54 x 37cm). *Sotheby's.*

Horses

The horse, which traditionally represented a favourite branch of animal painting, continued throughout the nineteenth century as an important and popular subject for artists. It was a period of contrast and change, however; a broad perspective of the hundred years from 1800 to 1900 indicates that up to about 1850 English supremacy in the field was largely unchallenged, while the second half of the century, for a variety of reasons, saw a decline in Britain and the emergence of a number of talented horse painters on the Continent. Earlier on, of course, Delacroix and Géricault turned their attentions to the horse extensively, and might be claimed to have painted the most memorable examples of the century, but it is significant that even Géricault was a fervent admirer of the English achievement. Indeed his visit to the Royal Academy in 1821 was a revelation, and he reported: 'You can have no idea of the animals painted by Ward and Landseer — the Old Masters produced nothing better in this genre.'

It is difficult for us in the latter part of the motorised twentieth century to appreciate the extent to which the horse was a pervasive and functional feature of the landscape in the nineteenth. Pictures of the subject can be divided into six main areas: hunting scenes, racing scenes, coaching scenes, horse portraits, cavalry scenes, and what may broadly be termed 'horse genre', themes like horse-markets, early morning rides, or everyday life in the stables. The first four of these sub-sections were to all intents and purposes English inventions of the eighteenth century or before. English specialists of the first half of the nineteenth century could build on the tradition of Wootton, Seymour and Sartorius, of Stubbs and Gilpin, and it was a time of continuing richness as Ben Marshall, James Ward, J.F. Herring senior and James Pollard created another golden age. In his heart of hearts, the archetypal English country gentleman of the period would probably have preferred a portrait of his favourite hunter by Ferneley to a portrait of his wife by Lawrence. Indeed, one cannot overestimate the tremendous popularity of hunting in England; it is also significant that racing was not developed as an organised sport on the Continent till the second half of the nineteenth century, while it enjoyed a flourishing vogue considerably earlier in Britain. Perfect familiarity with the highly bred racehorse, the ability to see with the trainer's eye, was a talent therefore possessed by painters like Herring and Marshall (who was also, incidentally, a racing journalist), but denied to their counterparts on the Continent.

The French tended to take a less obsessive view of the horse in art than the English. One of the foremost horse painters of the middle of the century in France was Alfred de Dreux; in his own country, critics marvelled at his single-mindedness in relegating human interest in favour of the equine in a picture. 'The dandy, the amazon and the groom were only secondary — they were the excuse, the pretext for the horse,' Charles Blanc wrote in wonder of de Dreux in 1865. Such a sense of priority would have been the source of no surprise in England. Another French horse painter, John Lewis Brown, was alleged to have been the victim of an even stranger prejudice in 1869 when commissioned to make some drawings for an illustrated paper. The editor, Pointel, promptly withdrew his invitation when he discovered that Brown proposed to depict horses, exclaiming: 'Horses! Horses lead to whores. Whores lead to the death of the family. There will be no horses in my paper.' Whether or not this story, recounted by the Goncourts in their journal, had any basis in truth, its implications would have been quite foreign to the Englishman, accustomed to the sporting or military functions of the horse but not to its significance as a conveyance on or through which to meet ladies of easy virtue. For the Englishman, a horse could be its own justification in a picture; for a Frenchman it more often needed human association.

That there was a decline in English horse painting from about 1850 onwards is incontestable: the reaction of some important English owners as the century progressed was to resort to horse painters from abroad, a sign of desperate times indeed. One of the first of these 'foreigners' was Alfred de Dreux, until he met a somewhat bizarre death in a duel in 1860, while a painter who enjoyed remarkable popularity, particularly amongst owners of classic winners in the last part of the century, was Emil Adam from Munich. There are several factors which must have contributed to this falling-off of power and quality. Technological inventions such as the railway and photography compromised on the one hand the supremacy of the horse as a means of transport and on the other the supremacy of the painter as a means of accurately recording it. Photography even revealed that since the beginning of time artists had incorrectly depicted the action of the horse's legs at the gallop. Such considerations may to a certain extent have shaken the confidence of a literal-minded patronage.

The horse painter symbolised the old order, anyway: his milieu was rural rather than urban, and as the Industrial Revolution shifted the emphasis from country to town, severely squeezing agriculture in the process, animal painters were inclined to make concessions to the tastes and demands of the city. Horse painting became in some senses démodé. If the first half of the century was typified by animal painters like J.F. Herring, Wilhelm Kobell, Ben Marshall and Albrecht Adam, the second half belonged to Henriette Ronner-Knip and Julius Adam, urban bourgeois cat painters, more at home in the town house or apartment than in the country estate.

This is not, of course, to deny that popular horse painters continued to emerge throughout the century. On the Continent, most countries had their favourite masters: there was for instance Wouter Verschuur in Holland, von Pettenkoffen and Ludwig Gedlek in Vienna, Carl Steffeck in Berlin and Otto Bache in Denmark. Horse painters were not oblivious to changing times and artistic trends, and some tried to adapt their work to meet new demands. There was a temptation to increase the emotional content, and although the equine soul was rarely sentimentalised to the level of some cow, sheep and dog paintings, a more intrusive narrative element sometimes made itself felt. Cart-horses break free of their shafts to join the hunt; cavalry officers weep over their dying chargers; and woebegone workhorses whose lives have been passed in toil and misery are conjured up on canvas to wring sympathy from the public. These horses are the equivalents of the poor beggar children, the applicants for admission to a casual ward, the exhausted seamstresses who featured in many late nineteenth century genre scenes as artists discovered that the affection of a 'social conscience' might conveniently open up revelations of the picturesqueness of poverty. Painters like Ludwig Hartman in Germany and Lucy Kemp-Welch in England preferred to treat humble workhorses rather than highly-bred champions of the turf in order to increase the pathetic impact of their pictures. Such changes in emphasis represent yet another instance of a powerful new patronage imposing its priorities on a traditional branch of subject matter, a recurrent feature of the nineteenth century.

Index of Artists

GILBERT, Joseph Francis (British, 1792-1855)
GILBERT, W. J. (British, fl.1830-1870)
GILES, Godfrey Douglas (British, 1857-1941)
GILES, James William (British, 1801-1870)
GILLARD, William (British, 1812-?)
GODDARD, Charles (British, mid-19th Century)
* GOUBIE, Jean Richard (French, 1842-1899)
GRAEME, Colin (British, late 19th Century)
* GRANT, Sir Francis (British, 1803-1878)
* GRAVIER, A. du (French, late 19th Century)
GRÜNLER, Louis (German, 1809-?)
GRUNWALD, Adalbert Bela Ivanyi (Austrian, 1867-1940)

HADDEN, Nellie (British, fl.1885-1893)
HAIGH, Alfred Grenfell (British, 1870-1963)
* HALL, Harry (British, 1814-1882)
HALPEN, Francis (British, fl.1845-1868)
HANCOCK, Charles (British, 1802-1877)
* HARDY, Heywood (British, 1842-1933)
HARDY (Jun.), James (British, 1832-1889)
* HARROWING, Walter (British, fl.1877-1904)
* HART, T. R. (British, mid 19th Century)
* HARTMANN, Ludwig (German, 1835-1902)
HAVELL, Edmund (British, 1819-1894)
* HENDERSON, Charles Cooper (British, 1803-1887)
* HERBERTE, Edward Benjamin (British, 1857-1893)
HERMANSTOERFER, Josef (German, 1817-1901)
HERRING (Sen.), Benjamin (British, 1806-1830)
HERRING (Jun.), Benjamin (British, 1830-1871)
* HERRING (Sen.), John Frederick (British, 1795-1865)
* HERRING (Jun.), John Frederick (British, 1815-1907)
HOLT, Edwin Frederick (British, fl.1850-1865)
* HOPKINS, William H. (British, ?-1892)
HORLOR, George W. (British, fl.1849-1890)
HORNER, Christopher (British, fl.1857-1867)
HUGGINS, William (British, 1820-1884)
HULL, Edward (British, fl.1827-1877)
* HUMBERT, Jean Charles Ferdinand (Swiss, 1813-1881)
* HÜNTEN, Emil Johann (German, 1827-1902)

JACKSON, George (British, fl.1830-1864)
JANCK, Angelo (German, 1868-?)
* JONES, Charles (British, 1836-1892)
JONES, Paul (British, fl.1856-1888)
JONES, Richard (British, 1767-1840)

* KEELING, E. J. (British, fl.1856-1873)
KEMP-WELCH, Lucy Elizabeth (British, 1869-1958)
* KEYL, Friedrich Wilhelm (German, 1823-1871)
KILBURNE, George Goodwin (British, 1839-1924)
* KOBELL, Wilhelm Alexander Wolfgang von (German, 1766-1855)
KRÜGER, Franz (German, 1797-1857)
KÜBLER, Ludwig (Austrian, fl.1850-1868)
KUYCK, Jan Louis Lodeijk van (Belgian, 1821-1871)

LAMI, Eugène Louis (French, 1800-1890)
* LANDSEER, Sir Edwin Henry (British, 1802-1873)
* LAPORTE, George Henry (British, 1799-1873)
LEDIEU, Philippe (French, fl.1827-1850)
LEEMPUTTEN, Frans van (Belgian, 1850-1914)
LEEUW, Alexis de (Belgian, fl.1848-1883)
LIEBERMANN, Max (German, 1847-1935)
* LIER, Adolf Heinrich (German, 1826-1882)
LLOYD, Edward (British, ?-1891)

LODER of Bath, James (British, fl.1820-1860)
LOS, Waldemar (Polish, 1849-1888)
* LOTS, Karl (German, late 19th Century)
* LUCAS-LUCAS, Henry Frederick (British, ?-1943)
LUKER, William (British, 1820?-1892)
* LUMINAIS, Evariste Vital (French, 1822-1896)

McLEOD, John (British, ?-1872)
* MAGGS, John Charles (British, 1819-1896)
MAIDEN, Joseph (British, 1813-1843)
MALLEBRANCHE, Louis Claude (French, 1790-1838)
* MARCKE DE LUMMEN, Jean van (French, 1875-1917)
* MARÉES, Hans von (German, 1837-1887)
MARSHALL, Ben (British, 1767-1835)
MARSHALL, Lambert (British, 1809-1870)
* MARSHALL, William Elstob (British, fl.1859-1881)
* MARTIN, A. Anson (British, fl.1840-1872)
* MARTIN, Sylvester (British, fl.1867-1878)
MARTINDALE, G. T. (British, early 19th Century)
* MELCHIOR, Wilhelm Johann (German, 1817-1860)
MELVILLE, Harden S. (British, fl.1837-1879)
MEW, Thomas Hillier (British, fl.1850-1868)
MICHALOWSKI, Piotr von (Polish, 1801-1855)
MILLNER, William Edward (British, 1849-1895)
* MONTEMEZZO, Antonio D. (Italian, 1841-1898)
MONTEN, Dietrich Heinrich Maria (German, 1799-1843)
MOODY, Fannie (British, 1861-1897)
MORLEY, George (British, fl.1832-1863)
MORRIS, John (British, late 19th Century)
MORRIS, William Bright (British, 1844-1896)

NAKKEN, Willem Carel (Dutch, 1835-1926)
NEDHAM, William (British, mid-19th Century)
NEIL, Marie Joseph Ernest le (French, late 19th Century)
NIGHTINGALE, Robert (British, 1815-1895)
* NOERR, Julius (German, 1827-1897)
NORTON, Benjamin Cam (British, 1835-1900)

OSBORNE, William (British, 1823-1901)

PAICE, George (British, 1854-1925)
* PALMER, James Lynwood (British, 1868-1941)
PANERAI, Ruggero (Italian, 1862-1923)
PARKER, Henry Perlee (British, 1795-1873)
PAUL, John (British, fl.1867-1886)
* PEARCE, Stephen (British, 1819-1904)
* PÈCHAUBÈS, Eugène (French, late 19th Century)
PENNE, Olivier Charles de (French, 1831-1897)
PÉRIGNON, Alexis (French, 1806-1882)
* PETIT-GÉRARD, Pierre (French, 1852-?)
PETTENKOFFEN, August Xaver Karl von (Austrian, 1822-1889)
PFEIFFER, Wilhelm Friedrich (German, 1822-1891)
PICHAT, Olivier (French, 1820-1912)
* PICOLA Y LOPEZ, Manuel (Spanish, 1850?-1892?)
PITTARA, Carlo (Italian, 1836-1890)
POCK, Alexander (Austrian, 1871-1950)
POLLARD, James (British, 1792-1867)
* PRADES, Alfred Frank de (British, fl.1862-1879)
* PRATÈRE, Edmond Joseph de la (Belgian, 1826-1888)
PRINCETEAU, René Pierre (French, 1844-1914)
PRINGLE, William (British, fl.1834-1858)

* QUAGLIO, Franz (German, 1844-1920)

RANDEL, Friedrich (German, 1808-1888)
RAUCH, Ferdinand (Austrian, 1813-1852)
* RENTZELL, August von (German, 1810-1891)
* RICHTER, Wilhelm (Austrian, 1824-1892)
* ROBBE, Louis Marie Dominique Romain (Belgian, 1806-1887)
ROLOFF, Alfred (German, 1879-?)
ROSEN, Jan (Polish, 1854-1936)
* ROWLANDSON, George Derville (British, 1861-?)

* SANGUINETTI, Eduardo (Italian, late 19th Century)
SCHMITSON, Teutwart (German, 1830-1863)
* SCHOUTEN, Henry (Dutch, 1864-1927)
* SCHRADER, Julius Friedrich Anton (German, 1815-1900)
SCHRAMM-ZITTAU, Max Rudolf (German, 1874-1950)
SCHREYER, Adolf Christian (German, 1828-1899)
SCHWANFELDER, Charles Henry (British, 1774-1832)
SEBRIGHT, George (British, mid-19th Century)
* SEXTIE, William (British, late 19th Century)
SHAYER, Charles Waller (British, 1826-1914)
SHAYER, Henry Thring (British, 1825-1864)
SHAYER, William Joseph (British, 1811-1891)
* SIMMLER, Wilhelm (German, 1840-1914)
* SIMPSON, Charles (British, early 19th Century)
* SMITH, Frederick Sheldon (British, fl.1877-1880)
* SMYTHE, Edward Robert (British, 1810-1899)
* SMYTHE, Thomas (British, 1825-1906)
* STEFFECK, Carl Constantin Heinrich (German, 1819-1890)
* STEINACKER, Alfred (Austrian, 1838-?)
STEWART, Charles Edward (British, fl.1890-1930)
STOFF, Alois (Austrian, 1846-?)
STONE, Rudolph (British, late 19th Century)
STOTZ, Otto (German, 1805-1873)
STRUTT, Alfred William (British, 1856-1924)
* SWEBACH, Bernard Edouard (French, 1800-1870)

* TANNER, C. (British, fl.1839-1847)
* TASKER, William (British, 1808-1852)
TAVERNIER, Paul (French, 1852-?)
* TAYLER, John Frederick (British, 1802-1889)
THOMPSON, Algernon Alfred Cankerien (British, 1880-1944)
THOREN, Otto Karl Kasimir von (Austrian, 1828-1889)
TOLLEY, Edward (British, fl.1848-1867)
* TOMINZ, Alfredo (Italian, 1854-1936)
TOMSON, Clifton (British, 1775-1828)

* TOWNE, Charles (British, 1781-1854)
TOWNSHEND, Arthur Louis (British, fl.1880-1912)
* TROYE, Edward (Swiss, 1808-1874)
* TSCHAGGENY, Charles Philogène (Belgian, 1815-1894)
TSCHAGGENY, Edmond Jean Baptiste (Belgian, 1818-1873)
TURNER, Francis Calcraft (British, 1782?-1846)
* TURNER, William Eddowes (British, 1820?-1885)

VAGO, Paul (Austrian, 1853-1928)
* VERBOECKHOVEN, Eugène Joseph (Belgian, 1799-1881)
VERNET, Carl (French, 1758-1836)
* VERSCHUUR, Wouter (Dutch, 1812-1874)
VERSCHUUR (Jun.), Wouter (Dutch, 1841-1936)
VINE, John (British, 1808-1867)
VISKI, Janos (Austrian, late 19th Century)
VOLKERS, Emil Ferdinand Heinrich (German, 1831-1905)
VOLKERS, Fritz (German, 1868-1944)
VOLKERS, Karl (German, ?-1949)
VOLTZ, Ludwig Gustav (German, 1825-1911)

WAHLBLOM, Johann Wilhelm Carl (Swedish, 1810-1858)
WALKER, Joseph Francis (British, fl.1857-1889)
WALLER, Samuel Edmund (British, 1850-1903)
WALTON, Frank (British, 1840-1928)
WARD, James (British, 1769-1859)
WARD, Martin Theodore (British, 1799-1874)
WARDLE, Arthur (British, 1864-1949)
WEAVER, Thomas (British, 1774-1843)
* WEBB, Byron (British, 1831-1867)
WEBB, Edward Walter (British, 1810-1851)
WEBB, William (British, 1780-1846)
* WEEKES, William (British, fl.1865-1904)
* WELLS, John Sanderson (British, 1872-1955)
WHEELER, John Arnold (British, 1821-1903)
WHEELRIGHT, W. H. (British, fl.1857-1897)
WIDDAS, Richard Dodd (British, 1826-1885)
* WILLOUGHBY, William (British, fl.1857-1888)
WOLSTENHOLME, Dean W. (British, 1798-1882)
WOODHOUSE, William (British, 1805-1878)
WOODWARD, Thomas (British, 1801-1852)
WOOLLETT, Henry A. (British, fl.1857-1873)
* WRIGHT, George (British, 1860-1942)
* WRIGHT, Gilbert Scott (British, 1880-1958)

ALBRECHT ADAM. The kill;
Count Halm hunting on his
Basedow estate. Signed and dated
1827. 27¼ x 39½ins.
(69.5 x 100.5cm). *Christie's.*

BENNO ADAM. Donkeys playing
outside a stable. Signed and dated
1869. 22¼ x 28ins. (56.5 x 71cm).
Christie's.

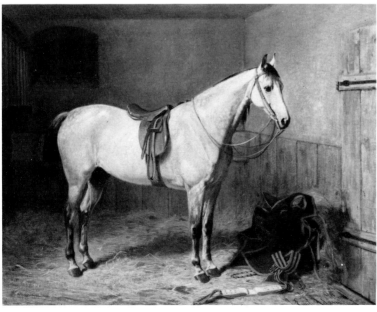

EMIL ADAM. A saddled grey horse
in a stable. Signed and dated 1869.
17½ x 23ins. (44.5 x 58.5cm).
Sotheby's.

ALFRED DE DREUX. A grey stallion. Signed. 42 x 51ins. (106.5 x 129.5cm). *Christie's.*

A. AKININOFF. A pony and poultry in a barn. Signed and dated 1872. 18 x 22ins. (45.5 x 56cm). *Christie's.*

HENRY ALKEN. View halloo. Signed. 17½ x 23ins. (44.5 x 58.5cm). *Christie's.*

LOUIS FELIX AMIEL. Le prix de l'Arc de Triomphe au Champ de Mars. Signed and dated 1840. 28 x 46ins. (71 x 117cm). *Private collection, New York.*

376

JOHANN GEORG ARSENIUS. Horses by a lake. Signed and dated 1868. 21 x 27½ins. (53.5 x 70cm). *Sotheby's.*

OTTO BACHE. The artist's family home from riding. Signed. 32 x 44ins. (81 x 112cm). *Christie's.*

HENRY BARRAUD. A grey hunter in a loose box. Signed. 17⅞ x 24ins. (45 x 61cm). *Christie's.*

WILLIAM BARRAUD. A chestnut hunter in a river landscape. Signed and dated 1843. 17 x 21ins. (43 x 53cm). *Christie's.*

JOHN BEER. Valentine's Brook. Signed, inscribed and dated 1901. 15 x 36ins. (38 x 91.5cm). *Christie's.*

ALEXANDER VON BENSA. Full cry. Signed, on panel. 8 x 10ins. (20 x 25.5cm). *Christie's.*

JOHN ALEXANDER HARRINGTON BIRD. An officer's charger of the Royal Horse Guards. Signed and dated 1895. 17½ x 23½ins. (44.5 x 59.5cm). *Christie's.*

JULIUS VON BLAAS. Carthorses. Signed and dated 1920, on board. 9½ x 13ins. (24 x 33cm). *Christie's.*

THOMAS BLINKS. Over the ditch. Signed.
34½ x 48½ins. (87.5 x 123.5cm). *Christie's.*

LOUIS CHARLES BOMBLED. Stag Hunting. Signed.
13 x 18¼ins. (33 x 46.5cm). *Sotheby's.*

ROSA BONHEUR. A Shetland pony. Signed.
15 x 21½ins. (38 x 54.5cm). *Christie's.*

Centre right: ERNST BOSCH. Rounding up. Signed and
dated Df 62. 31 x 39¼ins. (79 x 99.5cm). *Christie's.*

THOMAS BRETLAND. A grey hunter held by a
groom. Signed and inscribed Chentan(?) Hall.
24½ x 29½ins. (62 x 75cm). *Christie's.*

JEAN BAPTISTE ADOLPHE BRONQUART.
The Meet. Signed. 25½ x 32¼ins. (64.5 x 82cm).
Christie's.

GEORG HANS BÜTTNER. The Meet. Signed
and dated München 1889, on panel. 16½ x 25¼ins.
(42 x 64cm). *Christie's.*

WILLIAM FRANK CALDERON. Showery
weather. Signed, and signed and inscribed on the
reverse, on board. 22¼ x 30ins. (56.5 x 76cm).
Christie's.

SAMUEL JOHN CARTER. A lady riding sidesaddle. Signed and dated '63. 20½ x 23¼ins. (52 x 59cm). *Christie's.*

HENRY BERNARD CHALON. The Colonel, a chestnut racehorse with William Scott up, on a racecourse. Signed and dated 1829. 29 x 40¼ins. (73.5 x 102cm). *Christie's.*

JOHN CHARLTON. Mrs. C.J. Hoore on her bay hunter. Signed with initials and dated 1895. 24 x 30ins. (61 x 76cm). *Christie's.*

Centre right: DANIEL CLOWES. A grey hunter in a wooded landscape. Signed and dated 1825. 33½ x 47¼ins. (85 x 120cm). *Christie's.*

ABRAHAM COOPER. John Gully on his hack, with Hermit and John Wells up, and Andover with Alfred Day up. Signed with monogram, inscribed and dated 1854. 35 x 49½ins. (89 x 126cm). *Christie's.*

ALFRED CORBOULD. Fitzwilliam carriage horses. Signed and dated 1864. 41½ x 71½ins. (105.5 x 181.5cm). *Christie's.*

CONRADIJN CUNAEUS. The morning ride. Signed. 27¼ x 34¾ins. (69 x 88cm). *Christie's.*

DAVID DALBY OF YORK. Sezsle, a bay racehorse with jockey up in a landscape. Inscribed and dated 1843. 14 x 19ins. (35.5 x 48.5cm). *Christie's.*

JOHN DALBY OF YORK. Over the ditch. Signed, on board. 9½ x 11½ins. (24 x 29cm). *Christie's.*

RICHARD BARRETT DAVIS. Ernest Erle Drax, on horseback, with the Charborough hunt. Signed and dated Oct. 1844. 53¾ x 77½ins. (136.5 x 197cm). *Christie's.*

EUGÈNE FERDINAND VICTOR DELACROIX.
Two draught-horses, 11¼ x 15¼ins. (28.5 x 39cm). *Christie's.*

HENRI DELATTRE. The Percheron stud, Diligence, in a
stall. Signed and dated 1853. 12 x 14ins. (30.5 x 35.5cm).
Christie's.

M. DENARDE. Huntsmen in a landscape. Signed.
17 x 27¼ins. (43 x 69cm). *Christie's.*

OTTO DILL. Over the fence. Signed. 25½ x 46½ins.
(65 x 118cm). *Christie's.*

HERBERT CLAYTON DESVIGNES. A groom leading a
second horse to the hunt. Signed and dated 1831.
19 x 27¼ins. (48.5 x 69.5cm). *Christie's.*

EDWARD ALGERNON STUART DOUGLAS.
The Meet. Signed and dated 1918. 15¾ x 23½ins.
(40 x 59.5cm). *Christie's.*

JOHN DUVALL. A troop sergeant-major with his
charger. Signed. 14 x 18ins. (35.5 x 45.5cm).
Christie's.

WILHELM VON EMELÉ. A huntsman and
horses outside a country house. Signed and dated 1861.
18 x 26¾ins. (46 x 68cm). *Christie's.*

CLAUDE LORRAINE FERNELEY. 'Whitebait', a bay racehorse in a stable. Signed and dated Melton Mowbray 1877. 24 x 31¼ ins. (61 x 79.5cm). *Christie's.*

JOHN FERNELEY (JUN.). A chestnut hunter with other hunters and a spaniel in a landscape. Signed and dated 1861. 28¼ x 36ins. (71.5 x 91.5cm). *Christie's.*

JOHN E. FERNELEY (SEN.). 'Pussy' a dark brown racehorse with his trainer, 'Old John' Day, Mr. T. Crosby and W.B. Day at Epsom. Signed and dated Melton Mowbray 1834. 32 x 42ins. (81 x 107cm). *Christie's.*

JEAN RICHARD GOUBIE. The morning ride. Signed and dated 1890. 20¾ x 31ins. (53 x 78.5cm). *Christie's.*

A. DU GRAVIER. Full cry. Signed, on panel. 10¼ x 17⅞ins. (26 x 45cm). *Christie's.*

SIR FRANCIS GRANT. Queen Victoria riding with the Quorn. 1838. 35½ x 61½ins. (90.5 x 154.5cm). *Christie's.*

HARRY HALL. 'Voltigeur' with his trainer Mr. Robert Hill and his jockey, Job Marson, on the Epsom Downs. Signed and dated 1881. 21 x 30ins. (53.5 x 76cm). *Christie's.*

HEYWOOD HARDY. A huntsman and hounds in a wood. Signed. 36 x 24¼ins. (91.5 x 61.5cm). *Christie's.*

WALTER HARROWING. A group of mares in a landscape. Signed and dated 1882. 34 x 70ins. (86.5 x 178cm). *Christie's.*

T. R. HART. A gentleman driving a gig. Signed and dated 1860. 19¾ x 29½ins. (50 x 75cm). *Christie's.*

LUDWIG HARTMANN. The midday rest. Signed. 19½ x 27ins. (49.5 x 68.5cm). *Christie's.*

CHARLES COOPER HENDERSON. The Glasgow London coach halted on a country road. Signed with monogram. 24½ x 36¼ins. (62.5 x 92cm). *Christie's.*

EDWARD BENJAMIN HERBERTE. Over the fence. Signed. 17 x 23ins. (43 x 58.5cm). *Christie's.*

JOHN FREDERICK HERRING (SEN.). Three bay hunters by a stream. Signed and dated 1843. 47½ x 71½ins. (120.5 x 181.5cm). *Christie's.*

JOHN FREDERICK HERRING (JUN.). Horses, pigs and chickens in a farmyard. Signed. 16 x 24ins. (40.5 x 61cm). *Christie's.*

WILLIAM H. HOPKINS. A dark bay racehorse with a stable lad in a loosebox. Signed and dated 1879. 12¾ x 15½ins. (32.5 x 39.5cm). *Christie's.*

JEAN CHARLES FERDINAND HUMBERT. A grey stallion in a desert landscape. Signed and dated 1851. 13 x 17½ins. (33 x 44.5cm). *Christie's.*

EMIL JOHANN HÜNTEN. Full cry. Signed and dated 1869. 17 x 21¾ins. (43 x 55cm). *Christie's.*

E. J. KEELING. A groom with two hunters, the property of Robert Christie of Fulwood Park, Lancashire. Signed and dated Fulwood 1856. 27¼ x 35½ins. (69 x 90.5cm). *Christie's.*

FRIEDRICH WILHELM KEYL. A gentleman with his hunter and dogs outside his house. Signed and dated 1856. 34¾ x 48¼ins. (88 x 122.5cm). *Christie's.*

WILHELM ALEXANDER WOLFGANG
VON KOBELL. A landscape with sportsmen.
Signed and dated 1823. 17¼ x 24¾ins.
(44 x 63cm). *Mus. Folkwang, Essen.*

SIR EDWIN HENRY LANDSEER. No
more hunting till the weather breaks.
Inscribed on the reverse. 27½ x 36½ins.
(70 x 92.5cm). *Christie's.*

GEORGE HENRY LAPORTE. The vale of
Belvoir; over the ditch. Signed and dated
1833. 24½ x 37½ins. (62 x 95cm). *Christie's.*

ADOLF HEINRICH LIER. Full cry. Signed. 9½ x 16½ ins. (24 x 42cm). *Christie's.*

KARL LOTS. Horses resting at a well. 10¼ x 14½ ins. (26 x 37cm). *Sotheby's.*

HENRY FREDERICK LUCAS-LUCAS. Isinglass, a chestnut racehorse with T. Loates up, Signed and inscribed, and signed and dated Rugby 1893 on the reverse. 25¼ x 35½ ins. (64 x 90cm). *Christie's.*

EVARISTE VITAL LUMINAIS. Tipping the groom. Signed. 35¾ x 48ins. (91 x 122cm). *Christie's.*

JOHN CHARLES MAGGS. A mail coach in a snow drift. Signed and dated Bath 1885. 17½ x 29¼ ins. (44.5 x 74.5cm). *Christie's.*

THÉODORE GÉRICAULT. Cheval gris pommelé. Paper laid down on canvas. 18 x 17ins. (46 x 43cm). *Christie's.*

HANS VON MARÉES. A hunter.
14½ x 10½ins. (37 x 27cm). *Christie's.*

Top left: JEAN VAN MARCKE DE
LUMMEN. Over the fence. Signed.
23¼ x 32¼ins. (59 x 82cm). *Christie's.*

WILLIAM ELSTOB MARSHALL. New
Brighton hacks. Signed and dated 1881,
and inscribed on a label on the reverse.
19¾ x 35½ins. (50 x 90cm). *Christie's.*

A. ANSON MARTIN. A bay hunter and
a spaniel in a landscape. Signed.
25 x 30ins. (63.5 x 76cm). *Christie's.*

WILHELM JOHANN MELCHIOR. A grey and a bay hunter in a stable. Signed. 17 x 22⅓ins. (43 x 58cm). *Christie's.*

SYLVESTER MARTIN. In full cry. Signed and dated 1904. 20 x 30¼ins. (51 x 77cm). *Christie's.*

ANTONIO D. MONTEMEZZO. On the Hanoverian plain. Signed and dated Munchen 1874. 14 x 23ins. (35.5 x 58.5cm). *Christie's.*

JULIUS NOERR. Horse-drawn sleighs on a wooded path. Signed and dated München 1860. 20 x 27⅞ins. (51 x 70.5cm). *Christie's.*

JAMES LYNWOOD PALMER.
The Duke of Portland's
racehorses in a meadow. Signed
and dated 1900. 66 x 107½ins.
(167.5 x 274cm). *Christie's.*

EUGÈNE PÈCHAUBÈS.
The race. Signed. 10½ x 23½ins.
(26.5 x 59.5cm). *Christie's.*

STEPHEN PEARCE.
W.R. Stretton on a bay hunter
with the Monmouthshire hunt.
53 x 73ins. (134.5 x 185.5cm).
Christie's.

PIERRE PETIT-GÉRARD. A hunter leaping a hedge. Signed, on panel. 12½ x 9½ins. (32 x 24cm). *Sotheby's.*

EDMOND JOSEPH DE LA PRATÈRE. A woody landscape with a hunt in full cry. Signed. 46¾ x 72¾ins. (119 x 185cm). *Christie's.*

MANUEL PICOLA Y LOPEZ. Full Cry. Signed, on panel. 9 x 13ins. (23 x 33cm). *Sotheby's.*

ALFRED FRANK DE PRADES. A huntsman waiting at the edge of a wood. Signed, on board. 24¼ x 18ins. (61.5 x 45.5cm). *Christie's.*

FRANZ QUAGLIO. Noonday rest. Signed and dated 1887, on panel. 7 x 9½ins. (18 x 24cm). *Christie's.*

AUGUST VON RENTZELL. A gentleman on a bay horse coursing a hare. Signed and dated 1836, on panel. 15 x 19ins. (38 x 48.5cm). *Christie's.*

WILHELM RICHTER. A lady riding side-saddle out hunting. Signed and dated 1878. 23 x 28¾ins. (58.5 x 73cm). *Christie's.*

LOUIS MARIE DOMINIQUE ROMAIN ROBBE. A bay hunter in a landscape. Signed. 29½ x 37½ins. (75 x 95cm). *Christie's.*

BERNARD EDOUARD SWEBACH. A race meeting. Signed and dated 1819. 21 x 28½ins. (53.5 x 72.5cm). *Christie's.*

EDUARDO SANGUINETTI. Lord Suffield, Master of the Buckhounds, Lady Julia Follett and Frank Goodall, Whipper-in in full cry. Signed. 72 x 52ins. (183 x 132cm). *Christie's.*

Top left: GEORGE DERVILLE ROWLANDSON. Over the fence. Signed. 25 x 35¾ins. (63.5 x 91cm). *Christie's.*

Left: HENRY SCHOUTEN. The mid-day rest. Signed. 21¼ x 30¾ins. (54 x 78cm). *Christie's.*

JULIUS FRIEDRICH ANTON SCHRADER. A Horse Fair. Signed and inscribed Munchen. 33¾ x 56¼ins. (86 x 143cm).

WILLIAM SEXTIE. Tom Cannon and his sons on Danebury gallops. Signed. 29½ x 44½ins. (75 x 113cm). *Christie's.*

WILHELM SIMMLER. Gone away. Signed, on panel. 7 x 32½ins. (18 x 82.5cm). *Christie's.*

FREDERICK SHELDON SMITH. The London to Bristol mail coach on a road. Signed and dated 1880. 20 x 36ins. (51 x 91.5cm). *Christie's.*

CHARLES SIMPSON. A tandem cart and pair. Signed. 20½ x 34½ins. (52 x 87.5cm). *Christie's.*

GEORGE WRIGHT. Preparing for a game of polo. Signed. 8 x 12ins. (20 x 30.5cm). *Christie's.*

EDWARD ROBERT SMYTHE. A Shetland pony in a landscape. Signed. 19½ x 29½ins. (49.5 x 75cm). *Christie's.*

THOMAS SMYTHE. A pony and a spaniel in a landscape. Signed and inscribed Ipswich. 16 x 24ins. (40.5 x 61cm). *Christie's.*

CARL CONSTANTIN HEINRICH STEFFECK. The finish, Hoppegarten, Berlin, 15 June 1873. Signed. 29¼ x 51¼ins (74 x 130cm). *Christie's.*

ALFRED STEINACKER. Over the hurdle. Signed, on panel. *Christie's.*

Left: C. TANNER. A dark bay racehorse in a loose box. Signed and dated Dublin 1847. 24½ x 29½ins. (62 x 75cm). *Christie's.*

WILLIAM TASKER. Sir Rubens, a grey hunter, held by Jos. Hawkins, the groom, outside a stable. Signed, inscribed and dated 1835 twice. 18½ x 25½ins. (47 x 59.5cm). *Christie's.*

Bottom left: JOHN FREDERICK TAYLER. 'Granby' a chestnut racehorse with a groom in a loosebox. Signed and dated 1827. 28 x 36ins. (71 x 91.5cm). *Christie's.*

ALFREDO TOMINZ. Over the fence. Signed. 23¼ x 31ins. (59 x 78.5cm). *Christie's.*

CHARLES TOWNE. A chestnut hunter in a landscape with a hunt beyond. Signed and dated 1818. 19¼ x 26ins. (49 x 66cm). *Christie's.*

EDWARD TROYE. A chestnut stallion in a landscape. Signed and dated 1834. 17 x 21½ins. (43.5 x 54.5cm). *Christie's.*

WILLIAM EDDOWES TURNER. A mare and a foal in a paddock. Signed and dated 1889. 24 x 29ins. (61 x 73.5cm). *Christie's.*

CHARLES PHILOGÈNE TSCHAGGENY. Harvest time. Signed and dated 1875, on panel. 24 x 36¾ins. (61 x 93.5cm). *Christie's.*

EUGÈNE JOSEPH VERBOECKHOVEN. A grey stallion with sheep and poultry. Signed and dated 1851, on panel. 14 x 22ins. (35.5 x 56cm). *Christie's.*

405

WOUTER VERSCHUUR. The interior of a stable with travellers, horses and dogs.
Signed and dated 1846. 18¾ x 25¼ins. (47.5 x 64cm). *Christie's.*

BYRON WEBB. Into the river. On board. 15¼ x 20½ins. (39 x 52cm). *Christie's.*

WILLIAM WEEKES. Best of friends.
Signed, on board. 11½ x 8ins.
(29 x 20cm). *Christie's.*

JOHN SANDERSON WELLS. Huntsmen and hounds in a landscape. Signed. 15¼ x 23½ins. (39 x 59.5cm). *Christie's.*

WILLIAM WILLOUGHBY. Priam, a bay racehorse with Sam Day up. Signed and inscribed Boston. 20 x 23¾ins. (50.5 x 60.5cm). *Christie's.*

GEORGE WRIGHT. Up a tree. Signed, grisaille. 16½ x 24¾ins. (42 x 63cm). *Christie's.*

GILBERT SCOTT WRIGHT. Changing the leaders. Signed. 23½ x 36ins. (59.5 x 91.5cm). *Christie's.*

ISIDOR KAUFMANN. His first offence. Signed, on panel. 12½ x 15½ins. (32 x 39.5cm). *Christie's.*

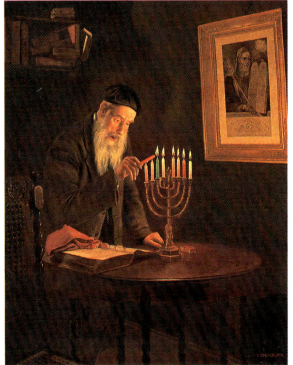

CHARLES SPENCELAYH. The last night of Hanuka. Signed. 20 x 16ins. (51 x 40.5cm). *Christie's.*

Jewish Genre

Paintings of Jewish genre — depicting synagogue ritual, merchants conducting business, rabbis instructing children, bar mitzvahs — were not uncommon in the nineteenth century. They tended to emanate from countries with large Jewish populations, and their increasingly widespread dissemination and exhibition is a measure of the broader process of emancipation of the Jews which continued across Europe throughout the century. The highest concentration of Jewish population by 1900 was to be found in middle and eastern Europe, Poland, Czechoslovakia, Hungary, and that part of the western Russian Empire designated as 'the pale of settlement'. In addition certain western capitals possessed large Jewish elements, notably Vienna, Berlin and Amsterdam. It is no coincidence that most paintings of Jewish life were produced in these areas. A leading specialist like Isidor Kaufmann was for instance born in Hungary and worked in Vienna.

It is not the whole truth to say that subjects of Jewish genre painted by Jewish artists for a Jewish clientele, although undoubtedly a fair number were. Painters also approached such themes with a wider public in mind, in search of a healthy helping of 'character' (Gautier's alternative aim of painting to 'beauty'), and a fair measure of the exotic, not to mention a frequent sprinkling of humour. The Jewish race was seen as a rich repository of 'character', with its worldly wisdom, its traditional business aptitude, and its exotic physical appearance. One of the Ludwig Knaus's best-known works, *A Shrewd Bargain,* elicited this response from an American critic when it was exhibited at the Paris International Exhibition in 1878:

> How beautiful and apostolic seems the doctrine of overreaching as embodied in this saintly bargain-driver! What philanthropy beams from his admirable old face as he teaches his disciple the doctrine 'Do others even as you know they would do you'.

The grasping Jewish businessman thus joins the grossly over indulgent friar and the idyllic rosy cheeked ploughman as victims of popular nineteenth century painting's fondness for stereotypes.

Index of Artists

* HART, Solomon Alexander (British, 1806-1881)
HERBSTOFFER, Karl Peter (Austrian, 1821-1876)
HETZ, Karl (German, 1828-1899)
HIRSZENBERG, Samuel (Polish, 1865-1908)
HOROVITZ, Leopold (Austrian, 1838-1917)
HUNTER, George Sherwood (British, fl.1855-1893)

ISRAEL, Daniel (Austrian, 1859-1901)
ISRAELS, Jozef (Dutch, 1824-1911)

* KAUFMANN, Isidor (Austrian, 1853-1921)
* KNAUS, Ludwig (German, 1829-1910)
KOHN, David (Austrian, 1861-1922)
KRESTIN, Lazar (Austrian, 1868-1938)

LIEBERMANN, Max (German, 1847-1935)
* LINDERUM, Richard (German, 1851-?)

MAKOWSKY, Constantin (Russian, 1839-1915)
* MESSER-KRITLAU, A. (Polish, late 19th Century)
MOYSE, Edouard (French, 1827-?)

* OPPENHEIMER, Moritz Daniel (German, 1800-1882)
OSTERSETZER, Carl (German, late 19th Century)

* PRIECHENFRIED, Alois Heinrich (Austrian, 1867-1953)
* PRUCHA, Gustav (Austrian, 1857-?)

* ROTTMANN, Mozart (Austrian, 1874-?)

SCHLEICHER, Carl (Austrian, fl.1859-1871)
SOLOMON, Simeon (British, 1840-1905)
* SPENCELAYH, Charles (British, 1865-1958)

WAPPERS, Egidus Karel Gustaaf de (Belgian, 1803-1874)
WOLLMANN, Christian Traugott (German, 1778-?)
* WOLMARK, Alfred Aaron (British, 1877-1961)

* ZAFAUREK, Gustav (Austrian, 1841-1908)

JAROSLAV COMAK. The Jews' Cemetery in Prague in the 17th Century. Signed and dated Paris 1857. 45 x 58ins. (114.5 x 147.5cm). *Christie's.*

KARIM BIENKOWSKI. A rabbi at prayer. Signed. 17⅞ x 11½ins. (45 x 29cm). *Sotheby's.*

O. EICHINGER. Portrait of a rabbi. Signed, on board. 10½ x 8ins. (26.5 x 20.5cm). *Christie's.*

CARL HAAG. A Jerusalemite shepherd at devotion. Signed and inscribed, and signed and inscribed on a label on the reverse, pencil and watercolour. 13½ x 9¾ins. (34.5 x 25cm). *Christie's.*

SOLOMON ALEXANDER HART. Reading of the law in a synagogue. Signed and dated 1831. 37 x 28½ins. (94 x 72.5cm). *Christie's.*

ISIDOR KAUFMANN. Portrait of the artist's daughter, Hannah. Signed and inscribed, on panel. 13½ x 10¼ins. (34.5 x 26cm). *Christie's*.

A. MESSER KRITLAU. A rabbi writing at a desk. Indistinctly signed, on board. 10½ x 11¾ins. (27 x 30cm). *Sotheby's*.

LUDWIG KNAUS. A shrewd bargain. Signed and dated 1878. 43¼ x 35½ins. (110 x 90cm). *Sotheby's*.

RICHARD LINDERUM. Reading the Scriptures. Signed and inscribed München, on panel. 8¼ x 10¾ins. (21 x 27cm). *Christie's*.

Opposite left: GUSTAV PRUCHA. The rabbi. Signed. 23 x 18ins. (58.5 x 46cm). *Christie's*.

Opposite right: MOZART ROTTMANN. The reading. Signed. 31¾ x 25½ins. (80.5 x 65cm). *Christie's*.

MORITZ DANIEL OPPENHEIMER. The
Barmitzvah. Signed and dated 1871, canvas laid down
on board. 19½ x 15ins. (49.5 x 38cm). *Christie's.*

ALOIS HEINRICH PRIECHENFRIED. A rabbi. Signed,
on panel. 16 x 12¾ins. (40.5 x 32.5cm). *Christie's.*

ALFRED AARON WOLMARK. The rabbis — waiting for the tenth, for Minian. Signed and dated 1900. 65¾ x 90ins. (167 x 228.5cm). *Christie's.*

GUSTAV ZAFAUREK. The new coat. Signed. 24 x 28¼ins. (61 x 72cm). *Sotheby's.*

Military Painting

It is not surprising that military painters should abound in a century which was devoted to imperialism, colonial expansion, and a good deal of sabre rattling. The political and more specifically nationalistic overtones of pictures representing armed conflict are not difficult to perceive. Chesneau remarked on the good fortune of military painters in this respect: 'Patriotism comes to the aid of battle painters, presenting them with a sympathetic public already fascinated by the subject.' On the other hand P.G. Hamerton, an Englishman, found fault with the bombastic chauvinism of the French military painter Isidore Pils, calling him 'the most coarse and truly vulgar of military painters...whose glaring daubs of gigantic dimensions are liberally purchased by the government, whilst their author receives the honours of his profession.' In fact military painting was calculated to stir up strong feeling: if its success was often based on considerations beyond the purely aesthetic, such as national pride, then its critics might find themselves debunking it on equally inartistic grounds, such as national rivalry.

Three wars dominate the pictorial output of the century. The Napoleonic conflicts represent the first and foremost of these, capturing artists' imaginations for the succeeding one hundred years. If the French were prone to harking back to this era, then so also were the British with countless reconstructions of episodes at Waterloo, especially from Hillingford and Caton Woodville. At least France could boast some serious military painters like Horace Vernet who had actually lived through and worked in those stirring times. The Germans, too, were fond of emphasising their role in the victory at Waterloo, and there were probably political motives in the number of pictures on this theme which they produced in the last quarter of the nineteenth century. The aim was an alliance with Britain at the expense of France; so Camphausen gives us Blucher and Wellington at Belle Alliance, the symbol of two armies joined by the threat of a common foe. Then again, when French painters wished to build up a crescendo of nationalistic pathos and heroism, they could recreate pictorially Napoleon's retreat from Moscow, which they did repeatedly through the ensuing years of the century.

The second war which particularly stimulated artists was the Crimean; painters French as well as English recorded its major battles, Alma, Inkerman and Sebastopol. It is strange that a century which did its best to curb the wider ambitions of female artists, encouraging them only as painters of cats and flowers, should in England see one woman acknowledged as mistress in the very masculine field of the painting of battles. This was Elizabeth Thompson, later Lady Butler, and her first great success was *Calling the Roll after an Engagement, Crimea.* Although painted in 1874, twenty years after the war, it thrilled the whole nation with its poignancy and realism. For the stay-at-home masses, it provided an exciting and convincing whiff of the battlefield. For the rest of the century the public continued to be exhilarated by Lady Butler's pictures of war, Napoleonic, Crimean and Sudanese. Technological advances were certainly made in warfare during the nineteenth century, but nothing so drastic that war was appreciably different three generations after the Napoleonic struggle. Cavalry charges were still a part of military tactics; khaki, such a deadening influence on the attractiveness of battle pictures, had not yet been introduced. The spectacle of colourfully clad cavalry at full throttle could still be exploited to the maximum by Lady Butler and painters like her.

The third war important in a pictorial sense was disproportionately prolific in its inspiration of military pictures. This was the Franco-Prussian encounter of 1870. Artists on both sides incessantly relived the triumphs and disappointments of this relatively brief struggle for the next forty years. The Prussians were not slow to rub in their success, while the French were anxious to retrieve national pride by painting pictures of incidents which reflected their own heroism as against the brutality of the enemy. Alphonse de Neuville's famous *Le Cimetière de St. Privat* (Salon of 1881) was typical in this respect. It depicted the dogged resistance of the hopelessly outnumbered French under Marshal Canrobert against the implacable German force. Its sheer size (2.35 x 3.41 metres) makes a dramatic impact; in the absence of the newsreel and television reports of later wars, it was small wonder that crowds gathered round it entranced, and it was described contemporarily by Louis Enault as 'perhaps the most moving and dramatic document of the Salon of 1881'. Another similarly dramatic recreation of the war by de Neuville, *Dernières Cartouches* of the Salon of 1873, had moved the same critic to declare: 'If this picture does not make something beat beneath your left breast, then in truth the Good Lord has put nothing there' — another instance of patriotic fervour displacing normal artistic standards of judgement, one of the pitfalls of contemporary criticism of military painting.

German military painting reached its apogee in the years following the Franco-Prussian war, with artists like Meyerheim, Christian Sell, Anton Seiler, E. Mattschass and H. Kohlschein beating the drum increasingly loudly. Their strident tone contrasts with the gentler and more amusing renderings of soldiery produced by Bavarian artists in the earlier half of the century, painters like Peter Hess who treated soldiers less as sacred symbols of national glory and more as actors in the rural comedy: falling asleep on guard duty, quarrelling with monks over meals in inns, enjoying a practical joke or two. The Austro-Hungarian empire followed a similar development towards militarism in the second half of the century, and with it emerged painters like Wilhelm Richter, Eckhardt von Eckhardsburg, and A. and C. Schindler who produced battle pictures calculated to arouse pride in the imperial armies.

Spain and Italy had their own internal troubles to preoccupy their military painters in the nineteenth century. The wars of Italian liberation had their pictorial chroniclers such as Gerolamo Induno and Sebastiano de Albertis, although the most distinguished Italian military painter was probably Giovanni Fattori, whose works have presented a challenge to generations of Italian fakers since. At the time of the more widely reported Franco-Prussian conflict, Spain was engaged in the Carlist War, which was assiduously reproduced by José Cusachs, Domingo y Munoz, and Munoz y Cuesta.

Military painting did not, of course, depend on wars for its existence, and many artists achieved success through the recording of parades or even as painters of individual uniforms. A country like Holland was wise enough to avoid international military embroilment but still had its favoured masters, van Papendrecht and occasionally Breitner and Isaac Israels, to paint pictures of colourful military scenes. Actually, after Napoleon, wars in Europe during

OTTO BACHE. The King is coming. Signed and dated 1898. 26 x 38ins. (66 x 96.5cm). *Christie's.*

STANLEY BERKELEY. Gordons and Greys to the front. Signed. 61 x 96½ins. (155 x 245cm). *Christie's.*

the nineteenth century were localised and short lived. Apart from the Crimea and various colonial actions, the British army saw little concerted active service until the Boer War. For the time being military painters could glory in the colour and the spectacle of a good battle, and find any number of prosperous patrons prepared to buy their pictures and enjoy the vicarious thrill of arms, mixed with a measure of patriotism, partly because war was not an immediate reality. Harry Quilter, writing in 1886, noted the inability of English painters:

> to reproduce the ghastly inner life of battle and suffering. We like to have our conflicts painted with as little reminder of their true nature as possible, and so we get from our artists a sort of Easter Monday warfare, such as Mr Crofts shows us, or a sentimental rendering of special incidents such as made Miss Thompson famous.

This mixture of fantasy and exuberance came to an end in 1914, when it was superseded by the need for a new type of war artist, one for whom colour and spectacle had been replaced by khaki and mud.

Index of Artists

GIBB (Jun.), Robert (British, 1845-1932)
GIOLI, Luigi (Italian, 1854-1947)
GIRARDET, Eugène Alexis (French, 1853-1907)
* GIRARDET, Jules (French, 1856-?)
* GONTIER, L. (French?, late 19th Century)
GOW, Andrew Carrick (British, 1848-1920)
* GROLLERON, Paul Louis Narcisse (French, 1848-1901)
GROS, Antoine Jean (French, 1771-1835)
* GUYON, Georges (French, late 19th Century)

HEIDECK, Carl Wilhelm von (French, 1788-1861)
* HENSELER, Ernst (German, 1852-?)
HERRING (Sen.), John Frederick (British, 1795-1865)
HESS, Peter Heinrich Lambert von (German, 1792-1871)
* HILLINGFORD, Robert Alexander (British, 1828-1902)
HOFFBAUER, Charles C.J. (French, 1875-?)
HORSCHELT, Theodor (German, 1829-1871)
* HYON, Georges Louis (French, 1855-?)

* IMSCHOOT, Jules van (Belgian, 1821-1884)
INDUNO, Gerolamo (Italian, 1827-1890)
ISRAELS, Isaac (Dutch, 1865-1934)

JACQUIER, Henri (French, 1878-1921)
JANET, Ange Louis (French, 1815-1872)
* JAZET, Paul Léon (French, 1848-?)

KAISER, Friedrich (German, 1815-1890)
KAUFMANN, Joseph Clement (German, 1867-?)
KENNEDY, William (British, 1860-1918)
KOCH, Georg Karl (German, 1857-1936)
KOCH, Ludwig (Austrian, 1866-1934)
* KOEKKOEK, Hermanus Willem (Dutch, 1867-1929)
KOHLSCHEIN, Hans (German, 1879-?)
KOSSAK, Wojciech von (Polish, 1857-1942)
KOWALEWSKY, Pawel Ossipowitsch (Russian, 1843-1903)

LALAUZE, Alphonse (French, 1872-?)
L'ALLEMAND, Fritz (German, 1812-1866)
L'ALLEMAND, Sigmund (Austrian, 1840-1910)
LANG, Heinrich (German, 1838-1891)
* LAPORTE, George Henry (British, 1799-1873)
* LECLAIRE, Léon Louis (French, 1829-?)
LEDELI, Moritz (Austrian, 1856-1920)
LELEUX, Adolphe Pierre (French, 1812-1891)
* LESUR, Henri Victor (French, 1863-1900?)
LOUSTAUNAU, Louis Auguste Georges (French, 1846-1898)
LOVE, Horace Beevor (British, 1800-1838)

McIAN, Robert Roland (British, 1803-1856)
MAGNUS, James (British, late 19th Century)
MARCHANEL, Andre (French, 1877-1951)
* MARTENS, Henry (British, ?-1860)
MARTIN, Paul (German, 1821-1901)
* MASSE, Auguste Antoine (French, 1795-?)
MATTSCHASS, Erich Friedrich Karl (German, 1866-?)
MEDARD, Eugène (French, 1847-1887)
MEISONNIER, Jean Louis Ernest (French, 1815-1891)
* MEYERHEIM, Wilhelm Alexander (German, 1815-1882)
MICHALOWSKI, Piotr (Polish, 1801-1855)
* MOERENHOUT, Joseph Jodocus (Belgian, 1801-1875)
MONGE, Jules (French, 1855-?)
MONTEN, Dietrich Heinrich Maria (German, 1799-1843)
MOREAU DE TOURS, Georges (French, 1848-1901)

MOROT, Aime Nicolas (French, 1850-1913)
MUNOZ Y CUESTA, Domingo (Spanish, 1850-1912)

* NEUVILLE, Alphonse Marie de (French, 1835-1885)
NOIRE, Orlando (Anglo-Spanish, 1832-1901)
* NURSEY, Claude Lorraine (British, 1820-1873)

PALIZZI, Filippo (Italian, 1818-1899)
* PAPENDRECHT, Jan Hoynck van (Dutch, 1858-1933)
PARIS, Alfred Jean Marie (French, 1846-1908)
PAYNE, Henry Albert (British, 1868-1940)
* PERBOYRE, Paul Emile Léon (French, 1926-?)
PETIT-GERARD, Pierre (French, 1852-?)
* PHILIPPOTEAUX, Henri Félix Emmanuel (French, 1815-1884)
PICKERSGILL, Frederick Richard (British, 1820-1900)
PILS, Isidore Alexandre Augustin (French, 1813-1875)
PLOLL, Victor (German, late 19th Century)
POPPOFF, Alexej Nikolajewitsch (Russian, 1858-?)
POTT, Laslett John (British, 1837-1898)
PRANGEY, E. (French, late 19th Century)
PRANISHNIKOFF, Ivan (Russian, ?-1910)
PROTAIS, Alexandre Paul (French, 1826-1890)
PUTZ, Leo (German, 1869-1940)

RABE, Edmund Friederich Theodor (German, 1815-1902)
RAFFET, Auguste Denis Marie (French, 1804-1860)
RAGAMEY, Guillaume Urbain (French, 1837-1875)
RICHTER, Wilhelm M. (Austrian, 1824-1892)
* RÖCHLING, Karl (German, 1855-1920)
ROCHOLL, Theodor (German, 1854-1933)
ROE, Frederick (British, 1864-1947)
ROEBER, Ernst (German, 1849-1915)
ROSENSTAND, Vilhelm Jacob (Danish, 1838-1915)
ROUFFET, Jules (French, 1862-1931)
ROY, Marius (French, 1833-?)

SABATIER, Louis Anet (French, late 19th Century)
SCHELVER, August Franz (German, 1805-1844)
SCHINDLER, Albert (Austrian, 1805-1861)
SCHINDLER, Carl (Austrian, 1821-?)
SCHNEIDER, Friedrich August (German, 1799-1855)
SCHOTH, A. (French?, late 19th Century)
SCHUCK, Werner Wilhelm Gustav (German, 1843-1918)
SCHUSTER, Ludwig Albrecht (German, 1824-1905)
SCOTT, Georges Bertin (French, 1873-?)
* SECCOMBE, Colonel F.S. (British, late 19th Century)
SEGONI, Alcide (Italian, 1847-1894)
* SEILER, Carl Wilhelm Anton (German, 1846-1921)
* SELL, Christian (German, 1831-1883)
SERGENT, Lucien Pierre (French, 1849-1904)
* SIGRISTE, Guido (Swiss, 1864-1915)
SIMKIN, Richard (British, 1840-1926)
STRASSGSCHWANDTNER, Josef Anton (Austrian, 1826-1881)
SURIKOV, Vassily (Russian, 1848-?)
* SWEBACH, Bernard Edouard (French, 1800-1870)

TREML, Friedrich Johann (Austrian, 1816-1852)

ULMANN, Benjamin (French, 1829-1884)
UNCETA Y LOPEZ, Marcelino (Spanish, 1836-1905)

* VELTEN, Wilhelm (Russian, 1847-1929)
* VERESHCHAGIN, Vasili Petrovich (Russian, 1842-1904)

419

EMILE JEAN HORACE VERNET. La bataille du Pont d'Arcole. Signed and dated 1826. 77 x 103ins. (195.5 x 261cm). *Christie's.*

AUGUSTE ANTOINE MASSE. Une compagnie de la 2eme Legion. Signed and dated 1836. 52½ x 73ins. (132 x 186cm). *Christie's.*

420

VERNET, Emile Jean Horace (French, 1789-1863)
VIBERT, Jean Georges (French, 1840-1902)

* WALKER, James Alexander (British, ?-1898)
WERNER, Anton Alexander von (German, 1843-1915)
WOLLEN, William Barnes (British, 1857-1936)
* WOODVILLE, Richard Caton (Anglo-American, 1856-1926)

WRIGHT, George (British, 1860-1942)

YVON, Adolphe (French, 1817-1893)

ZELLER VON ZELLENBERG, Franz (Austrian, 1805-1876)

JAMES D. AYLWARD. The billeting party. Signed, on panel. 11½ x 8½ins. (29 x 21.5cm). *Christie's.*

OTTO BACHE. Horseguards in
Frederiksholmskanal. Signed and dated 1911.
27½ x 37ins. (70 x 94cm). *Christie's.*

JAMES PRINSEP BEADLE. The Royal
Hussars and the Household Cavalry. Signed.
27 x 50¾ins. (68.5 x 129cm). *Christie's.*

WILFRID CONSTANT BEAUQUESNE.
A skirmish in a town, Franco-Prussian War.
Signed and dated 1894. 18¼ x 21¾ins.
(46.5 x 55.5cm). *Christie's.*

RICHARD BEAVIS. An incident at Waterloo. Signed and dated 1873-4, and inscribed on an old label on the reverse. 44 x 72½ins. (111.5 x 183cm). *Christie's.*

ETIENNE PROSPER BERNE-BELLECOUR. A quiet smoke. Signed and dated 1893, on panel. 23¾ x 14½ins. (60 x 37cm). *Christie's.*

ALEXANDER VON BENSA. A cavalry encampment. Signed, on panel. 7¾ x 12¾ins. (19.5 x 32.5cm). *Christie's.*

FRANÇOIS AUGUSTE BIARD. The Inspection. Signed. 25 x 41½ins. (63.5 x 105.5cm). *Christie's.*

AUGUSTE BIGAND. An Austrian cavalry attack. Signed and dated 1852. 19 x 25¼ins. (48 x 64.5cm). *Christie's.*

ALBERT BLIGNY. The battle of Marengo. Signed, on panel. 17½ x 21¼ins. (44.5 x 54cm). *Christie's.*

JULIAN LE BLANT. A battle scene. Signed and dated 1880. 59¼ x 86ins. (150.5 x 218.5cm). *Christie's.*

EMILE BRISSET. The last shot. Signed and dated '88. 42½ x 61ins. (108 x 155cm). *Christie's.*

JOHN LEWIS BROWN. The return of Napoleon from Waterloo. Signed and dated 1874, on panel. 18 x 13¾ins. (46 x 35cm). *Christie's.*

LADY BUTLER. The roll call. 36 x 72ins. (91.4 x 182.8cm). *Reproduced by gracious permission of H.M. The Queen.*

WILHELM VON CAMPHAUSEN.
Wellington greeting Blucher after the
battle near Belle-Alliance, 18 June 1815.
Signed and dated 1862. 28 x 38ins.
(71 x 96.5cm). *Christie's.*

JOHN CHARLTON. The Shanghai
Volunteer Corps at a review. Signed with
initials and dated 1892. 35¼ x 62ins.
(89.5 x 157.5cm). *Christie's.*

JAN VAN CHELMINSKI. The duel.
Signed and dated München 1881.
39 x 58¼ins. (99 x 148cm). *Christie's.*

ALPHONSE CHIGOT. Military bandsmen on the ramparts at Valenciennes. Signed twice, inscribed, and dated 1863 and 1864. 9 x 15¼ins. (23 x 38.5cm). *Christie's.*

ERNEST CROFTS. French Cuirassiers on the march. Signed, on board. 14½ x 11¾ins. (37 x 30cm). *Christie's.*

JOSÉ CUSACHS Y CUSACHS. Spanish soldiers crossing a mountainous terrain. Signed and dated 1896. 19½ x 39ins. (49.5 x 99cm). *Sotheby's.*

NICOLAS LOUIS ALBERT DELARIVE. An Hussar officer mounted on a charger. Signed and dated 1805. 54 x 45¼ins. (137 x 110cm). *Christie's.*

JEAN BAPTISTE EDOUARD DETAILLE.
A French Infantryman. Signed and dated 1877.
13 x 8¾ins. (33 x 22cm). *Christie's.*

Above right: WILHELM VON DIEZ. Cavalry on
parade. Signed, on panel. 5½ x 7¼ins. (14 x 18.5cm).
Christie's.

Centre right: HENRY LOUIS DUPRAY. Soldiers
drinking at a bar. Signed, on panel. 10 x 13ins.
(25.5 x 33cm). *Christie's.*

JOSÉ DOMINGO Y MUNOZ. Soldiers at the
blacksmith's yard. Signed and dated Paris 1897, on
panel. 9½ x 12¾ins. (24 x 32.5cm). *Sotheby's.*

LUDWIG ELSHOLTZ. Greeting the cavalry.
Signed and dated 1840. 18½ x 23½ins.
(47 x 59.5cm). *Christie's.*

GIOVANNI FATTORI. Returning home. Signed and bears a second signature. 12¾ x 27¼ins. (32.5 x 69cm). *Sotheby's.*

CONRAD FREYBERG. The cavalry charge. Signed and dated 1869, unframed. 33 x 59ins. (84 x 150cm). *Sotheby's.*

ALFRED EMILE GAUBAULT. A portrait of a Cavalryman. Signed, on panel. 9¾ x 7¼ins. (24.5 x 18.5cm). *Sotheby's.*

JULES GIRARDET. French soldiers asking their way through the woods. Signed. 37½ x 53ins. (95 x 134.5cm). *Sotheby's.*

L. GONTIER. The battle of Lutzen, 1813. Signed and inscribed. 21½ x 36ins. (54.5 x 91.5cm). *Christie's.*

PAUL LOUIS NARCISSE GROLLERON. Skirmishers. Signed. 24½ x 17½ins. (62 x 44.5cm). *Christie's.*

ERNST HENSELER. The billet. Signed and dated 1894.
40¼ x 59¾ins. (102 x 152cm). *Christie's.*

GEORGES GUYON. French soldiers relaxing by a campfire.
Signed. 18 x 14¾ins. (45.5 x 37.5cm). *Christie's.*

ROBERT ALEXANDER HILLINGFORD. Napoleon's peril at Brienne-le-Château. Signed and dated 1891. 38¾ x 55½ins.
(98.5 x 141cm). *Christie's.*

GEORGES LOUIS HYON. Napoleon on the road from Moscow. Signed. 25 x 31½ins. (63.5 x 80cm). *Christie's.*

JULES VAN IMSCHOOT. A cavalry charge, possibly Garibaldi at one of his battles in the war of 1866. Signed and dated 1866. 11¾ x 17½ins. (30 x 44.5cm). *Sotheby's.*

HERMANUS WILLEM KOEKKOEK. Lancers of the Ulanen Regiment on a country road. Signed. 16½ x 23ins. (42 x 58.5cm). *Christie's.*

PAUL LÉON JAZET. The charge of the Cuirassiers. Signed and dated 1881. 29 x 21½ins. (73.5 x 54.5cm). *Christie's.*

GEORGE HENRY LAPORTE. Soldiers of the 3rd Dragoons and the 9th Lancers outside the Star and Garter inn. Signed and dated 1841. 40 x 50½ins. (101.5 x 128cm). *Christie's.*

LÉON LOUIS LECLAIRE. The trumpet practice. Signed and dated 1857. 26¾ x 41½ins. (68 x 105.5cm). *Christie's.*

HENRI VICTOR LESUR. The barracks of the XVIIEME Dragoons. Signed and inscribed, on panel. 22 x 18ins. (56 x 45.5cm). *Christie's.*

WILHELM ALEXANDER MEYERHEIM. Welcoming the Hussars. Signed and dated 1866. 16¾ x 21¾ins. (42.5 x 55.5cm). *Christie's.*

Top left: HENRY MARTENS. The first Bombay European Regiment and two mounted officers of the Bombay Light Cavalry in India. 20¼ x 29½ins. (51.5 x 75cm). *Christie's.*

Left: JAN HOYNCK VAN PAPENDRECHT. The prisoners. Signed with initials. 14¼ x 20ins. (36 x 51cm). *Christie's.*

ALPHONSE MARIE DE NEUVILLE. Le cimetière de Saint Privat. Signed and dated 1881. 82 x 132ins. (235 x 341cm). *Musée d'Arras. Photo: Leroy.*

CLAUDE LORRAINE NURSEY. Encampment of the First County Battalion of Norfolk Volunteers at Gunton Park. 27 x 54ins. (68.5 x 137cm). *Christie's.*

Top right: JOSEPH JODOCUS MOERENHOUT. Calvalrymen taking refreshment outside an inn. Signed, on panel. 19¼ x 15½ins. (49 x 39.5cm). *Christie's.*

PAUL EMILE LÉON PERBOYRE. The eve of the battle of Froeschwiller. Signed. 12½ x 9ins. (31.5 x 2?cm). *Christie's.*

HENRI FÉLIX EMMANUEL PHILIPPOTEAUX. A French artillery officer with a troop of horse artillery. Signed. 12½ x 8¾ins. (32 x 22cm). *Christie's.*

KARL RÖCHLING. Prussian Infantry storming a hill:
Franco-Prussian War, 1870. Signed and dated 1910.
40 x 73ins. (101.5 x 185.5cm). *Christie's.*

COL. F.S. SECCOMBE. The Coldstream Guards on
manoeuvres. Canvas laid down on board. 13 x 19½ins.
(33 x 49.5cm). *Christie's.*

CHRISTIAN SELL. A battle scene with a cavalry officer
directing infantrymen. Signed and dated 1880, on panel.
5½ x 6¼ins. (14 x 16cm). *Christie's.*

CARL WILHELM ANTON SEILER. Prussian soldiers in a
barn. Signed and dated 1905, on panel. 24 x 30ins.
(61 x 76cm). *Christie's.*

GUIDO SIGRISTE. The charge of the French
Cuirassiers at Waterloo. Signed. 10½ x 16ins.
(27 x 40.5cm). *Christie's.*

BERNARD EDOUARD SWEBACH. Soldiers of the French
Imperial army resting by cottages. Signed and dated 1829(?).
9½ x 15½ins. (24 x 39.5cm). *Christie's.*

WILHELM VELTEN. An extensive landscape with Prussian troops and peasants on a path. Signed and inscribed München.
20½ x 31½ins. (52 x 80cm). *Christie's.*

JAMES ALEXANDER WALKER. An artillery battle. Signed. 27½ x 39½ins. (70 x 100.5cm). *Christie's.*

VASILI PETROVICH VERESHCHAGIN. A French soldier smoking a pipe. Signed with initial, on board. 15¾ x 12ins. (40 x 30.5cm). *Christie's.*

438

RICHARD CATON WOODVILLE. Life-Guards charging at the Battle of Waterloo. Signed and dated 1899. 34¾ x 23¼ins. (88 x 59cm). *Christie's.*

Monkeys

'Singeries', pictures of monkeys engaging in human activities, often clad in comically human costume, were popular during the nineteenth century. Gabriel Alexandre Decamps who, besides being a leading Orientalist, earned a reputation as a consummate painter of such things, explained that 'the mania for animals which possessed me...forced me to make pictures in which these interesting animals are the actors'. Neatly though such pictures fit in with the prevailing fondness for anthropomorphism in animal painting, they were not in fact an invention of the time, having been widely produced as early as the seventeenth century.

Animals are the actors in these scenes, but they differ from the average sentimental dog or cat picture. The equivalent Henriette Ronner-Knip for instance shows an animal displaying quasi-human emotion, but remaining nonetheless a cat or a dog. Monkeys go further: they are actually dressed up in human clothes, engaged in specifically human activities. They work at artists' easels, sit at banqueting tables. The 'travestissement', or disguise, is the more effective for the fact that monkeys are of all animals the closest physically to the human race. Indeed the existence in English of the verb 'to ape' meaning to imitate closely and perhaps comically, indicates the monkey's facility for reproducing human actions and manners. 'Singeries' thus strike a dissonant note when compared with other animal paintings of the time. There is an element of the grotesque about them: they present monkeys as performers, and their appeal is that of the circus.

Index of Artists

EDMUND BRISTOW.
Monkeys in a tavern.
Signed and dated Windsor
July 1826. Canvas, laid
down on panel.
8¾ x 11¾ins. (22 x 29cm).
Christie's.

GABRIEL ALEXANDRE DECAMPS. The experts. Signed and dated 1837. 18¼ x 25¼ins. (46.4 x 64cm). *The Metropolitan Museum of Art, Bequest of Mrs H.O. Havemeyer, 1929. The H.O. Havemeyer Collection.*

E. CARPENTERO. Monkeys playing draughts. Signed,
on panel. 9½ x 13¼ins. (24 x 33.5cm). *Christie's.*

Top right: SIR EDWIN HENRY LANDSEER.
Impertinent puppies dismissed by a monkey in a barn.
Signed and dated 1821. 27½ x 35½ins. (70 x 90.5cm).
Christie's.

Centre right: GABRIEL CORNELIUS VON MAX. Die
Kunstkritiker. Signed. 33¼ x 42ins. (84.5 x 107cm).
Christie's.

ZACHARIAS NOTERMAN. The foolish pupil. Signed,
on panel. 19¼ x 16ins. (49 x 40.5cm). *Christie's.*

VINCENT DE VOS. Monkeys at play. Signed, on panel.
10¼ x 14ins. (26 x 35.5cm). *Christie's.*

Monks

A subdivision of ecclesiastical genre concerns itself with the monastery behind closed doors: scenes showing monks *en déshabille* were as popular as those exposing cardinals' private moments, and perhaps even more widespread. From Munich, where Eduard von Grützner specialised in unguarded incidents in closed orders, to London, where Walter Dendy Sadler built a huge reputation for similar work, a procession of lusty, drunken, accident-prone monks stretched out across the drawing room walls of Europe.

English painters stood aloof from painting cardinals in distress. The *Art Journal* viewed such pictures as some sort of Continental aberration, and noted disapprovingly that they were 'hailed with delight by the Italian civic flaneur'. Monks, however, were a different matter, and could be considered fairer game. The *Art Journal* elsewhere refers to Dendy Sadler's 'gentle jesting with monks and friars', and indeed Sadler's two masterpieces of monastery life — *Thursday* showing monks fishing for their next day's lunch, and *Friday* showing them eating it — both swiftly found their way into major public collections, the Tate Gallery and the Walker Art Gallery, Liverpool. Sadler's tone, while not explicitly abusive, nonetheless characterises monks as good-natured simpletons rather than beings of highly developed spirituality.

The iconography of the school of monastic genre is limited, by the very nature of the closed community depicted. One can isolate five main areas of subject matter. *Thursday* and *Friday* are arguably the masterpieces of the first, the piscatorial-monastic: fishing was an outdoor activity apparently widely practised by monks and frequently chronicled by nineteenth century painters. The second, the bibulous-monastic, found its greatest practitioner in Grützner, a specialist in scenes from the monastery wine cellar. He produced a finely-wrought series of rotund and rubicund monks at work amongst the vats, often in trances alcoholically rather than divinely induced. The culinary-monastic covers kitchen scenes in which monks prove themselves so prone to domestic mishaps that the life span of the crockery is patently miniscule, and also monks eating, one of the few activities they seem good at. A small but significant fourth subdivision exists in the ablutionary-monastic. Henry Stacy-Marks has two monks merrily performing their toilet in *Cleanliness is Next to Godliness*, a trivial emphasising of the everyday rather than the spiritual aspects of life in a closed community. Not surprisingly, it was bought by Pears for use in a soap advertisement rather than by a religious order anxious to preserve for posterity a pictorial record of life in the monastery in the nineteenth century. Finally, the amatory-monastic is a rarer, somewhat more risqué category, occasionally encountered in the work of artists of the French and Italian schools. Monks who are allowed into the outside world are occasionally portrayed making a pass at a serving wench. The reaction of the *Art Journal* reviewer is not recorded.

Why this widespread fascination with keyhole visions of the domestic life of the monastery? Three motives can be suggested. First there is the attraction, to be encountered frequently in popular nineteenth century painting, of the new picture buyer to all such invasions of privacy; and in this case the privacy to be invaded was a particularly protected one. The closed community of a monastic order was seldom to be penetrated by the ordinary man, and it was therefore all the more fascinating to him.

Secondly, there had been, particularly on the Continent, considerable agitation about the wealth of some of the orders. Those pictures which present monks as men whose occupations are idly irrelevant, whose ineffectual existences are supported by an unearned inherited wealth, are often indirectly making a political point. The ultimate implication is that state expropriation would be more beneficial to society.

Thirdly, the monastic way of life struck 'modern' man of the later nineteenth century as increasingly difficult to understand, and roused both his scorn and his unease. The age was materialistic, and, as it flexed the muscles of its new technological strength, occupants of monasteries could only be disdained as objects of ridicule and mistrust. Commentators on Grützner make much of the fact that he was himself a practising Roman Catholic and conclude on these grounds that there can be no anti-clerical intent in his merry, drunken monks. But perhaps the sugar coating of 'gemutlichkeit' distracts from the fundamental point. One did not have to be a godless materialist to reach with suspicion and mockery to an institution so out of step with the march of modern life. Even a young Church of England curate was not immune to such feelings after visiting a monastery in 1870. It was then that Kilvert wrote in his diary:

> It does seem very odd at this age of the world in the latter part of the nineteenth century to see monks gravely wearing such dresses and at work in them in broad day. One could not help thinking how much more sensible and really religious was the dress and occupation of the masons and of the hearty healthy girl washing at the chapel house, living naturally in the world and taking their share of its work, cares and pleasure, than the morbid unnatural life of these monks going back into the error of the dark ages and shutting themselves up from the world to pray for the world.

The Claudio Rinaldi monk who slurps his spaghetti and Arnaldo Tamburini's alcoholic friar are part of a rich literary tradition, stretching back to Chaucer and beyond, of monastic lapses from strict self-denial into avid partaking of worldly pleasures. But Rinaldi, Tamburini and company are also reflecting an insecurity distinctly nineteenth century, a strengthened suspicion of a way of life which, being in essence spiritual, is at variance with the materialist and scientific tendency of the times. Their reaction is one of mockery, expressed pictorially in comic monastic anecdote.

Index of Artists

* ANDREOTTI, Federigo (Italian, 1847-1930)

BALDO, Marin (Spanish, late 19th Century)
BARASCUDTS, Max (German, 1869-1927)
BAUMANN, Hans Otto (Swiss, 1862-?)
BAUMGARTNER, Pieter (German, 1834-1911)
BLOCH, Carl Heinrich (Danish, 1834-1890)
BORTIGNONI, Giuseppe (Italian, 1778-1860)
BUONGIORNO, C. (Italian, late 19th Century)

* CALOSCI, Arturo (Italian, 1855-1926)
CASANOVA Y ESTORACH, Antonio (Spanish, 1847-1896)
CEDERSTRÖM, Baron Ture Nikolaus de (Swedish, 1845-1924)
COLEMAN, Enrico (Italian, 1846-1911)
* COLEMAN, Francesco (Italian, 1851-?)
* COSTA, L. da (Italian, late 19th Century)

DAGNAN-BOUVERET, Pascal Adolphe Jean (French, 1852-?)
DAVIS, Frederick William (British, 1862-1919)

EICHINGER, Erwin (Austrian, late 19th Century)

FRANGIAMORE, Salvatore (Italian, 1853-1915)

GAYLER, L. (German, late 19th Century)
GLINDONI, Henry Gillard (British, 1852-1913)
* GRÜTZNER, Eduard von (German, 1846-1878)

* HUMBORG, Adolf (Austrian, 1847-1913)
HYDE, Frank (British, fl.1872-1885)

* KERN, Herman (Austrian, 1839-1912)
KRAMER, Pieter Cornelis (Dutch, 1879-1940)
KRAUS, August (German, 1852-1917)

* LANZONI, P. (Italian, late 19th Century)
LEYENDECKER, Paul Joseph (French, 1842-?)
LINDERUM, Richard (German, 1851-?)

* MASSANI, Pompeo (Italian, 1850-1920)
MEISEL, Ernst (German, 1838-1895)

* MORO, Ferruccio (Italian, 1859-?)
MÜHR, Joseph (Austrian, 1873-1912)

* NOWAK, Ernst (Austrian, 1851-1919)

OFFORD, John J. (British, late 19th Century)
ORFEI, Orfeo (Italian, fl.1862-1888)
ORTLEIB, Friedrich (German, 1839-1909)

PEROFF, Vassily Grigorevich (Russian, 1833-1882)
* PETROCELLI, Arturo (Italian, 1856-?)

RIEFSTAHL, Wilhelm Ludwig Friedrich (German, 1827-1888)
* RINALDI, Claudio (Italian, late 19th Century)

* SADLER, Walter Dendy (British, 1824-1923)
* SANI, Alessandro (Italian, late 19th Century)
* SCHAVEN, R. (German, late 19th Century)
SCHLEICHER, Carl (Austrian, fl.1859-1871)
SCHMIDT, Matthias (German, 1749-1823)
SCHOLZ, Max (German, 1855-1906)
SEEGER, Hermann (German, 1857-?)
* SEGONI, Alcide (Italian, 1847-1894)
SOMERS, Louis Jean (Belgian, 1813-1880)
SORBI, Raffaello (Italian, 1844-1931)
SPITZWEG, Carl (German, 1843-1908)
* SPRING, Alfons (German, 1843-1908)
* STACY-MARKS, Henry (British, 1829-1890)
STOITZNER, Constantin (Austrian, 1863-1934)
* STREITT, Franciszek (Polish, 1839-1890)

* TAMBURINI, Arnaldo (Italian, 1843-?)
* THEDY, Marc (German, 1858-1924)
* TILL, Johannes (Austrian, 1827-1894)
TORRINI, Pietro (Italian, 1852-?)

VIBERT, Jean Georges (French, 1840-1902)

WEEKES, William (British, fl.1865-1904)
WINTER, Pharaon Abdon Léon de (French, 1849-1924)

* ZIMMERMAN, Reinhard Sebastian (German, 1815-1893)

EDUARD VON GRÜTZNER. A quiet smoke. Signed and dated 95. 17 x 14ins. (43 x 35.5cm). *Christie's.*

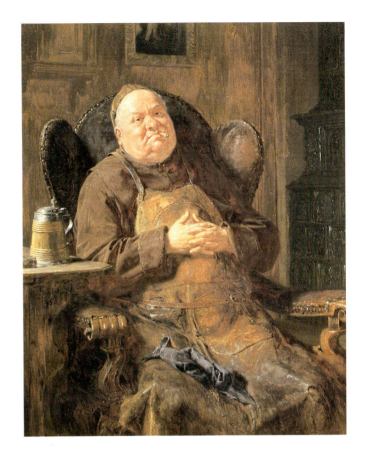

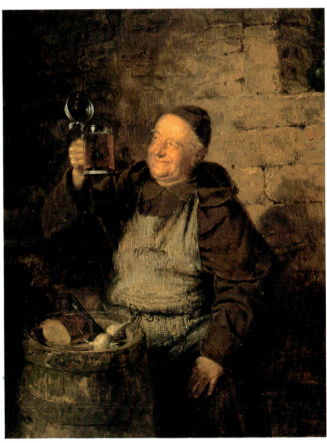

EDUARD VON GRÜTZNER. In a monastery kitchen. Signed and dated 87, on panel. 15 x 11¾ins. (38 x 30cm). *Christie's.*

FEDERIGO ANDREOTTI. Blessing the pot. Signed.
11 x 8¾ins. (28 x 22cm). *Christie's.*

ARTURO CALOSCI. The musical monk. Signed.
14¼ x 9¾ins. (36 x 25cm). *Sotheby's.*

L. DA COSTA. Cooling the pot. Signed. 19 x 14½ins.
(48 x 37cm). *Christie's.*

FRANCESCO COLEMAN. The lesson. Signed and dated
Roma 1891. 11½ x 14¾ins. (29 x 37.5cm). *Christie's.*

ADOLF HUMBORG. Leisure time at the abbey. Signed and inscribed München. 19¾ x 32½ins. (50.5 x 82.5cm). *Christies.*

P. LANZONI. A portrait for posterity. Signed, on panel. 13 x 17ins. (33 x 43cm). *Christie's.*

HERMAN KERN. A refreshing draught. On panel. 18¼ x 11¾ins. (46.5 x 30cm). *Christie's.*

447

FERRUCCIO MORO. A fine vintage. Signed and inscribed Firenze. 19 x 11½ins. (48 x 29cm). *Christie's.*

ERNST NOWAK. Admiring the catch. Signed. 19¼ x 25ins. (49 x 63.5cm). *Sotheby's.*

Top left: POMPEO MASSANI. A good smoke. Signed and inscribed Firenze. 12 x 15¾ins. (30.5 x 40cm). *Christie's.*

ARTURO PETROCELLI. A good stew. Signed. 8¾ x 12ins. (22.5 x 30.5cm). *Sotheby's.*

CLAUDIO RINALDI. The last drop. Signed and inscribed Firenze. 27 x 42¾ins. (68.5 x 108.5cm). *Christie's.*

WALTER DENDY SADLER. Thursday. Signed. 34 x 55½ins. (86 x 140cm). *Tate Gallery.*

ALESSANDRO SANI. Good advice. Signed. 17½ x 23ins. (44.5 x 58.5cm). *Christie's.*

R. SCHAVEN. A fine brew. Signed. 19½ x 25½ins. (49.5 x 64.5cm). *Christie's.*

ALCIDE SEGONI. A ticklish moment. Signed. 13½ x 11¼ins. (34.5 x 28.5cm). *Christie's.*

ALFONS SPRING. The sleeping monk. Signed and inscribed München, on panel. 29 x 19¼ins. (74 x 49cm). *Christie's.*

HENRY STACY-MARKS. The illuminated manuscript.
Signed and dated 1862. 25½ x 35½ins. (65 x 90cm).
Christie's.

ARNALDO TAMBURINI. His favourite pet. Signed and
inscribed Florence, on panel. 9½ x 7ins. (24 x 18cm).
Sotheby's.

FRANCISZEK STREITT. A pinch of snuff. Signed.
21½ x 17½ins. (54.5 x 44.5cm). *Christie's.*

JOHANNES TILL. Monastic produce. Signed and dated 1890. 30 x 18½ins. (76 x 47cm). *Christie's.*

Top left: MARC THEDY. The contented monk. Signed and dated München '81. 10¼ x 7ins. (26 x 18cm). *Christie's.*

REINHARD SEBASTIAN ZIMMERMAN. In the monastery library. Signed and dated 1876, on panel. 8¾ x 7¾ins. (22 x 19.5cm). *Christie's.*

Nudes

There can be few, if any, conventional nineteenth century painters who did not paint nudes at some early stage in their careers. Drawing from the undraped model, or from antique statuary, was an integral part of the training of the academy. Those who continued to treat such subjects for their living were an intrepid band, treading a minefield of potential moral obloquy. The unclothed human form presented serious problems in the climate of prudery which prevailed: but still there were artists who persisted and found it a profitable enterprise. It was necessary, however, to walk a tightrope of hyprocrisy.

The first essential of respectable nude painting was to establish some sort of convincing cover. This was normally achieved by setting the figure in a scenario which incorporated an element of distance from the spectator's own experience. This distance could be of time or of place. Thus antiquity was a particularly useful pretext. The many artists who painted classical nudes did so because it was an accepted fact that the ancients spent a fair amount of time divested of their clothes. Classical mythology was replete with Venuses, Nymphs (Sea, River, or Wood varieties) and Sirens, none of whom could exist satisfactorily unless naked. Then there were scenes like The Judgement of Paris, Gyges and Candaules, or The Rape of the Sabines which also demanded nudity. On a more prosaic, realistic level, the level of Alma-Tadema, settings such as the Roman baths, sculptors' studios, visits to medicinal springs, all gave ample opportunity for the removal of clothes.

The Bible was also consulted, and brought forth The Bath of Bathsheba, Joseph and Potiphar's Wife, and Susannah and the Elders. Further forward in history, Lady Godiva was also a tempting stimulus to both English and French painters. Then came a whole range of allegorical subjects: personifications of Truth took the form of nubile young ladies emerging unclothed from wells; The Seasons meant the same nubile young ladies frolicking amongst daffodils (Spring) or falling leaves (Autumn); and The Three Graces saw them once again as nature intended, this time dancing in loose embrace.

Distance from the present reality could also be established by place rather than time. Geographically the Middle East was far removed from most people's experience: even more so its seraglios and slave-markets (*see also* HAREMS). Yet such nudes, and those set in antiquity, had the same appeal of immediacy as much popular history painting of the nineteenth century, playing on the same intriguing premise that while times, places and societies change, certain human elements remain recognisably constant. In this case the abiding human element is the naked human form; thus artists were able to paint nudes (provided they were set in far-off situations) with an intimacy and realistic detail which a distant setting was alleged to compromise but could not in fact diminish.

What was less acceptable was nude painting for its own sake, the realistic depiction of a naked model in a contemporary setting. Only later in the century did a more progressive element introduce such practices on a wider scale; even then there was often a somewhat unconvincing emphasis on Health and Nature, as with the sturdy Swedish ladies cavorting *en plein air* in Anders Zorn's pictures of the 1880s and after. In the same category come the muscular male nudes of Henry Scott Tuke, the Cornish fisherboys who dive interminably from rowing boats. Other examples of nude painting set contemporarily, particularly if Parisian in origin, are unashamedly 'naughty'. Georges Croegaert and Carolus-Duran, for instance, produced pictures which are little more than expensive dirty postcards, showing *déshabillé* models relaxing accessibly in their boudoirs.

Many contemporary commentators addressed themselves to the question of the nude in art. Few made much sense of the problem. The French critic Ste-Beuve strikes a typical note of caution:

> The artist has of course rights, including even the right to paint the nude; but he requires, in order to absolve and justify him, a certain seriousness, passion, frankness of intention and force of truth.

All too often in England this caution in relation to the unclothed human form produced peculiarly anaemic, lifeless paintings of the Ideal, as is the case with Leighton and Watts. Perhaps they remained wary of the sanctimonious *Art Journal* critic who sharply reminded the unfortunate W.E. Frost that 'Nature, when least adorned, has a right to expect that the artist will take no advantage of her unprotected state'. The precise meaning of this cryptic jibe is elusive, but one catches the general drift. Then there was the bishop of Carlisle, profoundly concerned about Alma-Tadema's *The Sculptor's Model*:

> In the case of an Old Master much allowance has been made… for Old Masters it might be assumed knew no better… but for a living artist to exhibit a life-size life-like almost photographic representation of a beautiful naked woman strikes my inartistic mind as somewhat if not very mischievous.

There is a revealing and typically Victorian assumption underlying the Bishop's remarks about Old Masters knowing no better, a conviction of modern progress to a moral level unattainable by the nineteenth century's unfortunate ancestors. But in another way the Bishop was right to draw a distinction between an old master painting of the nude and one by Alma-Tadema. Alma-Tadema was exploiting a contemporary moral climate which did not exist for Titian: in withdrawing into the past for his setting but at the same time presenting a scene of 'almost photographic' vividness, Alma-Tadema was following the vogue for meticulous and life-like historical reconstruction and incorporating an element of titillation in the tension between past and present. Such a tension would have had less relevance to Titian and his contemporaries, who could approach the nude in a less devious and less hypocritical frame of mind.

On the Continent, nude painting was haunted by the ghost of David. Pupils as varied as Anton Wiertz in Belgium and C.W. Eckersberg in Denmark felt his influence, and in their turn passed it on to others. In France, through Ingres, successive generations of painters were made aware of his legacy of neoclassicism. As the century progressed, however, a change in emphasis is perceptible, a change which tended to underplay the ideal in favour of something more accessible and sensual. A new sort of follower of Ingres emerged, men like Cabanel, Baudry and Bouguereau whose nudes were vaguely classical and highly opulent. It was J.F. Millet who wrote a damning but not entirely unfair epitaph on most French Salon nudes of the second half of the century when he said of the work of Cabanel and Baudry: 'I have never seen anything that seemed to me a more frank and direct appeal to the passions of bankers and stockbrokers'. Such painters perfected a formula combining nudes and classical trappings for the titillation of 'City' patrons under the respectable guise of Art. They gave them the opportunity simultaneously to enjoy large expanses of female flesh and to gain reputations as art collectors and connoisseurs. But the *Art Journal* in London, ever vigilant for suspicious activities on the other side of the Channel, was not to be deceived, and declared in relation to Gérôme's especially-revealing *Phryne*: 'Cleverness of innuendo, a certain semblance of decorum preserved in the midst of sentiment dubious, such is the cunning subterfuge which has made French novelists, dramatists and painters notorious.'

For conventional nineteenth century art criticism, the problem posed by the nude arose out of the standards of judgement normally employed to define a picture's success or failure. These were direct and obvious criteria, one might almost say positivist standards. Elsewhere painters could be congratulated for pictures of peaches which made the mouth water, and for scenes of pathos which drew real tears to the eye of the spectator. So why withhold praise when a painting of a nude excited real lust? Perhaps this is what the French critic Burger is complaining about when he says of the 'Ingrist' ideal nudes of the Salon of 1864: 'All these sad images don't represent women at all; there's no flesh nor bone, no blood nor skin: they don't stir you, and they wouldn't know how to stir you.'

In fact, nineteenth century paintings of the nude set up and exploited a series of paradoxes between appearance and reality, art and pornography, distance and proximity, restraint and vulgarity, perhaps culminating in the old conflict between romanticism and realism.

PAUL BAUDRY. Muses of Mathematics.
Signed. 26½ x 16⅛ ins.
(67 x 41cm). *Sotheby's.*

JULIUS DE BENCZUR. Bacchante.
Signed. 77 x 46ins. (196 x 117cm).
Christie's.

SIR LAWRENCE ALMA-TADEMA. A sculptor's
model (Venus Esquilina). Signed and inscribed
Opus CLXXIX. 77 x 33ins. (195.5 x 84cm). *Christie's.*

JOHN WILLIAM GODWARD. Venus binding her hair.
89¼ x 49ins. (227 x 124.5cm). *Christie's.*

456

Index of Artists

INGRES, Jean Auguste Dominique (French, 1780-1867)

JALABERT, Jean (French, 1815-?)
JAMIN, Paul Joseph (French, 1853-1903)
JOBBE-DUVAL, Felix Armand Marie (French, 1821-1889)
JOURDAN, Adolphe (French, 1825-1889)
* JOY, George William (British, 1844-1925)

* KAHLER, Karl (Austrian, 1855-?)
* KASPARIDES, Edouard (Austrian, 1858-1926)
* KELLER, Albert von (Swiss, 1844-1920)
* KELLER, Ferdinand (German, 1842-1922)
  KIESEL, Conrad (German, 1846-1921)
  KRAY, Wilhelm (German, 1828-1889)

  LAEZZA, Giuseppe (Italian, ?-1905)
  LALIRE, Adolphe (French, ?-1905)
  LAMBRON DES PILTIÈRES, Albert (French, 1836-?)
* LANDINI, Andrea (Italian, 1847-?)
  LANGENMANTEL, Ludwig von (German, 1854-1922)
  LARD, François Maurice (French, 1864-1908)
  LAURENS, Paul Albert (French, 1870-?)
  LAVALLEY, Alexandre Claude Louis (French, 1862-1927)
  LEEKE, Ferdinand (German, 1859-?)
  LEFEBVRE, Jules Joseph (French, 1836-1912)
  LEHMANN, Heinrich Rudolf (German, 1814-1882)
  LEIGHTON, Frederic Lord (British, 1830-1896)
* LEMATTE, Jacques François Fernand (French, 1850-?)
  LÉVY, Emile (French, 1826-1890)
  LOOP, Henry Augustus (Italian-American, 1831-1895)
  LOTZ, Karl (German, 1833-1904)
* LOVERINI, Ponziano (Italian, 1845-?)
  LOWCOCK, Charles Frederick (British, ?-1922)

  MACLISE, Daniel (British, 1806-1870)
  MAINE, Georges Clemansin du (French, 1853-?)
  MAKART, Hans (Austrian, 1840-1884)
* MALMONT, Rene Mege du (French, late 19th Century)
  MARSTRAND, Wilhelm (Danish, 1810-1873)
* MERCIÉ, Marius Jean Antoine (French, 1845-1916)
  MERSON, Luc Olivier (French, 1846-1920)
  MERWART, Paul (Polish, 1855-1902)
  METEYARD, Sidney Harold (British, 1868-1947)
* MILLET, Jean François (French, 1814-1875)
  MILLOT, Adolphe Philippe (French, 1857-1921)
  MOORE, Albert Joseph (British, 1841-1893)
  MORGAN, Evelyn de (British, 1850-1919)
  MORTON, George (British, fl.1874-1904)
  MUCKLEY, Louis Fairfax (British, fl.1887-1901)

  NAISH, John George (British, 1824-1905)
  NAMUR, Paul Franz (French, 1877-?)
  NIGG, Hermann (Austrian, 1849-?)
  NORMAND, Ernest (British, 1857-1923)
  NORMAND, Henrietta (née Rae) (British, 1859-1928)

  OLIVER, William (British, fl.1867-1882)

  PAEDE, Paul (German, 1868-1929)
  PAULSEN, Julius (Danish, 1860-1940)
* PENOT, Albert Joseph (French, late 19th Century)
  PERRET, Felix (Swiss, fl.1865-1869)
  PIERREY, Louis Maurice (French, 1854-1912)
  POPELIN, Gustave Léon Antoine (French, 1859-?)

* POYNTER, Sir Edward John (British, 1836-1919)
  PROTTI, Angelo (Italian, late 19th Century)
  PRUSZKOWSKI, Witold (Polish, 1846-1896)

* QUERCI, Dario (Italian, 1831-?)
* QUESNE, Fernand le (French, mid-19th Century)

  RABES, Max (Austrian, 1868-1944)
* REA, Cecil William (British, 1861-?)
  RICHIR, Hermann Jean Joseph (Belgian, 1866-?)
* ROTH, Albert (German, 1881-?)
  ROUFFIO, Paul Albert Alexandre (French, 1855-1911)
  ROUGET, Georges (French, 1784-1869)
  ROYER, Louis (Belgian, 1793-1868)

  SCHACKINGER, Gabriel (German, 1850-1912)
  SCHÜTZENBERGER, Louis Frédéric (French, 1825-1903)
  SEIGNAC, Guillaume (French, late 19th Century)
  SERRALUNGA, Luigi (Italian, 1880-?)
* SIEFFERT, Paul (French, 1874-?)
* SMEDT, Joseph de (Belgian, late 19th Century)
  SOLOMON, Solomon Joseph (British, 1860-1927)
  STAAL, Gustave Pierre Eugène (French, 1817-1882)
  STOCK, Henry John (British, 1853-1931)

* TANOUX, Henri Adrien (French, 1865-1923)
* TASSAERT, Octave Nicolas François (French, 1800-1874)
  THIRION, Eugène Romain (French, 1829-1910)
  THIVET, Antoine Auguste (French, late 19th Century)
  THORNHILL, Philip J. (British, late 19th Century)
* THYS, Gaston (French, 1863-1893)
  TOULONGNE, Alfred Charles (French, mid-19th Century)
* TUKE, Henry Scott (British, 1858-1929)

  VEITH, Eduard (Austrian, 1856-1925)
  VERHEYDEN, Isidore (Belgian, 1846-1905)
* VOIGTLÄNDER, Rudolf von (German, 1854-?)

  WAGREZ, Jacques Clement (French, 1846-1908)
  WATERHOUSE, John William (British, 1849-1917)
  WATSON, George Spencer (British, 1869-1934)
  WATTS, George Frederick (British, 1817-1904)
* WEIGANDT, Ch. (German?, late 19th Century)
  WEINGÄRTNER, Pedro (South American-Italian, late 19th Century)
* WEISER, Joseph Emanuel (German, 1847-1911)
  WENCKER, Joseph (French, 1848-1919)
  WERTHEIMER, Gustav (Austrian, 1847-1902)
* WIERTZ, Antoine Joseph (Belgian, 1806-1865)
* WOOLMER, Alfred Joseph (British, 1805-1892)
  WYGRZYWALSKI, Feliks (Polish, 1875-1944)

  ZIEGLER, Jules Claude (French, 1804-1856)
* ZORN, Anders Leonard (Swedish, 1860-1920)
  ZULOAGA Y ZABALETA, Ignacio (Spanish, 1870-1945)
* ZWILLER, Marie Augustin (French, 1850-1939)

NIKOLAI CORNELOVICH
BODARERVSKI. A female nude on a
sofa in an artist's studio. Signed and dated
1886. 22½ x 31ins. (57 x 79cm). *Christie's.*

ARMAND BERTON. La Seduction.
Signed. 41 x 49¼ins. (104 x 125cm).
Christie's.

WILLIAM ADOLPHE
BOUGUEREAU. The first kiss.
Signed and dated 1890.
47 x 28ins. (119.5 x 71cm).
Christie's.

CHARLES EDOUARD BOUTIBONNE. Syrènes. Signed and dated 1883.
58 x 89¾ins. (147 x 228cm). *Christie's.*

HANS CANON. The bather. Signed and dated 1872.
54¼ x 42ins. (138 x 106.5cm). *Sotheby's.*

JEAN EUGÈNE BULAND. A wood nymph. Signed and
dated 75. 35 x 23ins. (89 x 58.5cm). *Christie's.*

CHARLES EMILE AUGUSTE CAROLUS-DURAN. La vie Bordelaise.
Signed and inscribed. 14½ x 21½ins. (37 x 54.5cm). *Sotheby's.*

F. CHALOIS. A look through the key-hole. Signed, on panel.
14½ x 8¼ins. (37 x 21cm). *Christie's.*

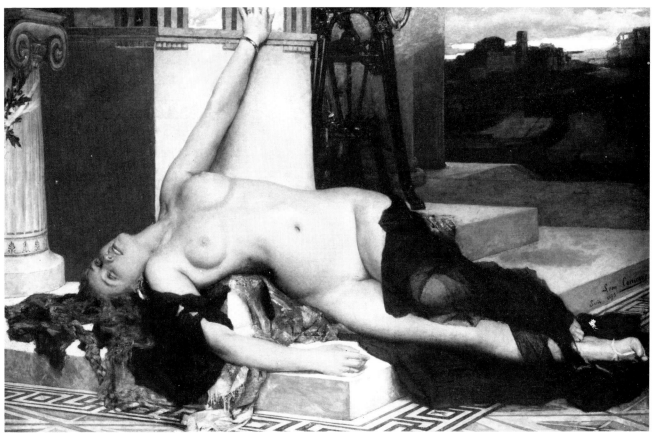

LÉON FRANÇOIS COMERRE. Cassandra. Signed and dated Paris 1875, and inscribed on the reverse. 52 x 79ins.
(132 x 200.5cm). *Christie's.*

GUSTAVE CLAUDE ETIENNE COURTOIS. L'amour au banquet. Signed and dated Paris 1898. 62 x 79½ins. (157.5 x 202cm). *Christie's.*

LOVIS CORINTH. Zwei weibliche akte. Signed and dated 1910. 35¾ x 28¼ins. (91 x 72cm). *Christie's.*

CHARLES EDOUARD DELORT. A voluptuous smoke. Signed and dated 1867, on panel. 10½ x 8½ins. (27 x 21.5cm). *Sotheby's.*

HENRI LUCIEN DOUCET. A female nude. Signed and dated 21 Feb 1876. 31½ x 21ins. (80 x 53.5cm). *Christie's.*

EDOUARD LOUIS DUBUFE. A reclining nude. 25¾ x 32ins. (65.5 x 81cm).

CLEMENTINE HELENE DUFAU.
A seated female nude in a landscape.
Signed. 47 x 35½ins. (119.5 x 90cm).
Sotheby's.

PIERRE DUPUIS. A water nymph. Signed and dated
1892. 25¼ x 15½ins. (64 x 39.5cm). *Christie's.*

KNUT EKWALL. The fisherman and the siren. Signed.
77½ x 59½ins. (197 x 151cm). *Christie's.*

WILLIAM ETTY. At the doubtful breeze alarmed. On board. 27⅞ x 21¼ins. (70.5 x 54cm). *Christie's.*

PAUL FISCHER. Nude bathers on a beach. Signed. 22½ x 29ins. (57 x 73.5cm). *Christie's.*

EMILE LOUIS FOUBERT.
La source. Signed and dated 1881.
79 x 37¼ins. (201 x 94.5cm).
Christie's.

ROBERT FOWLER. Woodland nymphs. Signed. 65½ x 89¼ins. (166.5 x 227cm).
Christie's.

WILLIAM EDWARD FROST. A woman bathing. Signed
and dated 1855, on board. 9¼ x 6½ins. (23.5 x 16.5cm).
Christie's.

JEAN LÉON GÉRÔME. King Candaules; or Queen Rodolphe observed by Gyges. Pen and ink and oil. 13 x 19¼ins. (33 x 49cm). *Christie's.*

NIELS CHRISTIAN HANSEN. A nude woman reclining on a sofa. Signed and dated 1906. 19¾ x 34¾ins. (50 x 88cm). *Christie's.*

JEAN JACQUES HENNER. A reclining nude. 18 x 31½ins. (45.5 x 80cm). *Christie's.*

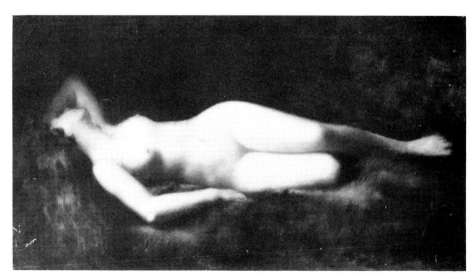

ANDERS LEONARD ZORN. Tva Vanner (two friends). Authenicated and dated 1918 on the reverse by Emma Zorn. 39½ x 29¼ins. (100.5 x 74cm). *Christie's.*

KARL KAHLER. The model. Signed. 23¾ x 17½ins. (60.5 x 44.5cm). *Christie's.*

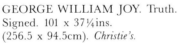

GEORGE WILLIAM JOY. Truth. Signed. 101 x 37¼ins. (256.5 x 94.5cm). *Christie's.*

EDOUARD KASPARIDES. A nude woman reclining on a couch. Signed. 37 x 61¼ins. (94 x 158cm). *Christie's.*

ALBERT VON KELLER. Study of a female nude standing in a leafy glade. Signed, on panel. 13 x 7ins. (33 x 17.5cm). *Sotheby's.*

469

FERDINAND KELLER. Stiftungsfest. Signed with monogram, inscribed, and dated 1874. 79 x 57½ins. (200.5 x 146cm). *Christie's.*

PONZIANO LOVERINI. The swing. Signed and dated 1884. 72¾ x 41¼ins. (185 x 105cm). *Christie's.*

JACQUES FRANÇOIS FERNAND LEMATTE. The water nymph. Signed. 19 x 38ins. (48.5 x 96.5cm). *Christie's.*

ANDREA LANDINI. The seductress. Signed and inscribed Firenze. 34½ x 56ins. (87.5 x 142cm). *Christie's.*

RENE MEGE DU
MALMONT. La cigale.
Signed. 21½ x 49½ins.
(54.5 x 125.5cm). *Christie's.*

MARIUS JEAN ANTOINE
MERCIÉ. A nude in a
landscape. Signed.
25½ x 39ins. (65 x 99cm).
Christie's.

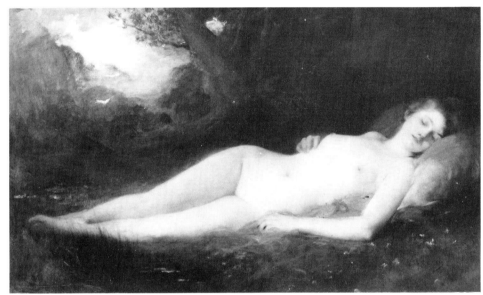

JEAN FRANÇOIS MILLET.
L'amour vainquer, on panel.
14½ x 9½ins. (37 x 24cm).
Christie's.

ALBERT JOSEPH PENOT
A female nude. Signed. 21½
x 15ins.
(54.5 x 38cm). *Christie's.*

SIR EDWARD JOHN POYNTER. The cave of the storm nymphs. Signed and dated 1903.
57 x 43ins. (146 x 110cm). *Christie's.*

DARIO QUERCI. The Pompeian bath. Signed and dated 1896. 22 x 18ins. (56 x 46cm). *Christie's.*

FERNAND LE QUESNE. The rescue. Signed. 74¾ x 62¾ins. (190 x 159.5cm). *Christie's.*

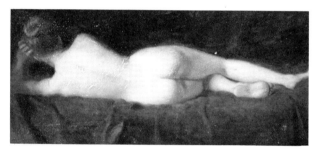

ALBERT ROTH. A reclining nude. Signed and inscribed München, on panel. 8½ x 18½ins. (21.5 x 47cm). *Christie's*

CECIL WILLIAM REA. Hylas. Signed. 49½ x 39¼ins. (125.5 x 99.5cm). *Christie's.*

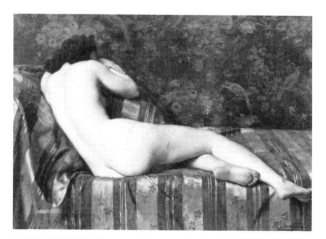

PAUL SIEFFERT. A reclining nude. Signed. 17⅞ x 25¼ins. (45 x 64cm). *Sotheby's.*

JOS. DE SMEDT. The odalisque. Signed and dated 1915. 38½ x 46½ins. (98 x 118cm). *Christie's.*

HENRI ADRIEN TANOUX. A seated nude. Signed and dated 1913. 21 x 14½ins. (53.5 x 36.5cm). *Sotheby's.*

OCTAVE NICOLAS FRANÇOIS TASSAERT. The bathers. Signed and dated 1837. 27⅞ x 23ins. (70.5 x 58.5cm). *Christie's.*

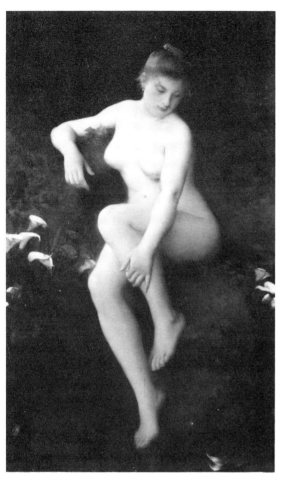

RUDOLF VON VOIGTLANDER. A nude model posing in a studio. Signed. 28¾ x 20¼ins. (73 x 51.5cm). *Christie's.*

Top left: GASTON THYS. The bather. Signed and dated Rome 1891. 89 x 34½ins. (226.5 x 87.5cm). *Christie's.*

CH. WEIGANDT. A reclining naked boy. Signed. 27 x 46½ins. (68.5 x 118cm). *Christie's.*

HENRY SCOTT TUKE. Summer pinks, a nude boy in the grass. Signed. 21 x 15ins. (53.5 x 38cm). *Christie's.*

475

ANTOINE JOSEPH WIERTZ. La belle Rosine. 21¾ x 15ins. (55 x 38cm). *Christie's.*

Top left: JOSEPH EMANUEL WEISER. Venus. Signed and dated 86, on panel. 28¾ x 16¾ins. (73 x 42.5cm). *Christie's.*

ALFRED JOSEPH WOOLMER. Eve. 24 x 20ins. (61 x 51cm). *Christie's.*

ANDERS LEONARD ZORN. Dagmar.
Signed and dated 1911. 34¾ x 24¾ ins.
(88 x 63cm). *Christie's.*

MARIE AUGUSTIN ZWILLER. A nude
woman reading a book. Signed. 28¾ x 39¼ ins.
(73 x 99.5cm). *Christie's.*

HUGO WILHELM KAUFFMANN. Zwei Männer an der Mauer. Signed and dated 72, on panel. 8¾ x 6½ins. (22 x 16.5cm). *Christie's.*

Old Men and Women

The gaze that was focused tenderly on children by popular painters of the nineteenth century was also turned with similar effect on to the old. A romance of charming, not to say heart-warming, old age was conjured up: sweet old men are shown reminiscing elegiacally about the past; 'real old characters' down a drink or two in a cosy inn; absent-minded gentlemen of advanced years potter about in libraries or studies. Such pictures might possibly be argued to reflect a deeper concern for the aged in the nineteenth century; more likely, they constitute yet one more example of the seemingly infinite capacity of the age to sentimentalise an image to the point where its connections with reality are all but severed.

Many paintings in this genre emanate from Germany and Austria, the Germany and Austria whose Biedermeyer legacy propagated such a taste for 'gemutlichkeit' in popular art. Golden old age was fertile subject matter for the realisation of that highly-prized mood of cosiness tinged with nostalgia. Prime examples are the old men of Carl Spitzweg who chase butterflies in sunny meadows or bend studiously over their books in musty attics. The titles of pictures by Spitzweg read like a list of suggested activities for the elderly in solitary circumstances: *Der Bücherwurm, Der Geologe, Der Kaktusfreund, Der Philosoph.* Spitzweg was a painter of genuine charm and originality, highly acclaimed in his own day as the number of fakes and imitations of his work attests. On a rather lower level of achievement are the grinning violinists which Hermann Kern made his stock-in-trade. Bankruptcy of imagination arrives with the apparently endless series of old Bavarian peasants depicted head-and-shoulders, smoking or drinking, by artists whose careers in several cases continued long into the twentieth century. Amongst these must be numbered the works of men like Oehring, Eichinger, Wagner, Rössler, Heuser and Thedy. In Italy, too, a similar degree of repetitiveness is achieved in certain — clearly commercially successful — works by Pompeo Massani, Eugenio Zampighi and others.

Old age was treated reverentially by English painters, too. A useful subject for eliciting maximum emotional response was the Chelsea Pensioner, a figure who combined patriotism (the trusty servant of his country, the old soldier), poignancy (the dignity of old age), and decorative appeal (the red of the uniform). Hubert von Herkomer's famous *The Last Muster* exploits all three to the full and adds a titillating narrative element in his touching scene of the pensioner who has passed quietly on in chapel. What better way to end a well-spent life? For Herkomer, old age was only one of several themes employed to play on his public's heart-strings, but the English painter most closely identified with the subject is Charles Spencelayh. He developed the genre to a high pitch of detail and finish with his scenes of old men in interiors, pottering about in a clutter of jumble.

With Spencelayh the spectator is asked to marvel not merely at the curious charm of the elderly magpie but at the meticulous rendering of the enormous variety of inanimate objects he has collected. Rather earlier in the century the

Dutchman Alexander Bakker-Korff made the same appeal to the public's appreciation of exquisite and distinctive technique. In his case it was exercised on old ladies doing nothing very much in comfortable bourgeois interiors. The models for these ladies were almost invariably the artist's unmarried sisters, preserved to unexpected immortality by their brother's efforts combined with the public's curious taste for geriatric domesticity.

Index of Artists

SMITH, Carl Frithjof (Norwegian, 1859-1917)
SOYER, Paul Constant (French, 1823-1903)
* SPENCELAYH, Charles (British, 1865-1958)
SPIELTER, Carl Johann (German, 1851-1922)
* SPITZWEG, Carl (German, 1808-1885)
* SPRING, Alfons (German, 1843-1908)
* STOLL, J. (German, late 19th Century)

* THEDY, Marc (German, 1858-1924)
TOZER, Henry E. (British, late 19th Century)

URBAN, Joseph (Austrian, 1872-1933)

VOLCKER, Robert (German, 1854-1924)

WAGNER, Fritz (German, 1896-1939)
WEATHERHEAD, William Harris (British, 1843-1903)
WERNER, Alexander Friedrich (German, 1827-1908)
* WOLFLE, Franz Xavier (German, early 20th Century)
WRIGHT, Robert W. (British, fl.1871-1906)

* ZAMPIGHI, Eugenio (Italian, 1859-1944)
ZIEBLAND, Hermann (German, 1853-1896)
ZIMMER, Wilhelm Carl August (German, 1853-1937)
ZIMMERMAN, Ernst Karl Georg (German, 1852-1901)
ZIMMERMAN, Reinhard Sebastian (German, 1815-1893)

EMMANUEL BACHRACH-BARÉE. The old campaigner. Signed, on panel. 7 x 5½ins. (18 x 14cm). *Christie's.*

ALEXANDER HUGO BAKKER-KORFF. Two women seated in an interior. Signed and dated '70, and signed, inscribed and dated 15 Juin 1870 on an old label on the reverse. 8 x 6¼ins. (20.5 x 16cm). *Christie's.*

HANS BEST. An old man. Signed, on board.
31 x 21¾ins. (78.5 x 55.5cm). *Christie's.*

LOUIS GEORGES BRILLOUIN. A musical companion. Signed
and dated 1861, on panel. 10 x 8ins. (25.5 x 20.5cm). *Christie's.*

ANTON BURGER. Good companions.
Signed. 10½ x 8¾ins. (26.5 x 22cm).
Sotheby's.

ARTURO CALOSCI. The violinist.
Signed and inscribed Firenze, on
panel. 12½ x 8ins. (31.5 x 20cm).
Christie's.

VINCENZO CAPRILE. The old
musician. Signed. 38¾ x 26ins.
(98.5 x 66cm). *Christie's.*

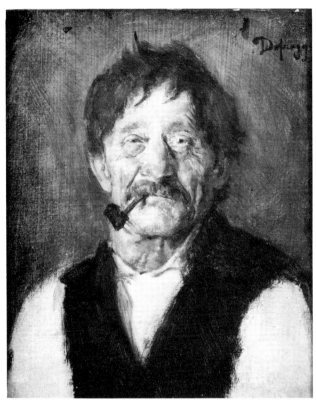

FRANZ VON DEFREGGER. An old man smoking a pipe.
Signed. 10 x 8ins. (25.5 x 20.5cm). *Christie's.*

THOMAS FAED. Nae anither drop. On panel, arched top.
12½ x 9¾ins. (31.5 x 24.5cm). *Christie's.*

CHARLES PAUL GRUPPE. A quiet smoke. Signed.
9½ x 13½ins. (24 x 34cm). *Christie's.*

JOHANN GRUND. Sampling the best. Signed and dated
'79, on panel. 12 x 8¾ins. (30.5 x 22cm). *Christie's.*

483

SIR HUBERT VON HERKOMER. The last muster. Signed and dated Mar. 75. 82 x 61ins. (208 x 155cm).
Merseyside County Art Galleries.

CARL HEUSER. An elderly pipesmoker. Signed, on panel. 6¼ x 4¼ins. (16 x 11cm). *Christie's.*

GEORG GREGOR HIRT. The Pipe Smoker. Signed and dated 1886. 8 x 5¼ins. (20.5 x 13.5cm). *Sotheby's.*

HUGO WILHELM KAUFFMANN. A quiet smoke. Signed and dated '86, on panel. 9 x 6¾ins. (23 x 17cm). *Christie's.*

ISIDOR KAUFMANN. The toper. Signed, on panel. 9½ x 7¼ins. (24 x 18.5cm). *Christie's.*

HERMANN KERN. The old clerk. Signed, on panel. 12 x 9½ins. (30.5 x 24cm). *Christie's.*

LUDWIG KNAUS. After the hunt. Signed and dated 1888, on panel. 12 x 9ins. (30.5 x 23cm). *Christie's.*

GUSTAV KÖHLER. A peasant wearing a loden costume. Signed and inscribed Mchn, on panel. 7 x 5½ins. (17.5 x 14cm). *Christie's.*

CARL KRONBERGER. An old man smoking a pipe. Signed, on panel. 6¼ x 4¾ins. (16 x 12cm). *Sotheby's.*

FRANZ LEITGEB. The old Bavarian. Signed, on panel. 10¼ x 8¼ins. (26 x 21cm). *Sotheby's.*

EUGEN LINGENFELDER. The snuff box. Signed, on panel. 8 x 6ins. (20 x 15cm). *Christie's.*

S. MASSARI. An old man holding bottles of wine. Signed. 12½ x 9¾ins. (31.5 x 25cm). *Christie's.*

FRANS MEERTS. Sharpening the quill. Signed and inscribed, on panel. 15¾ x 12ins. (40 x 30.5cm). *Christie's.*

FRITZ MÜLLER. A good smoke. Signed and inscribed Munchen, on board. 11¼ x 9¼ins. (28.5 x 23.5cm). *Christie's.*

WILLEM VAN NIEUWENHOVEN. Tea time. Signed. 11 x 13½ins. (28 x 34.5cm). *Christie's.*

HEDWIG OEHRING. A Bavarian peasant. Signed and inscribed München, on panel. 6¼ x 4½ins. (16 x 11.5cm). *Christie's.*

F. ORTNER. An interesting discussion. Signed, on panel. 7¾ x 11¾ins. (19.5 x 30cm). *Christie's.*

CHARLES SPENCELAYH.
The old curiosity shop.
Signed. 19½ x 23½ins.
(49.5 x 59.6cm). *Christie's.*

CARL SPITZWEG. Der
arme Poet. Signed and
dated 1839. 14½ x 17½ins.
(36.2 x 44.6cm). *Munich,
Neue Pinakothek.*

ALFONS SPRING. A quiet nap. Signed and inscribed München, on panel. 9½ x 7ins. (24 x 18cm). *Christie's.*

J. STOLL. The broken fiddle. Signed. 16 x 20ins. (40.5 x 51cm). *Christie's.*

MARC THEDY. An old man. Signed with initials, on panel. 6¾ x 5½ins. (17 x 14cm). *Christie's.*

FRANZ XAVIER WOLFLE. An old man holding a candle. Signed, on panel. 9 x 6¾ins. (23 x 17cm). *Christie's.*

EUGENIO ZAMPIGHI. An old peasant couple. Signed. 24 x 18ins. (61 x 46cm). *Christie's.*

489

Peasants and Country Life

For the purpose of easier identification, this section is subdivided by groups of nationalities. The interesting point is that were it not for reasons of sheer volume, such subdivisions would not be necessary; artists of all nations approached the peasantry and treated the genre of country life in a remarkably uniform fashion, be it Spanish, French, Norwegian, or Bavarian. There were certainly different elements in painters' attitudes to the rural working class, but none of these elements can be said to have been the sole preserve of one particular national school. The same three ideas recur almost universally: the peasant as enduring archetype, closer to the soil and therefore more natural and eternal than any city dweller; the peasant as being of picturesque charm; and the peasant as a victim of society, not without a certain picturesqueness of poverty, but ground down and deserving of the spectator's pity and concern.

European painters of peasants in the nineteenth century found themselves heirs to the inheritance of idyllic literature, which set up certain stereotypes of rustic life. George Eliot described this essentially romantic and unrealistic vision as follows in 1856:

> Idyllic ploughmen are jocund when they drive their team afield; idyllic shepherds make bashful love under hawthorn bushes; idyllic villagers dance in the chequered shade and refresh themselves, not immoderately, with spicy nutbrown ale.

Most artists of the first half of the century perpetuated this myth, beguiling and profitable in terms of sales to city dwellers as it was. How charming are the handsome shepherds of Mulready, the dancing harvesters of Leopold Robert, and all the fresh-faced children and frolicking villagers of the little Biedermeyer masters. How satisfyingly they reinforced the idyllic view of the countryside that the newly rich merchant, forced to spend his working life in urban surroundings, craved to have created for him.

Gradually this manifestly lyrical vision was transformed for the delectation of the new bourgeois clientele, by the use of certain superficial tricks of naturalistic technique, into an image of rural life which was claimed by its creators and their admirers to be a true one. In fact it was as sentimental and unrealistic as ever. Pretsch writes of Ludwig Knaus's *Dance Under the Linden Tree*:

> Everything here seems to be modelled on real life and its quickest movement is captured at a glance. Robust mirth, naïvely bashful joy, comical peasant awkwardness, and a delightful childlike charm are most truly reflected by the dancing figures. Elsewhere, even outside the circle of dancers, we see delectable and characteristic figures.

'Delectable and characteristic' — the combination of the two words sums up the desire of the new collector in his vision of rural life. He wants peasants to be made to seem charming and adorable, and furthermore he wants that vision to be true. In the same way that the new bourgeois imagination reinterpreted history painting, animal painting, and classical painting, it also made sentimental adjustments to the peasantry. Their antics could be humorous, but never unpleasant; they were to be treated sympathetically, but often this produced no more than a palpably patronising attitude in the artist and his public. The case of Waldmüller is typical in this respect. His 'Sittenbild' (records of morals and manners amongst the Austrian peasantry) are supremely accomplished pictures, and he himself was something of a revolutionary in his anti-academic stance which stressed the need to go back to nature; yet he was not enough of an objective realist to escape entirely the accusation of being merely the interpreter of the peasantry for the bourgeoisie. Roessler and Pisko wrote in 1909: 'The becoming, being, and passing of natural man — the peasant — was his preferred subject matter. He evolved it in many variations, and showed how beauty is always a part of our life.' This is the problem: although the middle classes might primly reassure themselves that 'beauty is always part of our life', there was no evidence that this was always the case in the peasant's existence. Such statements were merely sentimental wish-fulfilment, prompted by the idyllic happiness of Waldmüller's scenes.

George Eliot, again, pronounces emphatically against this fiction of the merriment of peasant life:

> That delicious effervescence of the mind which we call fun has no equivalent for the northern peasant, except tipsy revelry; the only realm of fancy and imagination... exists at the bottom of the third quart pot.

The Austrian and south German imagination, and its feeling for 'gemutlichkeit', was peculiarly responsive to sentimental renderings of peasant life. In its earlier Biedermeyer form, there remain elements of fantasy and romantic reverie which make such painting more palatable. It is later in the century that the materialist emphasis on naturalistic technique enters the equation and upsets it. The peasants of Waldmüller, Hugo Kauffmann and Franz von Defregger are indubitably real people reproduced with a photographic verisimilitude; yet they still behave as a sentimental bourgeoisie would want them to behave rather than as peasants did in reality. This reality was probably closer to George Eliot's grim view than the smiling world created so meticulously by many painters across Europe.

Certain other artists, particularly in France, turned to the genre of rural life not so much to lyricise it or sanitise it as to monumentalise. These were painters operating within the academic tradition who sought subjects which would offer some relief from the empty repetition of classical themes. They were not, however, prepared to sink to the vulgarity of painting contemporary life in all its ugliness, so they painted rural peasants, whose changeless devotion to the soil gave them a timelessness more suitable for the serious artist's brush. Italian peasants were considered particularly wholesome from this point of view. Edmond praised de Curzon's *Women of Piscinisco*, for instance, because the peasants 'busy in weaving linen make you enter one of those little corners of Italy where the ancient life and the primitive simplicity of manners are preserved by a happy anachronism'. Many the artist who travelled to Italy in the nineteenth century and sent home, not just to the Salon, but to the Royal Academy, to Berlin, to Copenhagen, to Brussels, renderings of the local peasants, who would no doubt have been mystified to learn that their appeal was their 'happy anachronism'.

France had in Jules Breton and Jean François Millet the two acknowledged leading exponents of 'peasant genre'. They too were both praised contemporarily for the solemnity, even the heroism, which they emphasised in peasant life. Gautier said of Millet:

> he loves the peasants whom he represents, and in their resigned figures expresses his sympathy for them. The seed-growing, the harvest, the grafting, are they not virtuous actions having their worth and their grandeur? Why have not peasants style as well as heroes?

Peasants arc no longer jolly; instead they are possessed of simple grandeur, even a sort of holiness. As Gautier remarked in connection with Breton:

> (he has) a profound sentiment for rustic beauty which separates him from some vulgar peasant makers... the nutritive labours of man have their grandeur and their sanctity.

The germ of realism à la Breton and Millet spread across Europe in the second half of the nineteenth century. Sometimes this realism was no more than a superficial naturalism grafted on to the old sentimental approach, as we have seen already. For other artists, however, grimness replaced jollity and they painted a succession of grey, depressing peasants in unremittingly grey, depressing landscapes. A new element in the air was the Social Conscience, and certain painters contracted a heavy dose of it.

In Holland, for instance, there was the Hague School, which was primarily a movement of realism in reaction against previous empty headed romanticism. Josef Israels won a huge contemporary reputation for his evocation of the lives of Dutch fisherfolk: he preferred to paint on days of heavy cloud cover, ideally when large sections of the fishing fleet were feared lost at sea. Gloom is indeed the watchword for the colouring and the mood of much Hague School painting. Sadee, Scherrewitz, Mauve and Maris do not do much to lighten it. It was fashionable for painters of other nationalities, too, to converge on Holland to paint the peasantry in the last quarter of the century: visitors included artists as varied as Rudolf Jordan, Hans von Bartels and Max Liebermann from Germany, Robert Gemmell Hutchinson and George Henry Boughton from Britain, and August Jernberg and Ferdinand Fagerlin from Sweden. By the 1880s, any aspirant painter of peasants who wished to acquaint himself with the avant-garde in his field could choose between going to the Holland of the Hague School and visiting France, where for a few brief years the star of Bastien-Lepage rose meteorically. His photographic realism, the product of rigorous 'plein-air' study, entranced Europe and had a direct influence on many of his contemporaries.

In England his closest followers were artists of the Newlyn school, Stanhope Forbes, Walter Langley, Frank Bramley and others. They painted Cornish fisherfolk in the same outdoor, photographic style which played down sentimentality without entirely eradicating it, and won them reputations in their own country for being dangerously advanced. There may be some sociological reason why fisherfolk particularly fascinated the peasant painters of the late nineteenth century. Apart from the Hague and Newlyn schools, there was also the Skagen school, a group of Scandinavian painters who worked in this small Danish fishing port in the 1880s and 90s. The leading lights were Peter Krøyer, Christian Krogh, and Michael Ancher, artists who painted everyday life of the maritime community about them. Oil-skinned worthies against grey seas and threatening skies are interchangeable pictorial motifs between Newlyn and Skagen, equally typical from the brush of Michael Ancher and Walter Langley. What also unites them is their admiration for Bastien-Lepage.

Across late nineteenth century Europe, no country was left untouched by the new realism in some form or another. Karoly Ferenczy is an example of a Hungarian painter who absorbed Bastien-Lepage via his teacher Simon Hollosy; in Italy, the work of artists like Angelo Morbelli strike a note of heightened seriousness and social commitment as against the frivolities of Eugenio Zampighi or Pompeo Massani; even in Spain, where picturesqueness and romanticism had long been the keynotes, realists like Sorolla and de Regoyos introduced a treatment of peasants which presented them as human beings rather than the grinning tailors' dummies they had previously become, with no more pretext for their existence than the exhibition of colourful local costume. And Wilhelm Leibl in Germany provided a more objective antidote to the unconvincing jollity of the popular Munich school; his attitude to the countryfolk he was portraying in his *Three peasant women in a Village Church* has taken on a new reverence, to judge from his letter of 1879:

> Even if the picture is not exhibited, it will have its effect. Several peasants came to look at it just lately, and they instinctively folded their hands in front of it. One man said, 'That is the work of a master'. I have always set greater store by the opinion of simple peasants than by that of so-called painters, so I take that peasant's remark as a good omen.

Peasants — British

Index of Artists

ABERCROMBY, John B. (British, fl.1873-1896)
ABSOLON, John (British, 1815-1895)
ALLAN, Sir William (British, 1782-1850)
ANDREWS, Henry (British, fl. 1830-1860)
ARCHER, James (British, 1824-1904)

* BANKS, J.O. (British, fl.1856-1873)
* BANNERMAN, Hamlet (British, fl.1879-1891)
* BARTLETT, William Henry (British, 1809-1854)
BEDFORD, John Bates (British, 1823-?)
BOUTWOOD, Charles E. (British, fl.1881-1887)
BOWKETT, Jane Maria (British, fl.1860-1885)
BRAMLEY, Frank (British, 1857-1915)
BROMLEY, William (British, fl.1835-1888)
BROWN, Frederick (British, 1851-1941)
BROWNLOW, George Washington (British, 1835-1876)
BRYANT, H.C. (British, fl.1860-1880)
* BUCHSER, Frank (Swiss, 1828-1890)
BURGESS, Adelaide (British, fl.1857-1886)
BURGESS, H. (British, fl.1857-1865)
* BURR, John (British, 1831-1893)

* CALDECOTT, Randolph (British, 1846-1886)
CALDERON, Philip Hermogenes (Anglo-Spanish, 1833-1898)
CAMERON, Hugh (British, 1835-1918)
CAMPOTOSTO, Henry (Belgian, ?-1910)
CHAPMAN, John Watkins (British, fl.1853-1903)
CLARK, Joseph (British, 1834-1926)
CLAUSEN, Sir George (British, 1852-1944)
* COBBETT, Edward John (British, 1815-1899)
COCKBURN, Edwin (British, fl.1837-1868)
COLLINS, William (British, 1788-1847)
COLLINSON, James (British, 1825-1881)
COPE, Charles West (British, 1811-1890)
CROSBY, William (British, fl.1859-1873)

DREW, J.P. (British, fl.1835-1861)
DUKES, Charles (British, fl.1829-1865)

ELLIOTT, Robinson (British, 1814-1894)

* FAED, John (British, 1860-1902)
* FAED, Thomas (British, 1826-1900)

* FILDES, Sir Samuel Luke (British, 1843-1927)
* FORBES, Stanhope Alexander (British, 1857-1943)
* FRASER, Alexander (British, 1828-1899)

* GILL, William (British, fl.1826-1869)
  GOOD, Thomas Sword (British, 1789-1872)
  GOODALL, Frederick (British, 1822-1904)
  GOODALL, Walter (British, 1830-1889)
  GRAHAM, Robert J.A. (British, late 19th Century)
  GRANT, William James (British, 1829-1866)

  HADDON, Arthur Trevor (British, 1864-1941)
  HALL, Frederick (British, 1860-1948)
  HARDIE, Charles Martin (British, 1858-1916)
  HARDY, Frederick Daniel (British, 1826-1911)
  HARRIS, Edwin (British, 1855-1906)
* HARVEY, Sir George (British, 1806-1876)
  HARVEY, Harold (British, 1874-1941)
  HAVELL, Charles Richards (British, fl.1858-1866)
  HAVERS, Alice Mary (British, 1850-1890)
* HAYNES, John William (British, fl.1852-1882)
  HEATH, Frank Gascoigne (British, 1873-1936)
  HEDLEY, Ralph (British, 1851-1913)
  HELCKE, Arnold (British, fl.1865-1898)
  HEMSLEY, William (British, 1819-1893?)
  HEMY, Charles Napier (British, 1841-1917)
* HENDERSON, Joseph (British, 1832-1908)
  HENZELL, Isaac (British, fl.1854-1875)
  HERKOMER, Sir Hubert von (German, 1849-1914)
  HILL, James John (British, 1811-1882)
  HILL, Rowland Henry (British, 1872-1952)
  HOLE, William Brassey (British, 1846-1917)
* HOLL, Frank (British, 1845-1888)
* HOLYOAKE, William (British, 1834-1894)
* HOOK, James Clarke (British, 1819-1907)
  HOUSTON, John Adam P. (British, 1812-1884)
  HUGHES, Arthur Ford (British, 1856-1927?)
  HULME, Edith (British, late 19th Century)
  HUTCHINSON, Robert Gemmell (British, 1855-1936)

  JENKINS, Joseph John (British, 1811-1885)
  JOHNSTONE, Henry James (British, fl.1881-1900)
  JUNGMANN, Nico Wilhelm (Dutch, 1872-1935)

  KENNINGTON, Thomas Benjamin (British, 1856-1916)
* KING, Haynes (British, 1831-1904)
  KING, Henry John Yeend (British, 1855-1924)
* KNIGHT, William Henry (British, 1823-1863)

  LANGLEY, Walter (British, 1852-1922)
  LANGLOIS, Mark W. (British, fl.1862-1873)
* LA THANGUE, Henry Herbert (British, 1859-1929)
* LAURANCE, Tom (British, late 19th Century)
  LEE, John (British, fl.1850-1860)
  LEE, William (British, 1810-1865)
  LEGGETT, Alexander (British, fl.1876-1884)
  LOCKHART, William Ewart (British, 1846-1900)

* MACBETH, Robert Walker (British, 1848-1910)
  MACDUFF, William (British, fl.1844-1876)
* McGHIE, John (British, 1867-?)
  McGREGOR, Robert (British, 1848-1922)
* MACNAB, Peter (British, ?-1900)
* MARKS, George (British, 1876-1922)
* MARSHALL, Thomas Falcon (British, 1818-1878)
* MIDWOOD, William Henry (British, fl.1867-1871)

  MILLNER, William Edward (British, 1849-1895)
  MITCHELL, William (British, mid-19th Century)
* MORGAN, Frederick (British, 1856-1927)
* MORRIS, Philip Richard (British, 1836-1902)
* MORRISH, Sydney S. (British, fl.1852-1894)
* MULREADY, Augustus E. (British, fl.1863-1905)
  MULREADY, William (British, 1786-1863)

  NEWTON, John Edward (British, fl.1853-1883)
* NICOL, Erskine (British, 1825-1904)
* NICOL, John Watson (British, ?-1926)

* O'NEILL, George Bernard (British, 1828-1917)

  PARKER, Henry Perlee (British, 1795-1873)
* PASMORE, Daniel (British, fl.1829-1865)
  PETTIE, John (British, 1839-1893)
  PHILLIP, John (British, 1817-1867)
* POOLE, Paul Falconer (British, 1807-1879)
* PROVIS, Alfred (British, fl.1843-1886)
  PULLER, John Anthony (British, fl.1821-1866)

  RAINEY, William (British, 1852-1936)
  REDGRAVE, Richard (British, 1804-1888)
  REID, Sir George (British, 1841-1913)
  REID, John Robertson (British, 1851-1926)

  SANDERSON, Robert (British, fl.1855-1895)
  SANDERSON-WELLS, John (British, fl.1895-1940)
* SCHEERBOOM, Andries (Dutch, 1832-1880)
  SHAYER, William (British, 1788-1879)
  SHERWOOD-HUNTER, George (British, ?-1920)
› SHIELS, William (British, 1785-1857)
* SMITH, George (British, 1829-1901)
  SPENCELAYH, Charles (British, 1865-1958)
  STOKELD, James (British, 1827-1877)
  STOTT, Edward William (British, 1859-1918)
  SUTHERS, Leghe (British, fl.1885-1905)

  TAYLER, Alexander Chevallier (British, 1862-1925)
  TEBBY, Arthur Kemp (British, fl.1883-1892)
  TENNANT, John Frederick (British, 1796-1872)
  THOMPSON, Jacob (British, 1806-1879)
  TOPHAM, Frank William Warwick (British, 1838-1924)
* TURNER, Edward (British, fl.1858-1862)

  UNDERHILL, Frederick Charles (British, fl.1851-1875)

  VIGOR, Charles (British, fl.1881-1893)

  WAITE, James Clark (British, fl.1863-1885)
  WALKER, Frederick (British, 1840-1875)
  WATSON, John Dawson (British, 1832-1892)
  WEATHERHEAD, William Harris (British, 1843-1903)
  WEBSTER, Thomas (British, 1800-1886)
* WEIR, William (British, ?-1865)
* WELLS, George (British, fl.1842-1888)
  WETHERBEE, George Faulkner (Anglo-American, 1851-1920)
* WILLIAMS, John Haynes (British, 1836-1908)
* WITHERINGTON, William Frederick (British, 1785-1865)
  WORTLEY, Archibald James Stuart (British, late 19th Century)
* WRIGHT, Robert W. (British, fl.1871-1906)

  YOUNG, Alexander (British, fl.1889-1893)

494

WILLIAM HENRY BARTLETT. The harbour, St. Ives, Cornwall. Signed and dated 1885. 23 x 32½ins. (58.5 x 82.5cm). *Christie's.*

J.O. BANKS. Bringing the harvest home. Signed. 41¾ x 64ins. (106 x 162.5cm). *Christie's.*

HAMLET BANNERMAN. His first day at work. Signed and dated 1890. 40¼ x 64¼ins. (102 x 163cm). *Christie's.*

FRANK BUCHSER. The Irish fishergirl. Signed with initials. 30 x 19¾ins. (76 x 50cm). *Christie's.*

JOHN BURR. The village barber. Signed and dated 81. 11 x 7½ins. (28 x 19cm). *Christie's.*

RANDOLPH CALDECOTT. The bird trap. Signed with initials. 13 x 11ins. (33 x 28cm). *Christie's.*

EDWARD JOHN COBBETT. The birdcage. Signed. 24 x 20ins. (61 x 50.5cm). *Christie's.*

JOHN FAED. At the spring. Signed and dated 83. 20¾ x 16¾ ins. (52.5 x 42.5cm). *Christie's.*

FREDERICK MORGAN. Not far to go. Signed. 29½ x 19½ ins. (75 x 49.5cm). *Christie's.*

THOMAS FAED. Morning, reapers going out. Signed. 40½ x 54¾ins. (103 x 139cm). *Christie's.*

SIR SAMUEL LUKE FILDES. The village wedding. Signed and dated 1883, and signed and inscribed on the reverse. 60 x 100ins. (152.5 x 254cm). *Christie's.*

STANHOPE ALEXANDER FORBES.
The slip. Signed. 41¾ x 33½ins. (106 x 85cm).
Christie's.

Bottom left:
ALEXANDER FRASER. The piper's family.
Signed and dated 1830. 16¼ x 20½ins.
(41 x 52cm). *Christie's.*

Bottom right:
WILLIAM GILL. A village fête. Signed and
dated Leamington 1857, on panel.
8¼ x 6¾ins. (21 x 17cm). *Christie's.*

SIR GEORGE HARVEY. Hop picking; a
composition of Kentish scenery. Signed and
signed with initials, and signed and numbered
on the stretcher. 18¾ x 28¼ins. (47.5 x 71.5cm).
Christie's.

JAMES CLARKE HOOK. Milk for the
schooner. Signed with monogram and dated
1866. 26¾ x 41¾ins. (68 x 106cm). *Christie's.*

JOHN WILLIAM HAYNES.
Cribbage. Signed and dated 59.
17½ x 14ins. (44.5 x 35.5cm). *Christie's.*

JOSEPH HENDERSON. At the well.
Signed and dated 1863, and signed
and inscribed on an old label on the
reverse. 26¼ x 20½ins. (67 x 52cm).
Christie's.

FRANK HOLL. Eventide. Signed.
23¾ x 19½ins. (60.5 x 49.5cm). *Christie's.*

WILLIAM HOLYOAKE. Waiting for the
boats. Signed. 39½ x 27ins.
(100 x 68.5cm). *Christie's.*

WILLIAM HENRY KNIGHT. The game of draughts. Signed and dated
1846. 16½ x 21½ins. (42 x 54.5cm). *Christie's.*

HAYNES KING. Mending the nets. Signed.
18 x 14ins. (46 x 35.5cm). *Christie's.*

HENRY HERBERT LA THANGUE. The violin lesson. Signed.
34 x 38ins. (86.5 x 96.5cm). *Christie's.*

JOHN McGHIE. The fishergirl. Signed.
29½ x 24½ins. (75 x 62cm). *Christie's.*

Top right:
PETER MACNAB. The end of the day.
Signed. 30 x 50ins. (76 x 127cm). *Christie's.*

Centre right:
GEORGE MARKS. Barley cutters
returning from work. Signed and dated
1882, and signed and inscribed on an old
label on the reverse. 26½ x 43½ins.
(67 x 110.5cm). *Christie's.*

TOM LAURANCE. The story. Signed, on
board. 8 x 12ins. (20.5 x 30.5cm). *Christie's.*

THOMAS FALCON MARSHALL. The midday hour. Signed and
dated 1855. 18 x 25ins. (45.5 x 63.5cm). *Christie's.*

WILLIAM HENRY MIDWOOD. The tired seamstress. Signed and dated
1866. 27½ x 35½ins. (70 x 90cm). *Christie's.*

PHILIP RICHARD MORRIS. Feeding
the turkeys. Signed. 29 x 19½ins.
(74 x 49.5cm). *Christie's.*

SYDNEY S. MORRISH. Sabbath evening in a shepherd's cottage. Signed and
dated 1872. 18 x 23¾ins. (45.5 x 60.5cm). *Christie's.*

AUGUSTUS E. MULREADY. Black
and white. Signed and inscribed, and
signed, inscribed and dated 1894 on the
reverse, on board. 24¼ x 17⅞ins.
(61.5 x 45cm). *Christie's.*

JOHN WATSON NICOL. Lochaber no more. Signed and dated 1883, and signed and inscribed on an old label on the reverse. 43½ x 33¼ins. (110.5 x 84.5cm). *Christie's.*

Top left: ERSKINE NICOL. Had a nibble. Signed and dated 1866. 39 x 29ins. (99 x 73.5cm). *Christie's.*

GEORGE BERNARD O'NEILL. Grandfather's visit. Signed and dated 1854 on the reverse. 20½ x 15¼ins. (52 x 38.5cm). *Christie's.*

DANIEL PASMORE. The fair pedlar. Signed and dated 1873. 24½ x 29ins. (62 x 73.5cm). *Christie's.*

ALFRED PROVIS. A woman and child in an interior. Signed and dated 1866, on panel. 11¼ x 16¼ ins. (28.5 x 41.5cm). *Christie's*.

PAUL FALCONER POOLE. Fetching water. Signed and dated '41. 24 x 19½ ins. (61 x 49.5cm). *Christie's*.

ANDRIES SCHEERBOOM. Harvester's rest. Signed and dated 1865. 24½ x 29½ ins. (62 x 75cm). *Christie's*.

EDWARD TURNER. A musical evening. Signed and dated 1872. 23½ x 35½ ins. (59.5 x 90cm). *Christie's*.

ROBERT WALKER MACBETH. Sedge cutting in Wicken Fen, Cambridgeshire — early morning. Signed and dated 1878. 39 x 78ins. (99 x 198cm). *Christie's.*

GEORGE SMITH. The gamekeeper's courtship. Signed. 20 x 30ins. (51 x 76cm). *Christie's.*

507

WILLIAM WEIR. The crofter's
kitchen. Signed and dated 1860, shaped
top. 20½ x 25¼ins. (52 x 64cm).
Christie's.

GEORGE WELLS. At the well.
Signed and dated '59. 13½ x 17½ins.
(34 x 44.5cm). *Christie's.*

WILLIAM FREDERICK WITHERINGTON. The woodman's dinner hour. Signed. 34 x 45ins. (86.5 x 114.5cm). *Christie's.*

JOHN HAYNES WILLIAMS. Her favourite treasure. Signed. 32½ x 25¼ins. (82.5 x 64.5cm). *Christie's.*

ROBERT W. WRIGHT. Late for tea. Signed and dated 1876. 12½ x 16ins. (31.5 x 40.5cm). *Christie's.*

MAX LIEBERMANN. A Dutch peasant woman knitting in an interior. 27 x 18ins. (68.5 x 45.5cm). *Christie's.*

Index of Artists

RUYTEN, Jan Michiel (Belgian, 1813-1881)

* SADEE, Philippe Lodewyck Jacob Frederick (Dutch, 1837-1904)
* SCHEERBOOM, Andries (Dutch, 1832-1880)
  SCHERREWITZ, Johan (Dutch, 1868-1951)
  SCHMIDT-CRANS, Johann (Dutch, 1830-1907)
  SIMPSON, Henry (British, 1853-1921)
* SIMPSON, William (British, 1823-1899)
* SNOECK, Jacques (Dutch, 1881-1921)
  STARKENBORGH, Jacobus Nicolas Tjarda van (Dutch, 1822-1895)

* TAYMANS, Louis Joseph (Belgian, 1826-1877)

* TEN KATE, Jan Marie (Dutch, 1831-1910)
* TONGE, Lammert van de (Dutch, 1871-1937)
* TROMP, Jan Zoetelief (Dutch, 1872-?)
  TSCHAGGENY, Charles Philogène (Belgian, 1815-1894)

  VERCAUTER, Jacob (Belgian, ?-1838)
* VERHEYDEN, François (Belgian, 1806-1890)
  VERSTRAETE, Theodor (Belgian, 1850-1907)
* VERVEER, Elchanon (Dutch, 1826-1900)
  VIGNE, Felix de (Belgian, 1806-1862)
* VREEDENBURGH, Cornelis (Dutch, late 19th Century)

* WEILAND, Johannes (Dutch, 1856-1909)

HANS VON BARTELS. The tulip girl. Signed, gouache. 39½ x 31½ins. (100 x 80cm). *Christie's.*

EMANUEL SAMSON VAN BEEVER. Lighting the fire. Signed, on panel. 8¼ x 10¼ins. (21 x 26cm). *Christie's.*

KATE BISSCHOP. Motherly love. Signed and dated 1881, on panel. 21½ x 29½ins. (54.5 x 75cm). *Christie's.*

EUGÈNE FRANÇOIS DE BLOCK. Waiting for the boats to return. Signed and dated 1874. 30¾ x 23¼ins. (78 x 59cm). *Sotheby's.*

BERNARDUS JOHANNES
BLOMMERS. The farmer's
daughter. Signed, on panel.
16½ x 12ins. (42 x 30.5cm).
Christie's.

CONSTANT BOON. The matchmaker. Signed and
dated 1857, on panel. 18½ x 23½ins. (47 x 60cm).
Christie's.

GEORGE HENRY BOUGHTON. The return from market. Signed
with monogram and dated 1866. 15¾ x 25½ins.
(40 x 64.5cm). *Christie's.*

CORNELIS BOUTER. The centre of attraction. Signed.
19¼ x 23ins. (49 x 58.5cm). *Christie's.*

FERDINAND DE BRAEKELEER. The trapped mouse.
Signed and dated Antwerpen 1851, on panel. 15 x 19ins.
(38 x 48cm). *Christie's.*

CHARLES BRIAS. The gamekeeper's bag. Signed, on
panel. 16¼ x 12¼ins. (41 x 31cm). *Christie's.*

JACOBUS FRANCISCUS BRUGMAN. An old woman
spinning wool in an interior. Signed, on panel. 15¾ x 11½ins.
(40 x 29cm). *Christie's.*

EVARISTE CARPENTIER. The kitchen artist. Signed. 28½ x 36½ins. (72.5 x 92.5cm). *Christie's.*

SIR GEORGE CLAUSEN. A young Dutch girl on a seashore. Signed and dated 1876. 18 x 14½ins. (45.5 x 37cm). *Christie's.*

ADOLF ALEXANDER DILLENS. The kissing bridge. Signed, on panel. 20½ x 17¼ins. (52 x 44cm). *Christie's.*

JAKOB JOSEPH EECKHOUT. Waiting for the fishermen. Signed, and signed, inscribed and dated 1859 on the reverse. 39 x 31ins. (99 x 79cm). *Christie's.*

THÉODORE GÉRARD. Returning from the fields. Signed and dated 1869 on panel. 23 x 28ins. (58.5 x 71cm). *Christie's.*

FRANS GONS.
An unexpected arrival.
Signed and dated 1859,
on panel. 24 x 19¼ins.
(61 x 49cm). *Sotheby's.*

PAUL HAESAERT. First steps. Signed and dated
1845, on panel. 19¼ x 22¾ins. (49 x 58cm).
Christie's.

THÉODORE BERNARD DE HEUVEL. The pancake dinner. Signed and dated 1838. 20 x 25¼ins. (50.5 x 64cm). *Christie's.*

PAUL HOECKER. A girl seated at a spinning-wheel. Signed with monogram, on panel. 12½ x 10½ins. (32 x 26.5cm). Christie's.

Left: BERNARD DE HOOG. At table. Signed. 24 x 30ins. (61 x 76cm). *Christie's.*

HUBERTUS VAN HOVE. A man with a kitchen maid in an interior. Signed, on panel. 14½ x 19ins. (37 x 48cm). *Christie's.*

JAN MARIE TEN KATE. Sorting the catch. Signed and dated '49. 22¾ x 29ins. (58 x 73.5cm). *Christie's.*

JOSEF ISRAELS. Looking out to sea. Signed, on panel. 13¼ x 17ins. (33.5 x 43cm). *Christie's.*

ELIZABETH KIERS. The poultry seller.
Signed and dated 1845, on panel, arched top.
20 x 15¼ins. (51 x 39cm). *Christie's.*

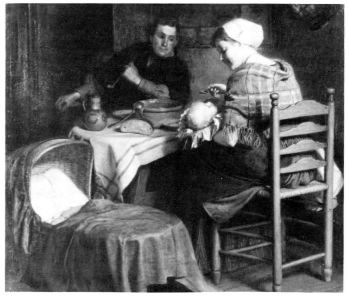

HERMANN KNOPF. Feeding baby. Signed and inscribed
München. 31 x 36ins. (79 x 91.5cm). *Christie's.*

FRANS PIETER LODEWYK VAN KUYCK. The harvest.
Signed and dated 1880. 51¼ x 92½ins. (130 x 234cm). *Christie's.*

ROBERT McGREGOR. Fisherfolk on the seashore.
Signed. 33¼ x 43¼ins. (84.5 x 110cm). *Christie's.*

ADRIEN JEAN MADIOL. A
stitch in time. Signed and dated
1873, on panel. 21¾ x 17⅞ins.
(55 x 45cm). *Christie's.*

DAVID DE LA MAR. A peasant
woman carding wool. Signed and
dated 1889. 33¾ x 23½ins.
(86 x 59.5cm). *Christie's.*

JULES LÉON MONTIGNY. La bergère.
Signed, on panel. 16¾ x 12¾ins.
(42.5 x 32.5cm). *Christie's.*

DAVID EMIL JOSEPH DE NOTER. A maid in a kitchen. Signed and dated '61, on panel. 30½ x 25¼ins. (77.5 x 64cm). *Christie's.*

ALEXIS NYS. Prayers for the dying. 47½ x 63¼ins. (120.5 x 160.5cm). *Christie's.*

PIERRE OYENS. The milkmaid's secret. Signed and dated '80. 9¼ x 12½ins. (23.5 x 32cm). *Sotheby's.*

EVERT PIETERS. Making a daisy chain. Signed. 24 x 19¾ins. (61 x 50cm). *Christie's.*

EDWARD ANTOON PORTIELJE. The dress makers.
Signed. 18 x 15ins. (45.5 x 38cm). *Christie's.*

GÉRARD PORTIELJE. In disgrace. Signed and dated
Anvers 1888(?), and stamped with the artist's seal on
the reverse, on panel. 15½ x 12½ins. (39.5 x 32cm).
Christie's.

EDUARD C. POST. Awaiting the return of the fishing fleet near
Scheveningen. Signed and dated '62, on panel. 20½ x 30ins.
(52 x 76cm). *Christie's.*

BERNARD JEAN CORNEILLE POTHAST.
Playing with baby. Signed. 29½ x 25¾ins.
(75 x 65.5cm). *Christie's.*

PHILIPPE LODEWYCK JACOB FREDERICK SADEE.
Fishergirls on a beach. Signed. 27¼ x 22ins. (69 x 56cm).
Christie's.

ANDRIES SCHEERBOOM. At the cottage door. Signed
and dated 1862, on panel. 12½ x 10ins. (32 x 25.5cm).
Christie's.

WILLIAM SIMPSON. A Dutch family. Signed and
dated 1839, and signed, inscribed and dated on a label on
the reverse. 44½ x 56ins. (113 x 142.5cm). *Christie's.*

JACQUES SNOECK. A woman sewing in a cottage interior.
Signed, on panel. 9¾ x 12¾ins. (25 x 32.5cm). *Sotheby's.*

524

LAMMERT VAN DE TONGE. A mother and child in an interior. Signed. 11½ x 13½ins. (29 x 34cm). *Christies.*

LOUIS JOSEPH TAYMANS. The shepherdess. Signed, on panel. 20 x 15¾ins. (51 x 40cm). *Christie's.*

JAN ZOETELIEF TROMP. The potato pickers. Signed. 26¾ x 43¼ins. (70 x 110cm). *Christie's.*

FRANÇOIS VERHEYDEN. The vagrants.
Signed and dated 1874. 29 x 43ins.
(74 x 109.5cm). *Christie's.*

Left: ELCHANON VERVEER. The fisherman's
family. Signed and dated 1877. 15¼ x 22ins.
(39 x 56cm). *Christie's.*

JOHANNES WEILAND. The love letter.
Signed, on panel. 14 x 9½ins. (35.5 x 24cm).
Christie's.

CORNELIS VREEDENBURGH. The turf
field. Signed and dated '08, on panel.
14¼ x 22½ins. (36 x 57cm). *Christie's.*

Index of Artists

PABST, Camille Alfred (French, 1821-1898)
* PATTEIN, César (French, late 19th Century)
* PERICHAU, Elisabeth (French?, late 19th Century)
PERRAULT, Léon Jean Basile (French, 1832-1908)
* PERRET, Aimé (French, 1847-1927)
* PINCHART, Emile Auguste (French, 1842-?)
POITTEVIN, Eugène Modeste Edmond le (French, 1806-1870)
PUIGANDEAU, Ferdinand de (French, 1874-1933)

RAFFAELLI, Jean François (French, 1850-1924)
RIBOT, Germain Théodore Clément (French, ?-1893)
RIBOT, Théodule Augustin (French, 1823-1891)
ROBIN, Louis (French, 1845-?)
ROEHN, Jean Adolphe Alphonse (French, 1799-1864)
ROLL, Alfred Philippe (French, 1846-1919)
* RONOT, Charles (French, 1820-1895)

SALMON, Thèodore Frédéric (French, 1811-1876)
SALOMÉ, Emile (French, 1833-1881)
SCHRYVER, Louis Marie de (French, 1863-1942)
* SEIGNAC, Paul (French, 1826-1904)
SERUSIER, Louis Paul Henri (French, 1864-1927)
* SIMON, Lucien (French, 1861-1945)

TASSAERT, Octave Nicolas François (French, 1800-1874)
TAUNAY, Nicolas Antoine (French, 1755-1830)
THIRION, Eugène Romain (French, 1839-1910)

* VALLAYER-MOUTET, Pauline (French, late 19th Century)
* VEYRASSAT, Jules Jacques (French, 1828-1893)
VILLAIN, Eugène Marie François (French, 1821-?)

* WATSON, John Dawson (British, 1832-1892)

LOUIS EMILE ADAM. The faggot gatherers. Signed. 20¾ x 28¾ins. (52.5 x 73cm). *Christie's.*

HENRY BACON. Returning home. Signed and dated Etretat 1882. 33¾ x 48½ins. (85.5 x 123cm). *Christie's.*

VICTOR GABRIEL GILBERT. In the market. Signed and dated 1882. 31½ x 48ins. (80 x 122cm). *Christie's.*

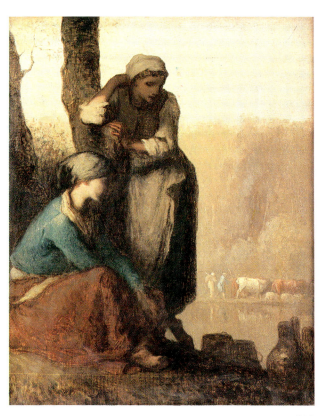

JEAN FRANÇOIS MILLET. Peasants resting. Signed.
21 x 28ins. (53 x 71cm). *Christie's.*

JOSEPH BAIL. Servants at work. Signed.
39½ x 32ins. (100.5 x 81.5cm). *Christie's.*

JULES BASTIEN-LEPAGE. The potato gatherers. Signed,
inscribed and dated 1878. 71¼ x 77¼ins. (180.7 x 196cm). *National
Gallery of Victoria, Felton Bequest 1928.*

FRANÇOIS BONVIN. A peasant
woman pouring a drink. Signed with
initials and dated '54. 8½ x 6½ins.
(21.5 16.5cm). *Christie's.*

JULES ADOLPHE AIMÉ LOUIS BRETON. Le départ pour les champs. Signed
and dated 1857. 29 x 49½ins. (73.5 x 126cm). *Christie's.*

F. BUCHERON. The vegetable seller.
Signed. 36½ x 29½ins. (93 x 75cm).
Sotheby's.

ADOLPHE FELIX CALS. The sabot maker. Signed and dated 1861.
22½ x 27½ins. (57 x 70cm). *Christie's.*

EDMOND CASTAN. Sheared. Signed
and dated 1873, on panel. 10 x 8ins.
(25.5 x 20cm). *Christie's.*

GASTON CHARPENTIER. The
frugal meal. Signed and dated 1890.
34¾ x 27ins. (88 x 68.5cm). *Christie's.*

PIERRE CHARLES COMTE.
The granddaughter's visit. Signed,
on panel. 12½ x 9½ins.
(31.5 x 24cm). *Christie's.*

EUGÈNE COURTEILLE. The faggot gatherers. Signed.
37 x 29ins. (94 x 73.5cm). *Christie's.*

PASCAL ADOLPHE JEAN DAGNAN-BOUVERET.
Young Breton girls. Signed and dated 1887. 21½ x 16ins.
(54.5 x 40.5cm). *Christie's.*

EDOUARD BERNARD DEBAT-PONSAN. At the well.
Signed and dated 1889. 28¼ x 39ins.
(71.5 x 99cm). *Christie's.*

FRANÇOIS AUGUSTE CLOVIS DIDIER. Picking
flowers. Signed and dated 1888. 58¾ x 78¼ins.
(149 x 199cm). *Christie's.*

GUSTAVE DORÉ. Alsace. Signed and dated 1869.
74¾ x 50ins. (192 x 127cm). *Christie's.*

LOUIS DOUZETTE. Milkmaids. Signed and dated 1898, on
board. 16½ x 13ins. (42 x 33cm). *Christie's.*

MARIE DUJARDIN-BEAUMETZ. Plucking geese. Signed
and dated 1885. 60 x 74½ins. (152.5 x 189.5cm). *Christie's.*

JULIEN DUPRÉ. The harvest. Signed. 25½ x 32ins.
(64.5 x 81.5cm). *Christie's.*

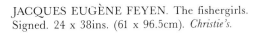
JACQUES EUGÈNE FEYEN. The fishergirls.
Signed. 24 x 38ins. (61 x 96.5cm). *Christie's.*

ADOLF ECHTLER. The centre of attraction.
Signed and inscribed Paris, on panel.
21¼ x 16¼ins. (54 x 41cm). *Christie's.*

Centre left: CHARLES EDOUARD FRÈRE. A
kitchen interior. Signed, on panel. 8 x 12¼ins.
(20.5 x 31cm). *Christie's.*

JULES GIRARDET. The flirtatious stranger.
Signed and dated 1883. 21 x 25ins.
(53 x 63.5cm). *Christie's.*

FRANCISQUE MARTIN GRENIER DE SAINT-MARTIN. Feeding the dog. Signed and dated 1840. 32 x 25½ins. (81 x 64.5cm). *Christie's.*

AUGUST WILHELM NIKOLAUS HAGBORG. Fisherfolk on the seashore. Signed. 17½ x 21¼ins. (44.5 x 54cm). *Christie's.*

ANTOINE AUGUSTE ERNEST HEBERT. A woman in an interior churning butter. Signed and dated 1848. 15½ x 12½ins. (39.5 x 32cm). *Christie's.*

EUGÈNE LÉON LABITTE. A girl harvesting hay. Signed. 23¼ x 18½ins. (59 x 47cm). *Christie's.*

GEORGES FRANÇOIS PAUL LAUGÉE. The gleaners. Signed and dated 1882. 26 x 32ins. (66 x 81cm). *Sotheby's.*

Top right: LÉON LEGAT. A farmyard with labourers. Signed. 59¼ x 34¾ins. (150.5 x 88.5cm). *Christie's.*

LÉON AUGUSTIN LHERMITTE. The gleaners. Signed and dated 1901. 38¼ x 48½ins. (97 x 123cm). *Christie's.*

LÉON HENRI ANTOINE LOIRE. The Flower Girl. 14 x 10½ins. (35.5 x 26.5cm). *Sotheby's.*

ANTOINE EDOUARD JOSEPH MOULINET. The concert. Signed. 29 x 39½ins. (73.5 x 100.5cm). *Christie's.*

GUSTAVE FRANÇOIS MORIN. Fishwives on the seashore. Signed and inscribed Rouen. 27⅞ x 36¾ins. (70.5 x 93.5cm). *Christie's.*

JULES ALEXIS MUENIER. The harvesters' rest. Signed. 35¾ x 47¾ins. (91 x 121.5cm). *Christie's.*

CÉSAR PATTEIN. Harvesters by the road side. Signed and dated 1904. 21½ x 32ins. (54.5 x 81.5cm). *Sotheby's.*

AIMÉ PERRET. The potato harvest. Signed. 25¾ x 32¼ins. (65.5 x 82cm). *Christie's.*

LUCIEN SIMON. Breton women picking potatoes. Signed. 40¼ x 54ins. (102 x 137.5cm). *Christie's.*

ELISABETH PERICHAU. Consolation. Signed and dated 1865. 26¼ x 22ins. (66.5 x 56cm). *Sotheby's.*

EMILE AUGUSTE PINCHART. On the terrace. Signed. 18½ x 14¼ins. (47 x 36cm). *Christie's.*

CHARLES RONOT. The flax workers. Signed and dated 1874. 21¼ x 16¾ins. (54 x 42.5cm). *Christie's.*

PAUL SEIGNAC. Feeding the chickens. Signed, on panel. 15 x 11ins. (38 x 28cm). *Christie's.*

PAULINE VALLAYER-MOUTET. The family meal. Signed. 60 x 46ins. (152 x 117cm). *Sotheby's.*

JULES JACQUES VEYRASSAT. After the harvest. Signed and dated 1879. 23½ x 39½ins. (59.5 x 100.5cm). *Christie's.*

JOHN DAWSON WATSON. A winter landscape with a faggot-gatherer and a young girl. Signed and dated Giverny 1890. 65½ x 51ins. (166.5 x 129.5cm). *Christie's.*

CASPAR KALTENMOSER. Advice from the curé. Signed and dated 1865. 35½ x 30ins. (90 x 76cm). *Christie's.*

Index of Artists

HUGO WILHELM KAUFFMANN. An amusing discussion. Signed and dated '87, on panel. 6 x 8ins. (15. x 20.5cm). *Christie's.*

KÜHL, Gotthardt Johann (German, 1850-1915)
KURZBAUER, Eduard (Austrian, 1840-1879)

* LAUPHEIMER, Anton (German, 1848-1927)
* LEIBL, Wilhelm (German, 1844-1900)
LIEBERMANN, Max (German, 1847-1935)
* LITSCHAUER, Karl Joseph (Austrian, 1830-1871)
LÜBEN, Adolf (German, 1837-1905)

* MAKLOTH, Johann, (Austrian, fl.1876-1894)
* MALLITSCH, Ferdinand (Austrian, 1820-1900)
MARC, Wilhelm (German, 1839-1907)
MARR, Joseph Heinrich Ludwig (German, 1807-1871)
MAYR-GRAETZ, Carl (Austrian, 1850-1929)
MELNIK, Camillo (Austrian, 1862-?)
MELZER, Franciscus (Belgian, 1808-?)
MENZEL, Adolf Friedrich Erdmann von (German, 1815-1905)
MERCKE, Eduard (German, 1816-1888)
MEYER, Diethelm (German, 1840-1884)
MEYERHEIM, Friedrich Edouard (German, 1808-1879)
* MEYERHEIM, Wilhelm Alexander (German, 1815-1882)
MICHAEL, Max (German, 1823-1891)
MINOR, Ferdinand (German, 1814-1883)
MODELL, Elisabeth (Austrian, 1820-1865)
MOLITOR VAN MÜHFELD, Josef Johann von (German, 1856-1890)
MORODER, Josef Theodor (Italian, 1846-1939)
MÜCKE, Karl Emil (German, 1847-1923)
MUHLIG, Hugo (German, 1854-1929)
MÜLLER, Adolf (German, 1853-?)
MÜLLER, Anton (Austrian, 1853-1897)
MÜLLER, August (German, 1836-1885)
* MÜLLER, Carl Friedrich Moritz (German, 1807-1865)
MÜLLER, Emma von (German, 1859-?)
MÜLLER, Moritz (German, 1841-1899)
* MÜLLER-LINGKE, Albert (German, 1844-?)

NEUSTATTER, Louis (German, 1829-1899)
NICZKY, Eduard (German, 1850-1919)
NIEDMANN, August Heinrich (German, 1826-1910)
NÜTTGENS, Heinrich (German, 1866-?)

* OBERSTEINER, Ludwig (Austrian, 1857-?)
* OEHMICHEN, Hugo (German, 1843-1933)
ORTLIEB, Friedrich (German, 1839-1909)
OSTERSETZER, Carl (German, 1850-1914)

PACHER, Ferdinand (German, 1852-1911)
* PILTZ, Otto (German, 1846-1910)
PISTORIUS, Eduard Karl Gustav Lenbrecht (German, 1796-1862)
POCK, Hans (Austrian, 1855-?)
* PRAM-HENNINGSEN, Christian (Danish, 1846-1892)
PRÖLSS, Friedrich Anton Otto (German, 1855-?)

RANFTL, Johann Mathias (Austrian, 1805-1854)
RASCH, Heinrich (German, 1840-1913)
RAU, Emil Karl (German, 1858-?)
RAUPP, Karl (German, 1837-1918)
RETTIG, Heinrich (German, 1859-1921)
RHOMBERG, Hanno (German, 1820-1869)
RIEDER, Wilhelm August (Austrian, 1796-1880)
* RIEFSTAHL, Wilhelm Ludwig Friedrich (German, 1827-1888)
RITTER, Caspar Johann (German, 1861-1923)

RÖGGE, Wilhelm (German, 1870-?)
RÖGGE, Wilhelm Ernst Friedrich (German, 1829-1908)
ROLOFF, Otto (German, late 19th Century)
ROMAKO, Anton (Austrian, 1832-1889)
ROSENTHAL, Toby Edward (German-American, 1848-1917)
RUMPLER, Franz (Austrian, 1848-1922)
RUSTIGE, Heinrich Franz Gaudenz von (German, 1810-1900)

SALENTIN, Hubert (German, 1822-1910)
SCHAD-ROSSA, Paul (German, 1862-1916)
SCHILDKNECHT, Georg (German, 1850-?)
SCHLATER, Alexander Georg (German, 1834-1879)
* SCHLEICH, Robert (German, 1845-1934)
SCHMAEDEL, Max von (German, 1856-?)
SCHMID-BREITENBACH, Franz Xaver (German, 1857-1927)
SCHMID-REUTTE, Ludwig (Austrian, 1863-1909)
SCHMIDTMANN, Hermann (German, late 19th Century)
SCHNEIDT, Max (German, 1858-?)
SCHNITZLER, Fritz (German, 1851-?)
SCHRÖDL, Anton (Austrian, 1823-1906)
* SCHULTZE, Wilhelm (German, late 19th Century)
SCHÜZ, Théodor (German, 1830-1900)
SIMMONDS, Julius (German, 1843-1924)
* SONDERMANN, Hermann (German, 1832-1901)
SPECKTER, Heinrich (German, late 19th Century)
SPERL, Johann (German, 1840-1914)
* SPRING, Alfons (German, 1843-1908)
STIELER, Eugen von (German, 1845-1929)
STREITT, Franciszek (Polish, 1839-1890)
* STUHLMÜLLER, Karl (German, 1851-1930)
SWOBODA, Eduard (Austrian, 1814-1902)

* TILL, Johannes (Austrian, 1827-1894)
TÖPFFER, Wolfgang Adam (Swiss, 1766-1847)
TSCHELEN, Hans (Austrian, 1873-1964)

UHDE, Fritz Karl Hermann von (German, 1848-1911)

* VAUTIER, Benjamin Marc Louis (Swiss, 1829-1898)
VENNE, Adolf van der (Austrian, 1828-1911)
VOLLMAR, Ludwig (German, 1842-1884)
VOLZ, Hermann (German, 1814-1894)

WACKSMUTH, Maximilian (German, 1859-?)
* WALDMÜLLER, Ferdinand Georg (Austrian, 1793-1865)
WEBER, Heinrich (German, 1843-1913)
WEIDNER, Josef (Austrian, 1801-1871)
WEIGAND, Konrad (German, 1842-1897)
WEYDE, Julius (German, 1822-1860)
WIESCHEBRINK, Franz (German, 1818-1884)
* WOPFNER, Joseph (German, 1843-1927)

* ZAFAUREK, Gustav (Austrian, 1841-1908)
ZIERNGIBL, Hans August (German, 1864-1906)
* ZIMMERMANN, Reinhard Sebastian (German, 1815-1893)
ZOLL, Kilian Christoffer (Swedish, 1818-1860)
* ZUBER-BUHLER, Fritz (Swiss, 1822-1896)

CARL JOHANN ARNOLD. Caught. Signed and dated 1873. 28½ x 37¼ins. (72.5 x 94.5cm).
Christie's.

FRITZ BERGEN. An amusing tale. Signed and dated '83, on panel. 10½ x 13¾ins. (26.5 x 35cm).
Christie's.

HANS BEST. A tavern interior. Signed. 40½ x 52¾ins. (103 x 134cm). *Christie's.*

HERMANN BETHKE.
Watching baby. Signed
and dated 1873.
24 x 20ins. (61 x 51cm).
Christie's.

ADOLPH BÖHM. The harvester. Signed.
37 x 27ins. (94 x 68.5cm). *Christie's.*

FERDINAND MAX BREDT. A lovers' tiff.
Signed and inscribed Munchen, on panel.
15¼ x 19¼ins. (38.5 x 49cm). *Christie's.*

HEINRICH BRELING. Fisherfolk on a beach.
Signed, on panel. 6¾ x 4¾ins. (17 x 12cm).
Christie's.

ALBERT CONRAD. Figures in a Bavarian inn.
Signed, on panel. 37 x 30ins. (94 x 76cm).
Christie's.

HANS BRUNNER. The meeting. Signed.
16 x 21¼ins. (40.5 x 54cm). *Christie's.*

FRANZ VON DEFREGGER. A family in an interior. Signed and dated 1872. 18 x 21ins. (45.5 x 53.5cm). *Christie's.*

LÉON DELACHAUX. Tasting the butter. Signed. 24 x 29½ins. (61 x 75cm). *Christie's.*

JOHANN FRIEDRICH ENGEL. The fisherman's girl. Signed and inscribed München. 28 x 21½ins. (71 x 54.5cm). *Christie's.*

FRIEDRICH FRIEDLÄNDER. The customer's favourite. Signed, on panel. 12 x 9ins. (30.5 x 23cm). *Christie's.*

FRIEDRICH TRAUGOTT GEORGI. The wood gatherer. Signed. 28¾ x 22¾ins. (73 x 58cm). *Christie's.*

JOHANN HAMZA. The itinerant vendor. Signed and inscribed Wien. 19 x 24½ins. (48 x 62cm). *Christie's.*

Right: ERNST HANFSTANGL. Flowers for mother. Signed and dated '76. 14½ x 11ins. (37 x 28cm). *Christie's.*

EDMUND HERGER. Playing with baby. Signed and dated Muchn '80. 31 x 23ins. (79 x 58.5cm). *Christie's.*

CARL HEINRICH HOFF. The lament. Signed, on panel 25½ x 19ins. (64.5 x 48cm). *Christie's.*

CARL WILHELM HÜBNER. The love letter. Signed and dated 1865. 27 x 21¼ins. (68.5 x 54cm). *Christie's.*

KARL JACOBY. A peasant family in an interior. 49 x 65½ins. (124.5 x 166.5cm). *Christie's.*

JULIUS JURY. Mischief. Signed. 21¾ x 16¾ins. (55 x 42.5cm). *Christie's.*

HUGO WILHELM KAUFFMANN. The Intermezzo. Signed and dated 1878. 7½ x 9ins. (19 x 23cm). *Christie's.*

WALTER KESSLER. The painter's respite. Signed
and dated 1904. 26¼ x 32ins. (66.5 x 81cm).
Christie's.

Centre right: THEODOR KLEEHAAS.
The proposal. Signed and dated München 1887.
29¾ x 49ins. (75.5 x 124.5cm). *Christie's.*

ANTON LAUPHEIMER. Supper. Signed.
35½ x 41ins. (90 x 104cm). *Christie's.*

KARL JOSEPH LITSCHAUER. Peasants carousing in a wine cellar. Signed. 14½ x 11½ins. (37 x 29cm). *Christie's.*

WILHELM LEIBL. Three women in church. Signed, on panel. 44½ x 30¼ins. (113 x 77cm). *Hamburger Kunsthalle.*

FERDINAND MALLITSCH. Maternal love. Signed and dated 69. 18½ x 15ins. (47 x 38cm). *Christie's.*

CARL FRIEDRICH MORITZ MÜLLER. The betrothal.
Signed and dated 1840. 29 x 25ins. (73.5 x 63.5cm). *Christie's.*

JOHANN MAKLOTH. Mending the scythe. Signed, on
panel. 7 x 9ins. (17.5 x 23cm). *Christie's.*

WILHELM ALEXANDER MEYERHEIM. Playing with
baby. Signed and dated 1871. 12½ x 15½ins. (32 x 39.5cm).
Christie's.

ALBERT MÜLLER-LINGKE. An unappreciative audience.
Signed. 23 x 33¾ins. (58.5 x 86cm). *Christie's.*

LUDWIG OBERSTEINER. The friendly innkeeper.
Signed and inscribed Munchen, on panel.
6¾ x 8¼ins. (17 x 21cm). *Sotheby's.*

HUGO OEHMICHEN. His first drink. Signed and dated 94.
25 x 32ins. (63.5 x 81cm). *Christie's.*

OTTO PILTZ. The fair bell ringer. Signed and
inscribed Weimar, on panel. 25½ x 19¾ins.
(64.5 x 50cm). *Christie's.*

CHRISTIAN PRAM-HENNINGSEN. Putting her socks on.
Signed and inscribed Munchen. 41 x 29½ins. (104 x 75cm).
Christie's.

EDUARD KARL GUSTAV LENBRECHT
PISTORIUS. A good song. Signed and dated 1835, on
pnael. 19¾ x 25¾ins. (50 x 65.5cm). *Christie's.*

WILHELM LUDWIG FRIEDRICH
RIEFSTAHL. Am Allerseelentag auf dem
Friedhofe zu Egg im Bregeuzer Walde.
Signed and dated 69. 40¼ x 66¼ins.
(102 x 168.5cm). *Christie's.*

ROBERT SCHLEICH. Haymaking.
Signed, on panel. 3¼ x 5½ins.
(8 x 14cm). *Christie's.*

WILHELM SCHULTZE. Home from the
fields. Signed and inscribed München.
30¾ x 24¼ins. (78 x 61.5cm). *Christie's.*

HERMANN SONDERMANN. The fair
spinner. Signed and dated Düsseldorf
1865. 25 x 28½ins. (63.5 x 72.5cm).
Christie's.

KARL STUHLMÜLLER. A meeting on the highway. Signed and dated München 1889. 16¼ x 26¼ins. (41.5 x 66.5cm). *Christie's.*

ALFONS SPRING. In church. Signed and inscribed München, on panel. 12¼ x 8¾ins. (31 x 22cm). *Christie's.*

BENJAMIN MARC LOUIS VAUTIER. The funeral. Signed and dated Duss. '67. 30 x 55½ins. (76 x 141cm). *Christie's.*

JOHANNES TILL. The goose girl. Signed. 30 x 45ins. (76 x 114.5cm). *Christie's.*

FERDINAND GEORG WALDMÜLLER. A group of children playing outside a cottage. 18½ x 23¾ins. (47 x 60.5cm). *Sotheby's.*

JOSEPH WOPFNER. Figures in a boat on a lake. Signed, on panel. 6½ x 9¼ins. (16.5 x 23.5cm). *Christie's.*

GUSTAV ZAFAUREK. At the cottage window. Signed, on panel. 6½ x 8¾ins. (16.5 x 22cm). *Christie's.*

REINHARD SEBASTIAN ZIMMERMANN. The village council. Signed. 15¾ x 22ins. (40 x 56cm). *Christie's.*

FRITZ ZUBER-BUHLER. A mother and child with a goat on a path. Signed. 27 x 19¼ins. (68.5 x 49cm). *Christie's.*

Index of Artists

MARTINUS RØRBYE. A terrace on the Neapolitan coast, with Amalfi beyond. Signed and dated 1844.
28½ x 40½ins. (72 x 103cm). *Christie's.*

GIOVANNI BATTISTA TORRIGLIA. Helping mother. Signed. 28¼ x 43½ins. (71.5 x 110.5cm). *Christie's.*

GIUSEPPE VIZZOTTO ALBERTI. Spring love. Signed and dated
Venezia 1898. 22 x 31½ins. (56 x 80cm). *Christie's.*

GIUSEPPE AURELI. Roman dalliance.
Signed and dated 1889, on panel.
11¼ x 8¾ins. (28.5 x 22cm). *Christie's.*

GUIDO BACH. The fisher family. Signed and
dated 1883. 18¼ x 26½ins. (46.5 x 67cm).
Christie's.

LUIS ALVAREZ CATALA. On the river bank.
Signed and inscribed Roma. 29¾ x 15¼ins.
(75.5 x 39cm). *Christie's.*

MASSANI, Pompeo (Italian, 1850-1920)
MAZZOLINI, Giuseppe (Italian, late 19th Century)
MAZZOTTA, Federico (Italian, late 19th Century)
MENTA, Edouard (French, 1858-?)
* MICHALLON, Achille Etna (French, 1796-1822)
MICHETTI, Francesco Paolo (Italian, 1851-1929)
MILESI, Alessandro (Italian, 1856-1945)
MONTESSUY, Jean François (French, 1804-1876)
MORA, Francis Luis (South American-Italian, 1874-1940)
MORADEI, Arturo (Italian, late 19th Century)
* MORBELLI, Angelo (Italian, 1863-1919)

NAVEZ, François Joseph (Belgian, 1787-1869)
NITTIS, Giuseppe de (Italian, 1846-1884)
NONO, Luigi (Italian, 1850-1918)
NOVO, Stefano (Italian, 1862-?)

PAJETTA, Pietro (Italian, 1845-1911)
PAOLETTI, Sylvius D. (Italian, 1864-1921)
PASTEGA, Luigi (Italian, 1858-1927)
PELLEGRINI, Riccardo (Italian, 1866-1934)
PELLICCIOTTI, Tito (Italian, 1871-1950)
PELLIZZA DA VOLPEDO, Giuseppe (Italian, 1868-1907)
PETERSEN, Edvard Frederick (Danish, 1841-1911)
* PHILIPPEAU, Karel Frans (Dutch, 1825-1897)
* PINELLI, Bartolomeo (Italian, 1781-1835)
PITTARA, Carlo (Italian, 1836-1890)
POINGDESTRE, Charles H. (British, ?-1905)
PRATELLA, Attilio (Italian, 1856-1932)

QUADRONE, Giovanni Battista (Italian, 1844-1898)

RICCI, Giuseppe (Italian, 1859-1901)
RIEDEL, August Heinrich Johann (German, 1799-1833)
RIPARI, Virgilio (Italian, 1846-1902)
ROBERT, Leopold Louis (Swiss, 1794-1834)
ROHDE, Niels Frederick Martin (Danish, 1816-1886)
* RØRBYE, Martinus (Danish, 1803-1848)
* ROSSI, Luigi (Italian, 1853-1923)
* RUGGIERO, Pasquale (Italian, 1851-1916)

* RUHL, Ludwig Sigismund (German, 1794-1887)

SACCAGGI, Cesare (Italian, 1868-1934)
* SALTINI, Pietro (Italian, 1839-1908)
* SANDRUCCI, Giovanni (Italian, late 19th Century)
* SANI, Alessandro (Italian, late 19th Century)
* SCAFFAI, Luigi (Italian, 1837-?)
* SCHMITT, Guido (German, 1834-1922)
SEGANTINI, Giovanni (Italian, 1858-1899)
SERRA, Ernesto (Italian, 1860-?)
SERRANO, Emanuele (Italian, late 19th Century)
SHERWOOD-HUNTER, George (British, ?-1920)
* SIGNORINI, Giuseppe (Italian, 1857-1932)
SIGNORINI, Telemaeo (Italian, 1835-1901)
SOLENGHI, Giuseppe (Italian, 1879-1944)
* SONNE, Jörgen Valentin (Danish, 1801-1890)
SORBI, Raffaello (Italian, 1844-1931)
SOTTOCORNOLA, Giovanni (Italian, 1855-1917)
* STAGLIANO, Arturo (Italian, 1870-1936)
STEFFANI, Luigi (Italian, 1827-1898)
STRUTT, Arthur John (British, 1819-1888)

TAFURI, Raffaele (Italian, 1857-1929)
* TIRATELLI, Aurelio (Italian, 1842-1900)
TIRATELLI, Cesare (Italian, 1864-?)
* TITO, Ettore (Italian, 1859-1941)
TOMMASI, Angiolo (Italian, 1858-1923)
TOPHAM, Frank William Warwick (British, 1838-1924)
* TORRIGLIA, Giovanni Battista (Italian, 1858-?)
TURLETTI, Celestin (Italian, 1845-1904)

UWINS, Thomas (British, 1782-1857)

WIGAND, Friedrich (Russian, 1800-1853)
WYLIE, Michail Jakowlewitsch de (Russian, 1838-1910)

ZACHINETTI, E. (Italian, late 19th Century)
* ZAMPİGHI, Eugenio (Italian, 1859-1944)
* ZINGONI, Aurelio (Italian, 1853-1922)
ZO, Achille Jean Baptiste (French, 1826-1901)
ZOPPI, Antonio (Italian, 1860-1926)
* ZUCCOLI, Luigi (Italian, 1855-1876)

EDGAR BARCLAY. Roman
peasant feeding turkeys. Signed
and dated Rome 1875.
22½ x 35¾ins. (57 x 91cm).
Christie's.

Left: PIETRO BARUCCI.
Market day. Signed.
22¾ x 43½ins. (58 x 110.5cm).
Christie's.

LUIGI BECHI. The mid-day
walk. Signed. 39 x 29ins.
(99 x 73.5cm). *Christie's.*

RICHARD BEAVIS. Shores of
the Adriatic: fishermen
preparing for the sea. Signed
and dated 1877, and signed and
inscribed on an old label on the
reverse. 23 x 36ins.
(58.5 x 91.5cm). *Christie's.*

MOSÈ BIANCHI. Autumn. Signed, and signed with initials and numbered 760 on the reverse, on panel. 19¼ x 29½ins. (49 x 75cm). *Christie's.*

NICOLO CANNICCI. A girl feeding turkeys. Signed. 17½ x 8ins. (44.5 x 20.5cm). *Christie's.*

A. CUNELLA. The station waiting room. Signed and dated 1877. 23¾ x 34ins. (60.5 x 86.5cm). *Christie's.*

GAETANO CAPONE. Going home. Signed. 33½ x 16½ins. (85 x 42cm). *Christie's.*

FRANÇOIS ALFRED DELOBBE. The flower seller. Signed. 17¼ x 21ins. (44 x 53.5cm). *Sotheby's.*

EDMUND EAGLES. Fording a stream.
Signed and dated Roma 1856.
52 x 35ins. (132 x 89cm). *Christie's.*

ISIDORO FARINA. The flower girl.
Signed and dated 1892, on panel.
16½ x 11ins. (42 x 28cm). *Christie's.*

ARNALDO FERRAGUTI. A foggy
morning. Signed. 21¾ x 18ins.
(55 x 45.5cm). *Christie's.*

C. FERRANTI. The fair harvesters.
Signed, on board. 18 x 11½ins.
(45.5 x 29cm). *Christie's.*

PIER GIUSEPPE FERRARINI. Return to Naples. Signed and dated Roma 1882.
28¼ x 38¾ins. (71.5 x 97cm). *Christie's.*

LUIGI FERRAZZI. Decorating a tabernacle in Lower Stiria. Signed and dated 1887. 49 x 19¼ ins. (124.5 x 49cm). *Christie's.*

Top right: V. FODARO. Feeding the geese. Signed and inscribed Firenze. 25½ x 32ins. (65 x 81.5cm). *Christie's.*

Centre right: E. GALLI. Two girls on a sunny terrace. Signed. 14 x 21ins. (35.5 x 53.5cm). *Christie's.*

BARTOLOMEO GIULIANO. On the seashore. Signed and dated 1883, and signed and inscribed on an old label on the stretcher. 24 x 34½ins. (61 x 87.5cm). *Christie's.*

G. GIUSTO. Peasants in a farmyard.
Signed. 39 x 59ins. (99 x 150cm).
Christie's.

HANS JULIUS GRUDER. By the well.
Signed and dated 1856. 25½ x 21¾ins.
(64.5 x 55cm). *Christie's.*

KEELEY HALSWELLE. At the well.
Signed, inscribed and dated Rome
1869. 24 x 39¼ins. (61 x 99.5cm).
Christie's.

DIETRICH WILHELM LINDAU.
Travellers on the way to Rome. Signed
and dated Roma 1825. 19½ x 27½ins.
(49.5 x 70cm). *Christie's.*

GIACOMO. MANTEGAZZA. Passa il re. Signed and inscribed Milano. 35½ x 59ins. (90 x 150cm). *Christie's.*

VICENTE MARCH. The fruit seller. Signed, and inscribed Roma and dated '84, on panel. 12 x 18ins. (30.5 x 45.5cm). *Christie's.*

ANDREAS MARKO. An Italianate rocky landscape with a peasant family and their flock on a path. Signed and dated 1868. 16¾ x 21ins. (42.5 x 53cm). *Christie's.*

ANGELO
MORBELLI.
Alba domenicale.
Signed and dated
1890. 29½ x 44ins.
(75 x 112cm). *Christie's.*

KAREL FRANS PHILIPPEAU.
The draper. Signed, on panel.
13 x 17⅞ins. (33 x 45cm). *Christie's.*

ACHILLE ETNA MICHALLON.
An Italian peasant. 13 x 9¼ins.
(33 x 23.5cm). *Christie's.*

BARTOLOMEO PINELLI. After the highwayman's attack. Signed and
dated Roma 1820. 26¾ x 26¾ins. (68 x 68cm). *Christie's.*

LUIGI ROSSI. A peasant scything.
Signed, on panel. 23 x 14¼ins.
(58.5 x 36cm). *Christie's.*

PASQUALE RUGGIERO. Winding thread. Signed and indistinctly dated.
15 x 19ins. (38 x 48cm). *Sotheby's.*

LUDWIG SIGISMUND RUHL. Dressing for the first
communion. Signed and dated Roma 1859. 28¾ x 24ins.
(73 x 61cm). *Sotheby's.*

PIETRO SALTINI. At the cobblers. Signed. 33 x 27ins. (84
x 68.5cm). *Christie's.*

GIOVANNI SANDRUCCI. Mending the umbrella. Signed.
20 x 15¾ins. (51 x 40cm). *Christie's.*

ALESSANDRO SANI. An appreciative audience. Signed.
23½ x 18½ins. (59.5 x 47cm). *Christie's.*

LUIGI SCAFFAI. The stubborn mount. Signed.
25½ x 33½ins. (65 x 85cm). *Sotheby's.*

GUIDO SCHMITT. The wayside shrine. Signed and dated
1867. 17½ x 22ins. (44.5 x 56cm). *Christie's.*

GIUSEPPE SIGNORINI. The gypsy wagon. Signed and inscribed. 39 x 70ins. (99 x 178cm). *Christie's.*

JÖRGEN VALENTIN SONNE. A fair in the Roman Campagna. Signed and dated 1843. 19½ x 28½ins. (49.5 x 72.5cm).
Christie's.

ARTURO STAGLIANO. A boy with turkeys. Signed and dated Capri 99. 13½ x 15½ins. (34 x 39.5cm). *Christie's.*

ARTHUR JOHN STRUTT. The wine cart. Signed and dated Rome 1878. 28 x 43¾ins. (71 x 111cm). *Christie's.*

ETTORE TITO. A beggar. Signed and dated 1905. 25½ x 18ins. (64.5 x 45.5cm). *Christie's.*

AURELIO TIRATELLI. An Italian fair. Signed. 26 x 53ins. (66 x 134.5cm). *Christie's.*

EUGENIO ZAMPIGHI. First steps. Signed.
29¼ x 41ins. (74 x 104cm). *Christie's.*

AURELIO ZINGONI. A peasant family in an
interior. Signed. 26¾ x 39¼ins. (68 x 99.5cm).
Christie's.

LUIGI ZUCCOLI. The engagement. Signed
and inscribed Roma. 13¾ x 16½ins.
(35 x 42cm). *Sotheby's.*

Index of Artists

MICHAEL PETER ANCHER. The fishermen. Signed and dated 1890. 49½ x 80¼ins. (126 x 204cm). *Sotheby's.*

HANS ANDERSEN
BRENDEKILDE.
A cabbage seller in a
village street. Signed and
dated 1879. 33½ x 39ins.
(85 x 99cm). *Sotheby's.*

HANS DAHL. Letter from lover — two girls in
a mountain landscape. Signed. 23¼ x 15ins.
(59 x 38cm). *Christie's.*

CHRISTOFFER WILHELM ECKERSBERG. Langebro with figures
running. 17½ x 12½ins. (44.5 x 32cm). *Christie's.*

DAGMAR FURUHJELM . The weavers. Signed. 59¾ x 86½ins.
(152 x 220cm). *Sotheby's.*

FERDINAND JULIUS FAGERLIN. The
fisherman's cottage. Signed and dated Df. '83.
22 x 19¼ins. (56 x 49cm). *Sotheby's.*

ANDERS LEONARD ZORN. Orsakulla i Hogtidsdragt. Signed and dated 1910. 48 x 35¾ins. (122 x 91cm).
Christie's.

SVEN VICTOR HELANDER. A peasant woman spinning in an interior. Signed and dated Ddf. 1895. 26¼ x 32ins. (66.5 x 81cm). *Christie's.*

CARL HANSEN. Family prayer. Signed and dated '76. 21 x 16ins. (53.5 x 40.5cm). *Christie's.*

Centre left: FRANTS PIETER DIDERIK HENNINGSEN. A woman carrying faggots. Signed and dated '84. 23½ x 29¾ins. (60 x 75.5cm). *Sotheby's.*

CHRISTIAN KROHG. Mother and child. Signed and dated Skagen 1883. 21 x 19ins. (53 x 48cm). *National Gallery, Oslo.*

RUDOLF JORDAN. A marriage proposal in Helgoland. Signed with monogram. 34¼ x 54¾ins.(87 x 136.5cm). *Sotheby's.*

LUDWIG MUNTHE. A wooded winter landscape with peasants on a path at sunset. Signed. 32¼ x 49½ins. (82 x 125.5cm). *Christie's.*

PETER SEVERIN KRØYER. The departure of the fishing fleet. Signed with initials. 31½ x 24½ins. (80 x 62cm). *Christie's.*

GERHARD HEINRICH NANNINGA. Looking out to sea. Signed and dated 1845. 9½ x 11½ins. (24 x 29cm). *Christie's.*

BENGT NORDENBERG. A tot of rum. Signed. 14 x 18½ins. (35.5 x 47cm). *Christie's.*

LAURITS ANDERSEN RING. June-girl blowing dandelion seeds, Frederiksvaerk, 1899. Signed and dated 1899. 34½ x 48½ins. (87.5 x 123.5cm). *Christie's.*

JÖRGEN ROED. In the stable. Signed and dated 1852.
24½ x 19¼ins. (62 x 49cm). *Christie's.*

AUGUST SCHIÖTT. A peasant family. Signed and dated
1846. 15¼ x 13½ins. (39 x 34cm). *Christie's.*

HERMAN CARL SIEGUMFELDT. Landing the catch, Hornbaek
beach. Signed with initials and dated 1858. 35 x 55½ins. (89 x 141cm).
Christie's.

SIMON SIMONSEN. Fishermen by a beached
boat. Signed and dated Masnedře 1873.
15 x 21ins. (38 x 53cm). *Christie's.*

ADOLPH TIDEMAND. Woman at the loom.
Signed, inscribed and dated 74. 17¼ x 21¾ins.
(43.5 x 55cm). *National Gallery, Oslo.*

KNUD SINDING. Friendly gossips. Signed with monogram and dated
1931-32. 37 x 50½ins. (94 x 128cm). *Christie's.*

FRITS THAULOW. Haymaking, Stord. Signed
and dated 1889. 26½ x 39½ins. (67 x 100cm).
Christie's.

ERIK WERENSKIOLD. The country funeral.
Signed and dated 1885. 40¼ x 59¼ins.
(102.5 x 150.5cm). *National Gallery, Oslo.*

Peasants — Spanish, including Bullfighting Scenes

Index of Artists

CESARE ALVAREZ-DUMONT. A bull fight. Signed and dated Madrid 1894, on panel. 19 x 14¼ins. (48 x 36cm).
Christie's.

RICHARD ANSDELL. On the road to Seville. Signed and dated 1862. 29 x 54ins. (73.5 x 137cm). *Christie's.*

FRANK BUCHSER. A spanish bandit. Signed with initials and dated Sevilla 1857. 13½ x 18ins. (34 x 46cm). *Christie's.*

JOAQUIN BECQUER. The matador. Signed. 15¾ x 11ins. (40 x 28cm). *Christie's.*

JOHN BAGNOLD BURGESS. The shawl seller. Signed and dated 1870. 28¼ x 36ins. (71.5 x 91.5cm). *Christie's.*

GEORGES LOUIS
CHARLES BUSSON.
The arrival of the bulls at
Saintes Maries de la Mer.
Signed. 25½ x 39½ins.
(65 x 100cm). *Sotheby's.*

JOSÉ DENIS. A musical interlude. Signed and dated
Malaga 1904. 37 x 26ins. (94 x 66cm). *Christie's.*

CARL D'UNKER. Horsemen at a well. Signed. 28 x 22½ins.
(71 x 57cm). *Sotheby's.*

VICENTE ESQUIVEL. The call to the Arena. Signed and
inscribed Madrid, on panel. 19¼ x 26ins. (49 x 66cm).
Christie's.

MARIANO FORTUNY Y CARBO. Preparing for the
carnival, Valencia. Signed and dated 1860. 19½ x 23½ins.
(49.5 x 59.5cm). *Christie's.*

JOSÉ GALLEGOS Y ARNOSA. The matador's respite.
Signed and dated 1909, on panel. 9½ x 16ins. (24 x 40.5cm).
Christie's.

MANUEL GARCIA Y BARCIA. The country dance.
Signed and dated Cadiz 1859, oval. 24 x 32ins. (61 x 81cm).
Christie's.

GABRIEL GOMEZ. Making scent. Signed, on panel.
12 x 8½ins. (30.5 x 21.5cm). *Christie's.*

ARTHUR TREVOR HADDON. A Spanish street scene.
Signed. 30 x 22ins. (76 x 56cm). *Christie's.*

RICHARD ANSDELL. Goatherds, Gibraltar — looking across the Strait into Africa. Signed and dated 1871. 47½ x 74½ins. (120.5 x 189cm). *Christie's*.

JULES WORMS. A Spanish courtyard. Signed. 25 x 35½ins. (63.5 x 89cm). *Christie's*.

JOSÉ MARIA JARDINES. The harvesters. Signed. 15 x 21¾ins. (38 x 55cm). *Christie's.*

ARTHUR KAMPF. A Spanish dancer. Signed. 77¼ x 61¼ins. (196 x 155.5cm). *Christie's.*

EDWIN LONG. The Spanish betrothal. Signed with monogram and dated Burgos 1860. 46 x 37½ins. (116.5 x 95cm). *Christie's.*

ENRIQUE MARTINEZ-CUBELLS Y RUIZ. The stable. Signed and dated 1907. 30¼ x 42½ins. (77 x 108cm). *Christie's.*

JOSÉ MIRABENT Y GATELL. Catalonia — in the mountains. Signed, and signed and inscribed on a label on the reverse, on panel. 27½ x 19¾ins. (70 x 50cm). *Christie's.*

FRANCIS LUIS MORA. The card players. Signed and dated 1905. 14 x 10ins. (35.5 x 25.5cm). *Christie's.*

THOMAS KENT PELHAM. A minstrel of the Basque Provinces. Signed, and signed and inscribed on the reverse. 44 x 34ins. (111.5 x 86.5cm). *Christie's.*

JOHN PHILLIP. Youth in Seville. Signed with
monogram and dated 1858, and signed and inscribed
on the reverse, on panel. 32½ x 24½ins.
(82.5 x 62.5cm). *Christie's.*

MANUEL RAMIREZ IBANEZ. Flirtation. Signed.
15¾ x 12ins. (40 x 30.5cm). *Christie's.*

DARIO DE REGOYOS. Soleil aux Courses de
Taureaux. Signed, on panel. 19 x 13ins. (48 x 33cm).
Christie's.

EDWIN ROBERTS. A reverie. Signed. 37¼ x 29½ins.
(94.5 x 75cm). *Christie's.*

AUGUSTIN SALINAS Y TERUEL. Gypsy dancers in a café. Signed and inscribed Roma, on panel. 9 x 15¾ins. (23 x 40cm).
Christie's.

GONZALO SALVA SIMBOR. Figures in the courtyard of an inn. Signed and dated 1870, on panel. 11 x 18ins. (28 x 45.5cm).
Sotheby's.

JOAQUIN SOROLLA Y BASTIDA. La vuelta de la pesca. Signed, canvas laid down on board. 18 x 24ins. (45.5 x 61cm). *Christie's.*

PEDRO VEGA Y MUNOZ. A Spanish courtyard. Signed and inscribed Sevilla, canvas laid down on board. 17⅞ x 25ins. (45 x 63.5cm). *Christie's.*

Venetian Genre

The development of international tourism in the nineteenth century meant that a new breed of traveller penetrated to the beauty spots of Europe. High on the list of desirable destinations was Venice, and pictures depicting Venice were increasingly popular as memorials of visits there for the new tourist. This section takes no account of the huge number of straight views of the city painted by an enormous range of marine and townscape artists. Such an undertaking would demand a book in its own right. Only compositions showing the picturesque Venetians themselves as the dominant element are included here.

There is no shortage of these, either. Besides native Italian painters like Antonio Paoletti, Giacomo Favretto and Antonio Rotta, there were foreign artists whose fascination with the city extended to a specific concentration on its colourful inhabitants, especially if they were attractive young women or children. The presence of painters from Vienna such as Eugène de Blaas or Alois Schonn is not surprising in view of the fact that Venice was under Austrian rule for part of the century. Englishmen like Henry Woods and Luke Fildes also stayed for extended periods, painting endless gondoliers, ragazzi, and fair fruitsellers.

Perhaps it is a reflection of an element peculiar to the imagination of the nineteenth century that whereas travellers on the Grand Tour to Italy a century earlier had largely been content with straight 'veduti' as records of the places they visited, now demand arose for a more anecdotal reportage which featured human interest. The new traveller was no less taken with the beauty of the city of Venice than his ancestor; but he had been conditioned to ask for an additional element in his pictures of the place, to demand that the inhabitants as well as the stones of Venice should perform for his pleasure.

Index of Artists

* LEVORATI, Ernesto (Italian, fl.1880-1893)
LOGSDAIL, William (British, 1859-1944)
LONG, Edwin (British, 1829-1891)

* McINNES, Robert (British, 1801-1866)
MALEMPRÉ, Leo (French, fl.1887-1901)
* MAURA Y FONTANA, Francisco (Spanish, 1857-?)
* MILESI, Alessandro (Italian, 1856-1945)
MONTALBA, Ellen (Swiss, 1872-1902)

* NERLY, Friedrich (German, 1807-1878)
* NOCI, Gaston (Italian, late 19th Century)
NONO, Luigi (Italian, 1850-1918)
* NOVO, Stefano (Italian, 1862-?)

* PAOLETTI, Antonio (Italian, 1834-1912)
* PAOLETTI, Silvius D. (Italian, 1864-1921)
PASSINI, Ludwig Johann (Austrian, 1832-1903)
* PASTEGA, Luigi (Italian, 1858-1927)
PUIG RODA, G. (Italian, late 19th Century)

RAYMOND, Lodovico (Italian, 1825-1898)
* RHYS, Oliver (British, fl.1876-1893)

* RIOS, Luigi da (Italian, 1844-1892)
ROTTA, Antonio (Italian, 1828-1903)
* RUBEN, Franz Leo (Austrian, 1842-1920)
* RUBEN, P. (Italian, late 19th Century)

* SALINAS, Pablo (Spanish, 1871-1946)
* SANCTIS, Giuseppe de (Italian, 1858-1924)
* SCHONN, Alois (Austrian, 1826-1897)
* SERENA, Luigi (Italian, 1855-1911)
* SÜHS, Joseph (German, late 19th Century)

TAFURI, Raffaele (Italian, 1857-1929)
* TITO, Ettore (Italian, 1859-1941)
TORNOË, Wenzel Ulrik (Danish, 1844-1907)

* VIANELLO, Cesare (Italian, late 19th Century)

WERNER, Alexander Friedrich (German, 1827-1908)
* WOOD, Charles Haigh (British, 1856-1927)
WOODS, Henry (British, 1846-1921)

ZEZZOS, Alessandro (Italian, 1848-1914)

EUGÈNE DE BLAAS. The rivals. Signed and dated 1886. 44 x 26½ins. (112 x 67.5cm). *Christie's.*

ANTONIETTA BRANDEIS. A Venetian street girl. Signed and inscribed Venezia. 19 x 12½ins. (48 x 32cm). *Christie's.*

ALCESTE CAMPRIANI. A gondola in the Venetian Lagoon. Signed and inscribed Venezia. 14 x 22ins. (35.5 x 56cm). *Christie's.*

PIETRO FRAGIACOMO. Fishermen in their boats on the Venetian lagoon. Signed. 17½ x 26¼ins. (44.5 x 66.5cm). *Christie's.*

CESARE LAURENTI. The fruitseller. Signed and dated 1889. 48 x 27ins. (122 x 68.5cm). *Christie's.*

ERNESTO LEVORATI. Lonely thoughts. Signed and dated Venezia 1882. 37½ x 25½ins. (95.5 x 65cm). *Christie's.*

Right: ROBERT McINNES. Venice —
'the pleasant place of all festivity. The
level of the earth, the masque of Italy'.
Signed and dated 1841. 21 x 36½ins.
(53 x 92.5cm). *Christie's.*

FRANCISCO MAURA Y FONTANA.
The courtyard of the Abbazia, Venice.
Signed and dated Venezia 1883.
39 x 27ins. (99 x 68.5cm). *Christie's.*

Centre right: ALESSANDRO MILESI.
The fisherman's return. Signed and
inscribed Venezia. 36½ x 50½ins.
(92.5 x 128cm). *Christie's.*

ELLEN MONTALBA. At the well.
Signed and dated '77. 30½ x 45ins.
(77.5 x 114cm). *Christie's.*

FRANZ LEO RUBEN. Campiello delle Mosche, Venice. Signed and dated 1880. 34 x 56ins. (86.5 x 142cm). *Christie's.*

PABLO SALINAS. On a Venetian canal. Signed, on panel. 9¼ x 15¾ins. (23.5 x 40cm). *Christie's.*

FRIEDRICH NERLY. On the balcony. Signed and dated 1845.
21½ x 17ins. (54.5 x 43cm). *Christie's.*

STEFANO NOVO. The Venetian vegetable seller.
Signed and dated Venezia 1890. 28 x 19½ins.
(71 x 49.5cm). *Christie's.*

GASTON NOÇI. A funeral in Venice. Signed, on
panel. 9¼ x 37¾ins. (23.5 x 96cm). *Christie's.*

ANTONIO PAOLETTI. Venetian urchins on a bridge
over the Grand Canal. Signed and inscribed Venezia.
21¾ x 31½ins. (55 x 80cm). *Christie's.*

SILVIUS D. PAOLETTI. A Venetian
street. Signed and inscribed.
35¼ x 25¼ins. (89.5 x 64cm). *Christie's.*

LUIGI PASTEGA. A fruit market in the
Campo Dei Gesuiti, Venice. Signed. 65½
x 46½ins. (166.5 x 118cm). *Sotheby's.*

OLIVER RHYS. A Venetian
beauty. Signed and dated '95, on
board. 17 x 13ins. (43 x 33cm).
Christie's.

LUIGI DA RIOS. At a Venetian well. Signed and dated Venezia 1873. 29 x 49ins. (73.5 x 124.5cm). *Christie's.*

P. RUBEN. A Venetian roof top. Signed and dated 1884. 24 x 36ins. (61 x 91.5cm). *Christie's.*

GIUSEPPE DE SANCTIS. A woman crossing St. Mark's Square. Signed and inscribed Venezia, on panel. 14½ x 11¾ins. (37 x 30cm). *Sotheby's.*

ALOIS SCHONN. The fish market, Venice. Signed and dated 1869. 72¾ x 54¾ins. (185 x 139cm). *Christie's.*

LUIGI SERENA. Sunday morning in Venice. Signed. 47½ x 27½ins. (120.5 x 70cm). *Christie's.*

JOSEPH SÜHS. A Venetian fruit seller. Signed. 24 x 30ins. (61 x 76cm). *Sotheby's.*

ETTORE TITO. A Venetian market scene. Signed and dated Venezia 1884. 12 x 15¼ins. (30.5 x 39cm). *Christie's.*

CESARE VIANELLO. Girls watering flowers on a terrace. Signed. 24½ x 33ins. (62 x 84cm). *Sotheby's.*

CHARLES HAIGH WOOD. The Venetian flower seller. Signed and dated '88. 15¾ x 11½ins. (40 x 29cm). *Christie's.*

Wildlife and Birds

The urge to paint wildlife in the nineteenth century was very often an extension of the urge to shoot it. The subjects encompassed generally appealed to the patrons' sporting interests rather than their zoological ones, although there were occasional pictures produced as contributions to natural history rather than for the adornment of hunting lodges. It is probably true to say, however, that the medium of the natural historian tended to be watercolour rather than oil.

Sporting subjects included foxes, stags, chamois, elks, reindeer and wild boar. Artists who seemed equally at ease in the mountains with a gun under their arm as with a paintbrush in their hand were an international phenomenon: there were Landseer and Ansdell in Scotland, Bruno Liljefors in Sweden, Deiker and Kröner in Germany, and von Pausinger and Max Correggio in the Bavarian Alps. Then there were the specialists in winged targets such as pheasant, partridge, grouse and blackcock, artists like Archibald Thorburn, Piet van Engelen, and George Lodge. The more exotic big game — elephants, tigers, and lions — was treated pre-eminently by Kuhnert, Vastagh, Wertheimer, and the Englishmen Swan, Nettleship and Dollman.

The inherent threat to all animal painting in the nineteenth century, the peril of anthropomorphism, was succumbed to less frequently by painters of wildlife than by those specialising in the more domestic species, the cow, the sheep, the cat or the dog. In so far as emotion enters into such painting, artists were fond of emphasising the heroism of the fallen stag, or the arrogance of the reclining lion. It was difficult for even the most sentimental to imbue a partridge's features with much profundity of character, and birds were in the main depicted dispassionately; a curious exception to this rule is Henry Stacy Marks whose speciality was comic scenes involving birds behaving in an absurdly human fashion.

The increase in interest in wildlife for its own sake during the nineteenth century is perhaps reflected in the growing popularity of zoos as places of public entertainment and education. Then again, a taste for pictures of the rarer wild animals can loosely be tied in with the taste for other exotica in the imagination of the time — Arab subjects, harems, and cossack scenes. But the majority of pictures in this section would have been painted for a patronage to whom the subjects had significance primarily as sporting prey; this was a patronage now considerably increased by newly acquired urban wealth, which sought the respectability conferred by the pursuit of such traditional rural activities.

Index of Artists

RICHARD ANSDELL. Addaxes in an extensive landscape. Signed and dated 1842. 30½ x 49½ins. (77.5 x 125.5cm). *Christie's.*

WRIGHT BARKER. Wolves by a cave. Signed. 15¾ x 24¼ins. (40 x 61.5cm). *Christie's.*

CARL FREDERICK BARTSCH. A herd of deer in a wooded landscape. Signed and dated 1881. 9 x 12¼ins. (23 x 31cm). *Christie's.*

JOHN CLEMENT BELL. Ptarmigan in a winter landscape. Signed and dated 1861. 22½ x 30¼ins. (57 x 77cm). *Christie's.*

ROBERT COLLINSON. Squirrels in a wood. Signed and dated 1874. 18¼ x 25¼ins. (46.5 x 64cm). *Christie's.*

GUSTAVE COURBET. Stags at a wooded river. Signed and dated '68. 38 x 51ins. (96.5 x 129.5cm). *Christie's.*

606

WILHELM KUHNERT. Elephants in an extensive landscape. Signed. 49 x 92ins. (124.5 x 234cm). *Christie's.*

BRUNO LILJEFORS. A fox flushing partridge. Signed. 13¾ x 19½ins. (35 x 49.5cm). *Christie's.*

BEN HOLD. Pheasants in a wood. Signed and dated 1903.
23½ x 33¼ins. (59.5 x 84.5cm). *Christie's.*

CARL FRIEDRICH DEIKER. Deer in a mountainous
landscape. Signed and dated 1865. 25½ x 30½ins.
(64.5 x 77.5cm). *Christie's.*

JEAN LÉON GÉRÔME. A tiger with its prey. Signed.
35½ x 28ins. (90 x 71cm). *Christie's.*

G.F. DAY. A pheasant. Signed and dated 1873. 27⅞ x 21½ins.
(70.5 x 54.5cm). *Christie's.*

WILLIAM HUGGINS. Giraffes in a
landscape. Signed and dated 1861.
35 x 27½ins. (89 x 70cm). *Christie's.*

CHRISTIAN JOHANN KRÖNER.
Deer in a wooded landscape. Signed
and dated D. 0'3. 24 x 31½ins.
(61 x 80cm). *Christie's.*

PAUL FRIEDRICH MEYERHEIM. A tiger in his lair. Signed and dated 1907.
42 x 75¼ins. (107 x 190cm). *Sotheby's*.

MICHELANGELO MEUCCI.
A pair of jays. Signed and
inscribed Firenze 1877. 31 x 22ins.
(79 x 56cm). *Christie's*.

GEORGE EDWARD LODGE. Broken slumbers; two tigers in a landscape. Signed. 19½ x 29½ins. (49.5 x 75cm). *Christie's*.

MORITZ MÜLLER. The kill. Signed and dated '93, on panel. 9¾ x 7¾ins. (25 x 19.5cm). *Christie's.*

FRANZ XAVER VON PAUSINGER. A chamois in a mountainous landscape. Signed and dated 1875. 54 x 43¼ins. (137 x 110cm). *Christie's.*

WILHELM PRENZLER. A wooded landscape with deer. Signed and dated Cop.22. 23¾ x 32½ins. (59 x 82.5cm). *Christie's.*

PHILIPPE ROUSSEAU. Storks and a peacock near a pond.
Signed and dated 1863. 102 x 70½ins. (260 x 179cm).
Christie's.

HENRY STACY MARKS. A pelican and a heron by a wall.
Signed. 29½ x 30ins. (75 x 76cm). *Christie's.*

JOSEF
SCHMITZBERGER.
Deer in a forest
clearing. Signed and
inscribed Munchen.
31¼ x 39½ins.
(79.5 x 100cm).
Sotheby's.

612

CUTHBERT EDMUND SWAN. A lioness and her cubs. Signed and dated 1905. 24 x 49ins. (61 x 124.5cm). *Christie's.*

EUGÈNE JOSEPH VERBOECKHOVEN.
A lion attacking a horse. Signed and dated
1855. 29 x 23½ins. (73.5 x 59.5cm). *Christie's.*

ARTHUR WARDLE. A lion. Signed, on board. 14½ x 19½ins. (37 x 49.5cm). *Christie's.*

BYRON WEBB. A winter landscape with a herd of red deer. Signed.
15½ x 26½ins. (39.5 x 67cm). *Christie's.*

JOSEPH WOLF. A thrush devoured in a falcon's nest. Signed and dated 1886.
34¾ x 24½ins. (88 x 62cm). *Christie's.*

GUSTAV WERTHEIMER. A pride of lions outside an Egyptian temple, by moonlight. Signed. 46½ x 60ins.
(118 x 152.5cm). *Christie's.*

WILLIAM WOODHOUSE.
Wolves attacking reindeer.
Signed and dated '96.
19½ x 29½ins. (49.5 x 75cm).
Christie's.

Select Bibliography to Text

C. Baudelaire, *Oeuvres Complètes,* 1961

R.M. Bisanz, *The René von Schleinitz Collection,* 1980

R.R. and C.B. Brettell, *Painters and Peasants in the Nineteenth Century,* 1983

A. Brookner, *Greuze,* 1972

G. Cavalli-Bjorkman and B. Lindwall, *The World of Carl Larsson,* 1982

C.C. Clement and L. Hutton, *Artists of the Nineteenth Century and their Works,* 1884

R. Curzon, *Visits to Monasteries in the Levant,* 1865

G. Eliot, *Adam Bede,* 1859

A. Fish, *Sir J.E. Millais,* 1923

G. Flaubert, *L'Éducation Sentimentale,* 1869

E. Fromentin (trans. A. Boyle), *Masters of Past Time,* 1948

T. Gautier, *Les Beaux-Arts en Europe,* 1855; *Abécédaire du Salon de 1861,* 1861

E. and J. de Goncourt (trans. R. Baldick), *Journals,* 1962

V.C.O. Gréard, *Meissonier,* 1897

P.G. Hammerton, *Views on Art,* 1882

J.D. Hunt, *The Pre-Raphaelite Imagination,* 1968

P. Jullian, *The Orientalists,* 1977

P. Lambotte, *H. Evenpoel,* 1908

C. Lemmonier, *La Vie Belge,* 1905; *A. Stevens...* 1906

B. Lytton, *The Last Days of Pompeii,* 1835

F. Mathey, *Equivoques, Peintures francaises du XIXe siecle,* Exhibition catalogue, Paris 1973

C. Moreau-Vauthier, *Gérôme, peintre et sculpteur,* 1906

R. Muther, *A History of Modern Painting,* 1907

L. Nochlin, *Realism and Tradition in Art, 1848-1900,* 1966; *Realism,* 1971

H. Quilter, *Sententiae Artis,* 1886

L. Robinson, *Life and Works of J.L.E. Meissonier,* 1887

M. Rooses (ed.), *Dutch Painters of the 19th Century,* 1898

J. Ruskin, *Academy Notes,* 1875

A.T. Sheppard, *The Art and Practice of Historical Fiction,* 1930

N.N. Solly, *W.J. Muller,* 1875

M.H. Spielmann, *Millais and his Works,* 1898

F. Steegmuller (trans.), *The Letters of Gustave Flaubert, 1830-1857,* 1979

G.A. Storey, *Sketches from Memory,* 1899

E. Strahan, *Chefs d'Oeuvre d'Art,* 1878

R. Strong, *And When Did You Last See Your Father?,* 1978

V. Swanson, *Sir L. Alma-Tadema,* 1977

H. Ward and W. Roberts, *Romney,* 1904

Further Reading

EUROPEAN ARTISTS (General)

E. Benezit, *Dictionnaire des Peintres etc.,* 10 vols., Paris 1973

J. Busse, *Internationales Handbuch aller Maler und Bildhauer des 19. Jahrhunderts,* Wiesbaden 1977

R. Hislop (ed.), *Auction prices of 19th century artists 1970-1980,* 2 vols., Weybridge 1982; *Annual Art Sales Index,* Weybridge from 1981

U. Thieme and F. Becker, *Allgemeines Lexicon der Bildenden Künstler,* 37 vols., Leipzig 1907

AUSTRIAN ARTISTS

H. Fuchs, *Die Österreichischen Maler des 19. Jahrhunderts,* 4 vols., Vienna 1972

BELGIAN ARTISTS

P. and V. Berko, *Dictionary of Belgian Painters born between 1750 and 1875,* Brussels 1981

BRITISH ARTISTS

A. Graves, *A Dictionary of Artists 1760-1893,* London 1895

S. Mitchell, *The Dictionary of British Equestrian Artists,* Woodbridge 1985

C. Wood, *The Dictionary of Victorian Painters,* Woodbridge 1978

DANISH ARTISTS

Weilbachs Kunstnerleksikon, 3 vols., Copenhagen 1947

DUTCH ARTISTS

P. Scheen, *Lexicon Nederlandse Beeldende Kunstenaars 1750-1950,* 2 vols., The Hague 1969

GERMAN ARTISTS

F. von Boetticher, *Malerwerke des Neunzehnten Jahrhunderts,* 4 vols., Dresden 1891-1901

H. Ludwig and others, *Münchner Maler im 19. Jahrhundert,* 4 vols. Munich 1981

ITALIAN ARTISTS

G. Bolaffi, *Dizionario Enciclopedico dei Pittori, etc.,* 11 vols., Turin 1972

SPANISH ARTISTS

M. Ossorio y Bernard, *Galeria Biografica de Artistas Españoles del siglo XIX,* Madrid n.d.

Index of Artists

Note: This index features only those artists listed at the beginning of each section. Numbers in italics indicate an illustration.

617

620

The Antique Collectors' Club

The Antique Collectors' Club was formed in 1966 and now has a five figure membership spread throughout the world. It publishes the only independently run monthly antiques magazine *Antique Collecting* which caters for those collectors who are interested in widening their knowledge of antiques, both by greater awareness of quality and by discussion of the factors which influence the price that is likely to be asked. The Antique Collectors' Club pioneered the provision of information on prices for collectors and the magazine still leads in the provision of detailed articles on a variety of subjects.

It was in response to the enormous demand for information on 'what to pay' that the price guide series was introduced in 1968 with the first edition of *The Price Guide to Antique Furniture* (completely revised, 1978), a book which broke new ground by illustrating the more common types of antique furniture, the sort that collectors could buy in shops and at auctions rather than the rare museum pieces which had previously been used (and still to a large extent are used) to make up the limited amount of illustrations in books published by commercial publishers. Many other price guides have followed, all copiously illustrated, and greatly appreciated by collectors for the valuable information they contain, quite apart from prices. The Antique Collectors' Club also publishes other books on antiques, including horology and art reference works, and a full book list is available.

Club membership, which is open to all collectors, costs £14.95 per annum. Members receive free of charge *Antique Collecting,* the Club's magazine (published every month except August), which contains well-illustrated articles dealing with the practical aspects of collecting not normally dealt with by magazines. Prices, features of value, investment potential, fakes and forgeries are all given prominence in the magazine.

Among other facilities available to members are private buying and selling facilities, the longest list of 'For Sales' of any antiques magazine, an annual ceramics conference and the opportunity to meet other collectors at their local antique collectors' clubs. There are nearly eighty in Britain and so far a dozen overseas. Members may also buy the Club's publications at special pre-publication prices.

As its motto implies, the Club is an amateur organisation designed to help collectors get the most out of their hobby: it is informal and friendly and gives enormous enjoyment to all concerned.

For Collectors — By Collectors — About Collecting

The Antique Collectors' Club, 5 Church Street, Woodbridge, Suffolk